GENTE DECENTE

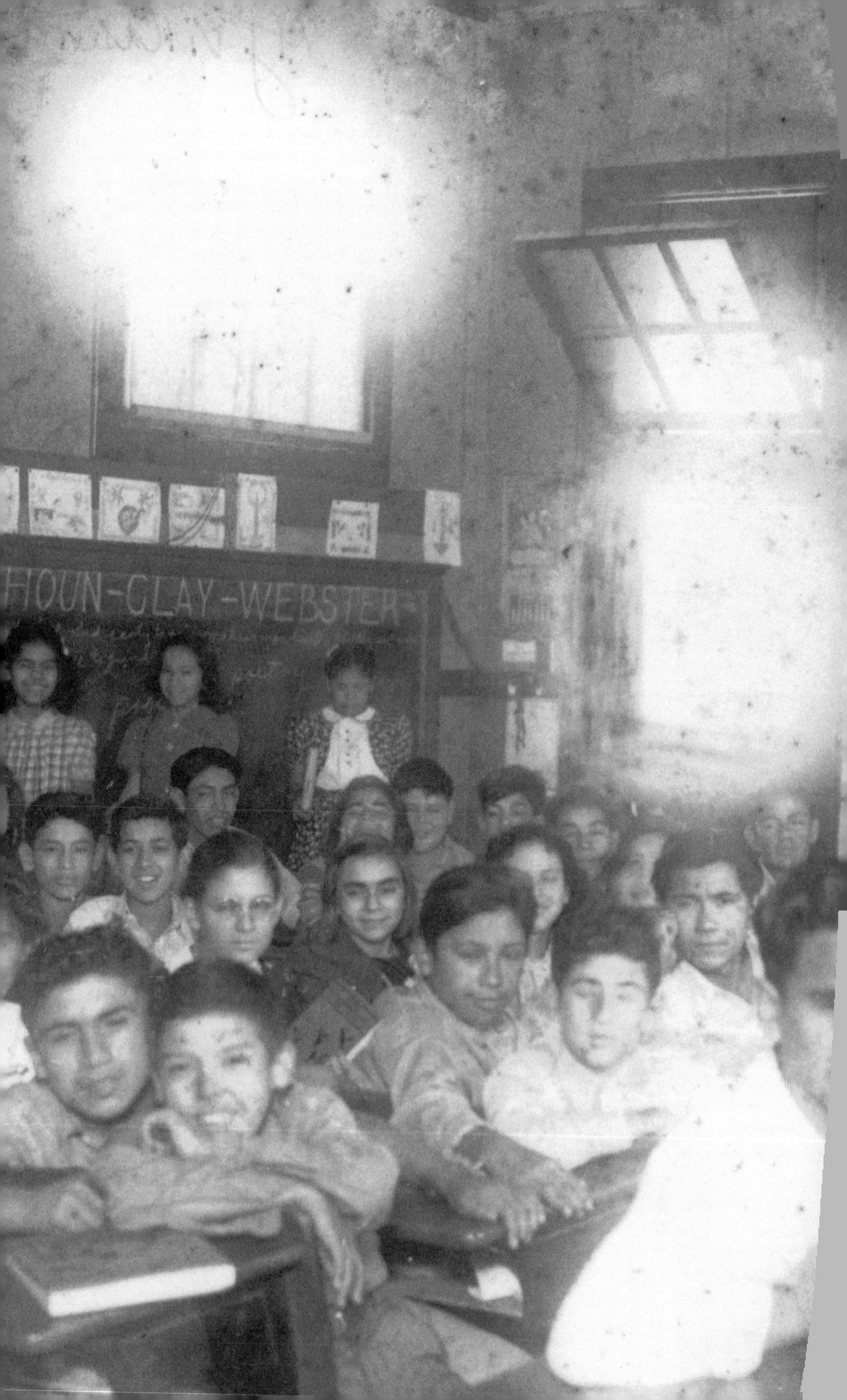
HOUN-CLAY-WEBSTER

GENTE DECENTE

A Borderlands
Response to the
Rhetoric of Dominance

o

BY LETICIA MAGDA
GARZA-FALCÓN

UNIVERSITY OF TEXAS PRESS
Austin

Requests for permission to reproduce material from
this work should be sent to Permissions, University of
Texas Press, P.O. Box 7819, Austin,
TX 78713-7819.

⊗ The paper used in this publication meets the mini-
mum requirements of American National Standard for
Information Sciences—Permanence of Paper for
Printed Library Materials, ANSI z39.48-1984.

Library of Congress Cataloging-in-Publication Data

Garza-Falcón, Leticia.
    Gente decente : a borderlands response to the rhetoric of
dominance / by Leticia Magda Garza-Falcón. — 1st ed.
        p.   cm.
    Includes bibliographical references and index.
    ISBN 0-292-72806-9 (alk. paper). — ISBN 0-292-72807-7 (pbk. :
alk. paper)
    1. American literature—Mexican American authors—History and
criticism.   2. Mireles, Jovita González, 1904–1983—Criticism and
interpretation.   3. Mena, María Cristina, 1893–1965—Criticism and
interpretation.   4. Viramontes, Helena María, 1954–   —Criticism
and interpretation.   5. De La Garza, Beatriz Eugenia—Criticism and
interpretation.   6. Paredes, Américo—Criticism and interpretation.
7. Mexican-American Border Region—In literature.   8. Dominance
(Psychology) in literature.   9. Mexican Americans in literature.
10. Ethnic relations in literature.   11. Texas—In literature.
I. Title.
PS153.M4G37   1998
810.9′86872—dc21   97-48906

DEDICATION

*With all my love, to my beautiful children, Alicia Margarita
Falcón, Laura Beatriz Falcón, Sara Eliza Falcón, Román
Gabriel Falcón; and to my little Gregorio Garza Sánchez, for all
the precious time I did not spend with you during the writing of
this book.*

IN MEMORIAM

*To Doña Barbarita Salinas (October 14, 1927–September 30,
1996) from the neighborhood, for the "calditos" she brought me
when I was recovering from surgery, for the tangos that she sang,
and for the still unwritten story of her life.*

CONTENTS

PREFACE

 Wɪᴛʜ this work I question a certain dominative history of the U.S. West and Southwest and explicate a number of literary works, hitherto little known, which challenge that history. Writing during the 1930s, Walter Prescott Webb foregrounded the pioneers' struggles in the great plains to the exclusion of the history and struggles of the Mexican people of the Southwest. Webb's discourse includes features of a particular type that can be unearthed to reveal what amounts to a rhetorical strategy that constructs a familiar, reiterated story. His narrative rhetoric provided fictions which made believable, when it was most needed, a cohesive picture of North American heroism and progress. On the other hand, literary works were being written, by people of Mexican descent, before, during, or after this same epoch; these works constituted a vital response to that emergent construction of history and to Webb's writing as it became sanctioned as "proper" history within institutions of higher learning. Accordingly, those literary works became a kind of historical writing, "an ideological rewriting of a banished history" (Saldívar 1990b: 19), and, in M. M. Bakhtin's sense, an opposition to the official "unitary language" (271). The work of these writers captures, in Henry Fielding's terms, "the great variety of the world" which has been flattened out by official histories written in the service of a particular ideology; those histories still persist in public school pedagogy and popular culture.

Precursors of what has been generally thought of as the burgeoning of Chicano letters are Jovita González, María Cristina Mena, and Fermina Guerra. Their works could be said to embody the perspective of the Mexicana elite, but they also portray social relations and transformations as they affected working people. Directly challenging the Webbian rhetoric of dominance, Américo Paredes is one of the writers whose literary works are discussed at length here along with later narratives by Helena María Viramontes and Beatriz de la Garza, who flesh out the dialectic of Chicana/o struggles. In so doing, they provide a more current response on questions of history as it is taught in public schools and on immigration, social relations, and violence in the inner city. Especially in the work of Jovita González, but integrated into all of these literary works, is the recurring motif of "*decencia*," as a set of values that manifests itself especially during a struggle for a decent life as it relates to any people's need to live with dignity and to preserve a cultural identity. Retrospectively and in our own times, the stories of a "gente decente" assert themselves against the grain of a particular epoch's Anglo American supremacist views, which include a continued construction of the "other" and the scapegoating that inevitably follows. The stories these writers offer have the potential of filling a void left empty long ago. They can now answer questions arising out of the minds of today's youth when they look around and find no explanation of where their people have been or how they came to be placed at the margins of this country's greater story, its heritage of struggle and success. The works examined here, like many others that remain to be recovered or re-viewed in this light, have not yet been credited or accounted for in the prevailing concepts of what makes up the U.S. literary canon. A revision of that canon is called for if we are to truly recover the diverse constructions of reality that lie within our national history and to nurture the soul of our national identity.

ACKNOWLEDGMENTS

I am grateful first and foremost to my children for their understanding of my not always being there for them when they needed me—I know that time can never really be replaced—and to my parents, Roberto Garza Maciel and Alicia Treviño Garza de Garza, who nurtured my love of story and pride in my Mexicana identity. Also I offer this book in honor of Dr. Américo Paredes and Mrs. Amelia Nagamine de Paredes for their courage and the inspiration and warmth they give us all.

I would also like to thank my friends and colleagues at Southwest Texas State University in San Marcos who took the time to review drafts of sections of this manuscript as it was being finalized: Mark Busby, Allan Chavkin, Frank de la Teja, Lawrence Estaville, Israel Nájera, and Charles Peak, visiting professor and scholar of the Great Plains, the University of Nebraska at Kearney. For their encouragement, friendship, and support during stressful times, I thank María de Jesús Páez de Ruiz, Stella Kerl, Luan Brunson, Elvin Holt, Nancy Grayson, Lydia Blanchard, Rumaldo Juárez, and Jack Gravitt. To Jody Dodd, my administrative assistant at the Center for Multicultural and Gender Studies, many thanks for her help with the formatting of this book and for her ongoing encouragement. I owe many thanks to Ramón Saldívar, professor of English and comparative literature at Stanford University; he was my first dissertation director at the University of Texas at Austin. He inspired my work both through his superb teaching of graduate courses on theory and literature and with the quality of his fine character. I must also thank José Limón, whose patience and perseverance saw me through the completion of my dissertation. For his comments on an earlier version of this book I also want to thank Raymund Paredes, professor of literature at UCLA.

For assistance with my research, I thank Margo Gutiérrez, of the Benson Collection of the University of Texas at Austin, and Thomas Kreneck and Grace Charles, of the Texas A&M University–Corpus Christi Mary and Jeff Bell Library Archives, for their care of the materials essential for my research and for the friendliness with which they gave their assistance. I also want to thank Isabel Cruz and Ray García of Corpus Christi for their insight into the lives of Jovita González and her husband, Edmundo E. Mireles. Also many thanks to Yolanda R. Zerda of the Oblate Missions in San Antonio for her help in locating the 1935–1936 publications of González's

"Among My People." I must express my deepest appreciation to Héctor Falcón and Crispino Sánchez for their encouragement of my continued studies and for their love and care of our children. And thanks to my *hermanas* in the struggle, Beatriz de la Garza, Oralia Garza de Cortés, Ana Juárez, Naomi Quiñónez, Helena María Viramontes, and María Herrera Sobek, for their help and support and to Vickie Ruiz, Pat Zavella, Olga Nájera, Barbara Cox, Antonia Castañeda, Judy Liskin-Gasparro, and Theresa May for reading and offering their criticism on earlier drafts of this work.

A final and most heartfelt thanks goes to my dearest friend, Christopher Middleton, for a decade of love and friendship given generously to me and my children and for listening to my ideas before they could be articulated in any logical manner. None of this would have been possible without you.

PERMISSIONS

Excerpts from *Recent Theories of Narrative* by Wallace Martin used by permission of the publisher, Cornell University Press, Ithaca, New York, © 1986, Cornell University Press.

Excerpts from Jovita González's "Dew on the Thorn" courtesy of E. E. Mireles and Jovita González de Mireles Papers, Special Collections & Archives, Texas A&M University–Corpus Christi Mary and Jeff Bell Library.

Excerpts from *George Washington Gómez* by Américo Paredes are reprinted with permission of Arte Público Press, University of Houston, 1990.

Excerpt from "Alma Pocha" by Américo Paredes is reprinted with permission of Arte Público Press, University of Houston, 1991.

Excerpts from *Anglos and Mexicans in the Making of Texas, 1836–1986* by David Montejano reprinted with permission of the University of Texas Press, Austin, 1987.

Excerpts from *Lenin and Philosophy and Other Essays by Louis Althusser,* New York, Monthly Review Press, © 1971 by NLB, Reprinted by permission of Monthly Review Foundation.

Excerpts from *Tropics of Discourse: Essays in Cultural Criticism* by Hayden White reprinted by permission of The Johns Hopkins University Press, 1987.

Excerpts from *The Content of the Form: Narrative Discourse and Historical Representation* by Hayden White reprinted by permission of The Johns Hopkins University Press, 1987.

"¡Ah, cuánto rinche cobarde para un solo mexicano!"
[Ah, how many cowardly Rangers against one lone Mexican!]
—Variant E of "El Corrido de Gregorio Cortez" as cited by Américo Paredes.
The Texas Rangers (circa 1880) with a "Mexican Bandit." Courtesy of the Walter Prescott
Webb Papers, 1857–1966, CN # 06060, the Center for American History,
the University of Texas at Austin.

CLASS OF SERVICE

This is a full-rate Telegram or Cable-gram unless its de-ferred character is in-dicated by a suitable symbol above or pre-ceding the address.

WESTERN UNION

1220

A. N. WILLIAMS
PRESIDENT

JAN 11 49

SYMBOLS

DL = Day Letter
NL = Night Letter
LC = Deferred Cable
NLT = Cable Night Letter
Ship Radiogram

The filing time shown in the date line on telegrams and day letters is STANDARD TIME at point of origin. Time of receipt is STANDARD TIME at point of destination

DA494 WU09

W.SMD165 LONG GOVT PD=SM WASHINGTON DN 11 537P=

DR HECTOR P. GARCIA, PRESIDENT=   1949 JAN 11 PM 4 59

        AMERICAN GI FORUM=CORPUS CHRISTI TEX=

RETEL. I DEEPLY REGRET TO LEARN THAT THE PREJUDICE OF SOME
INDIVIDUALS EXTENDS EVEN BEYOND THIS LIFE. I HAVE NO
AUTHORITY OVER CIVILIAN FUNERAL HOMES, NOR DOES THE FEDERAL
GOVERNMENT. HOWEVER, I HAVE TODAY MADE ARANGEMENTS TO HAVE
FELIX LONGIRIA BURIED WITH FULL MILITARY HONORS IN
ARLINGTON NATIONAL CEMETERY HERE AT WASHINGTON WHERE THE
HONORED DEAD ON OUR NATIONS WARS REST. OR, IF HIS FAMILY
PREFERS TO HAVE HIS BODY INTERRED NEARER HIS HOME HE CAN BE
REBURIED AT FORT SAM HOUSTON NATIONAL MILITARY CEMETERY AT
SAN ANTONIO. THERE WILL BE NO COST. IF HIS WIDOW DESIRES TO
HAVE HIM REBURIED IN EITHER CEMETERY, SHE SHOULD SEND ME A
COLLECT TELEGRAM BEFORE HIS BODY IS UNLOADED FROM AN ARMY
TRANSPORT AT SAN FRANCISCO, JANUARY 13 THIS INJUSTICE AND
PREJUDICE IS DEPLORABLE. I AM HAPPY TO HAVE A PART IN
SEEING THAT THIS TEXAS HERO IS LAID TO REST WITH THE HONOR
AND DIGNITY HIS SERVICE DESERVES=

        LYNDON B JOHNSON USS=

13=1.

THE COMPANY WILL APPRECIATE SUGGESTIONS FROM ITS PATRONS CONCERNING ITS SERVICE

o o o

Left Top: Fifth-grade class at Southgate School, Corpus Christi, Texas, 1939–1940. Their teacher was Edmundo E. Mireles. Courtesy of the Mireles Papers, Mary and Jeff Bell Library, Texas A&M University—Corpus Christi.

Left Bottom: Children at the Presbyterian Sunday School, Corpus Christi, Texas. Courtesy of the Russell Lee Photograph Collection, 1935–1997, CN # 09189, the Center for American History, University of Texas at Austin.

Above: Telegram from U.S. Senator Lyndon Johnson to Hector García (president of the G.I. Forum) regarding the burial of Felix Longoria. Courtesy of the Hector García Papers, Mary and Jeff Bell Library, Texas A&M University—Corpus Christi.

○ ○ ○

Top: Center trio from left to right: Henry B. González, John F. Kennedy, and Hector García, during the "Viva Kennedy" campaign, 1960. Courtesy of the Hector García Papers, Mary and Jeff Bell Library, Texas A&M University—Corpus Christi.

Bottom: Left to right: Dr. Hector García, Lyndon Johnson, Agustín Flores (National Chairman of the GI Forum), and Corky González in the Rose Garden at the White House in 1965. Courtesy of the Hector García Papers, Mary and Jeff Bell Library, Texas A&M University—Corpus Christi.

○ ○ ○

Top: Dr. Hector García. Courtesy of the Hector García Papers, Mary and Jeff Bell Library, Texas A&M University—Corpus Christi.

Bottom: From left to right: Hector García, George Sánchez, and Gus García (who took the Pete Hernandez case to the Supreme Court). Courtesy of the Hector García Papers, Mary and Jeff Bell Library, Texas A&M University—Corpus Christi.

∘ ∘ ∘

Left Top: Jovita González (center) with her sister, Tula (left), and an unidentified friend. Courtesy of the Mireles Papers, Mary and Jeff Bell Library, Texas A&M University—Corpus Christi.

Left Bottom: Jovita González–Edmundo E. Mireles wedding, 1935, at Mission Concepción, San Antonio, Texas. Courtesy of the Mireles Papers, Mary and Jeff Bell Library, Texas A&M University—Corpus Christi.

Top: Edmundo E. Mireles and Jovita González de Mireles at their home in Corpus Christi. Courtesy of the Mireles Papers, Mary and Jeff Bell Library, Texas A&M University—Corpus Christi.

◦ ◦ ◦

Top: Our Lady of Refuge parish church in Ciudad Guerrero (Old Guerrero), Tamaulipas. Courtesy of the family of Dr. Ignacio H. Sánchez (photographer).

Right Top: Beatriz de la Garza (age 7) with family friends in front of Our Lady of Refuge church, Old Guerrero, during bicentennial celebrations, October 14, 1950. From the collection of Beatriz de la Garza.

Right Bottom: Don Lorenzo de la Garza (left) with an unidentified visitor in front of his house in Old Guerrero. Don Lorenzo, who was Beatriz de la Garza's grandfather, wrote a history of Old Guerrero. She grew up in this house. From the collection of Beatriz de la Garza.

○ ○ ○

Municipal Plaza in Old Guerrero during *Diez y seis* celebration, 1926.
From the collection of Beatriz de la Garza.

GENTE DECENTE

INTRODUCTION

*Among the experiences from which we learn nothing that we didn't
know already, there is to be counted the insight that the reality we
consider as all-dominating in truth consists mostly of fictions.*

—GREGOR VON REZZORI, *THE SNOWS OF YESTERYEAR*

 FOLLOWING the Texas War for Independence, in which the newly
arrived Anglo Texans fought side by side with native Texans
against the Mexican forces of Santa Anna, a particular history of
the Texas Mexican as a part of a larger history of the U.S. West was projected into the future from the basis of a history written in the service of
current trends. After the turn of the century, with Anglo colonization almost complete and the last of the Mexican American and Native American
resistance having been put down, the time was ripe for a historian such as
Walter Prescott Webb to arrive on the scene and legitimize as "proper" history a story already in construction, a story which he, as a character in his
own narrative, would help to perpetuate. Webb's brand of history serves as
an excellent example of how scholarship considered academically sound
during a particular epoch can be revealed as a justification for racism and
serve to anesthetize a national consciousness. Webb built a great reputation
for himself as historian and eminent scholar, while writing fictions. Incor-
porating an Anglo American worldview of exclusion, Webb's brand of history epitomized the spirit of the West while it perpetuated stereotypes and
misinformation, as in the following: "Without disparagement, it may be
said that there is a cruel streak in the Mexican nature, or so the history of
Texas would lead one to believe. This cruelty may be a heritage from the
Spanish of the Inquisition; it may, and doubtless should, be attributed partly
to the Indian blood. . . . The Mexican warrior . . . on the whole, is inferior
to the Comanche and wholly unequal to the Texan" (Webb 1935: 14). Ideas
stemming from statements like this were well received as history by the
academy and the general public, and, worse, they perpetuated restrictive racial, ethnic, and class identities through reiteration in state-sanctioned, public school history texts.

Webb's work effectively re-created the enemy, even though the last confrontation between Anglos and Mexicans had occurred almost two decades

earlier. His romanticized version of history recalled in the mind of his audience portrayals revealing the "cruel streak" in the resurrected enemy, reflecting as well as reinforcing popular Anglo attitudes toward Mexicans. Webb offered to his audience a cheering nationalism that was tainted with notions of Aryan supremacy, much like the attitudes based on ideological racism that were gaining strength at the same time in Europe: "The 'scientific racism' of such European writers as De Gobineau in the mid-nineteenth century was used to justify the spread of European colonialism in Asia, Africa, and the Americas. A long line of racist theorists followed in De Gobineau's footsteps, including the Nazi leader Adolf Hitler. They even applied the ideology of racial inferiority to culturally distinct white European groups, such as Jewish Europeans. In a racist ideology real or alleged physical characteristics are linked to *cultural* traits that the dominant group considers undesirable or inferior" (Feagin and Feagin 1996: 7).

Today, similar, repeated patterns in the construction of similar stories reappear in the dominant media for a public wanting to be reminded of its "exclusive" participation in the American Dream. In retrospect, we see that "history" comes to be considered through a selection of significant forces that shape the current order of things: "It made history," we often say, without realizing that the factors that "make history" are socially and politically controlled. During the past half-century, the network of metaphors articulating history as a straight but embattled track carved through time by the "forces of progress" has come to look threadbare, if not conceptually mistaken. We realize that certain voices, considered at one time to be insignificant or threatening, were silenced, and we recognize retrospectively that what did not fit before, what was relegated to lower importance in the hierarchy of events called history, had a shaping significance. After certain concepts of history have been selectively rigidified, unselected forces may come to light and change our perspective. Analyzed afresh, the past and present relevance of those factors challenges historians to revise the previous view. The antecedent historian's linear, one-track narrative may come to be viewed as an ideologically induced fiction. Yet the partial truths of such fictions may be so entrenched that the (re)appearance of the suppressed past hardly shakes them.

It is my central purpose in this work to discuss U.S. writers of Mexican descent in relation to Webb and the dominative history he helped perpetuate. Specifically, I examine the works of several significant pre– and post–World War II writers who wrote "against" Webb even as he was producing his history. Hitherto, the literary works of these writers—Jovita González, Fermina Guerra, María Cristina Mena, Américo Paredes, Helena María Viramontes, and Beatriz de la Garza—have been largely unexamined in this light. I do not want to posit polarities but instead try to achieve an acknowledgment, in the Bakhtinian sense, of the polyphonic "voices" still unheard and unrecognized by the histories written in the service of a rhetoric of dominance. Private, previously unpublished histories such as those recently unearthed by Rosaura Sánchez and Genaro Padilla or the oral histories still alive in our communities reveal how empty some of the spaces were left and how they could have shaped history more fully. Those voices, I hope to show, can also be recovered through a channel of fictions that has not yet gained its legitimate place in American letters. While revisionist historians have made many alternative views available recently, for the most part these remain inconspicuous or "tokenized" in the public school curriculum and thus the national consciousness.

Chapter 1 examines how language in fictional narrative counters the collapsing effect of a certain kind of historiography. Given eighteenth-century ideas of progress and the general positivist nature of Western History, I discuss how Henry Fielding's view of "private history" (i.e., the novel) anticipates the Bakhtinian idea of the novel standing in direct opposition to the "official unitary language." Bakhtin alerts us to the centrality of language and its creative functions in narrative (150–151). Just as fairy tales function as a mythology, setting forth culturally upheld norms and beliefs, a narration such as Webb's within historical texts posits—on the level of "deep structure"—a certain ethic of imperialism. Bowing to the fashion of the times, we superficially affirm our freedom to differ, but nothing really shakes up and topples the deep structure of a belief system still in construction.

When Ramón Saldívar states, "In Chicano narrative the history of [Mexican Americans and Chicanos of twentieth-century America] is the subtext which must be recovered from the oblivion to which American social and literary history have consigned it" (1990b: 19), he engages the dialectic of how a banished history is somehow more recoverable through narrative, "through the narrativization of the political unconscious," than through traditional history (1991: 15). The recent and current political strife in Latin America has indicated how literature is often the only means of recovering the ongoing subtext of events—a pressing reality—at the very moment in which it is being erased from normal channels of documentation and communication. Mario Vargas Llosa writes: "In Argentina, in Chile and in Uruguay the Departments of Sociology have been closed indefinitely, because the social sciences are considered subversive. Academic knowledge in many Latin American countries is, like the press and the media, a victim of the deliberate turning away from what is actually happening in society. This vacuum has been filled by literature" (163).

Against this backdrop, the present study examines the process by which a set of collective beliefs become the constructions of an individual historian (here, Webb) who refashions and clarifies those beliefs, making them available for a new collective, and thus transmits them. In so doing, the historian not only puts forth the repetitive compulsions of a historic process as such but also perpetuates inadequate fictions which confuse the collective beliefs and empty history of alternatives. Some histories are shaped by the concept of "progress" or evolution, something we very willingly accept if in our own lives we have experienced progress as it came to many during the post–World War II and Vietnam War eras. This conceptualization of history as progress, reinforced by many linear, single-voiced historical narratives, may be inadequate when it faces or even clashes with what has been relegated to "lesser" classifications of oral history, folklore, anthropology, legends, personal narrative—that is, a borderlands heteroglossia, or cultural/sub-cultural production, much of which our students bring with them into the classroom.

All stories or events as recounted by history, reduced to basic plot lines or chronicles, have the capacity for being turned into fuller accounts through fictional narrative. The themes of the narratives examined here coincide with a very widespread postmodern analysis of mass alienation. Helen Carr, in her study of the fiction of Anglo Creole Jean Rhys, notes, "Cultural criticism has been transformed by a burst of intellectual creativity and energy which has brought together those two conditions of being—on the one hand, creolization, marginality, hybridity, assimilation, syncretism, and, on the other, migrancy, exile, diaspora, dispersal, traveling" (1996: 23). As with the literature examined here, Carr argues that Rhys's fiction registers what has come to be the representative postmodern experience—"the sense of disorientation and the uncertain identity of those who live the ambivalent, uncentred, dislocated existences which some now argue have become paradigmatic of our postmodernist times" (1996: 23).

In Chapter 2 I attempt to unearth some of the rhetorical, narrative, and linguistic devices employed for a historiography that succeeded in banishing the history of the Mexican American: the work of Walter Prescott Webb. Elements of those linguistic patterns and of the narrative elements embedded within the rhetoric of such a narrativized history reappear for the same purpose in some of today's popular culture and especially in today's public educational system. Exact linguistic patterns are applied reiteratively within these constructions for purposes of intellectual, ideological, political, and economic dominance.

With the Industrial Revolution technology became our means of perfectibility and reinforced our faith in eighteenth-century concepts of progress which excluded other ways of looking at historical events. As I show in Chapter 2, Walter Prescott Webb invokes the inventions of the Industrial Revolution to "explain" the success of his Anglo pioneers in the Southwest in his book *The Great Plains*. Embedded in this explanation is a larger story of how, with civilization now advanced to this point through inventions as well as travel and acquisition of land, the West could be won by these "unique" characters of this particular story. "Stories" appear repeatedly throughout the construction of a history situated within the ideologically tilted framework of an evolutionary theory of progress.[1] In a longer retrospect, Webb's story is not unlike the Whig positivist history launched in eighteenth-century England, not against a different race but against the common man perceived as a threat to the propertied class, those for whose protection the laws had been written. It would appear that eighteenth-century England provided the model for the great Anglo colonization of Texas; its descendants, the oppressed, became the oppressors during the nineteenth- and twentieth-century Anglo-Mexican struggles over property and human rights. Indeed, Webb strictly defines his pioneers of pure American stock as descendants of the English, the Scots, or the Scots-Irish. English law and the history being written in the service of that law protected the "freedom not of man, but of men of property." Douglas Hay, writing on the Glorious Revolution of 1688, describes a situation that is repeated in the southwestern frontier of the New World and that echoes the growing cynicism of our own times: "Henceforth among triumphant Whigs, and indeed all men on the right side of the great gulf between rich and poor, there was little pretense that civil society was concerned primarily with peace or justice or charity. Even interests of state and the Divine Will had disappeared. Property had swallowed them all: 'Government,' declared Locke, 'has no other end but the preservation of property.' Most later writers accepted the claim uncritically" (18). Thus a historian selects significant data, based on a type of "scientific" history that has been validated for his time, to support the "rightness" of the values manifested in his history.

While Ramón Saldívar proposes a "reconstructing of American literary history" (1991: 19), I propose a critique of the process by which this "American ideological consensus" has taken hold. I also attempt to show how, against the grain of a history written in the service of and within a specific and narrow ideological framework, the literary texts—in other words, the aesthetic and cultural productions—of the peoples bereft of a sanctioned history eventually come to the fore as "the ideological rewriting of [their] banished history" (Saldívar 1990b: 19). I inquire whether the real features of that process can be lifted from their flattened contextualizations, made identifiable, and matched against the world of values that Chicano/a narrative recovers.[2] My aim is not so much to present an alternative conception of the "Real," but rather to help reshape the consensus that, as Saldívar points out, has failed to "take into account the ways that class origins and racial and gender difference [have affected] literary and social history" (1991: 19).

I shall also note effects on our society that result when literary constructions not only banish the history of a people but also serve to marginalize ethnic groups psychologically, groups who later resist socialization by an educational system upholding this history through its adoption of state-sanctioned textbooks. As a present-day artist and activist, but especially as an educator, Yreina Cervántez speaks of her own painful memories as a student of color in a U.S. educational system which evoked in her feelings of intimidation and alienation resulting from institutionalized racism:

> As a child growing up in Kansas and later rural San Diego county, it was obvious that there existed two standards of education within the same classroom—standards applied by mostly white educators. One standard, based upon the precepts of "potential and possibilities," was imparted to the white children, the sons and daughters of ranchers and landowners. Another standard of inferior or lower expectation was inflicted on the Mexican and Indian children, those from families of migrant laborers, workers and the descendants of the original inhabitants of the land.
>
> Sadly, it is no surprise that children internalized either feelings of entitlement and superiority or those of alienation and a profound disappointment in their limited life choices. These extremes reveal the racist structure imposed by the colonizer, the powerful upon the

powerless. They are still reflected in the policies of many mainstream
institutions, particularly the institutions of higher education. (Cervántez 200)

Taught a history full of the complexities involved in the coming together of several cultures, students may not be so persuaded or inclined to disdain their own culture, nor will the privileged take their experience to be the norm or even the standard by which to measure achievement. The suppression or marginalization of "the other" is a dialectical process, both ways: "the other" is infected by the poor view taken of him or her, but the viewer can also be trapped in an exalted construction of himself or herself, only to be stricken when that construction fails. Efforts to maintain or reaffirm a distorted curriculum in the name of "essential skills" and "history standards" continue to our own day. In a discussion over the most recent proposed curriculum by the Texas State Board of Education, Donna Ballard and four other members of the fifteen-member State Board of Education proposed "paring down the proposed standards to the basic core subjects. . . . History standards should focus on the study of patriotic periods and heroic figures," reflecting Webb-style, hero-worship instruction of exclusion and dominance. On the other hand, board member Mary Helen Berlanga of Corpus Christi said that "schoolchildren should not only study American and Texas patriots, but also 'those who were there to greet Stephen F. Austin when he arrived in Texas'" (A. Phillips Brooks: A14). Some of the writings I examine feature this very dialectic in fictionalized yet nonfictive narratives; others recover history by directly opposing habitual ways of interpreting events from the point of view of a dominator; yet others offer more subtle opposition by restoring contours to the flattened picture of borderlands Mexicanos and their history.

Following Chapter 2 I turn to the literary works themselves to explore their challenge and response to a Webbian rhetoric of dominance. Chapters 3 and 4 thus approach the "unselected factors" that had been overlooked in the shaping of the canon of literary works recognized as responding to events as viewed in the optics of the dominative history—the women, "Mexicana" writers of the early twentieth century. "Chicano" literature has been defined primarily as the work of "an ethnic working-class minority of opposition and struggle," many times with folk roots in the *corrido* (Saldívar 1990b: 10–11), for much of the literary production that first came to the fore resulted from the first wave of Mexican American writers, whose university education was obtained by virtue of military service in the second World War or Korea. Such is the case with Américo Paredes, José Antonio Villareal, Tomás Rivera, Rolando Hinojosa, Rudolfo Anaya, and many other male writers. Thanks to the "GI Bill," and with the exception of Paredes, who wrote much before serving in Japan, these mostly working-class men could seek a university education a generation before or in the very midst of a cultural awakening and ethnic minority struggle for equal rights. Their literary production was born of this struggle and was the result of their personal and communal resistance to the dominative cultural hegemony. Their works represent a reinscribing of what is theirs, or perhaps what *was* theirs before the war, and a physical and psychological distancing from their communities prompted them to adopt a tougher stance of resistance in order to reinforce their culture through its literary re-creation.

Yet, before these male writers made their appearance in this seemingly initial phase of the Chicano literary movement, significant women's writings had already begun the re-creation. For several reasons, some of which will also be discussed in Chapters 3 and 4, their work did not come to the fore as "Chicana" literary production. These two chapters are devoted to a discussion of the writings of three women authors of Mexican descent who preceded the first wave of Chicano male writers. Note that, without the benefit of the GI Bill, the educated or university-trained women writers could hardly come from anywhere except from the Mexican elite, a term that in this case defies normal definition. This was the case for María Cristina Mena, Jovita González, and Fermina Guerra, the last two of whom are descendants of South Texas land grantees and students of J. Frank Dobie (see Chapter 2).[3] These "Mexicana" women writers do not overtly write about or represent a specifically working-class struggle or opposition as is thought to define Chicano literature, yet they offer contradictions to the restrictive, flattened pictures of Mexicanos that have for the most part prevailed in U.S. history and narrative fiction. Nonetheless, this canon, which has been taking shape for over three decades now, is gradually being redefined, thanks to many Chicana writers and scholars who have entered the field of literary criticism and history since the late 1970s. "The 1980s decade witnessed an explosion in the literary output of Chicana authors. The initial success of vanguard writers such as Alma Villanueva, Bernice Zamora, Lucha Corpi, and Lorna Dee Cervantes in the late 1970s and early 1980s encouraged Chicano-oriented publishing houses to "risk" investing in Mexican American women writers" (Sobek and Viramontes: 1).

In this book I take a thematic approach to various aspects of literary, folkloric, and autobiographical writings of authors of Mexican descent seldom acknowledged for their response of resistance to the male-dominated and historically inaccurate portrayals of their people. Their writings constitute a response to the reductive portrayal of their people that has been drawn by dominative historical and literary narratives. Women writers like Jovita González, María Cristina Mena, and Fermina Guerra who lived during Webb's time have been given little credit for doing what male writers who came after them accomplished in either fictional works or revisionist histories countering the dominative history.

Chapter 3 focuses on the literary writing of folklorist and historian Jovita González, who in her two novels written between the 1920s and 1940s, *Dew on the Thorn* (unpublished) and *Caballero: A Historical Novel* (1996), examine the meeting, or clash, between older traditional ways of life and new Anglo ways as a result of the annexation of Texas to the United States. Like María Amparo Ruiz de Burton's novels *The Squatter and the Don,* originally published in 1885 (see Garza-Falcón-Sánchez 1993), and her *Who Would Have Thought It?,* originally published 1872, but only recently recovered in 1992 and 1995, respectively, or Leonor Villegas de Magnón's early-twentieth-century autobiographical account of her struggles, *The Rebel,* finally published in 1994, González's never before published works have only recently been recovered. As such they serve as sources of extraordinary value in light of how they engage the themes of war, land loss by Mexicanos, the patriarch, and the woman struggling against and with a patriarchy, which played a prominent role in these authors' lives and in their historical accounts. Paralleling each other, Ruiz de Burton's patriarch in *The Squatter and the Don,* Don Mariano Alamar, and González's Don Santiago in *Caballero* fail tragically in their attempts to deal with the new social and economic order despite the two very distinct forms their resistance to oppression takes. They can thus be contrasted to show how, despite the attempts at litigation and generous compromise on the part of one and the unyielding and even violent oppositional stance taken by the other, both are defeated, their lives and way of life destroyed. Together, the works of these two authors, who were unaware of each other's existence, create a literary historical representation of the limited options available to the landowning Mexicanos shortly after the signing to the Treaty of Guadalupe-Hidalgo in 1848. I alert the reader to the voice of "the new leader" in González's *Dew on the Thorn,* which offers hope through an approach to education that defies the indoctrination of Mexican Americans into subculture mentalities. This theme gains increasing prominence in the works later examined.

As descendants of landowning families, both Ruiz de Burton and González offer another parallel: they succeed in telling a larger story of their own life struggles as elite women in relation to the patriarchy of their times. Jovita González's two fictional representations of the changing social and family structures of Mexican Americans due to their declining economic and political power are infused with her own personal struggles to negotiate her identity within a world where her people's place was already inscribed in the mind of the academicians into whose world she had gained admittance. Ruiz de Burton, on the other hand, struggles to maintain a dignity suitable to her landowning background despite her declining financial conditions. González struggles with her desire for intellectual pursuits, which tend to silence a voice that would otherwise speak more loudly for her people. She also negotiates between her own people's sense of *decencia* and the patriarchy of the Anglo-dominated academy of her time. Though in this study I do not include Ruiz de Burton or Leonor Villegas de Magnón together with Jovita González, their narratives and their struggles reveal important historical realities that provide some insight into how the present-day socioeconomic conditions of many Mexican Americans came to be. For our own times, the story of the representative struggles of Jovita González between her identity as a South Texas Mexicana of limited financial means, with a strict *gente decente* consciousness, and that of a scholar wanting to fit within the Anglo academic world encircling the University of Texas during the 1920s and 1930s is most valuable.

In Chapter 4 I show how two writers from distinct social classes and regional experiences contradict the stereotypical portrayal of Mexicano life, both in Mexico and on the South Texas border. I discuss a short narrative by an early-twentieth-century writer, María Cristina Mena, the only one of these authors whose writings originally appeared in prestigious magazines, and a brief literary work by folklorist and educator Fermina Guerra. Few of Guerra's writings have surfaced, but "Rancho Buena Vista" presents a historic scene, from a Texas Mexican perspective, of South Texas ranch life during an important epoch. These two writers' works contrast the value system of the Mexican elite with that of the South Texas Mexicanos of approximately the same period in history. This contrast is particularly telling because of how the Mexican elite exiles would have their destinies joined with the descendants of the South Texas original settlers with the coming of the

Mexican Revolution of 1910, a story told later by Beatriz de la Garza in her "Temporary Residents" (see Chap. 7). The Texas-Mexican border, in fact that space south of San Antonio and north of Monterrey, Nuevo León, México, is a unique place for this reason. It is a place that is neither all U.S. American nor all Mexican in its identity because many Mexicanos on both sides of the river have retained centuries-old ways and traditions while also feeling the threatening, growing influence of the surrounding, increasingly dominating cultures. In fact, a desire to sustain traditions, as pointed out in González's novels, is what brought many settlers to the isolated area of the Rio Grande Valley during the eighteenth century. Mena's and Guerra's depictions of a former world speak to changing class and gender relations. Mena, through her subtle use of irony, and Guerra, with her blatant telling of occurrences seldom depicted in the history of the Southwest, recover a banished history of internal and external class and gender distinctions.

In Chapters 3 and 4 I attempt to show how these women's writings signify "opposition" and "struggle," and I attend to these authors' particular challenge to the Webbian histories of the Southwest. In varying degrees of awareness of how this dominative history was being written, the three women writers I discuss responded either consciously or spontaneously. I contend that their presence and their literary statements, even when coming from within the Mexican elite, or from within an academic Anglocentric world, must be recognized. The picturing of their worlds, from their however privileged perspectives, provides a more complex and more complete picture which illuminates the dialectics of today's Chicano/a struggles.

Since I began working on this book, new anthologies of works and criticism, such as Tey Diana Rebolledo and Eliana S. Rivero's *Infinite Divisions* (1993) and Rebolledo's *Women Singing in the Snow* (1995), which include other early women writers, have been published. In these early narratives, this dialectic comes to the fore with a clarity hardly expressed by Chicano historians, and even less so by histories and literature rooted in the dominative culture.

I continue in Chapter 5 with the narratives presented in some of the poetry of Américo Paredes's early literary career, a poetry little known until the publication of *Between Two Worlds* in 1991. Also, I discuss Paredes's historical novel *George Washington Gómez,* which remained in manuscript form for half a century before being published in 1990 in relation to an earlier published short story, "The Hammon and the Beans" (1963). My discussion attends to the ways in which these works all more directly respond to a dominative history than do the women discussed in earlier chapters. The novel begins with the author's portrayal of the efforts of los Sediciosos ("the Seditionists") to resist colonialization and a repressive state order. Paredes would later further reflect upon this form of resistance in his in-depth studies of the South Texas and Northern Mexico folksongs and corridos that captured this spirit and thus provided early insight into today's frequently depicted "gang" violence:

> From the Anglo point of view, the Texas-Mexican was a lawless character who used intercultural conflict to excuse his natural bent for violence and disorder; and it must be admitted that the average *mexicotejano* of those days tended to see almost any act of resistance against the law as a protest against Anglo oppression. There is a close similarity between those Border attitudes and the current, so-called ghetto attitudes toward law and order, and for very much the same reasons. If people are not allowed to share in their own destinies, if they feel they are being governed from above by an alien group, then the 'law' is not considered their law, and flouting it becomes one more way of protesting against their inferior status. (Paredes 1976: 34)

Applying the Althusserian notion of an ideological state apparatus ensuring the provision of labor power, I examine in this novel the role of education in relation to labor. The "function" of this particular ideological state apparatus to reproduce a labor force and even a permanent underclass has been the underlying theme of many narratives by Chicano/a writers. Américo Paredes's novel is an important "fictional" description of the way the Chicanos were perceived and taught to perceive themselves in actual segregated school systems.

Interestingly, unlike the two patriarchs in González's and Ruiz de Burton's novels, Américo Paredes's Feliciano in *George Washington Gómez* succeeds, despite difficult negotiations, by accommodating to a new world order, but only to a certain extent. Because he refuses to be confined by only one norm of the new social, political, and economic system, he manages to save himself from total devastation during the Great Depression years. It is a message that can be drawn from many Chicano/a narratives, including those of the women writers examined here: "take from both worlds and draw from them something stronger and more sustaining, but never forget where you come from." The intelligence and survival instincts of *this* new leader dictate in pragmatic terms that a person divided between cultures, even when the cultures are dovetailed, can afford a little fraying at the edges as long as it does not induce erosion at the core. On the other hand, Feliciano's nephew, Guálinto, who for all intents and purposes is Feliciano's son, comes to represent the ultimate result of racism and the ideological state apparatus—self-hate. He is shamed into a denial of his origins and disparages his own community. This story is also telling of our own times, especially with today's second or third generation more "educated," an upwardly mobile minority that disdains being identified as Chicanos/as and that often becomes the mouthpiece for a reemerging rhetoric of dominance that justifies familiar policies of oppression.

Chapter 6 brings us sharply back to our own times as the author Helena María Viramontes takes us into the stark reality of the present-day inner city of a people without a history. Taking us west to southern California, the author closely focuses our attention on the violence and powerlessness felt by inner-city dwellers, Chicano/as and Central American political refugees who struggle with their past in the absence of a legitimate history in the present they simply endure. Though Viramontes is originally from California, her grandfather was a miner in Morenci, Arizona. I include her voice among these writers in my attempt to reveal how the reporting of inner-city events continues to have the same effects as Webb's history. The reiterated messages of violence and crime in the inner city where recent immigrants and Chicanos are caught up in day-to-day struggles come up against the lingering effects of a loss of history and memory in light of their current historical construction. In Viramontes's narratives we see how media language— drawn anyway to sensational events, as history is drawn to high points— tends to reduce those events by labeling, stereotyping, or configuring "history" as the history of only the dominant group.

In contrast to these images, the larger-than-life images of Anglos in the eyes of Mexicanos result in distortions of respective human value. Ed Montoya, a miner who grew up in the company towns of Clifton/Morenci, Arizona, and who saw the worst fighting in Okinawa, where he served during World War II, provides an example of this. In an interview conducted by Héctor Galán for his PBS documentary *Los mineros,* Montoya painfully remembers how he had internalized his perception of Anglos as superhumans in relation to his own community. Growing up in this Arizona mining community, where third- and fourth-generation Mexican Americans were relegated to the worst jobs, treated harshly, and forced despite three generations of struggles for equality to endure a dual-wage system imposed by the

Dodge Phelps Company, left him with little reason to trust his own courage over others. Experiencing the equalizing effects of war, Montoya recalls his astonishment in 1941 at the tears and faltering courage of the Anglos in his company whom he had previously seen in heroic proportion:

> On April 13, at 8:00 in the morning, there was 186 men in my company; by 5:00 in the afternoon, there was only 24 of us left. I remember a guy by the name of Thackery, "I knew there would be days like that," he would say, and tears started running down his eyes. "What's going on here," I said. "Hey, hey wait a minute. I'm the one who's supposed to be crying. You guys are Superman; you're Batman; you're Roy Rogers. You're super. You're not supposed to cry." I had never heard an Anglo cry in my life. Here in the neighborhood, I heard kids, Mexicanos, crying. I thought we were the only ones that cried.
>
> We went on a patrol and there were six of us. We were going to go on a reconnaissance patrol, and two of the Anglo boys didn't want to go. I told them, I said, "Hey, wait a minute. If there is a guy that is supposed to refuse, it would be me [Here Mr. Montoya begins to cry and he covers his face with a handkerchief; camera shot changes and then returns] . . . because back in the States, I was discriminated, and I should refuse to go right now. But no, I'm ready to go! Come on, bastards, let's go!" And they just bowed their heads and we went on the patrol. [You] see, those things are inside of you. (Galán 1991)

The internal effects of images resulting from a dominative history that invalidates one group's existence while it makes heroes of the others is evident in the stark reality that Viramontes's stories force the reader to (not just hypothetically) recognize. With this chapter, I also try to bridge the gap between narrative "fiction" and the fictions that present-day advertising, consumerism, and popular culture force upon our minds. That such stereotypification and reduction exists is validated by the fictive construction of Viramontes's characters' innermost psychological responses. The horror is brought back to its original immediacy; the cover of dominant media-imposed labeling is blown. Those fictions, like Webb's history, perpetuate the rhetoric of dominance.

In Chapter 7 I cover three short stories by Beatriz de la Garza that speak directly to Webb's history to reveal the internal diversity and historical distinctions within the Mexicano community that are wiped out by dominant media. In this analysis, I draw attention to the neglected story of Hispanic women in general. Beatriz de la Garza's female characters in her short story "Temporary Residents" speak to the particular struggles of women to resist family disintegration as a result of the Mexican Revolution of 1910 and pressures to acculturate to U.S. society. In "The Candy Vendor's Boy" de la Garza also inserts the missing story of Chicano military history with her depiction of a World War I soldier returning to Austin, Texas, his hometown in 1918. De la Garza extends her narrative beyond the theme of war to segregation and the lack of educational opportunities for Mexicanos during various periods. Even after their service in the military, Mexicanos were to find their return compromised by their being still confined to the menial, low-paying, low-status roles in a society in which they are still defined as "others." Her narratives depict dichotomous perspectives on the world that surrounds her protagonists. As Chicanos, her characters struggle against earlier constructions of themselves as they relate in uneasy ways to U.S. society.

Finally, all of the authors discussed in these chapters, as well as the various representations of gender and class struggle they create, are especially important because they succeed in offering their own versions of history by depicting the complex struggles of their people to survive and accommodate to change. Unknowingly responding to Webb's crediting of "his" pioneers as the sole participants in the carving out of a living on the American Western Frontier, these writers recover through literature what would have been a lost history of struggles that responds even to the most recent reemergence of the rhetoric of dominance voiced and perpetuated by what is known politically as the conservative right. I point, in Chapter 7 and in the epilogue, to the stories arising from a rhetoric of dominance that are still credited and continue to be constructed. In these final chapters, and especially as I examine de la Garza's story "The Kid from the Alamo," I pay particular attention to how present-day public school systems perpetuate an old story—the country's generally accepted narrative history (replete with present-day versions of the theory of Manifest Destiny, as theory of progress). This story carries with it a force that has laid the groundwork for ungrudging acceptance of certain attitudes about this country's account of the past. These attitudes still survive in popular culture and are carried out by some current media. The ideology reflected in the powerful image of the pioneering struggles prominent in traditional U.S. history (that view which prevailed before revisionist histories had made their influence felt) reinforces the prefabricated framework of an evolutionary theory, that is, a process in which we are always evolving, always succeeding in making things "better," without taking into account (except through occasional lip service) the destruction of civilizations along the way.

The conventional way of looking at the past maintains the hegemony, in turn an instrument of dominance. Major revisionist histories get published and receive some acknowledgment within the academy, yet the power of the original, essential story already inscribed within the minds of most Americans, particularly the history of the Texas Mexican in the service of Anglo colonialist ideology, still asserts itself in our schools. This became increasingly clear to me when I was teaching Chicano Literature at the University of Texas at Austin, and now as I teach U.S. Ethnic Studies and Chicano/a Narrative and Social History at Southwest Texas State University to increasing numbers of students from the Río Grande Valley. Many of these students express disappointment and a sense of having been somehow cheated out of the truth of their own identity and experience. At the university the process of devaluing their culture even further is often accelerated. As the Association of American Colleges and Universities (AAC & U) draft report "American Pluralism, American Commitments and the College Curriculum" notes: "It is at college, however, that students learn to devalue their cultures. Universities teach them to forget their particularities and local cultures. Sometimes that process of erasure is accelerated when the institution fails to challenge negative cultural stereotypes and media caricatures" (27).

Students closely identified with their culture, as are many of the students from the Río Grande Valley, are appalled that so many Chicano/as from the Valley have no sense of their own history; they realize how the schools have done their part to erase it. Sometimes even their parents, not wanting their children to suffer the discrimination which they underwent, have sheltered them from their history and consciously kept them from learning Spanish. In their attempts to have their children blend in more easily with the hegemony, and supposedly suffer less, they fear instilling hate or a victimization mentality. Many "minority" students experience these conflicts in our educational system, but with the particularly youthful population of Hispanics in the United States and the alarming dropout rate among them, these issues deserve crisis-level attention. The AAC & U put it this way: "Education for diversity requires that we encourage, rather than discourage, the exploration of origins and identity as a fundamental subject for college study. Students must learn to understand the metaphorical place of their birth and how that place and the specific identities rooted in it fit into an historically textured matrix of social relations" (27).

One subtextual concern throughout this work is to examine how the school systems have done their part in ensuring the establishment of a permanent underclass of Mexicanos. The process by which this has occurred has been the telling of a story, a story constructed out of the history, the literature, and the politically controlled media of an epoch; stories that gained credence at a particular time in history that called for and needed a justification for past and contemporary acts of suppressing and denigrating the borderlands Mexican. The power and influence that these stories have exerted serve as a subject for analysis. I wish to identify what in our educational system, and in our society as a whole, allows for the easy acceptance of these stories and perpetuates a cultural knowing of "one's place," even after the state apparatus ceases to be overtly oppressive.

The resulting experience for Chicano/a youth has been told over and over again with such literary depictions as the poems "History Class" by Tino Villanueva and "Rules of the Game" by Rogelio Gómez. But the Texas public education system, as it exists today, may still be generally if not directly linked to Webb because of the influence he exerted over the teaching of history, the writing of textbooks, and consequently the curriculum that has existed in the state of Texas since that time. As one of his biographers points out, in 1939 Webb conceived of *The Handbook of Texas* project while director of the Texas State Historical Association (TSHA): "When the two-volume work was published in 1952, the total cost was only $1 million—and Texas had the only book of this type in the United States" (Kingston: 2). About Webb's writing of Texas history textbooks and his influence over the way Texas history would be taught in the public schools this same biographer notes:

> Webb also was always active in attracting young Texans to the history of their state. He was concerned about the quality of instruction they received, and throughout his career he worked to improve the teaching. Webb began his university career by teaching the first course at the University designed to train Texas history teachers in the public schools. As director of the TSHA, he launched the Junior Historian program.
>
> While many historians disdained the writing of textbooks, Webb embraced the responsibility. Including textbooks, he wrote or edited more than twenty books during his career. The textbooks were a method of earning money, and they gave him access to students. The teaching of history should not be dull, he felt, and there were many

lessons for today to be learned from the state's past. He also wrote
numerous articles for popular history magazines. It was a major criticism of most historians, he argued, that they do not write for the public, but only for others in their field. Indeed, he felt that too many historians were not good writers. Webb was a good writer, for his style
was concise and he concentrated on content. (2–3)

As an educator, Webb must have been fully conscious of the power of textbooks, but how much that played into his motivations for writing them is yet
another matter for further exploration.

Today, the myths of Texas history continue to be perpetuated while the
Texas Mexican's history and perspective are never really taught. Instead, the
reverse is taught, causing the Chicano students of today to believe themselves inferior or to position themselves in an adversarial role to the ruling
culture in order to assert an identity—or, as we shall see in the dual identities developed in Parades's *George Washington Gómez,* they must pretend to
accept the lies.[4] Overt segregation as described by the protagonist's father in
de la Garza's "The Kid from the Alamo" or in Parades's novel continues into
our own time and in some cases is even worse. The paradigm is still active
and measures out in narrative terms an ongoing historical situation. At any
public school function where students congregate separately, even in the so-
called integrated schools, internal segregation becomes evident: the white
students take up leadership roles in the school community as almost the exclusive enrollees in the prestigious honors courses and societies, while minorities find themselves tracked in lower-level classes and receive little encouragement for higher education. According to a recent study reported in
the *Austin American Statesman,*

> Nearly six of 10 minority students attended schools in 1993–94 where
> more than 70 percent of the students were minorities, according to
> the computer analysis of Texas Education Agency data. Conversely,
> fewer than one in 10 whites attended predominantly minority schools
> that year. . . . An increasing number of low-income students are
> attending schools where more than 70 percent of students are poor.
> More than four of 10 low-income students attended such schools in
> 1993–94. About 45 percent of Texas' 3.4 million students were con-
> sidered low-income that year. (Phillips and South: A1)

Even programs designed to help, such as the bilingual program plagued
with inadequate funding for both teachers and curriculum, often become

dumping grounds for the "learning disabled" they sometimes create. The term "bilingual" in many cases becomes a stigma attached to those "other" students, while for white students in private or elite schools, learning Spanish becomes chic or at the very least a staple in their preparation to live and work in a pluralistic society, particularly in the Southwest.

Attention to resulting gaps in achievement of Mexican Americans is crucial as we approach the end of this century and enter a new one. The state of Texas, which has traditionally depended on its rich natural resources, faces a tremendous challenge entering the new millennium. With natural resources running out and with the shift to a knowledge-based service economy, the state's economic success will increasingly depend on the quality of its human resources (Hazelton: 13). According to current demographic projections and economic trends, and in the absence of major changes in public policy, the state's population will become more ethnically diverse, as 87.5 percent of the projected growth will be due to growth in minority populations: Hispanic population will rise by 257.6 percent. By 2030, Hispanics will account for 45.9 percent of the population. The number of elementary and secondary school students enrolled in Texas public schools will increase from 3.3 million in 1990 to 4.5 million in 2005, and to 5.4 million by 2030. Unless significant changes occur in the relationship between minority status and educational attainment, occupations of employment, and income, the state will find itself with a higher level of poverty, a lower level of income, greater demand for all public services, and reduced public revenues (Hazelton: 14).

Though it becomes obvious that a strong higher education system is essential to the country's prosperity and well-being, even with the Affirmative Action efforts by some institutions to at least sprinkle its faculty with the minimal, complying numbers of minority faculty, institutions are hardly altered. As Rosaura Sánchez indicates, minority faculty have become co-opted by oppressive "tenure-track" systems: "The absorption of some faculty into established departments does not however indicate that Chicanos, Blacks and Native Americans have gained access to the inner sanctum of academia. A look at educational attainment statistics, recruitment and retention figures on minority students at colleges and universities would indicate that, despite two decades of a liberal discourse on opportunity and affirmative action, we have not made great strides in higher education, unless a handful of academicians who now have tenure and a handful of minority Yuppies are considered meaningful change for the vast majority of ethnic minorities" (1989: 87).

Bakhtin's maps of heteroglossia in the novel can serve as a model for dy-

namic institutional change that goes well beyond the tolerated "celebrations" of diversity. He raises to a high level of discourse the plain facts of life,
insofar as he detects in the novel an image of language capturing, in many
facets, conflict as the pulse of articulate social life. The novel, he writes, is
"an artistically organized system for bringing different languages in contact
with one another, a system having as its goal the illumination of one language by means of another, the carving-out of a living image of another language" (361). It is through conflict by differing systems of meaning that new
meanings will be derived and learning and institutions can best engage, respond to, and refract a rapidly changing society.

But the messages we receive through various dominant media constructions continue to exercise a tremendous power over the minds of a public
untrained and unwilling to question, interpret, and analyze such constructions. The socialization process, the pressure to conform that takes place in
the schools, is specifically created by a curriculum still based on ideologically
constructed histories. The new Western history continues to challenge romantic notions of Anglo and European glory, but what meaningful changes
have occurred within the school curriculum? How accessible are these new
and different ways of looking at our past in the schools or in the general public? Stories such as Webb's, which present the myth of the Winning of
the West as American History, continue to be the pedagogical mainstay. As
Richard Slotkin points out, the myth perpetuated by these stories continues
to survive:

> It is by now a commonplace that our adherence to the "myth of the
> frontier"—the conception of America as a wide-open land of unlim-
> ited opportunity for the strong, ambitious, self-reliant individual to
> thrust his way to the top—has blinded us to the consequences of the
> industrial and urban revolutions and to the need for social reform
> and a new concept of individual and communal welfare. Nor is it by
> a far-fetched association that the murderous violence that has charac-
> terized recent political life has been linked by poets and news com-
> mentators alike to the "frontier psychology" of our recent past and
> our long heritage. (5)

Communication and thus understanding is necessary for that new concept of "individual and communal welfare" to occur. Together, the works I
examine here can represent a conversation, through time, between the authors and Webb. Though such a conversation unfortunately never took

place, the lives and the commentaries through story of these writers provide both a reiteration and a response to the rhetoric of dominance. In the absence of such a conversation, and given our history and our continual denial of the intimate stories of the repression of the soul that history required, it is no wonder that we presently live in such a violent society. With this book I hope to add to the already proposed redefinition of the canonical U.S. literary history: already the writings of Ramón Saldívar, Patricia Limerick, Norma Alarcón, David Montejano, Sarah Deutsch, Rosaura Sánchez, Antonia Castañeda, and many others have changed the horizon quite fundamentally. Such a definition is under way, and I believe it will eventually change perceptions of our country's literary and cultural history and bring about a more honest reckoning with our past.

1
HISTORY AS NARRATIVE

History is a fable mutually agreed upon.

—Napoleon Bonaparte

THE development of both historical and fictional narrative is marked by a concern, repeatedly renewed, with questions of "representation" or of "reality," as those terms are presumably or tacitly defined by these genres. According to Leo Braudy, since the eighteenth century historians and novelists alike have shared a concern for "true" representation (4). Novelists following Daniel Defoe, such as Samuel Richardson and Henry Fielding, not wanting their works to be confused with the romances discredited since the time of Cervantes for the "lies" they told, called their novels "histories," "expeditions," or "travels." Each writer tried in his own way to position himself as a writer in a particular nonromance genre. Despite the "distinct identities" that "the factual world of historical interpretation" and the "fictive world of the novel" eventually achieved (Braudy: 5), more recent approaches to historiography, such as that of Hayden White, have demonstrated that histories and novels employ similar elements of language. Though we may doubt that there is any such thing as historical objectivity in representing an event, a people, or a culture, whether in the construction of a history or in the telling of a story, the evidence often delivered as "facts" must be conveyed and rendered believable through narrative modalities of language.

Both historian and novelist, Fielding took issue with the apparent power of eighteenth-century historical accounts to render "official" a falsification of the past by applying what he called "falsely unified views." Seeing through these "public histories," he felt they "too often perpetuated falsely unified views that scanted the actual variety of the world; [whereas] private history displayed in fiction stands in opposition to public history" (Braudy: 94). In light of recent revisionist histories, Fielding's view of "private history" (i.e., the novel) anticipates the Bakhtinian theory of the novel standing in direct opposition to the "official unitary language." But Fielding also suggested how a novel could render a historical event more believable to the reader, capturing a more varied view of the world and of human experience. As I hope to show in subsequent chapters, the literary narratives of U.S. writers of Mexican descent accomplish just that when they specifically respond to historical events as well as to the writing of a dominative, public history. The narratives examined here, by responding to state-sanctioned histories, capture a more varied view of the human experience in the social world. Breaking up a "falsely unified view" and asserting the "variety of the world," Chicano/a writers recover a human complexity which would otherwise have been banished from the heterogeneous history of the people of Texas and the Southwest.

Fielding believed that fiction, through its power of imagination, could achieve a representation of reality unlikely to be conceptualized in any public history. In this way, we see how the defining of reality, or what constitutes the "natural" as defined by those in a position of authority, comes to be resisted as the aesthetic and cultural productions of peoples bereft of a sanctioned history come to the fore.[1] The achievement of a multiperspective view of events, rendered in the fictional narratives of people from outside the realm of dominative discourse, facilitates what is in essence a historical understanding that stands in direct opposition to public history as Fielding saw it or to what Bakhtin called the unified official language. In effect, with its complicated narrative fabric, fictional narration may also reject or at least call into question any clear-cut dichotomies between "literature" and "history." A certain degree of complex consciousness, which characters' voices achieve in narrative fiction, entails the convergence and "social intercourse" of several disparate inside interpreters of events. Measured against that complexity, the rigid, monological narrative of externality, found in histories such as those of Walter Prescott Webb, comes to look like a "romancing," and thus forfeits credibility. When various voices and distinct social languages are heard in the novel, each carrying with it a distinct worldview, the historical moment is filled out, "chronotoped" in time and space. A kind of truth, so often marred and banished from the "factual," historical narratives that we often accept as true, is revealed when a more complicated conceptualization of reality (and "the great variety of the world") is somehow recovered.

In choosing to write novels, Fielding deliberately and openly employed novelistic narrative rather than fashioning his "true" representation within a historical text as was the fashion during his time. In so doing, Fielding sought to draw the reader into moments in history to which she might not otherwise be drawn. As Braudy sees it, Fielding, through his "importation of themes and methods from history and biography, . . . [sought] to renovate in the reader of his fiction a sense of actuality that had been debased by the categories and assumptions of romancers, moralizers, party historians, and 'mere' chronologers—in short, anyone who screened life through literary and epistemological forms that were fixed, arbitrary and absolute" (94). Fielding thus anticipates Hayden White's concept of "discourse" in relation to both narrative and historical forms: "that form of verbal composition which, in order to distinguish it from logical demonstration on the one side and from pure fiction on the other, we call by the name of discourse" (1978: 2). As White points out, Northrop Frye also identifies the writing of history as a type of discourse that attempts to reconstruct past events. But in reconstructing "what happened," the historian faces the restrictions of his science and craft. He is concerned with events framed by the past political or party accounts (which concerned Fielding), or more obviously, as White would suggest, with the missing story of the nonsurvivors:

> the historian inevitably must include in his narrative an account of some event or complex of events for which the facts that would permit a plausible explanation of its occurrence are lacking. And this means that the historian must "interpret" his materials by filling in the gaps in his information on inferential and speculative grounds. A historical narrative is thus necessarily a mixture of adequately and inadequately explained events, a congeries of established and inferred facts, at once a representation that is an interpretation and an interpretation that passes for an explanation of the whole process mirrored in the narrative. (1978: 51)

While Northrop Frye launches harsh criticism against this type of historical interpretation, granted the historian's need to fill in the gaps during the construction of a historical narrative, Savoie Lottinville addresses another important "complication" concerning the narration of history—the question, "With whom do we march, the Indians or the army?" Lottinville writes: "In general, the white historian will place greatest reliance upon white (official) sources, using Indian testimony, when it has been preserved, as both countervailing and complementary evidence. This being so, he must find and rhetorically construct the cresting phases of his history. If he does not, he will have the straight line of 'How it happened' but the 'What happened' may forever remain obscure" (62). The tasks of the historian and fictional writer here begin to converge, for while we know that the historian consciously or unconsciously chooses "with whom to march" despite attempts at objectivity, the decision is much like that of the fictional writer who must choose a perspective or point of view from which the narration of events will emerge. While it cannot be overlooked that history is usually written from the point of view of the victors, we must still ask to what extent the history we read is a construct of a historical imagination and to what extent it is rigorously empirical historical interpretation. Walter Prescott Webb's histories soon make it obvious with whom the narrator marches and how he is filling the gaps with imagination; moreover, a history such as Webb's fills the gaps while allowing imagination to substitute for hard information that *was* available (as we shall see from Shannon's critique of *The Great Plains* in Chapter 2).

Webb is credited with a luminosity in his writing of history which draws into history readers who otherwise might have been turned away. In this way, Webb shared with Fielding some of the concerns for history as mere chronicle; like Fielding, he presumably sought to "renovate in the reader of his fiction a sense of actuality that had been debased by the categories and assumptions of romancers, moralizers, party historians, and 'mere' chronologers through an importation of themes and methods from history and biography." The important difference is that instead of turning to novel writing, Webb continued, with few exceptions, to represent himself as a "historian" at a time when the academy, as well as the general public, thought of history writing as a science rather than as an art form. Despite the art attributed to Webb's literary style, he continued to maintain that his narrative representations were factually based.

The manner in which Webb carries out his project will be explored in the next chapter. For now, the question of genre needs to be addressed more closely. Webb's narration reflects the prejudices of his time against a native population dominated not only by the victors but also by historical representations of those events which had vanquished the former. Webb's narrative representation too quickly satisfies his audience's perception of what constitutes history. Frye's criticism cautions against this type of "fiction," which, however "factual," may result from the play of imagination that White considers essential. As we have seen, in Frye's view, a history (or at least "proper" history) belongs to the category of "discursive writing," so that when the fictional element—or mythic plot structure—is "obviously" present (as will be shown in Chapter 2 to be the case in Webb's history), "it ceases to be history altogether and becomes a bastard genre, a product of an unholy, though not unnatural, union between history and poetry" (White 1978: 83).

Though this criticism serves Frye's purpose well when juxtaposing "ideal" history and myth, White challenges Frye's views by pointing to the historian's need to furnish the explanatory effect through "emplotment" by genre. Even then, Frye's historical theory sets up modes or divisions in narrative which define themselves according to certain characteristics, and the latter, despite White's challenge, are helpful in the study of Webb's kind of narration. Among the categories of myth (high mimetic, low mimetic, and ironic) is the category of romance. In a romance, the hero is superior in degree to others and to the environment. Narrative examples of this are found in "parts of classical and early European epics; romances; legends, folktales, marchen (fairy tales), and ballads" (Martin: 33). Webb's narration reads like a romance, with Webb himself and the Anglo colonizer as fairy-tale beings superior to others in and of the environment; the work sets forth a certain ethic of imperialism.

Yet without these "stories," or emplotments, according to White, historians could do little more than offer chronicles. In White's *The Content of the Form: Narrative Discourse and Historical Representation,* the question re-emerges more specifically in terms of the historian's use and "faculty" of the imagination, or what Frye would call the "fictional element." In his chapter "Narrative in Contemporary Historical Theory," White outlines various views on the role of narrative in historical theory, from Anglo American analytical philosophers to social-scientifically oriented historians, from hermeneutically oriented philosophers to historical defenders of a "craft notion of Historical studies who view narrative as a perfectly respectable way of 'doing history'" (1987: 31). White concludes the chapter by defending the use of imagination in any attempt to "realistically" represent "the human past," regardless of whether this endeavor be framed within a narrativized history or a historical narrative:

> One can produce an imaginary discourse about real events that may not be less "true" for being imaginary. It all depends upon how one construes the function of the faculty of imagination in human nature.
>
> The same is true with respect to narrative representations of reality, especially when, as in historical discourses, these representations

are of "the human past." How else can any past, which by definition comprises events, processes, structures, and so forth, considered to be no longer perceivable, be represented in either consciousness or discourse except in an "imaginary" way? Is it not possible that the question of narrative in any discussion of historical theory is always finally about the function of imagination in the production of a specifically human truth? (1987: 57)

Of course one's perspective depends upon one's school of history. White, for obvious reasons, is considered an outsider by most professional historians. Within the realm of history proper, it is generally agreed that "Narrative historians [give] their attention to story, to great events and human interest, and to individual heroism and depravity" (Shafer: 21–22). Narrative histories do indeed provide "a communication link between the scholar and the public": but the emphasis in a scholarly monograph is on "meticulous research into source material. Often—though not always—it presents an exhaustive treatment of a narrow subject" (Shafer: 22). In any case, historians cannot escape the question of evidence, how the available "evidence" is used "imaginatively," or how new "facts" can be imaginatively created, or why it is that certain "facts" are selected and foregrounded, making them more readily available for reiteration. A relationship between "facts" and the imagination presumably characterizes historical writings and distinguishes them from literary works. Narrative history, because "it is literary and dramatic in character," does accomplish some of what Fielding sought in the eighteenth century: a wider audience because of its greater appeal. However, that appeal, in good, scholarly history must not sacrifice the science for the literature. One genre depends on the other: "it must be said that some monographic literature is well written, even lively, and that in any event the best of narrative historians, who find large audiences must base their work on monographic literature" (Shafer: 21–22).

There is yet another feature of narrative in history that has much more to do with Fielding's concern, and later Bakhtin's, with public history or a "unified official language." From the present-day point of view of the historian, the role of history as a true explanatory picture of events is subject to doubt. Allan Megill, for example, has much to say of the perspectival factor in narrative history: "Upon recountings, explanations arise. Recountings and explanations presuppose an interpretive perspective, and, in the best histories, they modify and enrich such a perspective. The articulation of perspectives is a contribution to knowledge that historians too often over-look or view with discomfort" (653). Still, the recording of "facts" drawn from concrete evidence and the chronicling of social details, notwithstand-ing White (with Frye's criticism still valid), allows for the use of the imagi-nation. Without imagination, how could the past be told, especially the past of "non-historical" peoples or of peoples whose histories have been suppressed?

Emplotment entails two important functions, each of which is affected by the degree of imagination that comes to the fore in the construction of a history: one function is causality—the manner in which a historian, from his or her perspective, links events in sequences and patterns; the other is repetition—certain histories homologize fictions that recur to explain events otherwise inexplicable. Shlomith Rimmon-Kenan's analysis and syn-thesis of various theories of narrative fictions (1983) and Wallace Martin's further explanation of various distinctions (1986) are particularly helpful here. Rimmon-Kenan cites Gérard Genette's distinction between "histoire," "récit," and "narration," calling them story, text, and narration, respectively. The usefulness of these distinctions, as Martin points out, is that "we can't discuss the 'how' of storytelling without assuming a stable 'what' that can be presented in various ways" (108). "Story" designates the narrated events, abstracted from their disposition in the text, together with the participants or characters as well as their setting (Rimmon-Kenan: 3). Put another way, Genette's "story" consists of the preverbal raw materials in their chronologi-cal and causal order (Martin: 108). The "text," or the narrative, is what undertakes the telling of these events. Since the text is a spoken or written discourse, it implies someone who speaks or writes it. The act or process of production represents the third aspect—"narration." This, according to Martin, involves the relations between the speaker/writer (the narrative "voice") and the audience/reader: "Genette's 'discourse' contains all the fea-tures that the writer adds to the story, especially changes of time sequence, the presentation of consciousness of the characters, and the narrator's rela-tion to the story and the audience" (108).

My use of "story" in this work, then, really accrues from the common, everyday use of the word, referring to something we are told and remem-ber, something that results, when the raw material ("story" in Genette's terms) has been sorted out in the mediative "narration." The "text" is that upon which time and changing ideological stances have also had a formative influence. But it is with "narration" and how it "works" that I am most concerned. Richard Slotkin provides a concrete example not only of how familiar stories come to be repeated but of how historical events can culminate in a literary, cultural production of mythic proportions. He demonstrates what the Daniel Boone stories did for the construction of the "Mythology of the American Frontier" during an earlier period of U.S. history. Slotkin shows how the repetition of what is essentially the same story may have its origins in actual events, but is later transformed into a literary convention which in turn perpetuates itself. Referring to the first 250 years of American history, he states that "repetition is the essence of a process" in which the "problems and preoccupations of the colonists became transformed into 'visions which compel belief' in a civilization called American":

> Certain instances of experience consistently recurred in each colony
> over many generations; translated into literature, these experiences
> became stories which recurred in the press with rhythmic persistence.
> At first such repetition was the result of real recurrence of experi-
> ences. The Indian war and captivity narratives, for example, grew out
> of the fact that many pious and literate New Englanders were contin-
> ually falling into the hands of the Indians or attempted to explain
> their actions in battle. Once in literary form, the experience became
> available as a vehicle for *justifying philosophical and moral values* which
> may have been extrinsic to the initial experience but which preoccu-
> pied the minds of the reading public. Thus Cotton Mather and others
> wrote 'improvements' of the captivity narratives and used them in
> jeremiads and revival sermons. Through repeated appearances and
> recastings in the literary marketplace, a narrative which proved viable
> as a bestseller or a vehicle for religious and commercial persuasions
> would be imitated by more or less professional writers (where such
> existed) or those emulous of literary or ecclesiastical reputation. Thus
> the experience would be reduced to an imitable formula, a literary
> convention, a romantic version of the myth. When enough literature
> had been written employing the convention, it might become a sort
> of given between writer and audience, a set of tacit assumptions on
> the nature of human experience, on human and divine motivations,
> on moral values, *and on the nature of reality*. At this point the conven-
> tion has some of the force of myth: the experience it portrays has
> become an image which automatically compels belief by a culture-

wide audience in the view of reality it presents. Thus in tracing the development of the conventions of narrative literature, we are tracing the development—by accretion of symbols characteristic of cultural values—of a distinct world vision and an accompanying mythology emerging from the early experiences of Europeans in the wilderness. (20–21; my emphasis)

As we shall see, in Webb's work the functions of the characters serve as stable, constant elements in a tale, regardless of how or by whom they are fulfilled.[2] We might ask what these rhetorical strategies in "history" say politically, socially, and historically about a particular nation and culture. Given the rise of any new "contest for property and profit" (Limerick: 292), "how" these same constructions within different stories reemerge at the very moment in which they do so could become immediately apparent regardless of any specific geographical site or historical moment. Possibly, the "story" is in many cases already written or inscribed in consciousness through re-peated tellings that comfort audiences or reinforce their belief systems. In present-day dominant media, we recognize the familiar patterns that feed our assumptions on the nature of human experience. The historian, like the fictional writer's narration, is already controlled by this essential story that begs to be repeated. The writer who has experienced or at least witnessed the other side of the confirming "patterns of truth" (as Webb will call them) can bring to the surface a competing narrative truth, a story that opposes or at least complicates the overall picture. Such a writer may even succeed in unbinding the spell of the reiterated, dominative story. The task of the reader of history is to uncover the underlying strategies modeling accounts of events provided by a writing that serves a particular ideology. At stake is the complex and subtle reality of the individual cultures which are threat-ened and even eliminated by historical distortions. Before proceeding to explore Webb's narrative language, we should situate it within the context of a political discourse surrounding the writing of history as a rhetoric of dominance.

WEBB AND THE HISTORY OF THE WEST

Webb's story exemplifies a history which falls directly within the Turner school of historiography. As such, Webb's story provides a myth of a cohe-sive, unified American culture, one that became an important rehearsal of a rhetoric of repetition. Henry Nash Smith notes how well the writings of Frederick Jackson Turner helped promote the idea that through "nature," more specifically through struggles on a new frontier (like those which Webb places in the foreground), the individual as well as the American nation is reborn—or regenerated. This may partially explain the popularity of Webb's history, for as Smith shows, these concepts were ingrained in the "American" consciousness long before the "West" was "won." Smith quotes from Turner's *The West and American Ideals,* an address delivered at the University of Washington, June 17, 1914: "American democracy was born of no theorist's dream; it was not carried in the Susan Constant to Virginia, nor in the Mayflower to Plymouth. It came stark and strong and full of life out of the American forest, and it gained new strength each time it touched a new frontier" (253). Smith suggests that Turner's interpretation of history was shaped by a stock of poetic images he had at his disposal:

> The idea of nature suggested to Turner a poetic account of the influence of free land as a rebirth, a regeneration, a rejuvenation of man and society constantly recurring where civilization came into contact with the wilderness along the frontier.
>
> Rebirth and regeneration are categories of myth rather than of economic analysis, but ordinarily Turner kept his metaphors under control and used them to illustrate and vivify his logical propositions rather than as a structural principle or a means of cognition: that is, he used them rhetorically not poetically. (253)

Unlike Turner's, Webb's language, as we shall see in the next chapter, does not control this overflow into poetic language, nor does it resist the overuse of metaphors, yet his poetic coloring and the critique Shannon leveled against his work did not keep Webb's narration of events from being read as history. Webb's history and others like it continued to shape the American concept of the West consistent with earlier formulations. Yet, why, during this particular epoch of U.S. history, was Webb's "history" so acceptable? If we situate Webb's work within the particular moment in history in which it makes its appearance, we find various answers. Smith also provides one: he shows how the Turner thesis had been shaken and needed to be shored up. While it upheld a set of agrarian values that accorded with the "winning of the West" mythology, it could not be squared with the intervening industrial revolution: "The First World War had shaken Turner's agrarian code of values as it destroyed so many other intellectual constructions of the nineteenth century. He continued to struggle with the grievous problems of the modern world, but his original theoretical weapons were no longer useful" (Henry Nash Smith: 259).[3]

Webb's narrative of the Great Plains rushes to the assistance of Turner's weakening position:

> Turner's predicament illustrates what has happened to the tradition
> within which he worked. From the time of Franklin down to the end
> of the frontier period almost a century and a half later, the West had
> been a constant reminder of the importance of agriculture in Ameri-
> can society. It had nourished an agrarian philosophy and an agrarian
> myth that purported to set forth the character and destinies of the
> nation. The philosophy and the myth affirmed an admirable set of
> values, but they ceased very early to be useful in interpreting Ameri-
> can society as a whole because they offered no intellectual apparatus
> for taking account of the industrial revolution. A system which
> revolved about a half-mystical conception of nature and held up as
> an ideal a rudimentary type of agriculture was powerless to con-
> front issues arising from the advance of technology. Agrarian theory
> encouraged men to ignore the industrial revolution altogether, or to
> regard it as an unfortunate and anomalous violation of the natural
> order of things. (Henry Nash Smith: 259)

Through the emphasis he places on the hardships of the Plains on the pioneering settlers, Webb shows another war that was being fought, one that serves not only to glorify his heroes but also to continue to falsely present them as one unified people. In speaking to a Nebraskan audience in "The Story of Some Prairie Inventions," Webb's metaphor of battle or war abets his mystification of the Great Plains and its newly arrived people. The metaphor of battle introduces a picture of a unified and cohesive community, part of the myth of the ancestors which his audience holds dear. He tells the descendants of those pioneers what they want to hear. He proclaims for them a war against the terrain, whereas the only one they really fought was against the outnumbered and overpowered American Indian, whose main source of food, the buffalo, had been systematically destroyed:

> In speaking of this Battle of the Plains, I would not have you think
> that I speak of Nebraska alone. The battlefield was half as big as the

nation. It stretched from Mexico on the south to Canada on the north; it was several hundred miles wide, extending from the edge of the eastern woodland into and through the Rocky Mountains. All along the eastern edge of this land thousands of people were engaged in a common struggle. Fortunately, an occasional victory in any part of the country—in Illinois, Kansas, Texas or Nebraska—conferred its benefits on plainsmen elsewhere. The problem of one was the problem of all, and the fruits of success in one place were soon enjoyed in other places. (Webb 1969b: 28–29)

As for the industrial revolution, Webb reconciled agrarian philosophy with industrial America by upholding the important role that inventions such as the Colt, barbed wire, and the windmill played in the winning of the West.

At the crux of Webb's thesis is a reinforcement of a national identity associated with a people struggling against odds which are eventually overcome. The story sounds innocent enough, except that it is also a story of exclusion; the struggles of the "others," those who get in the way, are not taken into account. Their existence plays a role in these constructions only as they are written in as obstacles that, like the harsh environment, contribute to the struggle: The greater the obstacle, the more heroic the appointed people. Webb wrote a history which vindicated his people, also struggling with notions of class identity. In line with the character of his people, he wrote a history that challenged elitist academicians' view of how history should be written. By bringing poetry and romance into his narrative, Webb provided something his people could read enjoyably and with uplift. Putting his people "on the map" (so to speak), he makes them a part of the landscape they occupied; Webb's people could claim this history as their own. Rather than include the similar struggles of other communities within his view, Webb procures for his readers a sense of solidarity, the "us," along with the compulsory construction and scapegoating of the "other." This nationalistic, imperialist discourse, in the name of democracy, inevitably turns a blind eye to the struggles of those unfortunate enough to have been caught on the other side of the "progress" of a nation. The heroic myth would certainly have recalled, to some, that of the Hebrews as a "chosen people" in the desert. To others, it would have borne out the popular Spencerian notion of progress as a necessary (not accidental) means of perfectibility, the eradication of "immorality and evil."[4]

NARRATIVE REITERATION
AND CULTURAL ERASURE

Webb's history thus served his readers as a reminder of a destiny for which they had suffered and labored: it negotiated some kind of awakening, perhaps, of archetypes inscribed in their unconscious scheme of things. Analysis of the narrative elements in a reiterative history such as Webb's reveals certain rhetorical devices that are paramount not only in history but in political rhetoric as well. We should also observe that Webb's story is continually being reconstructed: a particular machinery of language is persistently used for the construction of the rhetoric of dominance. The historian's story is constructed within a prefabricated framework, the framework of an evolutionary theory of development that avoids the uncertain. Webb falls within a predictable cadence. The storyteller invents what the past meant; but the historian and/or politician seldom solves his real problem—to tell how it was not to know what was coming next.

Native Americans and Mexicanos may have been erased to a certain extent through language manipulation in this type of history, but as we shall see in subsequent chapters, the process of labeling or of assigning new meanings to words applied to the characters of history becomes itself a Proppian "function" in a larger narrative. The story of how histories conforming to the Turner school of historiography and of how the production of images supporting this view of U.S. history took hold is also told through a different type of historiography. Patricia Limerick points to the cycles of repetition as she surveys one "conquest" after another within the "unbroken past of the American West." With the temporal shifts she employs in constructing her narrative of history, Limerick draws parallels between the attitudes toward "the other" as they existed during the American Southwest of the eighteenth and nineteenth centuries and those of the Reagan Presidency and recent times generally. By exposing the repetitious nature of these cycles of conquest, Limerick also makes possible the extraction, from many stories, of a common pattern or "function" of narrative histories. The histories can be viewed as products of their times; they arise from an insatiable need for justification and are directly related to the upholding of the hegemony and especially to the exertion of dominance. Through various temporal shifts, Limerick shows how the actors represent constant elements in the larger narrative. Always present are the dominator and dominated, the aggressor and the unfortunate victim, the occupier and the displaced. The same attitudes are put in the foreground with essentially the same results. She reveals that the writing of history is bound together with the ideological worldview of scholars. History cannot be separated from the historian. Thus a certain brand of history making is due in large part to the use of shared rhetorical, narrative, and linguistic devices in the service of a specific ideology.

The aim of the present work is to approach historiography as narrative and to identify devices instrumental to the telling of a story that fulfills a cultural need to justify past as well as present events, a story which in its very essence belongs to a larger construction. With the reader's forbearance, I will next examine specific aspects of Webb's *The Great Plains;* but I relate them to a fierce spirit of resistance in Américo Paredes's literary works two chapters later. Together, these two chapters present a conversing through time between Webb and Paredes. Before and after these two chapters, I try to show how Webb's construction and Paredes's resistance are set in a different light by the literary texts of U.S. Mexicanas who subvert the limited vision imposed and perpetuated by various forms of the rhetoric of dominance.

2

WALTER PRESCOTT WEBB'S "THE GREAT PLAINS" AND "THE TEXAS RANGERS"

The Dissolution of History in Narrative

*The mixture of races meant in time that the common soldiers
in the Spanish service came largely from pueblo or sedentary
Indian stock, whose blood, when compared with that
of the Plains Indians, was as ditch water.*

—WEBB, *THE GREAT PLAINS*, *1931*

*A buzzard is circling slowly when we first meet Trace Jordan. He is a
hard man—a prospector and buffalo hunter—who is used to the harsh
conditions of the Southwest mountain ranges. Now he is dying from a
bullet wound—shot by a gang led by a famous half-breed tracker.
They have killed his partner and are about to finish him off, too.
But Trace has one slim chance . . . a dark-haired señorita
who gives him the opportunity to survive.*

—ADVERTISEMENT FOR *THE BURNING HILLS*, 1993,
BY LOUIS L'AMOUR

 WALTER Prescott Webb's *The Great Plains* (1931) and *The Texas Rangers* (1935) established the uniqueness of a special breed of men in an extraordinarily harsh environment. These two works typify the kind of historiography that laid the groundwork for the exclusion of "the other" from the larger story—the mythology of Manifest Destiny, or the American Dream. Webb's flair for colorful language and accessible concepts (of struggle, endurance, survival, and eventual triumph) and his reliance on oral tradition had a great popular appeal. In this chapter I attempt to isolate aspects of language Webb employs in his narration as well as reveal how his reiteration of recognizable situations tells a convincing story. Webb's language in *The Great Plains* has not yet been explored in a way that might elucidate how this book contributed significantly to the mythmaking of the American West; nor has the facility with which it was able to capture the public mind been investigated. The popularity of romantic narratives such as these falls within a tradition of mythmaking that is freely loaded with ideological language. Language servicing a dominant ideology accomplishes the task of confirming particular viewpoints by repeating similar constructions. These repeated constructions utilize linguistic and rhetorical devices that produce the same effects, and they can be identified. How *The Great Plains* "functions" outside its own narrative but within the narrative historiography of its time typifies the process, and so it is a matter of considerable importance.

Webb's rhetoric goes well beyond extolling the virtues of one cultural group and distinguishing it or showing a preference for it. His ethnocentric interpretation of the history of the West, the geographical region he identifies as the Great Plains area lying west of the ninety-eighth meridian, celebrates the superiority of a pure American stock and sets forth defining principles by which "the other" (more specifically the African American, the American Indian, and the Mexican American) would come to be socially and historically constructed. The success of Webb's histories is to a certain degree due to his exclusion of certain people from the history of the West on the basis of racist premises. Webb distorts historical reality by homogenizing the "West" as the land of the pure Americans, the white settlers, provided they were of English, Scots, or Scots-Irish descent. All other humans are deemed foreigners, inferiors, or wild animals. Webb's views thus represent a narrativized version of ideas about Aryan supremacy which were widespread also in Europe during the period in which *The Great Plains* was published and acclaimed as history. None of Webb's statements below are accurate:

> What is true of the "Indians" is in a measure true of the *wild animals*. The Great Plains afforded the last virgin hunting grounds in America, and it was there that the "most characteristic American animal" made its last stand against the advance of the white man's *civilization*.
>
> The West or the Great Plains, presents also a survival of the early American stock, the so-called typical American of English or Scotch and Scotch-Irish descent. The *foreign* element is prominent in the prairie region of the Middle West, as represented by "Germans" in Illinois and Iowa and by "Scandinavians" in Montana and in the eastern Dakotas. But once we go into the arid region of the Plains, partic-

ularly in the "Southwest," we find or did find until very recent times, the *pure American stock*—Smiths, Joneses, McDonalds, Harveys, Jameses, and so on. The *Negroes* did not move west of the ninety-eighth meridian, the Europeans were not attracted by their arid lands, the *Chinese* remained on the Pacific coast, and the *Mexican* element stayed close to the southern border. (1931: 509; my emphasis)

On the other side of literary historiography, Américo Paredes's *With His Pistol in His Hand* (1958) showed many of Webb's assertions in both his major works to be racially biased, *The Texas Rangers* more overtly so. Though in this chapter I am not as concerned with the racist nature of these histories as with how they function and contribute significantly to the mythmaking of the American West, it is important to recognize that there exists a debate regarding Webb's racism as well as the quality of his scholarship.

Rodolfo Acuña's *Occupied America* (1972) includes a note indicating feelings of regret that Webb may have had prior to his death in 1963 because "he would not have time to re-write his *Texas Rangers* and correct his comments and prejudices about Mexicans as reflected in that book," as they are recalled by historian W. E. Hollon in a letter to Larry McMurtry (Acuña: 51–52, endnote 57). While Américo Paredes has commented on how Webb probably hoped some bright, young, and perhaps "tame" Mexican would someday write the Mexican side of the matter, Hollon comes to Webb's defense, claiming environment as a major contributor to racial attitudes: "All of us who grew up in Texas on Texas history two generations ago, did not know any better in our attitudes toward the Negroes and Mexicans. It takes a long time to grow out of one's environment. So don't be too harsh on Webb. He grew into the most tolerant, intellectual giant that Texas ever produced" (Acuña 51–52, endnote 57).

On numerous occasions, Paredes has recalled the looks Webb gave him as their paths crossed almost daily on the West Mall of the University of Texas at Austin campus during the years when they both taught there. "I didn't expect for him to like me, but if looks could kill," he has stated, "I would have been dead a long time ago." Yet at the UT Texas Union faculty receptions, Paredes remembers how Webb was overly friendly in the company of others. It was only through colleagues and friends that Paredes heard of Webb's having been highly offended by his criticism. "Why did he pick on me?" Webb reportedly asked. To this, Paredes responds, "Why should I pick on some poor West Texas farmer? Webb was an educated man; he should have known better" (various talks given by Paredes at UT Austin, 1988–1993). With this personal experience and the fact that the only "revision" in *The Texas Rangers,* when it was reprinted in 1965, was a new introduction by Lyndon B. Johnson, Paredes is convinced and asserts that until the day he died, Webb was a racist (plain and simple), neither tolerant nor an intellectual giant as Hollon would have it (Paredes, personal interview, March 4, 1995).

THE GREAT PLAINS' "FORM AND CONTENT"

As far as I have been able to discover, Webb never expressed regret about his writing of *The Great Plains,* which is the main focus of this chapter. Though Webb denied having been directly influenced by Frederick Jackson Turner, his general view parallels Turner's and demonstrates how the historian himself really (if semiconsciously) believes in the truth of reiterative narratives. *The Great Plains* covers the history of white settlement of a geographic area beyond what Webb calls an "institutional fault," somewhere about the ninety-eighth meridian, from 1865 to 1900. Webb's thesis proposes that at this point, "the westward movement was halted until the Industrial Revolution had provided certain technological devices which made it possible for white men to occupy the Plains area and to develop a permanent mode of living there" (Bain: 215–216).

Out of this narrative emerges a symbolic hero, *"the* people." It is the people who struggle to overcome obstacles, finally gaining power over their new and strange environment through their innovation and technology: "Practically every institution that was carried across it [the ninety-eighth meridian] was either broken or remade or else greatly altered" (Webb 1931: 8).[1] The telling of the breaking or remaking of "practically every institution that was carried across" augments the struggles the heroes of this tale faced, thus elevating them to the larger-than-life status of mythological figures. The chapters of Webb's text are titled "The Physical Basis of the Great Plains Environment," "The Plains Indians," "The Spanish Approach to the Great Plains," "The American Approach to the Great Plains, The Cattle Kingdom, Transportation and Fencing," "The Search for Water in the Great Plains, New Laws for Land and Water," "The Literature of the Great Plains and about the Great Plains," and "The Mysteries of the Great Plains in American Life." Each chapter includes from three to seven subsections dividing the chapters into topics or concerns that Webb specifically addresses.

In his chapter "The Literature of the Great Plains and about the Great Plains," Webb situates himself as historian and literary critic. He attacks literary works that look back on the past as romantic and "softened by the glamour that diffuses and sometimes makes grotesque our view of distant things." He notes that the literary man, since "he was not a cattleman," had to view the Great Plains "from afar and it immediately took on for him much of the glamour which we attach to things little known or half understood" (455). Viewing himself as a "product of his environment," Webb discredits the literary man's version of history or historical events, while he also takes a stand against overtly scholarly ways of "doing history." Ronnie Dugger praised Webb's literary style and his courage in going against the current of views about what was and was not acceptable form in the scholarship of that time: "though his experiences went back to ancient scenes of travail on the farm and his attitudes on race were narrow then, he had no fear of radicalism, when it was called for" (Dugger: 114). Onto his own narrative fiction Webb projects himself as a writer uniquely qualified to present his own version of the history of the Southwest, a history of "his" people that in its form stands apart from other genres, while in its content confirms views already in the air. Before proposing a critique of Webb's narrative style and the particular features of his language, I need to assess Webb's identification with the subject/hero of his narrative history.

WEBB AS A CHARACTER AND HIS HISTORY AS ART

Webb saw himself as a pioneer in his academic field, a view that his own personal experience of growing up on the Great Plains, as the son of a farmer/schoolteacher substantiated. Webb becomes a character in his own fiction by inventing his own persona, the one he employs in his narration. His identification with the frontiersmen about whom he writes lends credence to the voicing of a particular ideology in his work. As writer and character, with only the English language at his disposal, he perpetuates some of the myths of the "other" that are still used to justify the process of domination. Describing his research on *The Texas Rangers,* Webb characterizes himself as one among the rangers, riding the range and carrying a Colt revolver, even on the "dangerous" Mexican border:

> Trailing the Texas Rangers, who in turn had trailed the ancestors of
> some of the best people in Texas, was a combination of drudgery and
> fun. It was my first work with sources, the faded letters and reports
> of a handful of men standing between the people and their enemies,

men better with a gun than with a pen. Though the records were
abundant, I did not stop with the records. Like Parkman I went to all
the places where things had happened. I sought out the old men, still
living then, who had fought Comanches and Apaches, killed Sam
Bass at Round Rock, and broken up deadly feuds inherited from the
more deadly reconstruction. With a captain and a private I visited
every Ranger camp on the Mexican border where there were still elements of danger; I carried a commission and had the exhilarating
experience of wearing a Colt revolver in places where it might have
been useful. At night by the campfires I listened to the tales told by
men who could talk without notes. (Webb 1969a: 7–8)

Webb's playing cowboy in what sounds more like the fulfillment of an
adolescent fantasy reveals his identification with the spirit he attributes to
the brave, pioneering settlers of the new frontier. He echoes their experience
when he describes how he, too, blazed new trails (if only metaphorically),
conducting his own style of research, gaining power over his environment—
the reward for his "long journey":

The Great Plains was published in 1931, and no more need be said
about it except that it has never been revised, never will be revised by
me, never has been imitated, and I am told by the publisher it never
will go out of print. I came out of the experience of writing it—doing
something in my own way—*with a sense of power* that comes to him
who has made "a long journey" for a purpose, *overcome the hardships,*
and returned to tell with appropriate exaggeration what to him is an
important tale. (1969a: 15; my emphasis)

Webb's manipulation of the genre of narrative history becomes clear.
Though *The Great Plains* is still considered Webb's best work and was legitimized as a scholarly history, it crossed over into a genre of imaginative writing that, nonetheless, can re-write history. Such narrativization occurred
during a period that called for this type of history as justification. As both
history and literature, Webb's *The Great Plains* exerted a tremendous influence on the U.S. conception of the West and helped construct the larger
myth of the American Dream. Webb's history, as the telling of a story, contains all the features of "cultural production"; its narrative elements make it
a "literary work."

Webb has it both ways as he manipulates both genres of history and
fiction. The 1939 meeting of the Social Science Research Council examined

The Great Plains as history when it reviewed a report by Fred A. Shannon, who had been commissioned by the council to appraise the text. Shannon's critique exposed numerous inaccuracies in the "evidence" Webb's research had produced. Much offended, Webb vehemently rejected the appraisal, claiming that Shannon was prejudiced against Texans.[2] Moreover, he stated that he had never asserted that *The Great Plains* was a history, but that it was a work of art, "one that came nearer satisfying the creative desire than all else I have done" (1940/1979: 114).

During the proceedings of this meeting, several members of the Social Science Research Council and participants of the meeting agreed with sociologist Louis Wirth that *The Great Plains* is "a work of art" and insisted on discussing *The Great Plains* for its "contribution to knowledge." Webb replied by modifying his previous statement: "I do not mean to imply that *The Great Plains* is art, but I think it has an artistic side to it in its construction and in the synthesis it attempts to make" (1940/1979: 143). Within the context of this discussion, historians Roy F. Nichols and John D. Hicks argued in favor of the "artistic element in its approach" and on behalf of "its readability and its capacity to awaken the interest of students." Both historians asserted that Webb's literary language breaks with past styles of history writing and constitutes a revolt against the traditional use of "monographitis." They credit his literary language as a "refreshing blast from the plains" (Shannon 143).

The same opinion of Webb's writing prevailed twenty-five years later when Walter Rundell, Jr., claimed that Webb made manifest his "consuming desire to present history in meaningful terms and with literary felicity." Rundell also credits Webb with speaking out against historians who were unwilling, or unable, "to write with clarity and vigor": "He indicted the 'high-level historical journals of national scope' . . . for publishing articles with 'little charm, few vivid figures of speech, and practically none of that soft luminosity . . . which suffuses good writing'" (1963b: 24). The American Historical Association through Rundell credits Webb with changing "our notion of history or historical writing" and for having "made a fundamental impact on American historiography." Thus, Webb is noted for having done more than ordinary historians whose "mere production of great quantities of conventional history, however meritorious in craftsmanship, was not enough to warrant the prizes" (Rundell 1963a: 1).[3] Ronnie Dugger also commends the literary style of this "original book of history" and states that one cannot read *The Great Plains* "without knowing from the occasional loveliness of language and the occasional flights of fancy that Webb never gave up wanting to write novels" (114).[4]

LITERARY "LUMINOSITY" AS RHETORIC IN WEBB'S HISTORY

An examination of Webb's narrative strategies demonstrates how close the historian comes to distinguishing his discourse from a "logical demonstration on the one side" and a "pure fiction on the other," either realistically representing a human past, or falling prey to romantic impulses, or perhaps a "mythic plot structure." It is important to ask whether Webb adequately presents and explains events and if his particular historical account survives as a credible history or "ceases to be a history altogether." Does it instead become a "bastard genre," a product of an "unholy union between history and poetry?" (White citing Frye: 83).

Two centuries after Fielding had taken up the question of narrative qualities in history, Webb conversely raises the same question and is taken to task for it. Webb as author-hero and his work are consciously set forth as essential "functions" or instruments applied in the construction of a myth essential in its time. Apparently because of a need for justification that such histories as Webb's were to fulfill, the U.S. public and academic historians were willing to ignore obvious major factual errors in Webb's work, errors that undermine his thesis. Moreover, two novelistic features in Webb's language are very similar to the writing in Fielding's novels and to a certain extent even to Laurence Sterne's *Tristram Shandy*. Webb frequently follows an anecdote of the Plains with moralizing commentary or reflection, and he continually weaves mundane and intimate details into a larger scene.[5]

Webb's "luminous" rendering of gray histories does not escape the romantic impulses he criticizes. His "clarity and vigor" are impregnated with an imagination that distorts realities that other historians are hard pressed to ignore. The appeal of Webb's style raises some questions: Is the luminosity Webb projects onto his narrative representation procured by stereotypical turns in the field of knowledge, turns from which this form derives its appeal? How much of the luminosity is actually a phosphorescence rising from shrunken remnants of bias disguised as knowledge? To what extent is his history, as form, an accommodation to readers' need for validation of the dominant ideology by history and not by "literature"?

Webb reveals a very personal commitment to *The Great Plains* when he calls it his "autobiography with scholarly trimmings." In response to a friend's question about where he began preparation to write *The Great Plains,* he recalls his early motivation and the inspiration he gained from the environment. In so doing, he offers an example symptomatic of the language he adopts for his narration:

> I answered that I began at the age of four when my father left the humid East and set his family down in West Texas, on the very edge of the open, arid country which stretched north and west farther than a boy could imagine. There I touched the hem of the garment of the real frontier; there I tasted alkali. I was not the first man, or boy; but the first men, Indian fighters, buffalo hunters, trail-drivers, half-reformed outlaws, and Oklahoma boomers were all around, full of memories and eloquent in relating them to small boys.
>   . . . . The Indians, the fierce Comanches, had so recently departed, leaving memories so vivid and tales so harrowing that their red ghosts, lurking in every mote and hollow, drove me home all prickly with fear when I ventured too far. The whole Great Plains was there in microcosm, and the book I wrote was but an extension and explanation of what I had known first hand in miniature, in a sense an autobiography with scholarly trimmings. (1969a: 14–15)

In this passage Webb's romanticizing rhetoric is obvious enough, beginning with the appeal to childhood as, implicitly, the springhead of a vision. He follows this with the use of biblical metaphor, "the hem of the garment" (Matthew 9:20), suggesting that the real frontier is too great for his imagination to wholly appreciate, for he has arrived too late. This reinforces his premise that no frontier like this had ever before existed. When mentioning Indians, Webb consistently applies adjectives such as *fierce,* effectively augmenting the bravery of the settlers. Adding drama to the narrative, Webb keeps the Indians present by having their red ghosts linger after they have *departed,* a euphemism for their having been driven out or exterminated. He then juxtaposes these *fierce* Indians with the first *real* men (for he never gives credit to any of the *real* women who came with them) that this *real* frontier has produced: "The first *men,* Indian fighters, buffalo hunters, trail-drivers, half-reformed outlaws, and Oklahoma boomers were all around, full of memories and eloquent . . ." (my italics).

Employing quasi-poetic language in his narrative, Webb unites history and the kind of poetry he admires when he criticizes the literature of the Great Plains in the same chapter noted above. Webb claims that the cowboy poets "have perhaps made the best contributions" (457) when he praises various poems, poems that reveal the attitude toward the land and the native inhabitants, the attitude from which he seeks to extract luminosity for his own writing. For example, for Webb, Badger Clark's verses from "The Plainsmen" have in them "the essence of the spirit of the cattle country" (457):

> *Born of a free, world-wandering race,*
> *Little we yearned o'er an oft-turned sod.*
> *What did we care for a father's place,*
> *Having ours fresh from the hand of God?* (458)

In these few lines a story emerges much like Webb's. The cowboy of the Anglo American West claims membership in a chosen race. Unlike the lowly natives, "Uncle Sam's Injuns" (as they are later labeled by Andy Adams, another writer Webb cites on page 462), he was born free and may therefore rightfully wander the world seeking new frontiers, taking possession of any place that suits his fancy. Though the frontiersmen did not anticipate the particularly harsh terrain of the Great Plains, their hard work and natural superiority will inevitably help them to overcome all obstacles. Unlike the Indians, Spaniards, and Mexicans before them, these superior men have no need for an inheritance from their earthly fathers; their claims are granted to them directly from "the hand of God"—Manifest Destiny! Holding this "the spirit of the cattle country" up for our admiration, there remains little doubt from what attitudes Webb derives the "clarity and vigor" with which he writes.[6]

In *The Great Plains* specific linguistic and rhetorical devices, such as its biblical structure, can be identified: a barren land lies wasting as the essential environment until the "people" arrive, are tested, survive, and are thus regenerated. Already we have seen a romanticized, literary language employed to record past events presented as history. Additionally, Webb's narrative style includes elaborate poetic metaphors; particular adjectives distinguish the heroes from the villains in his story, while euphemisms downplay the destruction of past civilizations and communities. With these literary features, Webb provides his audience with a lively, exciting, and convincing account of past events. The mythopoetic frames are here considered a category separate from purely linguistic devices; throughout Webb's narration, however, frames and devices continually overlap.

A quest or progress mythology is the paramount frame in Webb's text. As such it lends itself to the rhetorical creation of an illusion of a unified people setting forth against the tyranny of an elitist world, struggling forth as a group against an unfriendly terrain. A common enemy is inserted into the scheme, and the conquering cultural hero type then emerges. Repeated juxtapositions also establish Manichean dichotomies of hero versus villain, virtuous warrior versus immoral common enemy. The gods are invoked in this story as if the events were part of a religious ritual or in order to make evident the rightfulness of his heroes' cause. Finally, Webb employs a paternalistic authoritative voice as in mythic storytelling rituals to provide commentary or "translation" for his readers.

These "God is on our side," romanticized constructions of "reality" have a reiterative effect in today's political rhetoric as much as in popular culture. Like Badger Clark's verses which Webb so much admired for their representation of "the essence of the spirit of the cattle country" (457), many popular types of music today promote conceptions from the past of how the West was "won." In what was recently a very popular song and a television miniseries based on the novel by Larry McMurtry, "In Lonesome Dove," Garth Brooks sings a tale of hardship on the Plains similar to Webb's. A young woman falls in love with a Texas Ranger whom she sees for the first time when he rescues from a summer storm the wagon train in which she is traveling west. She stays on in Lonesome Dove and marries the ranger; they have a son. Soon her husband is killed, but her son, who "had an angel's heart," grows up to be just as brave and heroic as his father had been: "He was a Texas lawman legacy." The son then hears that the men who had killed his father have robbed a bank "in Cherico" and are headed for Lonesome Dove, "The only thing 'tween them and Mexico."

This image of the bandits headed for the Mexican border is quickly juxtaposed with the hardworking woman upheld as a heroine, "A farmer's daughter with a gentle hand / A blooming rose in a bed of sand." Much like Webb's settlers who struggle against their new environment, this "Christian woman in the devil's land" (who could the devils be but the Indians and Mexicans who were there before the arrival of such "Christians"?) epitomizes American agricultural values set in a hostile environment. Though she had "never learned how to beat the lonely nights," she had "learned the language and she had learned to fight." At the end of the narrative, the villains "lay at the ranger's feet" (her son's), but there is some doubt as to who really killed them, unless it was the older Ranger's ghost? Or might it have been the wife's/mother's six-shooter? The song ending indicates that only legend holds the truth and that truth is known beyond any doubt only by those "in Lonesome Dove."

Though the heroine has upheld all virtues, there is one virtue that is justified in its altered state and that is the right to violence or to take vengeance for acts committed on the devil's land against the Christians, its rightful heirs. Like Webb's institutions that changed once they crossed the ninety-eighth meridian, the law is also altered when the violence committed is against the devils of the land (Brooks and Limbaugh).

If there is any doubt as to who these devils might be, Garth Brooks's earlier recording of the song "Cowboy Bill" (Berghoff and Bastian) makes it quite explicit. This narrative tells a very specific story about a Texas Ranger's confrontation with the Mexican "bandidos," who of course outnumbered the Rangers. The narrator recalls his childhood in West Texas, when an old Texas Ranger "told a good story . . . 'bout his life on the border and the way it was then." The old man dies and the boys find him, "clutching a badge that said Texas Ranger" and in old "yeller" letters it said "Texas is proud." These songs follow the familiar narrative devices Webb employs: anecdotes are followed by moral reflections and direct clarification of motives or expectations. The storyteller first draws a portrait and then outlines lessons to highlight moral implications of historical events. The labeling device (bandidos, devils), for easy reference and acceptance of qualities attributed to that which is being labeled, comes in handy in order to soften, euphemistically, evidence of violent inhumanity.

Another device Webb employs to tell a convincing story is the passive voice. The passive voice is an exercise in avoidance which serves the purpose of preventing readers from recognizing the specific character who carries out certain actions. The protagonists of his story who perform acts that would inevitably paint them unfavorably remain unnamed and unspecified. Moreover, the passive voice makes events look divinely destined rather than a result of a conscious setting forth of policy. Finally, the readers' approval of these portrayals is made necessary; quick acceptance of the storyteller's views is essential if the reader is to be on the "right" side and if the continuation of the engaging narrative is to be possible. These features of Webb's language are the subject of the following sections of this chapter.

CULTURAL UNITY AND THE QUEST OR PROGRESS MYTH

Richard Slotkin's work on the frontier myth provides insight into Webb's adoption of myth as a social and political tool: "The narrative action of the myth-tale recapitulates that people's experience in their land, rehearses their visions of that experience in its relation to their gods and the cosmos, and reduces both experience and vision to a paradigm" (6). Slotkin's extensive work on "The Mythology of the American Frontier" shows that the "believer's response to his myth is essentially nonrational and religious." The believer, like the storyteller, sees himself as a character in his own story and recognizes in myth "his own features, the life and appearance of his ancestors, and the faces of the gods who rule his universe, and he feels that the myth has put him in intimate contact with the ultimate powers which shape all of life" (6–7). These mythologies provide a story of origin for a people devoid of one and fulfill both the psychological and social functions of providing cultural unity by reconciling and uniting individualities into a collective identity: "[myth] draws on the content of individual and collective memory, structures it, and develops from it imperatives for belief and action. . . . Myth describes a process, credible to its audience, by which knowledge is transformed into power" (6–7). If this is not the case, there is no myth: "A myth that ceases to evoke this religious response, this sense of total identification and collective participation, ceases to 'function' as myth" (p. 8).

But reiteration is also necessary. A tale such as this must be repeated "through the course of several generations—or even several retellings within one generation—in order for the myth to acquire the evocative power necessary for its evolution into myth" (Slotkin: 8). The essential "story," that which can be abstracted from Webb's text, is epistemological in nature. Like myths, it offers both an explanation and a description of how and why the West came to be dominated by the Anglo and in its essence tells of the white man's use of whatever means necessary to move west, and so explains why he now rightfully (as destiny manifested) dominates that region. Webb's "text" is the book itself, the only thing directly available to the reader. Through the text, we learn of the story (what happened in its raw form) and can discern its mode of narration. Webb's narration "dramatizes the world vision and historical sense of a people or culture," a mythological construct that can have the effect of "reducing centuries of experience into a constellation of compelling metaphors" (Slotkin: 6).

The impact that this written discourse had at the moment in which it made its appearance lies outside the text. Webb's direct "telling" of the Anglo occupation of the Great Plains, affirming the fact already within the frame of the new reality, is revealed to us through the "narration." The "narration" involves the relations between the writer and the audience/reader. Webb's identification with his heroes here becomes paramount in a narra-

tion containing the story of the terrain and the conditions of this frontier lying west of the ninety-eighth meridian. The terrain was unique, unlike any
other seen before in history. Because of the environmental hardships the
Great Plains presented to newcomers, every institution introduced to that
geography suffered drastic changes. As if to preface Webb, in 1844 Ralph
Waldo Emerson was claiming for modernity the frontier with "no past":
"America is the country of the Future. From Washington, . . . through all its
cities, states, and territories, it is a country of beginnings, of projects, of vast
designs, and expectations. It has no past: all has an onward and prospective
look. . . . Gentlemen, there is a sublime and friendly Destiny by which the
human race is guided" (quoted in Hills 97).

Having suffered and adapted, a special breed of man emerged. His
proven stamina and his ability to withstand these hardships, for he had assured the Anglo American of his "rightful" place, succeeded where others
had failed before him. But this "new" and difficult terrain also required the
construction and enforcement of a new set of rules for survival of the newcomers. A great many American Indians and Mexicans "abandoned" the
area, leaving property and cattle unattended, making it "necessary" once
again for the Anglo to take possession.

Wayne C. Booth, in his *The Rhetoric of Fiction,* points to the "authoritative telling" when he distinguishes two narrative methods in fiction: on one
hand the storyteller, author, or narrator will "authoritatively" provide insight into the mind and motives of a particular character in any given work,
and on the other hand, the character's actions are allowed to speak for themselves with the "showing" of events, reactions, and relationships: "One of the
most obviously artificial devices of the storyteller is the trick of going beneath the surface of the action to obtain a reliable view of a character's mind
and heart . . . unmistakably present whenever the author tells us what no one
in so-called real life could possibly know" (3). In *The Great Plains,* Webb
employs this fictional device when he consistently "tells" us the "mind and
heart" of the characters in his narrative history. This device is clearly at work
when Webb "translates" for us the sentiments of Coronado based on his (already translated from Spanish) letters, which he does not make available to
the reader: "If we might translate Coronado freely, here is about what he
meant to say: 'This is a country of great agricultural possibilities and very
much like Spain. But it is no place for Spaniards. There is no gold. . . . '"
(108). Before our eyes, the narrator presents a reductive picture of the whole
of Spanish ambitions in the New World, one that "rehearses the vision" that

sets up the Anglo American settlers' success story. Webb's explanation of the Spanish "failure" is a necessary preparation for the successful heroes he is about to bring into the picture, one that also makes logical the Spanish failure, according to his account.

Narrative control of the reader's beliefs comes through commentary often disguised as simile. Webb asks: "Why were the High Plains and their margins left to the undisturbed occupation of buffalo, coyotes, and Plains Indians? Why did the Spaniards in going from San Antonio to Santa Fe, detour south over a rocky road rather than take the direct route offered by a grassy plain little obstructed by either trees or mountains?" (87). Having reduced the Plains Indians to the same status as the buffalo and coyotes, Webb answers his own question. He brings his heroes to light as would a storyteller. He attempts to prove that the Spaniards, cowardly and less strenuous than his emerging heroes, circumvented the Plains because they shirked the harshness of the territory. Unlike the English (Webb's Europeans), the Spaniards were not made for these conditions: "It is apparent that the Spaniards avoided the Great Plains, or failed there for two reasons, both fairly independent of European politics. In the first place, the country itself did not attract them; in the second place, the Plains Indians repelled whatever efforts they did make at travel, occupation, or residence in the region. The result was that the Spaniards never did more than nibble around the margins of the Great Plains" (87).

With this stroke of his pen, Webb reduces the Spanish presence in the West to their characteristic "nibbling." Though this distortion did not go completely unchecked by historians other than Shannon, Webb's biographer, Necah Stewart Furman, attempts to explain Webb's biases on the grounds that he was a traditional Turnerian with a particularly Texan perspective:

> Criticism from friends and associates mainly evolved around his
> treatment of the Spanish period. His friend, George Fuermann,
> wrote, "To call our Spanish period 'thin and of little consequence'
> seems to me to put you on thin ice, but here you have the voice of
> inexperience." . . . In the opinion of Webb's associate and former
> president of Hardin Simmons University, Rupert N. Richardson,
> "Webb did not purposely minimize the influence of the Spaniard
> and Mexican, he just dealt with other matters and left them out of his
> thinking." Referring to Charles Hackett, a contemporary colleague

of Webb's at the university, as well as to Carlos Castañeda, Richardson observed that "Webb wrote about and admired the Anglos; the other men did the same for the Spaniards." John Francis Bannon, Borderlands specialist, noted that "Webb's departmental associations at Austin would have rubbed out any serious anti-Spanish bias," but, he added, "Webb was a Texan, and they do have their anti-Mex feelings." (Furman: 114)

Given the Spanish "failure" in Webb's narrative, the stage is set for a superior people to enter upon the scene. Juxtaposed in this way to the Spaniards is this "new breed of men" who squarely confront the harshness of the west—the fierce mounted Indians, the droughts, and the general environment of jackrabbits and prairie dogs, conditions unlike any other in the world and which only they could overcome. In order to survive they would have to use whatever means necessary to alter whatever institution they brought across Webb's "magic line" (Shannon's term for the ninety-eighth meridian). The Colt six-shooter, the windmill, the plough, and barbed wire would be the major inventions used to fight the "war" with the environment that lay ahead.

What Webb fails to mention is that it was the civilized Easterners, not his "special breed of men," who supplied these "major inventions," regardless of how they were altered once brought across the ninety-eighth meridian. What his "special breed of men" *did* invent on the Great Plains was a significant cultural altercation that contributed greatly to upsetting the balance of long-standing Spanish/Mexican–Indian relations. Instead of recognizing a web of established relations and interactions prior to the Anglo "arrival," Webb turns to the Indian and employs his narrative authority to argue that the Plains Indians were "'by nature' more ferocious, implacable, and cruel than the other tribes": "Perhaps this cannot be proved, but *certain well-established facts* make it certain that no other tribes, either in the woodland or in the desert, exceeded the Plains tribes in these respects. In the first place, *it may be stated* that the Plains Indians were the least civilized of all the tribes. . . . The frontiersmen on the Plains soon learned that one could not surrender to an Indian. The Indians rarely, if ever, surrendered themselves, and they had no concept of *the white man's generosity* to a vanquished foe" (59; my emphasis).

Thus early in the narrative Webb sketches his picture of heroes and villains while he ignores evidence available to historians of his time. That evidence points more to good old American industry and capitalism—the trade of guns and ammunitions in exchange for stolen Mexican goods—as the major factor contributing to the "fierceness" of the Indians he describes. Webb, instead, focuses our attention on the "inferiority" of the Plains Indians and on the Spaniards' having given the horse to the Comanches (as if they should have known better), despite Eugene C. Barker's own research (much of which Webb often cites for other purposes) regarding the lucrative trade Anglo Americans established with Comanches. Traders encouraged the Comanches and other tribes to raid on Mexicans and Tejanos by rewarding them with guns and ammunition, whiskey, and other goods in exchange for Mexican horses, mules, and other valuables: "The problem became so alarming that in 1826 Mexico's secretary of state asked the United States minister in Mexico City to stop the 'traders of blood who put instruments of death in the hands of those barbarians.' Years later, when the United States had still not stopped the traffic in armaments, one high-ranking Mexican official wondered if it was United States policy 'to use savage Indians to menace defenseless Mexicans in order to force them to abandon their lands or . . . request the protection of the United States government'" (Weber: 122).

Ignoring such evidence, Webb's agenda becomes clear. He is "emphasizing differences" to construct completely distinct cultural entities, as if these new and old inhabitants of the Plains had no influence on or interaction with each other. He augments the fierceness of the Plains Indians next to the Anglo American heroes, thus constructing the Plains Indians as "other" by presuming to define their cultural values with comments such as the following: ". . . the Indians counted their wealth in horses, paid their debts in horses, and bought their wives with horses. . . . The Indian rode his commissary into battle, and though it was only when he could obtain no other food that he ate his horse, his willingness to do so made him more formidable. . . . Where all men were mounted, the Indian's courage depended almost solely on the speed of his horse" (61–62). The practice of offering gifts on the occasion of marriage is reduced to a simple buying and selling of human life. The image of Indians eating horse flesh and their lack of natural courage are no less reductive in the construction of a slanted history. Like the fiction writer, Webb gets inside the minds and hearts of these ferocious Indians to tell us what they were thinking, what they had or had not dreamed of, and what they "felt," as well as what was their "natural" disposition:

Something had happened to revolutionize the Plains Indians, to give
them a majesty and power that they had never known before....
The Indians had obtained horses and had learned to ride, and found
themselves possessed of a liberty and power which, when combined
with their natural fierceness ... made them a scourge and a terror. It
was indeed a momentous event when a Plains Indian, half afraid and
uncertain, threw his leg for the first time across the back of a Spanish
horse ... and found himself borne along over a grassy plain with an
ease and speed he had never dreamed possible of attaining. (115)

By focusing our attention on the terrifying enemy, Webb calls for "sympa-
thetic involvement in [the] plight" of the pioneering settlers (Booth 5). One
can ungrudgingly appreciate the finely focused detail of the leg thrown
across the horse. Even then, without presenting any evidence to support his
views, and forgetting that the Pueblos lived in highly developed cities, Webb
characterizes the Indians of the Plains as less civilized than other Indians.
Unlike their white counterparts, the Plains Indians took no mercy on their
captured or defeated enemy; their courage came only from the speed of their
horses, which they used to buy their wives and to make meals of when food
was lacking. In this way, the storyteller's apparently intimate and detailed,
almost godlike knowledge of the physical Indian, someone he admittedly
never knew except as "ghost-like presences," makes the unfamiliar familiar
to the reader as if we were eyewitnesses to momentary, imaginary incidents
of conflict where the heroes and villains are clearly demarcated in advance.
Webb "encoded" the Indians as especially fierce with the acquisition of the
horse. He strategically builds heroes out of his white settlers and simultaneously justifies the failure of the Spaniard and the eventual elimination of the
American Indian "obstacle."

With the use of epic bard stratagems, a "form of artificial authority,"
Webb "writes scarcely a page without some kind of direct clarification of
motives or expectations, and of the relative importance of events. And
though the gods themselves are often unreliable, Homer—the Homer we
know—is not" (Booth 4). By denigrating the Spaniard and the Indian while
extolling the virtues of the "English," he places the "I" right in the middle
of his story and thus becomes a character in his own story. As the evidence
would indicate, Webb recognizes in the myth he helps to create "his own
features and experience, the life and appearance of his ancestors" (Slot-

kin: 7). He "blazes new trails" with his history, just as the settlers with whom he shares a cultural heritage had done before him on the Great Plains. Totally partisan in his outlook, he identifies with his white heroes and must therefore justify the actions of the characters he creates.

NARRATIVE DEVICES IN WEBB'S NARRATIVE, AND SHANNON'S CRITIQUE

With the help of narrative or linguistic devices, we see Webb's storytelling as "knowledge transformed into power" (Slotkin: 7) when he introduces phrases like "the truth was" (127) or states that certain factors in his "re-examination of well-known facts concerning the northern Spanish frontier" make a particular state of affairs "quite clear." In doing so, he invites his readers to assent to his villain-and-hero antithesis as a true-to-life stimulant for reading more about it: the antithesis serves as a Proppian "function." Though a substantiation of alleged "facts" appears nowhere in his study, Webb as paternalistic storyteller demands that we assent to his supposition that "the Plains Indians, Apaches and Comanches, became an insuperable *obstacle* to the northern advance" (117; my emphasis). In this way, Webb makes heroes of the settlers, and simulating the role of epic poet, he "works in the same explicit and systematic way to keep our judgments straight" (Booth 5). In the strategic deployment of innuendoes, notably slanted epithets, as for example the "adroit" and "unerring" skill attributed to Stephen F. Austin, Webb reveals his biases and storytelling skills. Moreover, he "properly" names or labels for us the various characters in his story, such as the "foreigners" in Texas (the French) at a time when the Anglo American had only recently and forcibly legalized his own foreign presence.

"Labeling" is a specific linguistic device frequently used rhetorically and reiteratively in texts such as Webb's.[7] Stereotyping, or—in the media—the frequent use of a "catchword," economizes on time. Catchwords also have the unfortunate effect of identifying persons or events by the qualifiers which are conveniently attached to them: nobody questions such haphazardly attached qualifiers. These catchwords cue the reader into a set of beliefs. By labeling, we practice a form of ideologically loaded name-calling. Whether applied deliberately or conventionally, this practice can be an instrument of intellectual, ideological, political, and economic domination, if not victimization. Webb's narrative devices, in which labeling is central, help him to "explain" past actions and in so doing propose the historical motivation for the "necessary" removal and extermination of the American Indian "obstacle" and for the glorification and mystification of those exceptional beings who removed them.

The absurdity of some of his attempts to explain complex circumstances of the West through generalizations becomes "quite clear" when, in trying to paint "a vivid impression of the effect of the horse upon the Comanches," Webb describes how it was possible for the "short-legged mountain Indian to come into and take possession of the most desirable portion of the Great Plains, take it from the long-legged Indians who had for centuries been trekking across the vast distances" (65). His "explanation" includes some astounding logic: "Is it not reasonable to assume that the Comanches found it necessary to become horsemen to compensate for their short legs?" (65). This explanation draws the portrait first and then offers his "logical" explanation afterward. As we shall see later with the story of the Colt six-shooter, Webb frequently follows anecdotes with moral reflection in order to highlight moral implications of historical events: a good ranger undoubtedly had long legs, but Webb does not care to account for how the Aztecs and Mayas managed to dominate a continent without the use of the horse.

Webb tells us what is "quite clear" when, by his own admission, "the problem is a complex one ... not all of which can be taken into consideration in this study" (117). Yet, he continues to clarify matters by making sweeping derogatory generalizations about cultures other than his own. Caught in the dilemma of the historian with a literary bent, Webb "gives pleasure by compromising truth" (Gay: 4). While the objective epic poet of tradition tells of events so old that his "evidence" cannot be verified, Webb's, to a much greater extent, can be. His linguistic device of telling us what is "quite clear" is convincing only to readers for whom the quasi-mythic tale reaffirms their already deeply held beliefs.

Shannon's critique of Webb's exaggerated comparisons of the Spaniards and the Indians with the English shows how quasi-mythical accounts of experience can turn out to be falsifications when evidence from history is available for scrutiny:

> It is an exaggeration to say that "No Spaniard produced his own
> wealth through manual labor," or to declare of the English that
> "... in no sense did they depend upon the natives to produce for
> them" (page 89). The English in the early days of settlement did
> enslave Indians whenever it was possible and there may have been at
> least one Spaniard who amassed goods by his own toil. The Spaniard

was spoiled, it is true, by finding *docile* Indians to take advantage of,
but Webb goes so far as to say (page 90) that ". . . without pueblo Indians in America the Spanish colonial system did not stand." The doc-
trine reaches its climax on page 94 with the generalization that Spain
made ". . . no headway in colonization where the colonies would
not be founded squarely upon a native people who would . . . 'do all
the work.'"

Webb realizes that the undesirable nature of the land was a deter-
rent force until 1700 but he over estimates the importance of the *fierce*
Indians on horses after that date. The chapter entitled "The Spanish
Approach to the Great Plains" could well have been reduced from
54 pages to two or three. The twenty pages on the Spanish explorers,
three fourths of which are based solely on Winship's *Coronado* and
Bourne's *De Soto,* might have been compressed into a footnote.
(Shannon: 32–33; my emphasis)

Notwithstanding Shannon's description of the Indians coming under
Spanish domination as "docile" (the Pueblos revolted in 1680 after a hundred years of Spanish domination), he reveals how in the face of the omitted evidence Webb encourages his reader to trust the historian to "tell" how
things were, to label properly the objects of his study, if not through his use
of imagination, then through the many "facts" he alludes to but then fails to
make available. Shannon comments on Webb's authoritative style and lack
of evidence:

> If an author intends to contradict a statement, opinion, or theory of
> long standing, as Webb so often does, he is at least duty bound to pre-
> sent his evidence. The assertions that no Indians except those on the
> Plains ever rode horses, that the range cattle industry never existed
> east of the ninety-eighth meridian, and that revolvers are the only fit
> weapons for horsemen are random examples of the author's unsup-
> ported contentions. In other cases, *the main point to be proved is
> merely asserted or implied,* while irrelevant matters are sufficiently
> fortified. The "patterns of truth" thus evolved are mere evasions of
> responsibility. (106)

Webb's patterns of truth lend credibility to his story; they originated and
manifested themselves in the frontier mentality and later in popular culture.
Giving "scholarly" support to extant prejudices, Webb becomes a popular
figure because he legitimized through "history" what people were already

believing, insofar as they were wanting and needing to believe. The dissolving of a larger, multiperspectival history become possible by means of his colorful narration. As a historian Webb played a significant role in creating an image of a cohesive nation, of a people united in their struggles to obtain the same goals. As Americans they were willing to endure whatever hardships were required to achieve their goal, and that, in itself, justified their occupation of the lands. For this myth, Webb posits himself as historian of the land but slants the record with the excited language of a writer of adventure stories.

WEBB'S INDIANS[8]

The paternalistic storyteller, while withholding significant evidence, asks that we trust his interpretations of what is "generally admitted" (Webb 1931: 69), frequently reminding us of what "we have to acknowledge" (118). In this manner, the reader is asked to assent to representations of the Plains Indians such as the following: By gaining the possession of the horse, "the obstacle[s]" had managed to raise themselves from a "position of inferiority in which the Spaniards found them" (115). We learn that they have a "proclivity for horse-thieving" (66) and are "a scourge and terror to the sedentary Indians." According to Webb, with the increased leisure time that the acquisition of the horse gave to the American Indian, he could now "strike with sudden fury and retreat out of danger before his enemy had recovered from the surprise, and with it all *he could enjoy himself*" (116; my emphasis). Webb's myth fits well into Slotkin's description of myth as a sort of "religious ritual [which] evokes in the people the sense of life inherent in the myth and all but compels belief in the vision of reality and divinity implicit in it" (7).

Webb describes the world of the American Indian in all its majesty as if God had his hand in the turn of events his retrospect foreshadows: "His world was enlarged and beautified, and his courage, never lacking, expanded with his horizon and his power. God save his enemies!" (1931: 116). Situating God's presence heavily on one side, Webb explains that the Spanish "failure" to convert the American Indians is due in part to the "fact" that "the Plains Indian took *his* religion with too much levity" (118; my emphasis). Providing no evidence by which he could have possibly judged the spiritual or religious life of any tribe or nation of American Indians, Webb leaves us with this generalization about all those who came in contact with the Spaniards. In making such a statement, the reader (of a more serious religion no doubt) is asked to participate in the perpetuation of a stereotype and thus gain entry to the insider group, another rhetorical device. As is often the case in epic, romance, and certain dime novels, war provides the general setting in Webb's history. As if with regret for the loss of what might have been a quaint, even pastoral presence of a few "red knights of the prairie," the historian remains uncritical of what brought relations between the American Indians and the "conquerors" to such a state: "Thus armed, equipped, and mounted the Plains Indians made both *picturesque* and dangerous warriors—the red knights of the prairie. They were far better equipped for successful warfare in their own country than the white men who came against them, and presented to the European or American conqueror problems different from those found elsewhere on the continent" (68; my emphasis).

Webb's exaggerated, warlike characterization of the American Indian coupled with his emphasis on the Spaniards' past record of inadequacies and failures in their dealings with the Indians, precedes the "success" story of his next chapter, "The American Approach to the Great Plains." Together, these chapters justify the displacement or elimination of the Mexican American and the American Indian. Moreover, they set the stage for the heroes of his next major publication, the more blatantly racist *The Texas Rangers* (1935). This chapter does, however, include a momentary diversion that reveals, though uncritically, nineteenth-century anti-immigration sentiment and its perceived threat to Anglo sovereignty. With emphasis on just how "fierce" Indians were thought to be, Webb recounts a plan devised by Anglo Texans to give up three million acres of land, mining, and international trading privileges to the French in order to establish a buffer zone on the ninety-ninth meridian against Mexicans and "marauding" Indians (see the subsection "The Franco-Texienne Company and Frontier Defense," 1931: 179–184). The myth of American heroism and bravery is turned upon itself in a striking way by a woman who reproves General Sam Houston for his support of the proposal and, especially, for admitting that "Texas was too weak to protect her frontiers" (Webb 1931: 183). Though Webb does not name the woman, he cites the description of her in the February 10, 1841, issue of the *Telegraph and Texas Register* as "a lady 'whose spirit would do credit to Lacedemon.'" Had she been a man, Webb would surely have credited her "sarcasm" with having saved Texas from the French. "The lady said, 'General Houston, how is it possible that the Texans, whose courage and prowess have become celebrated throughout the world, should now become so frightened with five hundred naked Comanches that they are willing to sell the republic for the sake of procuring eight thousand French soldiers to defend them?' The General is reported to have borne this sarcasm with his usual equanimity" (183).

Despite this slight detour, Webb in his chapter "The American Approach to the Great Plains" brings the western mythic hero more clearly into focus. The myth-hero "embodies or defends the values of his culture in a struggle against the forces which threaten to destroy the people and lay waste the land" (Slotkin: 269). Likewise, the myth-hero in Webb's narrative becomes the pioneer who must struggle not only against the difficulties of the terrain, but also, as if to add drama to the romance, against the common enemy— the "savage" Indian. By augmenting the threat this character presents to the hardworking pioneer, Webb also enlarges the hero and the heroic measures he must take in order to survive. Those measures, although drastic, become justified when put in the "proper perspective" of Webb's narrative. Concepts of justice, like many of the other institutions, changed when they crossed the ninety-eighth meridian. War is made necessary, but, as Shannon argues, battles with the Comanches and the presence of the Texas Rangers are imported themes into Webb's narrative. Neither belongs in Plains history. Webb's inclusion of them, however, puts his earlier research on the Texas Rangers to good use, making his story more dramatic, bringing it closer to achieving mythic proportions. Putting events such as the great boom in the cattle kingdom in their "proper perspective," Webb offers euphemisms for American greed for property and cattle as apologies for the "rough set"— the Western ranchmen and cowboys, "riding over green pastures on spirited horses and watching a fortune grow." Webb endorses U.S. expansionism by attributing to it a mystical quality. It is in this frame that he writes of the "irrational factor" at work in speculation, rather than naming such motives as rapacity and greed. Any attempt to explain a boom or a panic, he states, "fails in that we cannot weigh the irrational factor, the contagion which spreads from one member of a group to another until the whole is caught up in a frenzy of buying and selling" (233).

The "contagion" Webb depicts would fit well within a scene many times repeated in the Western films to which many present-day readers have been exposed. What later became a familiar scene in film and on television overtly presents Webb's thesis. Setting: a sleepy western town with tumbleweeds rolling down the dusty streets. Action: As the indispensable little Mexican takes a siesta under his hat and in the shade of a nearby cactus, a Walter Huston-like old-timer type runs out onto the middle of the main street shouting, "There's gold in them thar hills!" Panic strikes; all rush out in a great flurry of excitement. All reason is thrown to the wind, and what is more, who can blame 'em? They are the "rough set" who have had to adapt to difficult terrain and weather. A "contagion" takes over, and nothing in this scene speaks to the cold-hearted profit motive not altogether specific to this region and moment in history. Who the losers were and why they lost are matters not accounted for in *his* story. Webb explains his own lack of evidence: "Yet we must seek explanations in the tangible things, realizing at the same time that the intangible factor is dominant" (233). While any historian would surely like to know where Webb thinks there exists a plethora of "tangible" evidence when it comes to reconstructing past events, Webb is reluctant to consider the evidence that was readily available to him.

THE SIX-SHOOTER

Some of Webb's linguistic devices also become clear within the story of the Colt six-shooter: Hatred *"had been engendered"* (177); "the proposal *was fraught* with apparent danger" (181); "the Indian and the buffalo *had just been driven* [out]" (233); "The Indians *had all been reduced,* and people *were no longer held back* from the Plains by fear of the scalping knife and the tomahawk" (234); "government aid *was given* primarily to the Western roads" (275; all my emphasis). Note the use of the passive voice, which leaves unexplained how two peoples have come to have such hatred for one another. With the passive voice, Webb omits the protagonist of his story. The acting subject is removed and remote. No one is responsible for the destruction of the American Indian and the buffalo. The agent can become inanimate, a mechanism in "border strife." Already positioning this "strife" on the "border," Webb hardly takes into account the previous property rights or land grants of the Spanish/Mexicans, those who had apparently "abandoned" their lands. Instead Webb assumes that the conflict over land is between two separate nations, ignoring the long-standing presence and interaction between the American Indian and Mexican populations before Anglo occupation. Moreover, he credits the Anglo invaders with the creation of the range and ranch cattle industry, "perhaps one of the outstanding phenomena in American history" (225), as if nothing like it had existed there before the Anglo occupation: "the cattle kingdom spread from Texas and utilized the Plains area, which would otherwise have lain idle and useless. . . . From these conditions and from these elements emerged the range and ranch cattle industry, perhaps the most unique and distinctive institution that America has produced" (224). Webb refuses to see that the very elements of the ranching and farming industry he extols were brought into the Plains area by Anglo Americans who learned them from the Spanish/Mexican populations to the south and east of the Plains. He also ignores that many of those "half afraid and uncertain" Indians had escaped Spanish domination and had acquired their ranching and farming skills as well as their superior horsemanship long before the Anglo newcomers were to cross the ninety-eighth meridian.

Had Webb ever questioned the origins of loanwords already set by English speakers in a nineteenth-century American Southwest vocabulary, he would have found himself in the midst of the preestablished Spanish and Mexican societies that "depended to the backbone on farms and cattle," as Julio-César Santoyo points out: "They were men who lived in *haciendas* and *ranches;* who kept their crops in *silos* and their *burros, remudas* and *cavvies* in *corrals;* who used *quirts, lariats, cinches, hackamores* (Sp. jáquima) and *lassoes* to make their *mustangs* and *broncos* tame; . . . who were afraid of *stampedes* and of their animals becoming *loco* (= mad) by eating the toxic *locoweed,* and who hired the work of *peons* and *arrieros*" (722–723). Through lexicology Santoyo offers his own response to the rhetoric of dominance and the reiteration of the "Black Legend" by U.S. historians: "Where in this long list of Spanish words adopted by American English is anything referring to missionaries, friars and monks, crosses, swords or any other kind of weapon; anything related to the Inquisition, to the mountains of gold and silver so oftentimes alluded to by the 'black legend,' and where are the explorations and scouring of wide territories in search of treasures?" (724).

Given the evidence of the loanwords from Spanish so apparent in the English language, the Spanish/Mexican way of life hardly figures in the "Westward Ho" version of history. Ironically enough, the loanwords indicate that Hispanic settlers had much in common with the people whose history Webb's work tells of: "If words are, to a certain extent, the mirror of history," Santoyo notes, "the image we see reflected in these loan-words from Spanish speaks of a rather poor people living a plain, homely and unpretentious life; living in a small way, almost literally off the land, and habitually engaged in agricultural and ranching activities" (725).

Now Webb's story of the six-shooter offers a specific example of his general method. As cue epithets and reiterated situations underpin his narrative vision, so the six-shooter marks an epiphany of technological genius and becomes a kind of technoid fetish. With his story of the six-shooter Webb invites readers to imagine a battle between the Texans and the Comanches. Once within this imaginary scene, Webb establishes the Comanches' use of superior weapons against the "lawful" Texas Rangers, emphasizing especially the Indians' pursuit on horseback, their shooting of their enemies in the back, and the Texan's losing of "his scalp to the Indian, who left the mangled body to the birds and wolves" (170). (No doubt when a Texas Ranger killed an Indian he stopped, dismounted, and conducted a solemn burial rite for his enemy.)

Prominent in this cowboy-and-Indian scenario is Webb's tale of how Samuel Colt's invention, the six-shooter, found its way into the hands of the Texas Rangers, "those hard-pressed men who were most in need of it" (1931: 172). The six-shooter was the Rangers' answer to the "tremendous odds" against them. After having established their name as "a check and terror to the bands of our frontier Indians" (175), the Rangers had yet another challenge. This one concerned the war with Mexico. Following an anecdote with moralizing commentary, Webb dramatically describes how the Colt revolver, "the perfect weapon for waging war on the Plains Indians," is restored to prominence in the West when the "mills of the gods continued to grind." More than once the Colt had saved the Texas Rangers, and now they were to save the "Colt's life" from a "dark period between 1842 to 1847" (176).

Webb highlights moral implications of historical events when he draws the portrait first and then offers his "logical" explanation afterward. The rescue of this invention and its inventor are thus transformed into the greater story simply by Webb's narrative spice. In this greater story is embedded the U.S. War with Mexico, but that is less important than the telling of how the Texas Rangers "rejoiced at this turn of affairs, [for] if there was anything they relished more than fighting Indians, it was fighting Mexicans, hatred of whom had been engendered by a long period of border strife" (177).

Shannon disputes Webb's assertion that the Colt six-shooter played a significant role in victories against the Indians when he points to how Webb cites but a few victories in Texas. Demystifying Webb's generalizations, Shannon writes, "The fault of the account is that it omits all discussion of the very point that is intended to be made." Because Webb has no evidence that the revolver really did tame the Indians, Shannon asserts that the "struggles of a Connecticut inventor alone do not constitute Plains history" (59–60). Moreover, he refutes Webb's claims that the Colt was "the most effective horsemen's weapon yet invented" when he reveals that Webb had his Colts confused.

> In the first place, Webb's definition of the Colt in the early Texas days is insufficient. The weapon is "known and recognized the world over" (page 167), as he says, but not the primitive Colt used before 1865. Webb shows that he was not familiar with it himself. All the revolvers shown in the plate facing page 172, except the last one (and it was not invented till long after the period he describes), are of the semimuzzle-loading type. A paper cartridge had to be torn (usually with the teeth) and inserted into the cylinder from the end facing the muzzle. Then a percussion cap had to be placed on the nipple facing the stock. The loading of each of these cartridges was almost as slow as doing the same to a muzzle-loading rifle. When the horseman emptied both of his revolvers and his rifle he was just as helpless as if armed with horse pistols. His first advantage, though, in having thirteen shots in place of three, was a distinct one. The Indian just possibly might wait till both revolvers were empty. If he did, the white horseman was again at his mercy. (59–60)

Shannon's account of the inaccuracies in Webb's story about the skirmishes between Texas Rangers and Comanche exposes Webb's weakness for overdramatizing and romanticizing his heroes' plight on the Plains:

> This was not Plains fighting; at least it was not fighting for control of the Plains. It was just an effort to keep that "handful of naked, half-starved, unarmed savages" (page 181) from invading the wooded area of east Texas in search of food. There was little occupation of the Plains even in Texas, before 1867. Webb includes a quotation (footnote, page 183) to the effect that in 1876 there were probably not 3000 white people in the whole Plains area of Texas. . . . The answer is that, in the days of the real Indian wars, when federal soldiers, instead of Texas Rangers, did the fighting (that is, after the Civil War), the cavalry was armed with breech-loading, repeating Spencer rifles, and the Indians seldom got within revolver range unless they overpoweringly outnumbered the white men. R. I. Dodge speaks of a battle won against Indians as early as 1867 with improved Spencer and Winchester rifles. (Shannon: 60–61)

With Webb's work on the Texas Rangers already under way when he began his research for *The Great Plains,* it is small wonder that he felt compelled to include their "heroic" deeds and the "fictional" importance of

Samuel Colt in his presentation of the Plains history. Webb projects the same story onto a different setting, making the heroic cowboy synonymous with the heroes he would later construct in *The Texas Rangers*. Though Shannon asserts that neither Samuel Colt nor the Texas Rangers belong in Plains history, this feature of the controversy is never taken up at the proceedings, and Webb's tendency to celebrate the mythic hero, his romanticizing rhetoric and dichotomized history, goes unchecked.

> In line with his general tendency, Webb makes the cowboy himself just a little too perfect. The Six-shooter, to be sure, is credited with some sins, which are remitted because of its services. But any well rounded history of the range should contain at least a few references to wanton bloodshed at the muzzle of this weapon. Where are the hell-roaring cowtowns? The reader is treated only to the original love feast at Abilene. Abilene was not always thus. Neither was Newton or Dodge City. The latter has its "boot-hill" grave yard as an undying memory to the dead who were sacrificed to the savior of the Plains. McCoy says that Newton "gained a national reputation for its disorder and bloodshed. As many as eleven persons were shot down on a single evening and many graves were filled with subjects who had "died with their boots on." (Shannon: 78)

Ignoring evidence that does not suit his purposes, Webb invents within his narrative a system of values devoid of moral considerations. Rather than examine the long tradition of industrious farming/ranching society that preceded the history of his people, he chooses to emphasize war and fighting machines with a morality implicit and manifesting the favor of the gods. Yet "[Samuel Colt] did have faith, and he set to work overcoming obstacles.... He had made a better gun, it had blazed a pathway from his door to the Texas Rangers and the Plains, and the world was now to pave that pathway with gold" (Webb 1931: 178). God would reward Colt for his faith and perseverance. Yet, almost as if from second thoughts, Webb begins to rationalize: "Whatever sins the Six-shooter may have to answer for, it stands as the first mechanical adaptation made by the American people when they emerged from the timber and met a new set of new needs in the open country of the Great Plains. It enabled the white man to fight the Plains Indian on horseback" (179). Even when evidence abounds that contradicts popular visions of reality, the characters and events of a construction in the service of a dominant ideology are thus cast and fixed within these traditionally upheld notions, especially when there is a need to cushion evidence of actual killing.

THE WOMEN OF THE PLAINS

One cannot leave Webb's history without examining his perfunctory characterization of the women of the Plains. In the chapter entitled "Mysteries of the Great Plains," Webb offers as one of the *mysteries* the fact that "men of the West [as opposed to those of the East] were the first to grant to women the franchise [equal suffrage for women]" (505). Webb ponders the "problem that remains to be solved" and states that "its final solution will grow out of a better understanding of a peculiar psychology that developed in a region where population was sparse and women were comparatively scarce and remarkably self-reliant" (505).

Notwithstanding the "self-reliance" he attributes to women, Webb asserts that the solution to the conundrum lies not with the women of the Plains but that "hidden somewhere in the cause is the spirit of the Great Plains which made men democratic in deed and truth" (505). This spirit of renewal once again euphemizes the harsh treatment that the American Indians received at the hands of these putative democratic male heroes. At this point the best one can say about Webb is that he is complacent and conventional. The "spirit of the Great Plains" did nothing to keep women from struggling side by side with their men and enduring the same hardships. These hardships, Mormon leadership, and the influence of Spanish law which granted women considerably more civil rights and ownership of property than they were allowed under U.S./British law are but a few of the factors that influenced earlier women's suffrage in the West. Also significant but a fact Webb fails to mention is that Anglo men stood to gain much "property" by intermarrying with Mexican women, whose right to inherit land in their own name was upheld under U.S. law. Ignoring such possibilities but critical of Eastern mentality, Webb resorts to the conventional portrayal of women as soft, delicate creatures who could hardly withstand the same plight as their "tough and ready" male partners who protected them from all danger.

According to Webb, "the early conditions on the Plains precluded *the little luxuries* that women love and that *are so necessary to them*" (506; my emphasis). Again invoking imagination, Webb asks us to "imagine a sensitive woman set down on an arid plain to live in a dugout or a pole pen with a dirt floor, without furniture, music, or pictures, with the bare necessities of life!" In a book of 525 pages, Webb's entire commentary on women in the West occupies a one-and-a-half-page section entitled "What Has Been the Spiritual Effect of the American Adventure in the Great Plains on Women?" Despite his perfunctory analysis here, Webb apologizes for his attention to women: "Since practically this whole study has been devoted to the men, they [women] will receive scant attention here" (505). He then quickly returns to the qualities of his mythic, male hero: "The women were few; and *every man was a self-appointed protector of women* who participated in the adventures of the men and escaped much of the drabness and misery of farm life" (506; my emphasis). After taking up sixteen pages on the sign language of the Plains Indians, twenty pages on the prairie dog, the jack rabbit, and other plant and animal life, and ten pages on weather conditions, Webb devotes only one and a half pages to commonplace negative stereotypes of women. For example, one finds this characterization: "*If we could get at the truth,* we should *doubtless* find that many a family was stopped on the edge of the timber by women *who refused to go farther*" (505; my emphasis).

Again, his rhetorical devices demand assent to an unconvincing argument he substantiates with only one student's claim that his family refused to go further when "the women caught sight of the Plains" (505). He also cites an account from a work of fiction, *The Writings of John J. Ingalls,* typical of a literature which, according to Webb, "is filled with women's fear and distrust of the Plains. It is all expressed in Beret Hansa's pathetic exclamation, 'Why, there isn't even a thing that one can hide behind!' No privacy, no friendly tree—nothing but earth, sky, grass, and wind" (506; Webb makes no reference as to who Beret Hansa is).

Fred Shannon adds to his criticism of Webb his shortchanging of the women of the Plains: "Again he [Webb] stresses their loneliness, but he omits the *bravery* they showed in sticking with the men they loved and remaining because the men were contented" (106). Anglo women figuring as insignificantly as they did, one could hardly expect Webb to consider the history of struggles of the Hispanic woman on the frontier. Yet there certainly is no shortage of other accounts telling of the importance of Hispanic women on the frontier, in the village, in the family, and later in the fields and in the canneries, especially in times of war. During the time of early settlement, the Spanish government recruited women; "they traveled to what for them were unknown frontiers. They often walked up to ten miles a day and had little food and water, and, because their husbands were military men, many soon became widows" (Rebolledo and Rivero: 2). These accounts hardly support the stereotypical portrayals of women that Webb attributes to the pioneering Anglo women.[9]

SOME CONCLUSIONS

The impact of *The Great Plains* on the American concept of the West has been far-reaching. It was first published by Ginn and Company, principally a publisher of textbooks, but in 1936, Houghton Mifflin made arrangements for it to have a far wider sale. Achieving two printings as early as 1939, *The Great Plains* was in popular demand as a college textbook primarily in history courses, but it also had interdisciplinary appeal in geography, sociology, ecology, government, and other fields. "The American Library Association listed it as one of the Fifty Notable Books in 1931; it won second place in the Loubat award in 1933; it was twice listed as an alternate by the Book-of-the-Month Club; it was favorably reviewed, not only in the United States, but also in France and England. It still enjoys a steady sale as text, treatise, and trade book" (Shannon: ix).

Since the 1930s, Webb and the history he projected into the future have continued to exert a great deal of influence on U.S. perceptions of the West. The extent of this influence is noted by Howard Lamar when he recalls how in 1982 (a half-century after the book's initial publication) Professor Richard W. Van Orman, of Purdue University at Calumet, "surveyed teachers of courses on the history of the American West to ask which historian and which book they felt had been most influential in shaping their concept of the West": "Of the seventy-two who replied, the majority identified Walter Prescott Webb as the most influential historian, and his *The Great Plains* as the most important book. They also indicated that current textbooks followed Webb's ideas more closely than they did those of Frederick Jackson Turner" (Lamar: 25).

However emphatically Webb attributes artistic qualities to his writing, *The Great Plains* was legitimized as history; Webb achieved notoriety not as a creative writer but as a career historian. The story he tells, disguised as history, has had an impact. To this day, we see Webbian constructions in our public schools and in popular culture. The "same story" of romanticized heroism is repeated for one new generation after another, offering up strong messages as to who is included and excluded in our national identity. This distorted history is passed on through textbooks to schoolchildren, and through advertising and government agencies to the general public. How much of this particular instance of ignored history and what is written in textbooks is part of Webb's legacy would be difficult to prove; however, whatever influence his "history" has had is not limited to just these very important channels of information.

By his own account, the images Webb produced of the Great Plains filtered into the movie industry, beginning in 1935 with the publication of *The Texas Rangers:* "Since *The Texas Rangers* was the only book about Texas that appeared in 1935, Paramount bought it for the Texas Centennial picture of 1936. Paramount made full use of the title and little else. The picture was quite successful. I am not going to tell you what I got for it in the midst of the depression, but I will say this: what I got made the depression more tolerable" (1969a: 17). Of course we know that many Hollywood films (particularly Westerns) were adapted to television in series such as *The Rifleman, The Lone Ranger, Bonanza,* and *Wagon Train,* to name but a few. Webb's part in the creation of that manifestation of the American Dream is still another realm that could be explored. Webb's thesis of hardship overcome by those special people who came west and endured can be said to have lived on and been reinterpreted even in the later popular situation comedies many of us grew up watching, where within thirty minutes an obstacle is overcome, a problem is solved, and everyone is happier in the end.[10]

In places of entertainment and recreation such as Six Flags Over Texas, images of battle with the geographic terrain live on; images of Webb's pioneering heroes are engraved into children's minds in their most impressionable and formative years, when they are just beginning to learn their American heritage and history. E. C. Barksdale emphasizes Webb's influence in his introduction to "Geographical-Historical Concepts in American History," a paper Webb delivered in 1960 to the annual meeting of the Association of American Geographers:

> Particularly interesting is Webb's proposal that Houston build a great
> museum of natural history which would show the impact of land, of
> geography and of natural resources on the culture and architecture—
> and history—of Texas. Ignorance forces me to confess that I do not
> know whether the great city on the Ship channel has adopted and
> expanded on the Webb suggestion. I do know that it has built an
> Astrodome. Curiously, an amusement center in Arlington, Texas,
> "Six Flags Over Texas," sometimes called "The Texas Disney-
> land," has, in part at least, used some ramification of the Webb idea,
> a panorama of Texas presented as a carnival ride, and that as a

result "Six Flags" grosses several millions of dollars in admission fees annually. (Barksdale: xv)

Webb became an institution in Texas and the Southwest as well as a national figure. His depiction of the struggles on the Western frontier has continued to have its impact in all the major avenues of mythmaking available to the U.S. public, including schoolbooks that jump very quickly from the "conquistadores" to the Battle of the Alamo. The myth Webb helped promote, replete with images of fierce fighting Indians on horseback, has had a formative and detrimental effect on our society that works both ways. False self-images of U.S. Anglos based on their perceptions of others lead to cultural misunderstanding in the workforce and in social relations: people become afraid to talk to one another for fear of causing offense by unintentionally revealing stereotypical or racist knowledge.

Privilege and a good-ol'-boy–style affirmative action comes sharply into focus here when one considers the fact that Webb failed his Ph.D. preliminary oral exams at the University of Chicago, where he had been awarded a scholarship for a year, never completed his doctorate, and still lived with all the respect and honor due to a scholar in his field. Apparently, when Webb left Texas in an effort to acquire further credentials in his field, he did so with a mind already set and convinced of a history he would play a major role in perpetuating. According to Furman, Webb's failure was the result of the overconfidence he felt, due to his already having a position at the University of Texas as well as to his having "narrowly focused his area of interests on the history of the United States and to the West" (Furman: 82). In Webb's own view, however, part of his failure was due to the fact that he had had the effrontery to disagree with his committee's belief that immigration into Texas was "motivated by Southerners seeking to create a slave state. Rather Webb argued that people moved to Texas for land, with the result that the committee derided his view 'as being that of a biased Southerner'" (Furman: 83).

Returning to Texas in a dispirited state, Webb boarded a San Antonio train car of the *Texas Special* at St. Louis, where in romantic fashion he describes that he "heard again familiar voices of people I never knew talking in familiar accents of cotton, cattle, and oil. I was already home" (1969a: 12). Very happy to be back in Texas after dealing with illness, academic failure, and economic hardship in the North, Webb's influence grew when he participated extensively in the writing of Texas history books for children in the public schools: "I recouped my finances by participating in a series of highly successful textbooks, a wonderful antidote for academic anemia. Then I turned from textbooks and a small fortune to write history as I saw it from Texas. The road led west, and I now knew I had something to say" (1969a: 12). On Eugene C. Barker's suggestion, the University of Texas accepted *The Great Plains* as a dissertation and granted him "his professional 'union card' in 1932" (Furman: 88).[11] Webb was thus able to continue playing a major role in the shaping of Western historiography.

Throughout his career, Webb stated that he had spent ten years working on *The Great Plains,* indicating that he began work on it around 1921, just three years after the First World War had come to an end. This date could also be said to mark the completion of Anglo occupation and the establishment of dominance in the state of Texas, a symbolic closing of the final frontier. The final uprising of Texas Mexican seditionists in South Texas had been quelled in 1917: "armed insurrection of Texas Mexicans and its brutal suppression by Texas Rangers" was one of "the most dramatic episodes in the history of the Southwest. . . . The conflict turned the Valley into a virtual war zone during 1915–1917" (Montejano 117). Webb's research on the Texas Rangers, which was interrupted three or four years later by his work on *The Great Plains,* had begun almost immediately following this period of rebellion in South Texas. It was hearing that a lawyer and civic leader, José Tomás Canales, had charged this "law enforcement" agency with crimes committed against the Texas Mexicans of South Texas that motivated Webb to begin work on the history of the Texas Rangers. Speaking about his education, Webb describes his initiation of this project in 1918:

> The time came to start work on the M.A. It was necessary to choose a subject, and here good fortune attended me. A series of Mexican revolutions had made the Texas border a turbulent place; James E. Ferguson as governor had made all Texas turbulent. Ferguson increased the Ranger force, and the Rangers went to the border to commit crimes almost as numerous and quite as heinous as Pancho Villa bandits. These crimes were exposed in a legislative investigation led by J. T. Canales. The exposure made exciting headlines in all the papers. I read those headlines and asked myself an important question: Has anyone written the history of the Texas Rangers? The answer was no. I chose that subject and was off on the first lap of the great adventure, to write the history of the oldest institution of its kind in the world. The story led west, to the frontier, to vicarious

adventure of the body, and to real adventure of the mind. Though I
was not aware of it then, I had found my field. (Webb 1969a: 7–8)

Though what attracted Webb to South Texas were reports of the "hei-
nous crimes" Rangers committed against Texas Mexicans, Webb chose to
swim with the current and not against it. His narrative makes heroes of
those whose history he was to write. Interrupting his work on the Texas
Rangers, Webb began *The Great Plains* during an important historical moment—the end of World War I, the uprisings in South Texas, the rise of
social Darwinism pre-dating Hitler, and as a final ingredient, the period of
great economic depression that soon followed. By emphasizing the inventions that he believed essential to the success of the pioneering settlers of the
Plains, Webb wrote a timely American success story, and he became a character in the greater narrative of this historiography. His story reconciles
the agrarian philosophy behind Turner's work and the cultural identity
it promoted with a newly industrialized U.S. By hailing inventions such
as the Colt, barbed wire, the windmill, and agricultural implements as indispensable "weapons" against the hardships of the Plains (the war they
fight), Webb manages to bridge the gap between the two worlds by presenting the western mythology of a very special breed of people who "made the
West" side by side with an essential phase of U.S. history—the industrial
revolution.

Shannon refuted the two major elements of Webb's thesis. First, he stated
that there really was no thesis to develop out of the fact that population was
checked near the fringe of the High Plains: "It has been known by historians for a generation. . . . everybody knew that farmers avoided a cow country, ill adapted to farming, so long as there was land available elsewhere"
(36). Second, Shannon asserted that the Industrial Revolution "ruined more
farmers than it ever helped": "The question in recent years is whether he
[the frontiersman] ever did really overcome the obstacle [the Great Plains].
A dust bowl where once the buffalo and cattle roamed is no meritorious
achievement, either of the Industrial Revolution or of the indomitable frontiersman" (36). Although Shannon minimized the significance of Webb's
thesis and many of his claims, Webb, with the help of an academy all too
ready to defend and promote his work, succeeded in celebrating and digni-
fying the "Westward Ho" movement. Even when the frontier was no more,
new emphasis was given to a movement onward to a symbolic frontier.
Webb's interruption of his work on the Texas Rangers to write *The Great*

Plains suggests a need to establish the harsh conditions of the West as an important preliminary factor in the narrative creation of his mythic heroes—heroes who succeeded where so many others had failed.

Webb's faulty research and the erroneous generalizations were exposed more than once. The protection Webb received from his colleagues reveals how they shielded him from sound criticism, upholding his work as scholarship at a time when his "story" was required. However unprepared Webb was for being taken to task on his often shallow research and the biased attitudes from which his work is derived, it is evident from his having later become president of the American Historical Association and the monetary rewards he received that Webb became an instrument essential to a myth-creating process, a metaphor for his own work, a character in the historical narrative of his own making. He was a farm boy who achieved some learning, wrote a history for "his" people, as he was to state on several occasions, and was duly rewarded. Like his pioneers, he "succeeded" where no one of his social class and background had succeeded. The slant he gives his work was power for the cause of building a heritage where and when one was needed the most. The Anglo Southwesterners, surrounded by "foreigners" in an economically depressed and culturally depleted environment, were in need of a historian who could legitimize "their" story. The Great Plains history that Webb wrote (albeit from a Texas view), controversial in its form, anti–Eastern elitist in its tone, easily filled that void. Walter Prescott Webb thus perhaps unwittingly became a tool for far cruder justifications of U.S. imperialistic thinking.

Webbian histories have had an influence and done their damage to American thought, particularly as regards the way "the other" is viewed and continues to be constructed. The narrative elements and linguistic devices in his romanticizing rhetoric—the metaphors, euphemisms, adjectives, juxtapositions, quasi-poetic language, mythopoetic frames, epic bard stratagems—all invite the reader's assent to the "truth" in a peculiar story replete with images of the "rough set's" freedom gained at the expense and denigration of others. It is important to isolate these elements, for they reappear in various forms and especially in times of economic hardship to affirm the "rightness" of the domination of a particular group over the "others" who make up our nation's diverse population. Webb's "literary felicity" and "soft luminosity" reinforced a mythology of Western history that could easily be adopted by the Southwest and would be viewed as such for generations. His rhetorical and narrative strategies arose from a crucial moment, and at that crucial moment they reinforced politically and economically desirable myths, easily transported to our own times.

Webb's views have drawn a response from some Chicano writers. Webb gave scholarly and literary support to extant prejudices and thus dissolved a larger history by means of narration. Revisionist historians, notably Chicano/a ones, may also take a "moral" stand—in other words, a justification for their biases—whether artfully presented or not. The following chapters will examine how certain literary works adjust historical perspectives and tell another, more complex story than Webb's.

3
THE HISTORICAL FICTION OF JOVITA GONZÁLEZ
Complex and Competing Class Identities

A Mexican found stealing cattle from an American
was hung. An American doing the same from a
Mexican merely added a few head to his herd.

—González, *Dew on the Thorn*

Fuimos por las vacas de tatita.
[We went back for grandpa's cows.]

—An old South Texas saying

 Until very recently, little was known about Jovita González other than basic biographical data and the fact that as a student of history in the 1920s and '30s she distinguished herself as a folklorist by writing about the area and the people of her own Mexican American background and upbringing in South Texas. Though her papers had existed in the University of Texas Nettie Lee Benson Latin American Collection for almost half a century, few scholars had taken notice of her work. It was only when Teresa Palomo Acosta and Cynthia Orozco resurrected her at the 1990 "Mexican Americans in Texas History" conference in San Antonio that more scholars became aware of her importance.[1]

Jovita González (1899–1983) was born in the border town of Roma, Texas. Though the press in González's time described her as a "descendant of a family of wealthy Spanish landowners along the border" (see Walker), her own eighteen-page handwritten memoir indicates otherwise: "My father, Jacobo González Rodríguez, a native of Cadereyta, Nuevo León, México came from a family of educators and artisans. His father, Pablo González taught poor boys the trade of hat making" (Memoirs: 1).[2] This image of a wealthy Spanish landowner's daughter created for or by her is certainly one that made her presence more acceptable in academic circles, where imagined or desired perceptions of her identity could flow more freely if they were far removed from stereotyped images of working-class Mexicans.

The fact is that González began her education in a very humble one-room schoolhouse on the San Román Ranch. She recalls that shortly thereafter her father moved the family to San Antonio, so that his children could continue their education: "As a poor man my father felt that the only heritage he could leave his children was an education. . . . he decided that the family should move to San Antonio where we could be educated in English" (Memoirs: 7). Following elementary and high school, González acquired her teaching certificate in 1918. Because finances were always a problem, she continued her education during the following years, even while intermittently teaching school in Rio Grande City and Encinal and tutoring at Our Lady of the Lake College in San Antonio. She completed a B.A. in Spanish from Our Lady of the Lake in 1927 and became a full-time teacher at Saint Mary's Hall in San Antonio while working toward a master's degree in history at the University of Texas at Austin.

At the University of Texas González reestablished her relationship with Dr. Carlos E. Castañeda, an old family friend. She also met J. Frank Dobie. Both men were to shape her career as a folklorist, teacher, and writer of historical fiction: "Heretofore the legend and stories of the border were interesting, so I thought, just to me. However, he [J. Frank Dobie] made me see their importance and encouraged me to write them. Which I did, publishing some in the *Folk-lore Publications* and *Southwest Review*" (Memoirs: 13). On April 22, 1928, during the fourteenth annual meeting of the Texas Folklore Society, Professor Newton Gaines of Texas Christian University praised González as one of the folklore society "stars." That year, González served as vice-president and presented "Legends and Songs of the Texas-Mexican Folk." She was elected the society's president for two terms, from 1930 to 1932, and gave several lectures, most of which were included in the society's annual publications for almost a decade from 1927 to 1936. In 1930 González completed her master's thesis, "Social Life in Webb, Starr and Zapata Counties," under the direction of historian Eugene C. Barker. Though he was somewhat hesitant at first to approve her thesis because of its lack of historical references, yielding to Carlos E. Castañeda's comment that "this thesis will be used in years to come as source material," Dr. Barker gave his final approval, commenting to his student that it was "an interesting but somewhat odd piece of work" (Memoirs: 16).

Writings in the area of folklore appear to have breathed new life into the careers of both J. Frank Dobie and Jovita González. The academy with which Dobie had become disillusioned gained a new realm of knowledge from his efforts with the society, just when he had resolved that formal intellectual life was not for him. "When Dobie quit the University in 1920, he was disgusted with teaching [English] and resolved never to return. He was ready to return to ranching, the life he felt he was born to, so he took a job managing his Uncle Jim Dobie's Rancho de Los Olmos" (Abernethy 1992: 81). While it was J. Frank Dobie who inducted González into a world of knowledge that he was instrumental in building and revitalizing, he too had much to gain from her writings.[3] Book reviews of 1927, when her work first made its appearance, provide us with a clue to her increasing prominence in the field of folklore. A special mention is made of her "Folklore of the Texas Mexican Vaquero," published as part of *Texas and Southwestern Folklore,* edited by Dobie: "Miss González's study of the folklore of the Vaqueros is especially good. She gives the stories of 'The Cenizo,' 'The Mocking Bird,' 'El Cardo Santo,' and 'The Guadalupana Vine,' all strongly tinged with Latin religious fervor, and stories of ghosts and treasure" (*Times-Picayune,* Sunday, October 16, 1927). Another important review of Dobie's book appeared that same year in *The New York Book Review.* It praises González's "Folk-Lore of the Texas Mexican Vaquero," as "Perhaps the best piece in the collection," while it is generally uncomplimentary of the publications of the Folklore Society: "'Texas and Southwestern Lore' . . . contains some excellent new stuff. A great deal of it is extremely thin, but as a source-book for those interested in the Southwest it should prove useful. The same is true of many of the previous publications of the Texas Folk-Lore Society . . . much of it is made up of polite essays by persons who haven't much information to give" (Walker).

As a folklorist and a novelist, Jovita González's dual identity presents a complex case, insofar as her earlier folkloristic writings published by the Texas Folklore Society do not reject the dominant culture's general views of her people, while her recently recovered novels, *Dew on the Thorn* and *Caballero,* respond energetically to Webbian formulations of history.[4] Another significant contrast exists between her earlier folklore publications (by the Texas Folklore Society) and those published by the San Antonio Missionary Oblates in a journal entitled "Mary Immaculate" in 1935. Although much of her early and later folklore was derived from the same source—the manuscript of the novel presumed to be *Dew on the Thorn*—it is interesting to examine what was selected for the larger context and how it was tailored for the different audience and readership.[5] In her actual life and in her narratives, González remains both "among" and removed from "her" people. The South Texas Mexicans *are* her people, in the sense that she defends their history against commonplace stereotypes; and then too they are not. She writes about them from a distanced and sometimes even paternalistic viewpoint influenced by the ethnographic style that prevailed during the late 1920s and by the cultural climate at the University of Texas at Austin.

Jovita González and her husband, Edmundo E. Mireles, met in graduate school at the University of Texas and married in 1935. Although in the later years of their lives in Corpus Christi they were far removed from the Chicano Movement of the late 1960s and 1970s, among today's educators and intellectuals they continue to be viewed as forming a part of an elite group of intellectuals with a political consciousness in the context of education. Blandina Cárdenas, educator and former director of Minority Affairs in Washington, D.C., who grew up in Del Rio, Texas, and whose father was a cousin to Edmundo Mireles, tells how Jovita and her husband became closely identified with a group of Mexicanos responsible for the 1929 desegregation law suit (*Salvatierra v. Del Rio Independent School District*), the first suit to challenge the segregation of Mexicano children in school facilities. The couple's initiation into this very awkward political position came as a result of the significant role they played in shaping the newly formed San Felipe School District community, which had seceded from the Anglo School District in Del Rio. In 1935, on the recommendation of Carlos E. Castañeda to Alonso S. Perales (who founded the League of Latin American Citizens [LULAC] in 1929) and Santos Garza, president of the San Felipe School Board, Edmundo was appointed principal of San Felipe High School and Jovita was appointed as an English teacher.

Among these Mexican Americans in Del Rio was a group of Mexicano exiles from the 1910 Mexican Revolution, particularly from the state of Coahuila. Apart from their cultural refinement, these exiles brought with them a strong liberal tradition that produced Francisco Madero and Venustiano Carranza, the first Revolutionary presidents of México. As Cárdenas recalls, among these "élite" Mexicanos (as we would perceive them today), "there was advocacy and identification with the whole community" (personal interview, April 13, 1995). Recalling her upbringing in the San Felipe School District, Cárdenas is able to reflect upon this specific moment in the development of the Mexican American political struggle for social justice: "San

Felipe was about people who were *educada, preparada.* The question of being *gente culta* is not about race or class. Neither is it strictly related exclusively to social or economic status or to material worth. Though that may be a factor, it certainly was not the dominant factor. You could be high class economically and be without culture. Though these people may have a sense of superiority because of their *preparación* [their formal education], there was a solidarity with all Mexicanos in the pursuit of justice" (personal interview, March 13, 1995).

Though the question of social class begins to emerge strongly here, Cárdenas asserts that as well-read, formally educated *gente culta,* these San Felipe residents were concerned with the civil rights and education of *all* Mexicanos, regardless of class. They felt an urgent need to correct growing, but generally mistaken, notions about Mexicanos, especially regarding the history of their land usurpation. Walter Prescott Webb was at that very moment able to codify and thus perpetuate these notions as official history. The San Felipe educational advocacy was in effect a political response to the dominant culture's mistaken notions, which exacerbated cultural and racial conflict.

As educational leaders in Del Rio, during the next four years Jovita González and Edmundo Mireles were to play a significant role in shaping the public education of the community of San Felipe. They helped bring about a renaissance of language and culture and established a Latin Club which put on *zarzuelas,* or operettas, as a reinforcement of high culture as well as part of the formal education of young people. What lasting effects their identification with this community was to have on their later lives sheds some light on the complex question of Jovita González's class identity throughout her career. According to Isabel Cruz, who worked for and lived with the Mireleses from 1959 until their deaths in 1983 and 1987 and to whom they willed their house and personal belongings, E. E. Mireles's mother was a sister of Venustiano Carranza, while Jovita González remained very loyal to the pre-Revolutionary dictator of Mexico, Porfirio Díaz. *"Ella adoraba a Porfirio Díaz, se hincaba en la estatua de Porfirio Díaz en Querétaro. Haga de cuenta que el casamiento de ellos era un casamiento de un Carranzista con un Porfirista"* [She adored Porfirio Díaz; she would kneel at his statue in Querétaro (when we visited). It is as if their marriage was a marriage between a Carranzista and a Porfirista] (personal interview, August 2, 1996). Indeed, González's description of the Mexican Revolution gives us a strong clue as to her political affiliations: "The year 1910 saw the end of Mexico's *rule of iron* and the beginning of *anarchy and chaos* in the republic south of the Rio Grande. As might be expected this brought about a succession of raids and disturbances. As a result the Rangers were called and it is estimated that 'one hundred Mexicans were executed by the Texas Rangers and Deputy Sheriffs without process of law'" (1935–36, Feb.: 37).

Very likely it was during these years in San Felipe that Jovita González began writing her second novel, *Caballero*. Jovita González and Edmundo Mireles remained in Del Rio until 1939, when they relocated to Corpus Christi. There they continued as educators and as advocates of Spanish language teaching in the public schools until their retirement. In 1992, Isabel Cruz donated the "Mireles Papers" to what was then Corpus Christi State University Library Archives (now Texas A&M–Corpus Christi). Because Ray J. García, a member of the Nueces County Historical Society, had urged her not to throw the papers away and because he advised Thomas Kreneck, special collections librarian and archivist, about their existence, we now know of González's attempts at a literary career.[6] Later in this chapter I will delve more deeply into the Mireleses' later lives and their work in Corpus Christi. For now, because my main purpose here is to examine Jovita González's literary writing as a response to the rhetoric of dominance I outlined in the previous chapter, *her* story of negotiation between her identity and experience as a South Texas Mexicana of limited financial means and her role as a scholar of the 1920s and 1930s is most relevant. Her participation in the academic world at UT Austin gave rise to an already heightened class consciousness. Her constructed identity along class and gender lines in turn mediates her response to Webb's rhetoric of dominance, a response that asserts itself more boldly in her literary writings and her later folkore publications (those published by Mary Immaculate). They respond to Walter Prescott Webb's work at the very time he is gaining recognition. What we see here is the patterned response that has been evidenced throughout history whereby widespread notions generated by cultural or racial conflict too easily become legitimized; they infiltrate official scholarship, and they contribute to the construction and diffusion of the "same story"—the discourse of a narrative justifying exclusion and domination. González feels compelled to respond.

"AMONG MY PEOPLE":
THE FOLKLORIST AND NOVELIST

Like Walter Prescott Webb's writings on the Great Plains and Texas, Jovita González's earlier work for the academy of her times presents an idealized, romantic version of South Texas life during the late nineteenth and early twentieth centuries, one tailored to suit the Anglo audiences of the time. Her version of South Texas life is complete with "noble savage" images of the *vaquero* and the *peon*. Like Webb, she emphasizes environmental influences on these two types within a highly stratified class structure, and she refers to her own family as the aristocrats in a highly romanticized caste system that stretches the "historical" features of this "historical" novel: "On one side, he descends from the first Americans, the Indians; on the other his ancestry can be traced to the Spanish adventurer and conquistador. From the mingling of these two races a unique type has resulted, possessing not only salient racial characteristics of both but also certain peculiar traits created by the natural environment and surroundings in which he lives. This composite type is the vaquero of the Texas Mexican frontier" (González 1927: 7).

A dichotomous image emerges here, vaquero versus aristocrat. The author's footnote to this passage insists that "the vaquero is not the aristocratic, landed proprietor of the borderland, but the wandering cowboy whose only possessions are his horse, an unlimited store of legends and traditions, and the love for his *Chata* [his sweetheart]." Her description fits well into the already romanticized picture of the wild and untamed Texas cowboy. But one can only wonder how this deviant without any worldly possessions ever hopes to make a home with his *chata* or ascend to the level of the *patrón*, which according to Jovita's literary writings was his ambition. Moreover, what is a Mexican if not a racial mixture of at least the Spaniard and the Native American? The racial identity she ascribes to her "aristocratic" landowners leaves it clear that the author is identifying herself as something other than a "common" Mexican. According to her description of the mid-eighteenth-century settlements of the present day Valley of the Rio Grande, the "*'agraciados,'* holders of grants, founding the border towns were in the majority *'criollos'* or Spaniards. They were *'gente de razón,'* and the settlements they founded were destined to prosper because of the 'desirable character of its citizens' and because even though small in number they were of good quality and well to do" (1935–36, Feb.: 36). Her description still begs the question: What aristocrats? Where in this brush country is there anybody who wants to eat but does not work? One would be hard-pressed even among the landowning families to find "aristocrats" that in any way approximate that image of southern gentility and a life of leisure inscribed by literature into the minds of U.S. readers of that time. The author is again trying to fit the myth of South Texas "pure" Castilian heritage or playing up the idea of the wealthy Spanish dons such as those of eighteenth-century California. González may have perceived these images as being useful for the purpose either of separating herself from her people so as to gain easier acceptance into "Society" or of making her presentation seem more objective to her audience. Worse still, not being of a "wealthy" landowning family, with her ideas of self not matching her material conditions, the author may have imagined that this was how such families lived and thought of themselves.

Like Walter Prescott Webb, her identity, both strange and foreign to the academy, serves as the bridge by which she can have it both ways. She is both among and away from her people. While she asserts herself as an informant, because of her real life experiences with South Texas ranch life and its characters, she also sets herself apart from the common people like the vaquero, the peon, and even members of the artisan or merchant class, in order to create a source for her knowledge that is both intellectual and, by virtue of her birth, less raw and more cultivated, more palatable in its perspective than that of her subjects.

The Mireles Papers contain two major manuscripts: *Caballero,* which was eventually published in 1996 and which I will discuss later in this chapter; and another manuscript, *Dew on the Thorn,* with no title page, but which I believe the author wrote before *Caballero,* early in the 1920s, even before she met J. Frank Dobie in 1925.[7] Throughout the *Dew on the Thorn* manuscript, there are what appear to be handwritten instructions to a typist, indicating where several of the internal narratives could be excerpted and edited to stand independent of their connections with the plot or other characters in the novel. The ties between the characters and the larger narrative are deleted in revised drafts of the excerpted material. These editorial markings also indicate that most of the author's talks for the annual meetings and contributions to the Texas Folklore Society Publications were in fact derived from this earlier manuscript. Perhaps acting on Dobie's suggestions, the author is thus taking from her "fiction" and presenting folklore, inscribing her people into the scholarly imagination.

In *Dew on the Thorn,* a thinly disguised plot line ties a series of shorter folktales together. In terms of the novel, these folktales could be the author's attempt to provide digressions to a larger narrative, as in Cervantes's *Don Quixote.* For González, the technique fails to hold the novel together, though for our purposes the "novel" is no less valuable. These digressions later facilitated the author's numerous folklore presentations, publications, and eventual scholarship awards. For today's reader, the novel's lack of cohesion cannot be explained away as anticipatory signs of postmodern narrative experimentation, but the digressions do provide us with a fascinating though complex attempt to inscribe the people and the history of South Texas into the genre of the American novel.

There is evidence of much rewriting, with all the chapters numbered, renumbered, and renamed at least once. *Dew on the Thorn* shows signs of a writer struggling with the pull between her passionate interest in capturing and preserving the ways, the history, and the belief systems of her people and the kind of detachment from "reality" required by the craft of a mature novelist. González moves illogically at times from a loosely linked chain of events that form part of the romantic plot line, to a variety of apparent but not fully realized minor political treatises, to an often too intentional exposition of the "*vida cotidiana,*" the daily life, and the "*modales,*" the manners of South Texas Mexican ranch culture during the early part of this century. The series of internal shorter narratives also reveals a specific belief and value system, the "telling" of which is significantly modified for later presentation to a specific audience.

In this novel we meet many of the characters who bear the same name as those whom the author knew during her childhood and whom she later transposed into the independent shorter pieces for the Texas Folklore Society. As early as Chapter 2 (later Chapter 1), the author introduces Pedro de Urdemañas, the wandering vaquero, and the famous story of "The Devil in Texas." These stories are told while the shelling of corn by moonlight is taking place, an event she relates in her 1932 President's Address, "Among My People," delivered at the Texas Folklore Society's Eighteenth Annual Meeting, and published later that year in the society's publication *Tone the Bell Easy,* edited by J. Frank Dobie. In Chapter 4 we meet Tío Patricio, a major character from another one of her famous stories about the Devil on the Border. These stories emerge in her 1929 presentation at the fifteenth annual meeting of the Texas Folklore Society, "Legend and Song of the Texas-Mexican Folk," published in 1930 as "Tales and Songs of the Texas-Mexicans" in the society's publication *Man, Bird and Beast,* also edited by Dobie. In Chapter 5 we meet the famous unwelcome guest, Antonio Traga-Balas, the Bullet Swallower, who in 1935 reemerges in "The Bullet Swallower" in another Dobie-edited society publication, *Puro Mexicano.* In Chapter 6, "Nana Chita's Symptoms," we meet Pedro the Hunter; in Chapter 8, "The Cupid of the Brush Country," we meet Tío Esteban, the mail carrier, also characters in "Among my People" and elsewhere. In 1947 González presented "Nana Chita's Symptoms" at the thirty-first annual meeting of the Texas Folklore Society, held in Corpus Christi on April 18–19. This paper was never published (see Abernethy 1992: 49). Chapter 9 contains some Aztec legends, "The First Cactus Blossom" and "The Gift of the Pitahaya" stories, which also later appear in "Tales and Songs of the Texas-Mexicans." In the final chapter, "The Last of the Mendozas," we again encounter the famous Pedro de Urdemañas. Many of these characters appear repeatedly throughout the author's numerous presentations for the Texas Folklore Society and its subsequent publications.

Because this manuscript was just recently recovered, there is good reason to pause here and examine how González's portrayals of South Texas Mexicano ranch life appeared, both in her talks and in her first publications, before they could be re-placed within this larger context.

Typical of the tone in González's earlier published folklore is "Shelling Corn by Moonlight," a section of a much larger body of work, "Among My People." Originally published in *Tone the Bell Easy* in 1932, it was later excerpted for one of the first anthologies of Mexican American Literature, *Mexican American Authors,* compiled and edited by Raymund and Américo Paredes. Had the manuscript of *Dew on the Thorn* or the *Mary Immaculate* version of "Among My People" never surfaced (see note 5), readers might have been left with the very narrow image of Mexicanos that follows. "Shelling Corn by Moonlight" describes the "ranch folk," vaqueros, children, *pastores,* musicians, hunters, mail carriers, and finally the women all gathered at the "Big House" to shell corn. It begins with a traditional pastoral scene, describing the terrain, animal life, and the sounds of the evening. Each character (all happen to be male) is introduced with a brief history of the major events in his life: "All came: Tío Julianito, the pastor, with his brood of sunburned half-starved children ever eager for food; Alejo the fiddler; Juanito the idiot, called the Innocent, because the Lord was keeping his mind in heaven; Pedro the hunter, who had seen the world and spoke English; the vaqueros; and, on rare occasions, Tío Esteban, the mail carrier. Even the women came, for on such occasions supper was served" (9).

Taken out of the context of her first attempt at novel writing, the author's description of "her people," as it first appeared in this folklore selection, leaves it unclear whether the women appear on the scene only because they will be serving the supper, or because the serving of the supper makes it a social event which women are expected to attend. The narrative gives little indication as to why their presence is necessary, though it is clear that their presence is secondary to that of the men. The various characters tell a number of stories during the shelling, and eventually the music and merriment begin. The narrative follows with more sections whose titles bear the name or occupation of each of the characters, and it contains more detailed descriptions of what characteristic adventures they have had. Overall the internal narratives provide one quaint picture after another of the venturing out of these characters from their homeland or of their idiosyncratic ways. With the exception of that of the patriarch, the characterizations are not particularly complimentary; they seem more likely to be entertaining to outsiders, for whom preexisting notions call up a picture of Mexicanos as almost childlike, not too intelligent, not happy venturing outside of their small communities, frequently caught in their own tricks, dirty, scrawny, poor, but basically a contented people with food, music, and merriment a priority in their lives.

The story is completely uncritical of conditions in which these people lived or of what they witnessed. Although this is not the case in her novels, in these nine pages González hardly mentions women, but three times she mentions the impoverished condition of children, each time with no sympathy but rather with a tone of loathing: "'Bitter mesquites and poor folks' children are plentiful,' is an old Border saying. And Tío Pancho's flock was more plentiful than the mesquite beans. His brood of boys were never bothered about keeping clean, for during the first two years of their life they were miniature Adams—except they wore no fig-leaves—in a place far from being a Garden of Eden. . . . Once they came to grandfather's ranch, and a more raggedy bunch I have never seen" (15).

With this González provides the perfect stuff for the Anglo audiences of the time whose minds were more than receptive to her picture of these indigenous "savages." In similar terms, González describes what Pedro the Hunter had seen: "He had seen how convicts were worked on the plantations and how they were whipped for the least offense. Yes, he, Pedro, had seen that with his own eyes" (10). Like a folklorist who has quelled all political or critical consciousness, she fails to ask if these "convicts" by some remote possibility happened to be Mexican or African American. Could they have been imprisoned unjustly as "bandits" because they revolted or defended their land rights against Anglo occupation? Did the labor these prisoners provide become a convenient means by which to develop South Texas commercial farming? Raising none of these questions, González goes on to

describe with almost childlike wonder and uncritical innocence the picaresque nature of her people, from the perspective of an ignorant insider, unaware of the dominant culture's preestablished views of the Mexicano. Some
of her characters are reminiscent of the pícaro types in the tradition of Spanish letters; yet with all the errors in judgment the pícaro commits, there is
still in the genre proper (especially in the writings of the Mexican genius of
the genre, Fernández de Lizardi, 1774?–1827) a kind of double-edged satire
employed when a writer wishes both to delight an audience and to offer
sharp criticism of social and political systems. Jovita has no use here for this
form of criticism. Instead, in "Among My People," only the title becomes
unintentionally ironic. The narrative voice in these stories is undeveloped,
like that of a child who is shielded from the harsh realities of the surrounding socioeconomic system and the "history" of her land. Yet many of the
characters in "Among My People" who are also present in the novel emerge
out of her own life and childhood, where not even the names and places
have been changed to protect the "innocent":

> My sister Tula and I did everything together. We went horseback
> riding to the pastures with my grandfather, took long walks with
> father and visited the homes of the cowboys and the ranch hands. We
> enjoyed the last the most. There were Tío Patricio, the mystic; Chon,
> who was so ugly, poor fellow, he reminded us of a toad. Old Remigio
> who wielded the *metate* with the dexterity of a peasant woman and
> made wonderful *tortillas*. Tía Chita whose stories about ghosts and
> witches made our hair stand on end, Pedro, the hunter and traveller,
> who had been as far as Sugarland and had seen black people with
> black wool for hair, one eyed Manuelito, the ballad singer, Tío
> Camilo; all furnished ranch lore in our young lives. (Memoirs: 6)

Though her intimate knowledge repeatedly competes with the established
ethnographic styles of her times, this struggle eventually translates itself into
the diverse genres that profile competing narrative voices.[8]

Although in these folktales, as they came to be published in the 1920s and
early 1930s, Jovita González does not directly challenge the life and conditions of the majority of South Texans, she was acutely aware that her South
Texas Mexicanos, regardless of original class background, by the 1920s and
1930s "had generally been reduced, except in a few border counties, to the
status of landless and dependent wage laborers" (Montejano: 114). Noted
historian and sociologist David Montejano surmises the conditions at that

time: "Mexicans now found themselves treated as an inferior race, segregated into their own town quarters and refused admittance at restaurants, picture shows, bathing beaches, and so on" (114). In contrast to most of her folklore, in her 1930 publication in *Southwest Review,* "America Invades the Border Towns," González's competing voice speaks up to describe the extent to which her people had been displaced: "The farther one gets away from the River the worse the conditions are. In the towns along the boundary-line, where the descendants of the old grantees live, Mexicans have more or less demanded certain privileges, which they still retain. But segregation of the two races is practiced in every town north of the counties bordering the River" (as cited in Montejano: 114).

But what of the audiences for González's depictions of South Texas life and characters? Francis Edward Abernethy offers us perhaps the best glimpse of the spirit of receptivity with which the students and scholars of folklore in the 1920s and 1930s received González's stories. In political, economic, and social terms, it is hard for us today to fathom how such an interest could have been sustained isolated from the context of the cultural conflict, the cruel realities, and the disparity of opportunity that existed between Anglos and Mexicanos in Texas:

> Folklorists were interested in Mexican culture for the same reason that they were interested in Negro culture: it was something new and different. So while Mexicans (and Negroes) were denied Depression relief assistance in some of the Texas cities, they were still the objects of interest to scholars. We sang "South of the Border" and "Mexicali Rose," built houses in the Mexican style, and toured Mexico and brought back sombreros and serapes and metates to decorate our rooms with. I had lived in Texas all my life but I saw my first Mexican in 1937 when we took a vacation trip to San Antonio and the Valley. Dobie's attitude, and the attitude of most of the TFS writers, was that of a member of a dominant culture studying, enjoying, appreciating another culture. He and Riley Aiken and other collectors and writers of Mexican folklore would have been hurt if someone had accused them of not treating Mexicans fairly. That was another time and another world. (1992: 206–207)

Though this sounds similar to the apology that Walter Prescott Webb made in retrospect for his racist portrayals of Mexicans and Negroes (see Chapter 2), today even among those once very angry at Dobie's blindness to injustice, despite his youth spent in South Texas, there is agreement that he made significant contributions at least indirectly to an increased awareness of the plight and struggle of the Mexicano in Texas. "He was a very nice man," most will say, and argue that paternalism and perhaps even condescension earlier in his career, rather than racism, frames his depictions.

Notwithstanding her education, and especially after becoming a "star" among the academy of those times, González's identity as a "descendant of wealthy Spanish land-owners" plays well into the prearranged Anglo images of class stratification and good Mexican/bad Mexican dichotomies and consorts with a spirit of heartfelt sympathy for the injustice suffered by a few presumed elites admitted into the club. This is permissible, provided that the vast majority of these "others" is kept at a safe distance, where they at times can be studied as colorful subjects without disrupting their primary "use value"—the labor force they "happily" provide.

Regardless of class origins or family history, by the time González submitted her article "America Invades the Border Towns" to the *Southwest Review* (1930), or wrote her fiction, at least in economic and social terms "a Mexican was simply a Mexican," as Montejano notes (115). But for González, stressing class differences even across racial lines is ultimately more important. The notion of the original friendliness toward the first arriving Southern Confederacy families with whom the landed elite happily intermarried is still extremely important and deeply embedded in her psychology. Time and again she asserts that it was the later-arriving "white trash" from the North and Midwest that caused the conflict and resentment:

> We, Texas-Mexicans of the border, although we hold on to our traditions, and are proud of our race, are loyal to the United States, in spite of the treatment we receive by some of the new Americans. Before their arrival, there were no racial or social distinctions between us. Their children married ours, ours married theirs, and both were glad and proud of the fact. But since the coming of the "white trash" from the north and middle west we felt the change. They made us feel for the first time that we were Mexicans and that they considered themselves our superiors. (González 1930a as cited in Montejano: 115)

Perhaps fearing her audience might see themselves as the descendants of the "white trash" to which she refers, González tailored her views for an audience in many ways prepared by Dobie. They allowed her to speak not as a historian per se but as a folklorist claiming a share of history, in however compromised a fashion, for her people of South Texas. Let us now examine yet another side of that "double-consciousness," one in which the complexities of the author's own internal class identities become a poetics still in the process of defining itself.

THE GENTE DECENTE

Throughout her life Jovita González was preoccupied with class identity. Her writings and reflections bristle with terms like *gente decente* (literally, "decent people" but very often thought of as high-society people) or *gente culta* or *fina,* as opposed to *gente corriente* or *mal educada.* These terms distinguish social rather than economic status in the life of South Texas to this day, though to a lesser degree than in González's time. In other words, very poor people can have class, while middle-class people can be common; *corrientes,* have no class. To understand the internal social diversity of South Texas Mexican life during the 1920s and 1930s, we must go beyond standard Marxist concepts of class stratification or those images we associate strictly with middle-class prosperity during the post–World War II era or with the upward mobility of many Chicanos prior to and continuing after the Vietnam War. If we are to appreciate some of the nuances in class relationships, we must also consider the internal diversity of the South Texas communities. Though Jovita González's family, as she presents it in her ethnographic work, obviously owns land, and thus is better off than the laborers or the mail carrier, in her "Among My People" the landed wealthy are not so obviously taken with their own sense of power or status as the "aristocracy" she presents in her fiction. Traditionally, the main economic class distinctions in South Texas arise from the basic issue of whether you work for yourself or for a *patrón,* a patriarch. However, family history and origin entail a certain pride: in many cases landed property does not go hand in hand with moveable property. You can be land rich but cash poor in this life where everyone works with little pretension to any kind of wealth. González's interpretation for an Anglo audience rests on what she perhaps feels is the only thing they understand: a social class distinction of the *gente decente* from the *corriente,* with the former enjoying the benefit of their landowning heritage.

González's class identification becomes rather more complex when we consider the influences of her early career upon her later life experiences. All who recall González from Corpus Christi describe her as an energetic, courageous, strong, passionate, well-read, and intelligent woman. Reflecting upon her own career and perhaps as a result of the many years of con-

tact with the Mexican exiles in San Felipe, González consistently and officially identifies herself as *gente decente*. Though the term could be interpreted
simply to mean that she is a lady of good breeding, within the university it
takes on a limited meaning more likely determined by class and property:
she distinguishes herself from the dominant culture's view of the Mexicano
as *peon* or *vaquero*, both of whom she persistently presents as a "noble savage" type. Within her own community the term *gente decente* could simply
represent a set of polite values, mores, a certain comportment, or breeding;
but her use of this term within the university culture could represent her determination to define herself as a lady among the men of a male-centered,
male-dominated academy. In her attempt to show that Mexicanos also have
class, the poor uneducated and most often exploited Mexican gets lost in the
analysis. In her efforts to *hacerse al ambiente,* González is accommodating
and conforming to an environment with which she cannot fully agree. Yet
given the stereotypes set forth by Anglo American literature about the
women of her culture (see Cecil Robinson's remarks in the following chapter), González must have felt compelled to lessen her discomfort, to set herself apart from perceptions freely floating among these self-proclaimed
gentlemen of the South and within the academy; even so, the mark of a
"lady" does suggest a certain economic status.

Among her own people, González apparently also felt a need to identify
herself as a decent woman in contrast to "*esas otras,*" for all intents and purposes the feminized "other"—feminized along sexual and class structured
mores and also set against the standard of the highly contextualized term
gente decente. There exists among the Mexicano community a long-standing
cultural norm by which a woman alone is viewed as "open game," while a
woman accompanied by a relative, be it aunt, mother, sister or little brother,
is to be respected as *familia.* González's memoirs show evidence of her acute
awareness of this after she was awarded the Lapham Scholarship in 1928 at
the University of Texas for research on Texas history on the border and to
advance her studies toward her M.A. She spent that summer traveling in
Webb, Zapata, and Starr Counties of South Texas. An apparently necessary
step for her to be treated with respect as she gathered her materials among
mostly male storytellers was to secure letters of introduction from Catholic Archbishop Droessarts and Episcopal Bishop Capers of San Antonio
to clergymen of these border counties who would facilitate her research.
Recalling this event decades later in a taped interview (Barrera), she again
identifies herself with the *gente decente,* in this case a sexually chaste and

proper woman. In her own words, González describes the challenges of her work, the accommodations she made to the patriarchy of her own culture, as she presented herself among her people in her unusual role as woman scholar:

> Cuándo salí a tomar datos para mi tesis me valí de dos cosas—una fue que fuí con el Arzobispo de San Antonio y le dije, "quiero que me escriba una carta de recomendación para llevar a cada pueblo donde yo vaya y llevársela al pároco para que él les diga que soy una persona decente." Otra es que donde quiera que iba, llevaba mi hilo de tejer. Mientras que la gente estaba hablando, yo me ponía a tejer para que vieran que no era de las otras.
>
> [When I would go out to do research for my thesis, I depended on two things—one was that I went to the Archbishop of San Antonio and asked him, "I want you to write a letter of recommendation for me, so that I can take it to each town where I go and show it to the parish priest, so that he will tell the people of the community that I am a decent person." Another is that whenever the people were talking, I would take out my knitting needles and begin to knit so that they would not think I was one of those "other" women.] (my translation)

Keeping her hair long and rolled into a bun helped her to be distinguished from "*las otras*" (those other women), for these were the years of the short-haired, short-skirted flappers. Her carrying along a set of knitting needles and using them while she listened to the stories of her people provided another overt sign of a decent woman. In an audiotape by Aida Barrera for a radio series entitled *Sabor del pueblo,* Américo Paredes describes González as "a young woman traveling alone, acting as an independent professional and at the same time being a traditional model of propriety."

González's concern with appearances of *decencia* is coupled with tendencies in her attitude toward other Mexican American women who were also in the public eye. A reliable source recalls González's being asked if she knew Lydia Mendoza. Her response is quite telling of her interest in setting herself apart from the commonplace community: "¿Esa que grita en la plaza de zacate, que la voy a conocer?" [That (woman) who yells at the grass plaza (the Haymarket Plaza in San Antonio), how can you expect that I would know such a person?]. Here González appears to view Lydia Mendoza, who is well known and highly respected to this day by her community, and as a "lady" in every sense of the word according to an older definition of propriety and femininity, with disdain. An interesting version of the "town-gown" gap also emerges here between the popular culture or "folklore" celebrated and practiced in the daily life of the community and that practice, removed and codified, analyzed and formally presented to the academy anxious for a taste of the local color. An association that for her is unthinkable is transformed into the "decent" for González when it is *she* who "performs."

In 1927, several newspapers in the Central Texas and Dallas area reported on her address "Lore of the Texas Vaquero," which was delivered "with ballads sung to the accompaniment of guitars by native Mexican cowboys" and closed the thirteenth annual meeting of the Texas Folklore Society in Austin that year: "The stage was appropriately set on the University Y. M. C. A. auditorium for presentation of Miss Gonzales' address and the Mexican songs. There was a camp fire surrounded by cactus and mesquite thickets and about the fire were Mexican rifles, blankets, canteens, moorals [*sic*] and cow saddles" (*San Antonio Express,* April 24, 1927). For González, her own "performance" in this artificial setting, with boundaries firmly established, removing her from the place and the people she describes to an almost exclusively Anglo audience within the walls of the exclusive hotels and universities of the time, also validates and confirms her sense of *decencia.* This constructed border precludes even her remote association with Lydia Mendoza, who performs at the Haymarket Plaza for the public, for a people who intimately know and have lived the experiences related in songs sung for the Folklore Society, such as "Cuando yo salí de Kansas," ("When I Went Up the Kansas Trail") "and other ballads of the Texas *vaqueros* sung by Mexicans" on that closing night of the society's annual meeting (Abernethy 1992: 163).[9]

THE NOVELIST AND
MORE CLASS CONSIDERATIONS

In light of González's career as a folklorist and historian, her fiction is complex. As with her scholarly writings, one of the most important factors to consider is how she tenaciously clings to her distinctions between the landed families, her *gente decente,* and the "common" Mexicans. Given my own South Texas and northern Mexican origin, I find her depictions of this highly stratified South Texas system suspect; they are the views of someone who aspires to high-class status and "imagines" the rich condescending to the poor. At the very least her view is a highly romanticized view of a long-faded or never in fact strictly defined social system. I believe that rather than from claims to Spanish nobility or inherited class background, dignity in South Texas comes with more down-to-earth, practical concerns such as land ownership, however cash poor the owner of thousands of acres or a five-acre *ranchito* may be. To this day in South Texas, whether one is the owner of a *tendajito* (little store) or a chain of them, it is the autonomy and independence of working for oneself rather than as a wage earner or dependent of a *patrón* that bestows prestige. An example of this are the *colonias* of South Texas, where poor people have purchased plots of land to have their dream of ownership, a "place" that represents dignity in their society, even though they may not have running water and a sewage system. The irony is that middle-class America sees the *colonias* as emblems of America's poor and uneducated, a people without hope. But then, Jovita González's view is from a different epoch; she witnessed what none of us living today can testify to, and she did so from a truly unique perspective. However identified today's scholars of Mexican American literature, culture, and history may be with their "Chicanismo," we are all inescapably products of Anglo American dominance; whereas Jovita González, at least at a very early age, lived in a world still not completely infused with the new social, political, and economic system of the United States.

Both of her novels explore the in-between existences of the characters she creates, and it is in those characters that her hope for the future of Texas Mexicans lies, especially when it comes to their relationship with an emerging dominant culture. In *Dew on the Thorn* we have the son of an intermarriage offer hope precisely because of his dual perspective and multiple roles in a community, while in *Caballero* a patriarch who refuses to change from the old traditions meets with a tragic end and no heirs to carry on his proud name.

But Jovita González's case becomes even more complex when the study of her life experiences in relation to her writing concerns education. A scene in the final chapter of *Dew on the Thorn* (marked XVII) is most telling with regard to questions of identity and the author's alleged *Porfirismo* and belief in the education of all classes. A school had circulated among all the *ranchos* of South Texas: "*La escuela de español* for boys was beginning the fourteenth year of its existence and the third at the Olivereño ranch. Following a system of rotation, encouraged by the patrons, the school was moved from ranch to ranch, and for the second time since its foundation Don Francisco, as head of the board had brought it back to his ranch." Even though the school circulates in Texas, it opens with the singing of Mexico's national anthem. The schoolmaster, Don Alberto, asks himself, "What if the school was in Texas? He was paid by the parents to make good Mexicans out of these boys and he was doing it." As the boys reach the age of twenty-one they can make a choice: "either to cross into Mexico or if they were born in Texas either naturalize themselves as Mexican citizens; the other, to pay allegiance to the land of their birth and reinforce their citizenship."

Don Alberto has been educated in Mexico, "during the period when the French trend of thought predominated" and as a result his philosophy reflects the writings of Rousseau, Diderot, Montesquieu, Voltaire, and Hugo. Because he marries the daughter of a South Texas landowner, the ranchers persuade him "to stay in Texas and conduct a school for boys." Though the "father" of the ranches, Father José María, and Don Alberto disagree about every religious principle, they agree on one thing: that education should be for *all* children regardless of their class background. It is clear that the narrator is also critical of the attitude of most *rancheros:* "The *rancheros* believing themselves masters of everything, looked down from their self appointed eminence upon the *peones* as mere instruments to work for them. It had never ocurred to them that the *peones* were human beings, with a mental capacity to learn, and spiritual possibilities to appreciate the beautiful things."

The teacher persists in arguing on behalf of the *peones'* children that "fanciful imagination needs an outlet which only instruction can give them," and the priest insists that "their spiritual hunger and lack of proper religious environment makes them have a pagan soul," and Don Francisco makes a liberal concession, so for the first time, "the children of the *peones* joined the children of their masters in singing the national hymn." The mixing of classes is symbolically represented in Don Alberto's talk, which he prepares for this special occasion, and in which he represents the Indian ancestry in relation to that of the Spanish:

> He related to the boys the past greatness of the indigenous races; he
> told them of the city of Aztecs, the great Tenochtitlán that had sur-
> prised the Spanish conquerors with its splendor and its wealth. He
> told them of the valiant prince Cuautemoc, who, when tortured
> by the Spaniards, because he would not reveal the hiding place of
> Moctezuma's treasure, had merely said when his anointed feet were

placed over the burning coals: "Verily this is no bed of roses." He unfolded before their avid minds the miracle of the dark Virgin of Tepeyac, the Blessed Mother, who as an Indian maid appeared to the Indian, Juan Diego, as a proof of God's love for his Indian children. "It was an Indian boy, Pipila," he continued, "who set fire to the strong Spanish fortress of Granaditas when the patriot Father Hidalgo was fighting for our independence; it was Morelos a man with Indian blood who carried on when all hopes for freedom were lost. It was a pure blooded Indian, Benito Juárez, who struggled for our sovereignty, when French aggression threatened Mexico, and today," he ended, "it is a *mestizo,* Don Porfirio Díaz, who directs our destinies. So you see my boys, the heritage of this race of bronze, the race of strong heroic men. *Viva la raza de bronce! Viva México! Viva Don Porfirio Díaz!*"

In regard to social interaction between the classes, in her fiction González maintains the focus of the conflict on class rather than on race, but she struggles with what she portrays as her own class's treatment of *peones,* or common Mexicans, especially as it concerns education. González has crossed out throughout her two major manuscripts several scenes of mistreatment or pejorative depictions of the lower classes:

He stopped as though struck by a sudden thought; then cupping his hands in a manner of men used to speaking across stretches of the Texas plains he called out:

"Marcos, Marcos."

Hurried footsteps were heard in answer, and an Indian *peón* stood before him hat in hand.

"*Mande Vd.* Don Francisco. Did you wish something?"

"Yes, you Indian bastard; have all the guests left?"

"*Sí,* my master."

"Tell your mistress I have returned."

"Yes, Don Francisco."

"And do it immediately, you son of ten thousand devils! Why do you stand there like a scarecrow staring at me?"

"For nothing master, for nothing," answered the *peón,* retreating as quickly as he could.

Yet as we shall see in *Caballero, peones* are also shown to be decent people, *gente decente;* the author is even critical of how the daughters of the Mendoza y Soria family are taught not to trust them enough to be alone with them, as is the case during Susanita's ride into Matamoros with José, the peon, as her only companion:

> "Jose, you are good. Papa will reward you well, I know."
> Jose had a different opinion but he made no comment.
> What would Don Santiago say? He knew what Alvaro would say.
> Alvaro would not believe that even a peon like he could ride through
> the night with Susanita and *treat her with respect*. For a moment Jose
> hoped they would not arrive in time to save Alvaro, who judged all
> men by himself. (*Caballero:* 391; my emphasis)

Two contrasting views become evident here: the views of the enlightenment, which had affected prerevolutionary *"Porfirismo,"* and the post–Mexican Revolutionary cultural consciousness compete with the strict class system evident during the Porfirio Díaz dictatorship in Mexico prior to the Mexican Revolution of 1910. The author's presentation of these two contradictory images could be the result of her having lived in San Felipe and coming under the influence of the liberals of postrevolutionary México. Additionally, the fuller context of the novel *Dew on the Thorn* and even of *Caballero* also reveals at least a personal cultural poetics, well formed and already replete with strong women, an anti–Anglo American invasion history of domination, and a great deal of resentment. Most important are the author's class distinctions and her stress on the role of education in relation to the future of Texas Mexicans as Anglo American domination by intervention and investment was on the increase. Her role in later life as an educator reflects the sustaining effects of some of the same negotiations of identity between two irreconcilable worlds that unfold as she writes her novels.

HIGH SOCIETY, LOCAL COLOR, AND THE EDUCATOR

Having moved to Corpus Christi in 1939, Edmundo Mireles was successful in organizing the Spanish program for the third through sixth elementary grades during the 1940s. In González's words, they both confronted "a period when the walls of racial prejudice [were] still hard to be torn down." The Spanish language teaching movement was spreading through Texas and the Spanish Southwest before 1941 when, with Eleanor Roosevelt as a chief influence, the U.S. Congress revoked the 1917 law barring the teaching of all foreign languages in the state's public elementary schools. In 1941,

W. S. Benson & Co. in Austin published *Mi libro español,* an eight-volume textbook series based on courses Edmundo had introduced in the Corpus Christi Independent School District classrooms in 1940. Eventually used in Texas and other parts of the country to teach Spanish to elementary students, the series is a result of a collaborative effort by E. E. Mireles, Roy B. Fisher, and Jovita González de Mireles. It incorporates Mexican American historical figures and the contributions of the Spanish-speaking population to the United States and includes illustrations and songs with music.

Because of Mireles's advocacy for teaching Spanish in the public schools, the Corpus Christi community today views him as the father of bilingual education. Corpus Christi attorney and former national president of LULAC Ruben Bonilla recalls that when LULAC honored Mireles shortly before his wife's death, he seemed very proud and genteel, but Bonilla attributes this to *her* upbringing. Mrs. Mireles (Jovita González) was Bonilla's Spanish teacher between the years 1962 and 1964 at W. B. Ray High School, which had opened in 1950. In this school for the affluent, where only 20 percent of the students were Mexican American (there were no African Americans, and the remainder were Anglo), he recalls that every day during the second half of their split lunch period, she methodically drew down a map of Spain and proceeded to recite her usual litany on the Spanish nobility in the Hispanic community, Spain, and its provinces. "She used the class as a platform from which she could tell us anecdotes and folktales" (personal interview, August 6, 1996). This passion for an education that includes the stories of her people surfaces several times in *Dew on the Thorn,* as in the voice of the grandmother who tells the story of Doña Rita's possession and assures the disbelieving young listeners of the value of such knowledge transmitted through stories: "'Youth may have learning these days, but it does not have the wisdom that comes with gray hair,' answered Juana, the old grandmother, rolling her corn shuck cigarette. 'This young generation is ignorant of many things; you go to school and only learn to be ashamed of your beliefs, *getting nothing in turn to replace them'*" (291; my emphasis).

But Jovita González was also prepossessed with her lineage and heritage. According to Bonilla, she had students role-play to learn the proper ways in which to go courting. In this way, "she taught more about life, social mores, and origins, about respect, discipline, family values, and the church,"—all ideas that go with her image of the *gente decente,* though Bonilla does not recall her using that term (personal interview, August 6, 1996). Bonilla's general impression of the couple was that they certainly were not *of* the people;

"they seemed aristocratic." He remembers Mrs. Mireles as a tough and demanding teacher, and one with a good sense of humor, for they played a few pranks on her. Though she made a lasting impression on her students because of her concern for them, Bonilla also remembers another side of her complex personality: "She did not identify with Mexican American causes, certainly not the organizational leadership among Mexican Americans. The Mireleses championed the cause of bilingual education, but then the politicians took it over and took the credit. They were modest and unassuming and did not make attempts to claim their place in history" (personal interview, August 6, 1996).

Notwithstanding this tremendous accomplishment in the area of Spanish language teaching, in Corpus Christi, otherwise than in the San Felipe School District, the Mireleses' role becomes less politicized; in fact, their earlier pursuits of educational justice in time became less noticeable. Reduced to the function of adding local color to the mostly Anglo society within which she circulated, Mrs. E. E. Mireles, as she was now exclusively known and referred to in the society pages of the *Corpus Christi Caller,* continued to be ever increasingly distanced from the Mexican American local community and to reinvent herself among the Anglos. Dan Kilgore, local community historian, remembered her to Thomas Kreneck as a "blueblood" (personal interview, August 2, 1996). By Anglo community standards, she was viewed as "upper crust," while by the Mexicano community she was either not known or perceived as aloof, mixing only with the highly educated Anglo and Spanish/Mexican society.

This aloofness can be measured against the host of political activities that had been underway in the region. Organizers like Manuela Solis de Sager were combating unfair labor practices, and Alberto Perales was addressing the forced repatriations of Mexicans and Mexican Americans of the thirties and beyond. In the Mireleses' home town of Corpus Christi, Dr. Héctor García was organizing meetings to fight for the burial rights of World War II veteran Felix Longoria from Three Rivers and advocating rights to medical care and education for all veterans. Meanwhile, in 1943, Edmundo Mireles was organizing a local chapter of a Pan American Council, whose objectives among many others were to study Spanish, Latin America, its people, history, geography, population, customs, habits, and way of life; to foster good relations between Anglo Americans and Latin Americans; to cooperate with Latin Americans to help themselves; to encourage them to contribute to the welfare of their community; and to cooperate with the public schools in the organization and functioning of Pan American Clubs and parent-teacher associations. Likewise, the onetime "star" of the Texas Folklore Society was busying herself in 1946, directing *pastorelas,* pageants, and Christmastime *posadas* with local Mexican children as the pilgrims playing for the entertainment of a mostly Anglo audience, thus providing the local, nonpoliticized, color for an established community with a need to express occasional benevolence toward their surrounding indigenous population. According to Isabel Cruz, Mrs. Mireles enjoyed entertaining in her home, hosting bridal and baby showers for her friends, who, though racially mixed, all happened to be *"gente de prestigio, puras mujeres universitarias"* [people of prestige, only university women] (personal interview, August 2, 1996). Like those of some Chicano academics today who stay at arm's length from the Mexicano community, these social activities provided a niche for the Mireles couple while more overtly political pursuits of social justice through direct action were carried out in other circles.

On the other hand, even after the couple's relocation from the community of Del Rio to Corpus Christi, Blandina Cárdenas recalls, the San Felipe community continued to express respect and admiration for Jovita and Edmundo Mireles on their occasional visits during the next decades—mostly for weddings and *velorios*—up until the 1970s: "Edmundo was particularly proud of Jovita González's passion for teaching South Texas Mexicano history." In fact, Cárdenas recollects people commenting that she was a lot smarter than her husband. She especially recalls a long conversation that took place *en familia* in 1962 at a *velorio* in which the Mireleses had come to San Felipe to pay their last respects to Cárdenas's Tío Ramón Méndez: "Edmundo Mireles bragged quite a bit about his wife's work. He was so proud of her and her research and even spoke of her unpublished novel" (personal interview, April 13, 1995). Cárdenas was particularly struck by the tremendous joy Jovita took in her people's history and by her passionate desire to pass on the true history of land grants and how the land had been taken away from the Mexicanos, a favorite theme of hers, for she had done research on the families around the King Ranch. Cárdenas adds an important observation: "I am certain of two impressions: Edmundo Mireles celebrated his wife's intelligence, and brilliance. . . . When I saw them together, I said, 'I want that'" (personal interview, May 5, 1996). The other thing of which Cárdenas is certain concerns González's novel *Caballero,* to which I will turn after discussing her first novel.

DEW ON THE THORN

Embedded in the first chapter of *Dew on the Thorn,* "The Stronghold of the Olivares," is "Among My People," which provides interesting digressions from the larger narrative about the devil in Texas and various other characters introduced during the shelling of corn by moonlight. This manuscript, however, also contains another first chapter, "The Family of the Olivares." This original but deleted chapter more directly responds to Webb, for the author lays out the history of her South Texas in a perspective roundly contrasting with her later images of South Texas ranch life. All evidence indicates that, for her novel, González eventually opted for the softer, less politicized first chapter. Though the women remain strong and central to the story, the author's revisions to the original first chapter already signal an accommodation of the South Texas history of conflict behind a foreground of family history. While the second Chapter 1, "The Stronghold of the Olivares," begins with the aftermath of a family wedding, the deleted, original Chapter 1, "The Family of the Olivares," begins with a tone of impending loss, a history of conflict, mistrust of the invading *Americanos,* and above all, resistance to change:

> Rich in the traditions of a proud past, and still rich in worldly goods, the year of Our Lord 1904 found the Olivares in the land which His Excellency Revilla Gigedo, Viceroy of New Spain, had deeded to the head of the family in 1764. The grant which extended into territory destined later to become Texas, was located thirty miles east of the Río Grande, and ambled leisurely along through fertile plains and grass-covered prairies to within five miles of the Nueces river.
>
> Yet in spite of their long permanency in the country, this family, as was also true of all the border families, remained more Spanish and more Mexican than if they had lived in Mexico. A series of unfortunate circumstances which had made the Olivares cling tenaciously to the traditions of their people, had also made them look upon all Americans with distrust and dislike.

That the family remained more Spanish and Mexican than if they had lived in Mexico is certainly a defining feature of South Texas culture. Again, the Olivares are very much like the author's own family as she describes them in her memoirs. Though her grandfather purchased a ranch by the name of "Las Víboras" in Starr County at the close of the Civil War, González claims this was part of the land lost by her ancestors after the Treaty of Guadalupe Hidalgo, when "fearing the reprisals of the new conquerors, most of the colonizers on the Texas side crossed the Rio Grande to live among their kinsmen in Mexico" (Memoirs: 3). In her novels, as with the telling of her own family history, González tracks events according to the history of land loss by South Texas Mexicanos that occurred in waves of displacement at several different points: after Texas gained its independence from Mexico in 1836, after the Republic was annexed to the United States in 1845, immediately after the end of the U.S. War with Mexico in 1848, and finally with the coming of commercial farmers immediately before and after the turn of the century, when the latter bought up land for pennies an acre and put pressure on Mexicans to sell. González also claims that her maternal grandparents came from a long line of colonizers who had come with José Escandón to Nuevo Santander, the original name for the stretch of land from the Rio Grande to the Nueces: "One of my ancestors, Don José Alejandro Guerra had been surveyor to the Crown" (Memoirs: 2). In the novel, the Olivares family is also connected to the Escandón settlement: "The first of the Olivares, Don Juan José, had come in 1748 as surveyor to the Spanish Crown. At that time the Indian infested region north of Nuevo León had been created into the new province of Nuevo Santander. Later a military expedition led by Don José Escandón was sent by the Viceroy with a two fold purpose, namely to subdue the warlike Indian tribes and to look for suitable locations for settlements in the region between the Río Grande and the Nueces river" (*Dew on the Thorn:* chap. 1, pp. 1–2).

As a Mexicana from South Texas coming into an academic world at a moment in which the power structure and the land of her South Texas were still shifting into Anglo hands, González, like Webb, creates for herself a character right out of her own fiction — or perhaps a fiction right out of her own life and family history. This character which she creates and which she is to live out professionally and socially is born in 1904, the very year which she later gives as her birthdate at the University of Texas, though her earlier records with the Folklore Society indicate that she was born in 1899.

As if in direct response to Webb and all of Texas history symbolized by the ever present Battle of the Alamo, Don Cesareo, the patriarch of *Dew on the Thorn,* reflects on the dead *Americanos:*

> Don Cesareo was sorry they had all been killed. Like the good Catholic that he was he had even said a few prayers for the repose of their souls.

But that was as it should be, he thought. Why should they have come to a land that was not theirs? Did they not have a country of their own? Poor foolish men, these foreigners be, he mused to think they could take anything away from Mexico. Mexicans were courageous and could fight! Hadn't they heard how the Mexicans had driven out the mighty armies of the king of Spain from their country? He shuddered at the mere thought of the approach of these Americans. These men who were heretics should not come to Christian territory. He had read in a history his father left him that the Americans were the same as the English, and the English had always been enemies of Spain. One of his ancestors if he remembered right, a captain of a Spanish galleon, had been killed by the English pirate Drake. Not only were they enemies of Spain but at one time the English had even dared to oppose the Pope, and all because he would not allow their king to have more than one wife. And if history was true the king's lawful wife had been a Spanish princess. Ah! these *Americanos* had a deathly heritage. They were the born enemies of the Mexicans. Certainly, thought Don Cesareo, God, who was a Catholic, could not allow these people who were His enemies to take the land away from them! (chapt. 1, p. 7)

If we compare this with Webb's writing, we see that the Manifest Destiny or "God is on our side" construction of reality is present on both sides of the Mexican-Anglo conflict, as is the characterization of the enemy replete with similar linguistic and rhetorical elements. This labeling of the *Americanos* as heretics and foolish men and of a hero of English history, Sir Francis Drake, as a mere pirate, certainly serves to illustrate dichotomous constructions of reality, depending on one's context at the time of the events. A strange affinity in contrast appears between Webb's version of the mental state of the Anglo pioneer in Texas and on the Great Plains with whom he very much identifies and a contemporary *Mexicana* scholar's version of a character with whom she also very strongly identifies. These however slanted versions of history through fiction, when conjoined, propose a more nuanced picture of historical experience than that afforded by official histories that present only a single view of the past. In other words, through the multiperspectival fictions we gain a sense of historical reality not often procured by official histories, or by hero-worshipping monographs re-presenting but one view of the past.

RACIAL CONFLICT AND CLASS ALIGNMENT

A few years pass in silence after Santa Ana's eventual defeat, but then violence over land possession rights erupts at a time which González represents as the period between the aftermath of the U.S. War with Mexico in 1848 and just prior to the end of the Civil War. The clash between two races in her first deleted chapter appears in numerous violent episodes, as it does in one significant scene in the final chapter of her next novel, *Caballero*. However, in *Dew on the Thorn,* the roles of the killer and victim are reversed. A stranger who has come to take possession of the land kills Don Cesareo's *caporal,* his ranch foreman, when he tells the foreigner that the land belongs to Don Cesareo: "Let that be a lesson to you Mexicans," the man says, "that's how we shall deal with any one who opposes us, and unless you leave the country you shall be treated to the same" (*Dew on the Thorn:* deleted first chap. 1, "The Family of the Olivares").

With conflicts like these, Don Cesareo is forced to leave Texas, "the land won by the sweat and blood of his ancestors." This eventually "crushed his proud spirit" and kills him, leaving his wife, Doña Ramona, "a spirited, arrogant woman," a widow, and the matriarch who now has the responsibility of looking after the ranch, the *peones,* "the families who had been left fatherless by the Americanos," and their three orphaned children. She keeps two things in the minds of her children—that the Americans have despoiled them of their land, and that they must remain true to their traditions:

> "My son," she often told Francisco, "later in life when you are a man you are bound to meet the enemies of your family. When that happens there is only one thing for you to do. Kill—and kill without compassion. Spare no one; if one of these foreigners should fall into your hands—kill him. If he should ask you for mercy, kill him, if he should kneel at your feet and beg for his life, kill him. Did they have mercy on your uncle Juan? Did they show mercy to your father? Did they have compassion on the hundreds they despoiled of their land? The blood of your father and of your uncle calls for vengeance!"

Racial conflict gives way to class considerations when, at the close of the Civil War, "a new type of Americans" comes to the border. Doña Ramona's heart softens when she comes in contact with some people from Virginia, Alabama, Kentucky, and the Carolinas, "people of culture who had been impoverished by the Civil War." Because one of these men marries into the family, Doña Ramona learns that "not all Americans were cruel, heartless, avaricious men. He had the same fine sentiments as her husband had had." In *Caballero* this aligning of South Texas landowning families with these displaced, post–Civil War southern gentlemen, as opposed to what are described as riff-raff pioneer types (the "white trash" to which she later refers in her scholarly work), resurfaces to make the South Texas conflict over land appear more as a class war than one drawn along diverse racial, ethnic, and religious lines. Américo Paredes offers his own interpretation of this connection between some landowning families and the "southern gentlemen" of González's novel. "Not all Mexicans along the Rio Grande protested against Anglo exploitation. Some 'good' families made common cause with the Anglo fortune-seekers and were accepted as loyal citizens of the United States (and later of the Confederacy)" (1976: 22). Though in this novel González compares the complicity of some of the landowning families with that of the southern aristocracy at the end of the Civil War, her point about upper-class recognition, understanding, and "distinction" is well made.

In some ways the exaggerated fictional descriptions of this deleted chapter stress a class system that also affirms the separateness and distinctive superiority the author claims for herself. Some of the editorial markings indicate her movement toward creating an image of an aristocratic lifestyle for the landowners as well as a well-defined caste system by which the *patrón* ruled absolutely over the *peones,* who "led the same life of submission their brethren did in Mexico" (18). The Porfirismo speaks against the Mexican revolutionary ideals when González at one point emphasizes the *patrón*'s role: "With him he brought the system of peonage, perfected by centuries of existence and this he enforced at the ranch. As owner of the land he had certain duties toward his servants, and they in turn had specific obligations to perform. He was the protector in time of danger, the adviser and counselor, and not seldom the judge who tried the case as well as inflicted punishment" (17).

Besides providing for their living quarters, the *patrón* offers a salary (which the author crosses out) of *"dos reales y la comida o cuatro reales y comen de ellos"* [two bits and meals or four bits and furnish your own] (17).[10] Later, however, the author softly decries the inherited debt to the *amo,* the master, as one the *peones* "could never hope to pay." Realizing their position, they "grew pessimistic and developed a spirit of hopelessness and despair. There was no incentive for them to save, since whatever they might economize went to pay the inherited debt" (19). González's portrayal of strict class distinctions brings her *peones* close to the position of southern plantation slaves, while the landowning *patrón* approximates the status of the pre–Civil War southern aristocrat.

In contrast, the vaqueros resemble Webb's pioneers in their representation of the spirit of the West: "either mestizos or criollos . . . fiery spirited men, wild and untamed, over whom Don Francisco had no control. A product of the frontier, they disliked law and restraint and hated innovations and newcomers. The open prairie was their haven and as they galloped across the prairie both horse and rider appeared as one" (17–18). While the vaquero "might some day rise to the level of his more fortunate associate," the peon had no such hope of rising "to the dignity of being vaqueros, but became goatherds, worked the fields, performed all the menial and manual labor around the ranch, and sometimes became the personal servants of the master and his sons" (18).

The epigraph to this first chapter reads, "*Soy como el roble, me doblo, pero no me quiebro*" [Like an oak I may be bent but not broken] (in the author's own translation). It is the family motto and as such immediately signals the prevailing theme, which resurfaces as the central theme of her later novel, *Caballero*. That inability to change with the new times and with the new imposing ways of the invading *Americanos* comes more to the fore in *Caballero* in the character of the central figure, Don Santiago de Mendoza y Soria, patriarch and owner of Rancho La Palma. This first chapter ends with the same conclusion, however suppressed this theme of resistance may have become in her later writings. The theme of the Mexican being reduced to a foreigner in his or her own land is one that many Chicano writers are to revisit time and time again during the next half of the century. The deleted chapter ends with a description of the new patriarch, the eldest son, Don Francisco (also the name of González's own grandfather), who also appears as the patriarch in her folklore: "It was said of Don Francisco that he was so busy being busy that he had no time for work. For when he was not riding with his *caporal,* he was arranging a hunt, a cock fight, a *rodeo* or attending the races in town. Thus lived Don Francisco, in the midst of this rural splendor enjoying life to the fullest, never realizing that *he was a foreigner in his own land*" (my emphasis).

Crossed out from this final sentence is an indication of another prevailing theme, that of autonomy, harmony, and tradition being disrupted by the coming of the Anglo colonizer. Don Francisco was enjoying "the same things and doing what since the beginning of time had been the pastimes of a Mexican gentleman." More to the point, the impending disappearance of an old regime foreshadows the usurpation of land and civil rights that await many of the landed classes of South Texas. With the coming of the commercial farmers soon after the turn of the century, the period in which the novel begins, bending or breaking, accommodating or selling one's soul would become central issues.

The Women, the Devil, and the Land

In the new first chapter of the novel, "The Stronghold of the Olivares" (or "Don Francisco de los Olivares"), women are still strong and conspicuous. The chapter opens with the appearance of Don Francisco. He arrives at his ranch, angry with himself for not having attended his daughter's wedding, her leaving the "paternal roof" too much for him to bear:

> "Francisco my love, you are an idiot," echoed a woman's voice back of him.
>
> He whirled around. In the doorway, stood Doña Margarita, his wife, stately and serene, still wearing the silk dress she had worn at her daughter's wedding. The look of anger faded, and a shamed expression suffused his handsome face.
>
> "I know it my Pearl," he replied meekly.

As he rests, feeling the "Laguneño," the breeze from the Gulf of Mexico, his mind travels back to the memories of his mother and his having left the maternal fold of another very strong woman:

> He could see her so distinctly even now as head of her household, stern and severe; her pale face, clear cut, as an ivory cameo, contrasting with the snappy black eyes that saw everything and shone like burning coals when provoked to anger. And again her memory came to him, but in a different mood; not as the mistress to be feared, but as a mother, a Mater Dolorosa, ever anxious for her children. Dressed in black, a mother of pearl and silver crucifix on her breast, lace *mantilla* covering the soft wavy hair, just turning gray, he remembered going to church with her; he could still hear her words, as she led him to that altar, "My child pray for your father who lies buried here."

As if making love to the daughters of the *peones* were a rite of passage, this abuse is depicted in both novels, except that here, unlike in *Caballero,* the young Francisco is severely reprimanded by his mother for his misconduct: "Grown to early manhood he remembered making love to the servant girls with the ardor and impetuousness of youth. He saw himself facing Doña Ramona in her room; her hair almost white now, framed her deep lined face but the eyes had retained the fire and spirit of former times. Unable to stand the look of disgust and contempt in them he had stooped to kiss her hand, but she had withdrawn it away with violence, 'The kiss of one who is not a gentleman soils my hand,' he heard her say." This image of the strong, commanding woman is consistent with Doña Margarita, who appears in one of González's *Mary Immaculate* publications (June 1935). In this case, she is not a widow but the wife of Don Francisco, who is described as a lamb and a slave under her influence: "Doña Margarita was the undisputed mistress of her home, her eight children, and the women of the ranch. Every evening the ranch people gathered in the *sala* to hear music from the phonograph, or stories from Doña Margarita. The gatherings always ended with prayers, led by the mistress of the house, and were always punctuated by commands and reproofs" (175).

The prevailing theme of the weight and responsibility of being a *caballero* in every sense of the word was to be more fully developed in the novel thus titled. *Dew on the Thorn,* on the other hand, provides a fuller context for what it was to be a matriarch, a major figure in González's first novel as well as in her own life. It is clear in this first novel that the woman's strength and her sense of history gives courage to the patriarch. Remembering his own wedding day, and also the day of his departure from his birthplace, Don Francisco recalls how it was Doña Ramona who instilled in him a sense of a lost heritage he is destined to reclaim:

> "Francisco, my first born," she had said "dearer to me than life itself,
> tomorrow you will leave me to fulfill your father's wish. My heart
> bleeds for you when I see you go to another land. You will re-enter
> the heritage of your ancestors, it is true, yet you will be ruled by
> people who are the born enemies of your race. But remember my boy,
> that wherever you may be, wherever you may go, you are the heir
> of a proud name and a prouder race. Keep your faith and be what
> God destined you to be, a Mexican and a Gentleman."

The lasting resentment is marked when Francisco returns for his mother's blessing with his own firstborn in his arms, stating, "No child of mine will ever be born in Texas." That this child is born in "God's land" and registered in the *Palacio* (the municipal building), is significant for reasons the author explains in a footnote: "Because a number of Mexicans fought on the side of the Texas Revolution against Mexico, the Mexicans from the lower Rio Grande country called Texas a land of traitors."

Again, many of the characters and much of the plot are taken from González's own family history. Before moving to San Antonio, her family paid a final visit to her great grandmother, Ramoncita, from whom she directly draws her character Doña Ramona:

> I have a clear picture of her lying in a four poster bed, her clear cut ivory features contrasting with her dark sharp eyes.
>
> "Come closer to me children, so I can see you better," she said. "Your mother tells me you are moving to live in San Antonio. Did you know that land at one time belonged to us? But now the people living there don't like us. They say we don't belong there and must move away. Perhaps they will tell you to go to Mexico where you belong. Don't listen to them. Texas is ours! Texas is our home. Always remember these words: Texas is ours. Texas is our home."
>
> I have always remembered the words and I have always felt at home in Texas. (Memoirs: 8–9)

Those final words, spoken by her great-grandmother and recalled in her memoirs, provide the ending for González's *Dew on the Thorn.*

Several dark internal subnarratives in this novel bring women either under the spell of the devil or into his vicinity. There are at least three such narratives that bring women and the physical abuse their husbands administer in proximity with the devil on the border. Interestingly enough, none of these accounts shows up in her published folklore edited by Dobie. There is the story of how Don Ramón, Don Francisco's neighbor, cured his wife of a strange malady that made her turn yellow and kept her from sleeping or eating. "She just laid in the bed staring at the ceiling." Thinking the trouble is in her heart, Don Ramón administers various home remedies, such as making her drink *toronjil* [sweet lemon] and powdered deer blood for nine consecutive mornings, but that did not cure her malady. "This he followed with *cenizo* [Texas shrub, silvery gray in color] tea, which as you know, if left out doors to be cooled by the night dew will cure any liver trouble." Seeking and following the advice of Tío Anselmo, the witch healer, Don Ramón becomes convinced that his wife is under a spell and proceeds to burn chili peppers in an enclosed room with Doña Rita close to the fire. "The suffocating vapors would either choke or drive the evil spirits away."

This done, Tío Anselmo prescribes that he whip her "with a raw hide rope, folded three times, made from the hide of a black steer." This "cure" leaves Doña Rita close to death. Her son, Cristobal, having witnessed the horrible scene and hearing the excruciating cries of his mother, "sat by her bedside day and night," and as if affected, "looked with eyes that saw nothing." As a result of his strange behavior, the ranch folk believe that "the evil spirit that left the mother took possession of the boy." He goes about silent, "looking at the world with the haunted eyes of the possessed," and he also hates his father.

In another subnarrative, a woman named Paula is heard screaming in the night. Another woman, Margarita, cautions a concerned man not to "'meddle in other people's affairs, most probably she's been having 'loves' with another man and she is getting what she so well deserves.'" The screaming continues, however, and the next day, the woman is seen by the well with a towel wrapped around her face and shoulders. The narrator of this story approaches and tells what he saw when the towel is blown away by the wind.

> "Believe me or not, she was branded on the face! A cross, some two inches long, very definitely marked, showed an angry red on her dark skin. She dropped the bucket, and hurriedly covered her face again. I asked her who had done it and she told me an unseen hand had tortured her all night. She found herself unable to move, as though her arms and limbs were tied by a wire to the bed. She screamed in fear, but the worst had not as yet happened she had not felt the hot iron searing and scorching her face. She says she even heard the sizzling of the raw flesh, and smelled it burn. She must have fainted for she knew no more; but when she came to she was tormented by a pair of slanting, green eyes which shone luminously in a corner of the room. She thinks it was the Devil."
>
> "The Devil was no doubt the husband, as your wife so well suggested" said Don Alberto.

The rest of the conversation reveals that the husband was away at the time and the priest refuses to do anything about the incident, commenting, "I can explain a miracle but things like that are far beyond me," and that "it is not only the *peones* who have beliefs like these." It must have been a difficult thing for González to negotiate her knowledge of such stories with her academic world, especially because these stories relate the treatment of women, their defenselessness in the face of such denial and/or complicity on the part of both the community leadership and the law. What would academics make of such stories, and how would they perceive her for knowing them, if she did not distance herself from their source? [11]

THE NEW LEADER

The remaining plot circles around another whipping incident and the separation and reunion of two young lovers, Don Francisco's only remaining daughter, Rosita, and Don Ramón's son, Carlos. In Chapter 3, "Border Honor," Don Ramón carefully selects a *huellero,* a tracker, and fourteen men to pursue cattle thieves whom he suspects to be insiders. Astonished and shamed to find his own son, Carlos, among them, he begs consideration for his son apart from the others, who upon his orders are being tied up and delivered up for quick trial and punishment.

> "Friends," he said to his companions who witnessed the scene in
> astonishment, "you know what this means! You also know that I
> would prefer death to this. I do not kill this wretch because in my
> family there are no assassins. You also know that until now, my name
> was untarnished and beyond reproach. As your friend, I ask one
> thing of you. This unhappy father begs a favor from you; don't give
> up my son to be tried as a common criminal. He is a thief, I know,
> and my tongue burns when I say it. But don't allow his name which
> is mine to be dragged [through] the dust. Allow me to punish him as
> he deserves. I am his father, but I can forget it to become his judge.
> I do not need the interference of authorities to inflict the punishment.
> I know how to deal with him."

He publicly whips his son beyond consciousness, but then in a moment of fatherly tenderness he gathers "the blood-covered form of the youth gently in his arms, took him indoors, and placed him on a cot." He orders the women to bring water and salve, and he washes his son's wounds. As a result of this crime there remains another question between the two families which the two patriarchs settle quickly enough. Regarding the courtship between Rosita and Carlos, and as he comments on the stoicism of Mexican women, Don Francisco resolves this question simply and authoritatively as the two patriarchs discuss it in the final scene of this chapter:

> "Always a man of honor, my friend. Courage would have failed me to
> do what you have done. Your sufferings are my sufferings."
> "Yes, our poor Rosita, this will kill her!"

"No compadre, like the women of our race she will suffer but she will do her father's wishes."

"You mean?"

"I mean that the Olivares stand for no dishonor. She will do as I command."

With the impossibility of seeing Rosita again, Carlos leaves the hacienda only to return near the end of the novel, as a successful man, to clarify the mystery of what he was doing with the cattle thieves. The prodigal son is thus forgiven and the marriage finally takes place between Carlos and Rosita, who has waited patiently all these years.

All would end happily if not for the news that Don Francisco receives on the very happy day of his daughter's wedding, the only daughter whose wedding he has attended. Much as in the following novel, *Dew on the Thorn* ends with the foreshadowing of doom for the Texas Mexicans as the signs of change to be imposed by the *Americanos* begin to reveal themselves. In the final chapter, "We Stay," Don Francisco, feeling generous for having ordered the same food served to his ranch workers as to the guests at his daughter's wedding, receives word that his *vaqueros* have left his employment to work for the *Americanos,* who will pay them more in one day than what they get on his ranch in a week. As if to announce the 1910 Mexican Revolution, they proclaim upon their departure that "'The time of the monarchy and the Inquisition has ceased'" and that they "'are free men and as such have no master to obey.'" (They must have learned their lessons well at the *escuela de español.*) A conversation ensues between Don Francisco and Father José María regarding the future of South Texas Mexican Rancheros.

The only hope for the future that the priest offers lies in people like Don Alberto, the educator, and Fernando, the new leader who is a product of both races, a businessman, a rancher, and a politician. Having lived away from South Texas, Fernando has learned the ways of the Americanos and has even gone so far as to try to become one of them. Experiencing discrimination from the Americanos, he comes to the conclusion that he must remain a Mexican, for that is the only way they will ever see him, but that he must learn and teach his people all that he can about their ways so as to better prepare them to save their interests: "'but how can I do that when not for a moment am I allowed to forget that I am Mexican? That being the case I am not going to thrust my society where I am not wanted. I came prepared to become an American, but instead of that I am now more determined to remain what I have always been, a Mexican and a Gentleman.'"

His father's death brings him back home to South Texas. His South Texas identity, coupled with his experiences in the Anglo American world, has filled him with an urgent need to protect and lead his people through their inevitably changing world. His experience is a product of both worlds:

> The experiences that he had met, the history of his people, made him see that they needed a leader, and what better leader could they find than he who understood and knew the *Americanos?* It was fifty-five years since the land of his ancestors had become part of the United States and all this time the *rancheros* had lived happily ignorant that they were foreigners in a foreign land. He could see that they were unprepared politically and educationally to cope with the situation that would soon be theirs to solve. He saw what his work was to be: To awaken his people to the fact that they were a part of the country in which they lived, and to urge them to exercise their rights as American citizens. He told them to "send our children to American schools. It is our duty to learn English. Not that we are ashamed of our Mexican traditions, but because this will make us know how to protect ourselves against their snares and their wiles."

Strong women, the *caballero,* and an unyielding Texas Mexican "nationalism" become paramount themes in the next novel. But here these themes are mitigated by a love interest, as well as by folkloric digressions. In view of the recognition González achieved in the field of folklore regardless of her views, political, historical, or otherwise, her accommodation for the sake of penetrating the world of scholarship raises complex questions. In *Dew on the Thorn,* her rich and unusual descriptions are excerpted and brought forth in a more palatable form for an Anglo audience, with the political history removed along with the strong women figures. Stripped of the fuller, unpublished context, the remaining figures of the *caballero,* the *vaquero,* and the *peones* are foregrounded in the published folklore. Did the resulting overemphasis on an outdated and rigid class system in place of the concern for the education of all classes of children and the economic and political future of Texas Mexicans make González's scholarship more acceptable to the mostly Anglo folklorist audiences of the time? Did they take some comfort in viewing South Texas Anglo colonization and capitalistic endeavors as benevolent acts upon the indigenous populations, offering them "democracy" in place of their antiquated social systems?

A comparative approach to the author's novels, her folklore, and her academic writing offers us at least some insight into the author's negotiation of her "self" and her unique presence within the academy. The complex question of her identity gives way to the competing voices that manifest themselves in the different genres through which she examines her people. A struggle is evident. Though she remained unpublished long after her death, the novelist comes to fruition accompanied by a history of complex relations, a history that resists complete dichotomization along racial lines but lends itself freely to a consideration of class backgrounds and distinctions. The folklorist has a paternalistic and distanced viewpoint that preserves, and significantly so, some important stories, beliefs, and values that mediate between clearly drawn polarities. Jovita González's consistent criticism of the debt-peonage system in both novels was an important political theme, due in large part to the influence on her of the liberal political views of the exiles in Del Rio and of her husband. On the other hand, as if oscillating between two worlds, the author's persistent inscribing of the strict class system also lends itself to a parallel presentation of South Texas as a kind of antebellum South, something she perhaps thought would link her more to a U.S. readership. This feature becomes more obvious in the next novel.[12]

CABALLERO

In his introduction to this novel, one of the editors, José E. Limón, adds drama to the circumstances surrounding the disappearance of the original manuscript by implying that Jovita's own husband suppressed information of its existence or even destroyed it while Jovita hid the carbon copy in the hope of posthumous resurrection. While Limón notes that Mireles was concerned about "the reactions of both Anglo bigots *and* Chicano nationalists" of the sixties and seventies (1996: xxii), he ignores the profound effects that McCarthyism had on Jovita's generation. Mexican American intellectuals and labor activists had been singled out during the so-called "Pinko Scares," one more move in the tactics of repression of Mexicanos, one more distortion of their history. According to Cárdenas, Edmundo Mireles felt the need to protect his wife, though he had always taken pride in her work, precisely for its defense of South Texas Mexicano history: "He was afraid that the novel was too strong and would result in some kind of persecution, and I remember his using the word 'Pinko.' There were these accusations. In my memory, I link it to some persecution of Carlos Castañeda. This conversation occurred around '62 or '63 right after the first Crystal City takeover of land by Anglos. The impression was that 'they' would come after them, those opposed to any Mexicano self-valuing" (Cárdenas 1996, May 5). Cárdenas is certain that at this time the book had not been destroyed. While it is tempting, from present-day perspectives on earlier gender relations, to assume that Edmundo Mireles kept his wife from publishing the book because of the threat he may have thought her success posed to his position, it is the patriarchy in the form of his role as protector of his wife that here reveals itself, rather than any typical male insecurity in the wake of a woman's intellectual success.

The other important question surrounding the loss and delayed publication of this second novel is the extent to which Eve Raleigh (pseudonym for Margaret Eimer) served as co-author. In a March 8, 1993, interview I conducted with Austin historian Marta Cotera, she indicated that during the last visit that González and her husband paid to her during the mid-seventies, she had received the impression that Eve Raleigh's co-author role had served mainly to get the manuscript published. Cotera felt that this "co-author" contributed at most some editorial comments and suggestions. In his introduction to the now published book—and after having examined some correspondence between González and Eimer found with the manuscript—Limón proposes that Raleigh indeed "had a strong authorial hand in shaping the romantic plot" (xxi).

However, the prose in a letter Margaret Eimer wrote to González on June 29, 1946, contrasts sharply with González's style in both *Dew on the Thorn* and *Caballero*. This letter also reveals that Eimer held on to the original manuscript, while she sent González only the carbon copy typed on to the backs of used paper from the late 1930s and '40s, many of which were fliers announcing events of the times, but mostly letters addressed to a "Pop" Eimer in Joplin, Missouri, a much written-about and written-to gun shop owner and perhaps a relative of the "co-author." This is the copy recovered from her papers in 1993: "Herewith the revised edition—I just couldn't do what I wanted to and after wasting a number of precious hours on it during the week and getting nowhere decided to let it ride. However I would like to rewrite it all again, put back in what I left out, smooth her still more,—oh well, that could go on forever. It's a carbon and not all of it is corrected, and will you draw out a better chart of the hacienda?"

Because the correspondence to Pop Eimer is dated from the late 1930s to mid '40s, we know that this final version must have been typed after the dates on these letters. However, we also know from González's correspondence with Dobie that by 1935 she had written enough of it to send Dobie a portion. We can assume, then, that the novel was written during the 1930s at the same time that Webb was writing his histories of the West and particularly of Texas. The carbon copy includes many handwritten editorial changes to which Eimer refers in her letter, and which I indicate in the endnotes to this chapter whenever these involve changes in a passage cited. However, "To whoever reads this carbon copy" the "authors" leave the following message: "It is uncorrected. All flagrant mistakes in punctuation have been corrected in the original, many words changed and sentences bettered, to further the smooth flow. So if your mind "bumps," now and then, read on, secure in the knowledge that it is not there in the finished book. (We got so sick of the thing and had worked so hard to finish and get it on the market while the set-up is timely, that we could not bear the thought of correcting carbons. In the main the mistakes are trivial and obvious)." Indeed, most of the changes seem to have been erased only on the original and may have been the suggestions of Mrs. Eimer, who, I suspect, also wrote the above explanation, for it seems unlikely that Jovita González would have tired of her passion in life, her restoration, if only through fiction, of the history of her South Texas Mexicanos.

In her letter Eimer goes on to explain her efforts to get the manuscript published and the business about her name appearing first:

> Now regarding my name first instead of as in the original having yours first: that Messner outfit who was so snotty to me in that whatwas-her-name affair—oh, Keyes—and I got pretty well burned up and told them so, told me the name of the author should be first on a book and it was not their fault if they thot [*sic*] me merely the compiler given a certain sop by having my name put on. And might they suggest that I put my name first so another publisher be not confused. It matters not to me personally, particularly as I am still trying for more humility etc. It is of small importance and I only mention it so you won't think I seek aggrandizement or something above you.
>
> Doubtless I need not tell you to be careful into whose hands it falls as it contains valuable material. If a publisher wants to consider it I will be glad to send him the original.

Obviously, Margaret Eimer *was* in fact very much concerned about the matter of placing her name before González's or she would not have referred to the matter four times. Also, it is possible that González was never again in possession of the original. We see from her comments that Eimer was very much in control of the manuscript or at least wished to be, considering her warning to González, "be careful into whose hands it falls" and that it was she who would send the original to any "publisher who wants to consider it." Yet Eimer goes on in this letter to describe how she *has* shared the novel with several people, almost all of whom are clergy of the Catholic or Episcopal Church. She emphasizes how everyone is "enthralled with it," "how well it is written," how it was especially interesting to a Franciscan by the name of Tonne, because of the history. "Fr. Healy says it is the best book he has read (he is about a third thru as he goes back over the good parts and, says he, there are so many in it) and he must have it back to finish. So says everybody—sure is a mystery to me why the pubs throw it right back at me." Eimer closes the letter suggesting that González read the passage about Susanita's ride at a conference she will be attending because "everybody who has read the book picks that as something special." In this one item of correspondence between the "co-authors" there is not a trace of similarity with the prose of either of the two novels. In addition, González in her own writing never abbreviates the spelling of the kind of words Eimer so often does in words like "thot" or "thru" or "bec." for because, "pubs" for publisher, and "Fr." for Father. Hers is a fast-paced, almost Irish/English style of expression, whereas González's style is lengthy, slow paced, much more formal, and elaborate in its expression; even in her quickly written letters to her husband and friends, she is not given to these types of abbreviation. With all this, I can only conclude that Eimer cut large portions from the text and made some stylistic changes that would give it more market appeal. She serves more the function of editor, as evidenced when she regretfully reports to González that she "took out" quite a bit though it "should be put back but the too long—too long was a common publisher fault finding so I listened."

This conclusion on my part is supported by the conversation I had on March 8, 1993, with Marta Cotera. On the title page of this manuscript of *Caballero* (no date noted on manuscript) appear several suggested titles, including "This my House" and "Mine, Mine!," which are similar titles to that referred to in her correspondence with Dobie.[13] The names Eve Raleigh and Jovita González indeed appear as authors on the title page on this carbon copy. José E. Limón and María Cotera unearthed the lost manuscript in February 1993 from among the "González-Mireles Papers." For my dissertation at the University of Texas at Austin (1993), under Limón's direction, I read the novel a few weeks later and wrote the first criticism of the novel.

THE OLD WAYS VERSUS THE NEW

The novel is a treasure, abundantly rich in details of customs, traditions, and manners; attitudes toward marriage and sexuality, skin color, and class differences are particularized as well as the language, dances, and fashions of the time—in short, South Texas culture immediately before it was to be changed by the imposition of U.S. Anglo ways on the people living in the Texas border area around Matamoros (before Brownsville was to become a major city on the other side of the river). Providing a detailed account that perhaps only a native folklorist could offer of her own culture, González records the value systems of the South Texas landed élite, their festivities, their religious practices, their marital relations, their courtship procedures—down to the number of articles a bride takes to her husband upon their marriage, the number of sheets and pillowcases, the shirt and sash she will sew with her own hands, the blanket she will weave, the dresses of her trousseau, her lingerie—all are recorded with an expert precision. As the "authors" themselves stress the historicity of the novel, it becomes apparent that the recording of the manners of the time was also of the utmost importance to González, who recognized the passing of traditions and felt urged to record them in her work.

Some historical characters in the novel are merely mentioned: figures such as Santa Anna, Juan Seguin, Zachary Taylor, Stephen F. Austin. Others receive special and telling attention, such as Juan Cortina, whom she (or Eimer) minimizes though she had noted his significance as the "champion of the Mexican ranchmen" in the February 1935 issue of the *Mary Immaculate* version of "Among My People" (36), before and after the Civil War, and General Antonio Canales, leader of a guerrilla group who (according to the novel) recruits the sons of the landed elite to set out for Mexico in order to kill the Texas Rangers there in retaliation for their abuses.

In what follows, I offer an analysis of the novel based on several themes such as the new ways and the old, the loss of land, and violent conflict between the two races that emerge from it and respond directly to the kind of history offered by historians falling within the Turner/Webb tradition. As the plot of González's fictional narrative drama unfolds, so does a history full of conflicts: the U. S. Army, the Texas Rangers, the *Americanos,* the border Mexican elite, the women, the peon class, the clergy, and finally Webb's pioneers—all are principal actors.

The novel begins with Texas joining the Union, flashes back to the aftermath of the Battle of the Alamo, and then moves up through a period of about two years while the Mexican War is being fought, and ends with 1848, the year the Treaty of Guadalupe Hidalgo is signed. It opens on an evening of the spring of 1846, upon a scene in which the patriarch, Don Santiago de Mendoza y Soria, "lord of land many miles beyond what his eye could compass, master of this hacienda and all those that would soon gather before him" (2), leads his family, the *vaqueros*, and *peones* of his ranch, Rancho La Palma (de Cristo) in *El Alabado*, in their regular evening prayer service. In a time when news travels slowly, and not wanting to believe the "rumors" that Texas has won its independence from Mexico, Don Santiago, as we first look upon him, feels confident that the traditions and customs he and his forebears have always maintained will remain free from the interference of foreigners: "All these rumors that Texas no longer belonged to Mexico was the talk of fools easily frightened, who gave significance to the rout of the braggart Santa Anna. Because these blue-eyed strangers trespassing here had made a flag with one star—what did that mean? The fools! Making a flag and thinking this made a nation! It would not be long before they would be gone again, back to their own country" (2).[14]

It is during these daily prayers that the reader is introduced to the members of the patriarch's family, where another significant battle is played out—between Santiago's submissive wife, María Petronilla; his strong-willed, outspoken, and widowed sister, Doña Dolores, "a special cross for him to bear"; and his children. Alvaro, his oldest son, is a *ranchero* like his father, but he is violent, undisciplined, and tyrannical in his sexual abuse of the daughters of the *peones*. He stands in contrast to Luis Gonzaga, the second and effeminate son, who is a constant disappointment to his father, for he is an artist by vocation rather than a rancher. He must bear the constant criticism of his father, who thinks a "man" can only become a man in his image, only through the path taken by his oldest son. (Gonzaga's character provides a daring and early exploration of social attitudes toward homosexuality.) María de los Angeles, or Angela, the very pious and seemingly docile older daughter, wants to be a nun but is also denied her vocation by her unyielding father, while Susanita, the very lovely and feminine youngest daughter—special because of her blond hair and green eyes that remind her father of his mother—is of course her father's favorite and the heroine of the novel. This daily prayer service is interrupted by the arrival of the exhausted Don Gabriel, hidalgo and owner of a neighboring ranch. He brings news he has just received of Texas being taken by "*Los Americanos* (it happened last year)"—in other words, that Texas has now joined the Union, that they are all now *americanos*, and that "there is again war":

> "This Zacarias [Zachary] Taylor who was at the Nueces with his
> army last summer is now at Matamoros, building a camp in the chap-
> arral on this side of the Río Bravo. Our army is with Arista but what

of that? I have not heard of a battle, news coming to us slowly. This is May and Taylor only went to the Rio Bravo last month. What can Arista do? He has too small an army and if Texas now belongs to the United States what would be the sense of fighting? So many have already been killed, and if we are already Americanos it—" (13)

Soon after this scene, the novel flashes back eleven years through Don Santiago's memory to the return from the Battle of the Alamo of his younger brother, Ramón.[15] Upon his return, Ramón, whose father has built him into a hero, announces that "the Americanos are not cowards":

"They were a handful, only a hundred and fifty. We were an army, there were thousands of us. Thousands, papa, to less than two hundred, was that fair? We tried to get over the walls—is it not strange that it took us so long? Twelve days. Yes, twelve days. Santa Anna cursed like a madman and swore that . . .

"They were great! I wished, when I fought them, that I were one of them. I wished that I were there with them, fighting gloriously against a swarming horde, refusing to surrender. By San Pablo, but I wished to be with them! So could a man die in glory, his soul free forever! So could he die and leave a name that could never die!" . . .

"We, not they—were the cowards, papa."

Don Francisco de Mendoza y Ulloa struck his son on the mouth, so that he fell to the floor. And blood gushed from his opened lips and ran in a bright small stream onto the tiles. (21–23)

The family had not been aware that Ramón, during his ride of many days, had suffered from internal bleeding from a wound received in battle. The blow struck him by his father was the last he would suffer. Until his own death, Don Francisco would blame the *Americanos* for his son's death and instill a hatred for them within his heir, Santiago: "Allow no Americanos on this land. Have nothing to do with them, ever, build a wall between them and what is yours. Remember always that Ramon was killed because he defended his country against them. Fight them—fight them to the end!" (23). This opening scene is at best melodramatic, and strange for its praise of the *Americanos,* given some of González's depictions of them throughout the rest of the novel and especially given her note in the earlier novel about how Texas Mexicans fighting on the Texas side were looked upon as traitors by Mexicans. Yet it is important to note that in Eimer's 1946 letter she states, "I think the first chapter not so good and the scene in the *sala* most undramatic.

If a pub. [publisher] is interested I must be allowed to rewrite it." The father's final blow to his son and the praise for the *Americanos* while calling the Mexicans cowards at the Battle of the Alamo may be the result of Eimer's dramatizing touch.

It is thus that the authors establish the setting for the major conflict in the novel. The cause of Ramón's death is always remembered, but his last words are soon discarded—until the very end, when Doña Dolores reminds her brother of them after the treaty has been signed. Don Santiago, the *caballero* of the novel, with his sense of purpose clearly defined for him by his father, and as the one remaining "true" *caballero,* is uncompromising in his determination to keep the *Americanos* out, if not from Texas, at least from having any influence over his family. He persists in his convictions even when neighboring landowners have begun to make concessions to the first arriving Americans, in order either to preserve their land or to sell it at a reasonable price when through intermarriage these two hostile races may have begun to merge. We soon learn that the preservation of the old ways was by no means a new struggle for these early settlers. They had come into this area along the Rio Bravo for the precise purpose of keeping out the corrupting influence of Mexico City, an accomplishment that made the same struggle repeated a century later all the more determined:

> Given grants of the land by the Crown for its colonization, a group
> of rancheros had moved their small armies of peons, their herds of
> cattle and sheep, to the flower decked plain between the Nueces and
> the Rio Grande, in the year of grace 1748. They were men of vision
> and of courage innate with the culture of the mother country Spain,
> and Don Jose Ramon de Mendoza y Robles was their leader. And the
> reason they had come to this Indian infested new land was to pre-
> serve the old ways and traditions of family life, safely away from
> perfidious influence of Mexico City and the infiltration of foreign
> doctrines. (24)[16]

The emphasis from the beginning to the end of this history of South Texas is on the preservation of the old traditions. This significant parallel between white settlers and Mexicans who came earlier to the region for the same reasons is in large part ignored by history books reflecting upon Mexicano-Anglo relations. Mexicanos came and built up a region, only to be conquered by Anglo settlers seeking the same freedom the Mexicanos had previously sought. In the end, the battle to preserve the old ways and the autonomy of the region is of course lost. The novel in many ways presents a tragic tale of the decay of an old regime, either because it could not compromise or because it *does* compromise and make concessions.

Don Santiago becomes a symbol of this old regime and is thus a tragic figure. It is made clear to the reader that his unyielding ways have by no means been painless to him, but that he himself is a prisoner of tradition and is bound to uphold the sternness that a patriarch must exhibit even in the face of his own family's defiance. In the end, his oldest son, Alvaro, is killed by a band of Texas Rangers in a conflict his son instigates by shooting one of them; he disowns his second son for having left for Baltimore to study art under the tutelage of a Dr. Devlin who had been stationed at Fort Brown (across the river from Matamoros). Also without his blessing or consent, his older daughter, Angela, has married Alfred "Red" McLane, a politician and promoter, whose career would be well served by his marrying a Mexican of such breeding; and his youngest, favorite daughter, Susanita, is married to a Virginian, a Southern gentleman, Lieutenant Robert Warrener, U.S. Army, also stationed at Fort Brown. Don Santiago, this last *caballero,* as a tragic symbol of the fate that awaits many Texas Mexicans, dies, lonely and with no heir, clinging to a handful of dirt from his *rancho.* It is Warrener who finds him dead on a bluff overlooking the *hacienda,* his place of solace and prayer, from which he could view and take pride in all that was his. His death occurs the day Warrener and Susanita, seeking his forgiveness and a reconciliation, have returned to the ranch with Don Santiago's first granddaughter:

> It was a last irony that an American, and the man who took his most beloved child, should be the one to close the lids over the eyes of Don Santiago de Mendoza y Soria. . . .
> Warrener noticed that Don Santiago's hand was tightly clenched. He stooped and opened the fingers to see what they held.
> A scoop of earth, brown and dry, trickled from the palm and lost itself in the sandstones. (509)

Don Santiago had taken on the burden and obligation of upholding the old ways at the cost of isolating himself from the important events in the lives of the remaining members of his family.[17] With this powerful but sad picture of Don Santiago, the novel also presents a sort of apology for the eventual complicity of the Mexican elite with the Anglo invader and the assistance that some of them provided for the transition of power and land. This complicity is voiced in the novel by Don Gabriel, who disappoints Santiago.

He says: "If I have bent down from my pride it is because I thought it wiser to have pride suffer a little rather than have all the rest of me suffer. I am only forty-three, Santiago. It may be that I live that many years again and I prefer to live them in peace and with some pleasure if I can. My land, a wife, good will with my neighbors, they are things to enjoy even if one gives some pride in exchange for them" (495).

Showing in effective dramatic and tragic terms the fate of one who will not compromise and yet one with whom we are in sympathy, the novel thus attempts to justify for the reader the role that some of the Mexican elite would eventually play in the future oppression of the Mexican working class. The choices before the Mexican elite are made clear: They can move to the other side of the river and remain Mexican, starting over again on new land. If they comply, as Don Gabriel has, with the new regime, they may at least have an opportunity to maintain their old standard of life. Or they can risk losing their property and join the laboring class of people they have had as little to do with as possible other than in their roles as masters. The final choice, as we see with Don Santiago and his son, is death. Of course many of them do not freely choose this latter alternative, but have the choice made for them by what we know are far from ethical means, such as high taxation on their lands, the accusing of the patriarch of some crime, or simply his out-right murder. As Américo Paredes has reminded his listeners in some of his talks at the University of Texas, "There was an old saying, that if the owner would not sell his land, his widow would."

The novel in this way offers a history that can be situated before the history of border conflict and strife that would be recorded by the *corridos,* which later emerged from a Mexican laboring class when it came face to face with a new oppressive state during the early years of the next century, and which have often been recognized as providing the origins of a Chicano literature of struggle and opposition. With all its emphasis on resistance to change, throughout the novel there is a strong foreboding sense that the battle is lost before it has even begun. In contrast to the adventurousness foregrounded in U.S. versions of Western history, González's prose most ef-fectively reveals the history of Texas from the perspective of this sense of loss and impending violence:

> Trouble rode in Texas, on a fresh mount. It galloped over the plains,
> lay at ambush in the hills, stalked the mesquite thickets, camped at
> the water holes, swaggered and strutted in the towns. Trouble whis-
> pered to the domineering Anglo, to the marauding Indian, to the

mercurial, high-tempered Mexican. Trouble kindled the fire beneath
a pot where simmered racial antagonisms, religious fanaticisms,
wrongs fancied and wrongs real—[the brew salted with greed].[18]
And brought it from the simmer to boiling, up to the edge and
spilling over. The adventurer, the outlaw, the siftings of the East,
came to the new state and each took what suited his individual fancy.
Mexicans were killed for a cow or horse, for no reason at all. The
Texans, grabbing the spoils, fixed the southern boundary of the state
at the Rio Grande and marked it down with the black of gunpowder
and the red of blood. The Mexicans marked it at the Rio Nueces and
harassed the invaders of what they considered Mexican territory. The
Rangers, formed of dire necessity and recruited, too often, with men
whose sole virtue was a daring courage, were reluctantly recognized
by the army units which came now by water and by land; and were
rewarded for their hardships and courage by penurious dribbles from
a niggardly, non-understanding government. The Rangers hated the
Mexicans, who hated and feared them in return. Politics stretched out
its tenuous fingers and drew in the weak, the ignorant, and those lust-
ing for power.

> *There was turmoil and strife unending.*
> *There was blood. Texas dipped a pen deeply in it, and*
> *wrote its history with it.*

Yet slowly, relentlessly as Time, the indomitableness of the Americans laid its foundations for permanency and order and built firmly
upon them. The Mexican hidalgo and the high-bred ranchero, by
nature slow to recognize the logic of events, failed to gauge the future
by happenings of the past. Serene in the belief that his heritage of
conquest was a sort of super-bravery which must, inevitably, conquer
again, he built a wall against the Americans—against everything
American—and enclosed himself within it. (27–28)

As an antithetical statement to the struggles of this one class of people,
this novel also depicts the oppression of the *peón* class under the rule of the
Mexican patriarchy. This reveals some of the anti-Porfirismo critique of the
conditions that existed for the working poor in Mexico before the 1910 Revolution. We see the mingling of these histories in the novel when Don Santiago, as Don Francisco had done, begins to lose some of his most valued
workers, either because they seek wages from the Anglos, or because they

flee abuse, or because their daughters will not be left alone by the patriarch's son, Alvaro. The *Americanos,* on the other hand, will supposedly not be their master/owner, will not abuse their daughters, will not whip them into subservience, but instead offer them wages, an opportunity to vote, and mastery over their own destiny. All this presents itself as an optimistic new way of life: the coming of the Americans heralds the end of their lifetime servitude to the Mexican patriarch, who will never offer them any more reward than a home, subsistence, work, and a place to live, and perhaps schooling for their children.

THE FEMINIST SUBTEXT OF THE NOVEL

The strong female characters more prominent in *Dew on the Thorn* become little more than a subtextual concern in *Caballero.* The novel presents an account of the oppression of women under the old regime and their emerging liberation—their breaking away from the old ways that bind them to men they do not love and who restrict their ability to think for themselves and to plan their own lives. González here is making distinctions within her own culture. Maybe because war and the border conflicts that followed left few eligible Mexicano men, the liberation that the women characters experience is unfortunately limited to one form other than the convent, and that is intermarriage with the Anglo American, who presumably "treats his woman as his equal" and gives her more freedom within the domestic as well as the social world. Here again, Eimer's touch may be evident along with her constant portrayal of Anglo men as tall and formidable next to the short, unimpressive Mexican men. (Perhaps Eimer never had the occasion to meet tall borderlands Mexicano men like my grandfather, who stood six feet tall). Yet, it is important to note that it is because of the women's compromise with or acceptance of the new order that the old Mexican traditions (in however diluted a fashion) are maintained. It must also be noted that, as in *Dew on the Thorn,* the intermarrying men are not the Webbian pioneers of the Great Plains but emphatically both officers and gentlemen, men of good breeding, vision, and culture like the Mexicanos themselves, and who have learned to speak Spanish, have studied and respect the Mexican ways, and are used to deferring to the wishes of the women in their domestic lives. Class here overtakes race as a consideration for gender relations.

Doña Dolores is the strongest figure in the feminist subtext of the novel. Her independence of mind comes through early in the novel when she objects to Don Santiago's decision not to go on their usual journey to Matamoros and stay in their house there from the Day of the Dead early in November to the Epiphany early in January as is their custom. She is outspoken and rebellious against the Master of the house, as is revealed in many scenes like the following that contrast with Doña Petronilla's meekness:

> "A thousand evil spirits take wifely duty!" Dona Dolores crushed
> a hibiscus bloom and threw it away. "That's all you can talk about,
> duty, duty, to all but yourself! A wife has rights too and if I were in
> your place, Petronilla, the orders would not come from only one pair
> of lips, I can tell you that!"
>
> "What's this now?" asked Don Santiago, spurs clinking as he came
> across the patio floor. "What is it, Dolores?" (31)

In the ensuing argument between the siblings, the brother sides with the world in censuring the sister for helping her husband into the grave:

> "It is no secret that you helped him get to the other world with your
> independence and sharp tongue, my dear Dolores. . . . Our dead will
> have to manage with prayers from the ranch. We are not going to
> Matamoros. . . . My sainted mother would have taught you more sub-
> mission had she lived!" He stood opposite her, glaring at her. "I com-
> mand you to be silent! Sit down!"
>
> "Command all you wish, I shall not obey. I do not cringe before
> you as your wife does, I shall not blindly do your wish as does
> Angela, I shall refuse the abuse you heap upon Luis Gonzaga. I am
> a Mendoza and a Soria also and worthy of the name if you are not
> and though a woman I know my duty!"
>
> It was always so between these two when their wishes crossed.
> Don Santiago raised a hand, dropped it with a muttered curse.
> "Silence!" he thundered. "I command your respect if not your obe-
> dience. I am master here!" (33)

Dolores leaves him standing there as she exits, reminding him of what is imprinted on the rafter of their *sala*—"The Lord is Master Here"—and that the Lord's concerns (paying respect to the dead) come first. But Santiago knows it was mostly the festivities, courtship, and new dresses of this season that attracted the family to Matamoros each year. Moreover, he "had too much respect for his family to take them to a town polluted with alien soldiers and Rangers" (34).

Like many of the characters in González's fiction, it is very likely that Doña Dolores is inspired by a member of the author's own family. In her memoirs, she writes about her Tía "Lola" (short for Dolores): "I must add some one very special, Mi Tía Lola my mother's sister. As a young widow she had come to live at Las Víboras Ranch. She was a handsome woman with a will of iron and a vast store of family history. It was from her that we learned many things that made us proud of our heritage" (Memoirs: 6–7).

As in *Dew on the Thorn,* it is the women who carry the history and see that it is carried forward through story. Regarding questions of marriage and sexuality, the male characters in *Caballero* make it clear that women do not marry "to have an ornament in the house" (53), and that men do not marry women because they are sexually attracted to them. For that the mistresses, whores, and even the peons' daughters come in handy, while the wife, *la mujer decente,* exists for purposes of procreation, administration of the household, the raising of the children, and of course the dowry her father can bestow on the groom. As Don Santiago advises his son, Alvaro, who "wants" Inez for his wife, "She provoked you in the seguidilla you danced with her and now you want her. That is for a mistress, not a wife, and the men of our family do not marry a mistress. . . . you would not marry Inez if you could have her for mistress, . . . poor reason for choosing her to give her your name" (170). When Don Santiago also points out another problem with Inez, that "she is not submissive. Quite the contrary," Alvaro provides more arguments in favor of the marriage: "Another reason why I want her. I want the joy of taming a woman and breaking her to my will" (170).

The most flagrant scene of a woman crossing the barrier of what is considered *decencia* is when Susanita makes a heroic ride overnight into Matamoros only in the company of one of her father's *peones,* in order to save her brother who is to be made an example of by being hung along with other *guerrilleros* (also sons of the landed elite) who have been captured by the Rangers. She starts out in search of the father, but then it occurs to her to appeal to Warrener, with whom she has maintained a secret correspondence. Back at the ranch, after having saved her brother, she is made to undergo a sort of trial, with her father and brother presiding as judge and jury. Don Santiago maintains his role as stern patriarch and sentences his favorite child to either living isolated on the ranch with no communication with the other family members or to leaving the ranch, cast off and disowned. Susanita decides to leave and marry Warrener, whose plans are to establish a town around Fort Brown with his own inheritance.

Courtship and the Clashing of Two Races

Early in the novel, Don Santiago finally decides to go into Matamoros after all; there is to be a meeting of Mexican landowning rancheros for the purpose of discussing what actions they will take in the face of their changing situation. Don Santiago presides over this meeting, at which much anger is expressed regarding the abuses already suffered by some of them who have lost their property. Also present are historical figures like Juan Cortina, who wishes to continue fighting. Most striking is a defense of the Americans and even the Texas Rangers by Padre Pierre, a Frenchman, respected among the Mexicanos because he is their priest, but not completely trusted because he is not really one of them. After hearing of abuses suffered by some of the rancheros and by the daughter of a Spanish merchant, Padre Pierre comes to the defense of the Rangers by saying that not all the Americans are alike: "There is strife among the Americanos, one holding this is law, another that, and the lawless take advantage of it. . . . Don Pablo, the men who stole your race horses were doubtless renegades and in ill repute. The Rangers go after them and bring them to justice and—" (79). At the mention of the Rangers, the *Rancheros* become infuriated, but finally the Padre is permitted to continue, advising them to make friends with the newcomers and to invite them into their homes so that they can see that they have culture and do not fit the stereotypes already fixed in many of their minds:

> "There are men here to restore order, and if we align ourselves with
> them those who stole from us will be punished. General Taylor was
> disposed to peace and justice and there are many others equally dis-
> posed. Always remember, my friends, that we are a conquered people
> and pride will need to suffer. You hate the Rangers and it is true that
> you have had reason to be incensed at them, but remember that they
> were met with enmity by you. Remember that, for it is an important
> factor. Travel for you has been safer because of them, they have driven
> away the Indians again and again. Consider this—when the Rangers
> saved you the plundering of a dozen cows by Indians, you refused
> them even one for food. Didn't you? Not one of you ever offered
> them anything but hatred, what should they show you in return? . . . .
> Invite them, offer them friendship, let them see our worth. Put our
> problems before them and ask their help. Show them that it is your
> wish to be good Americanos though the name was forced upon you."
> (82–83)

The Padre's reasoning, in light of the violent confrontation and cost in lives that follow, contains the explanation why the Mexican elite eventually complied with the Anglo American occupation—and also why there were not many sons of wealthy ranchers left alive or north of the border to court the elite Mexicanas. The padre goes on to question their loyalty to Mexico, which has only served as a pretext for the Americans' war with Mexico and their eventual takeover:

> "What then has Mexico done for you? She gave your fathers land that was worthless to her, beset as it was with marauding Indians, and let you use your own money to build the towns and missions. "Royal grants" sounds very fine, be assured you would have received not a foot of ground had it been worth anything to Spain or the viceroy. The land's worth was in the taxes the Mexican government could collect after you had built your ranches. It was because of greed for more taxes to bolster a rotten, tottering regime that she betrayed you by inviting American colonists into Texas, and gave them huge tracts of land. *Gave* it, senores. When was it? Twenty-five years or so ago.
>
> "Now listen, all of you. After the Americans Mexico had invited into Texas had built their homes on the land given them, they were ordered out again—so that this improved land could be given again and a high tax charged upon it. The Americans did not go. Would you have done so, senores? Then Mexico declared war upon them and destroyed all the good will which had been built. There was good will, my friends. (84)

The Texas Mexicans here are indeed between two worlds, to neither of which the main characters want to belong. González adjusts this account (perhaps Eimer's) when she also offers us a view of Webb's pioneers later in the novel, those who will soon outnumber any Americans with any regard for the rights of the Mexicano. With this we see that indeed not all the Americans are alike and that, unfortunately for the Mexicans, the great majority who came to Texas were like those whom we see here, already with a fixed idea of what belonged to them and of how the Mexican had no rights in what they now considered "their" land.

A dramatic scene unfolds when Don Santiago confronts two men and a woman who have stopped their wagon and begun to build a house of stones on his land. When Don Santiago demands that the squatters leave, one of the men responds by shooting at him but is instead killed. The surviving man then tries to explain how having seen no markers, they thought, "the land belonged to the first who took it." Though Santiago has been warned by the more considerate Americans to record his property and set up markers, he responds, "'It is not necessary to have markers, all the land here has belonged to us for a hundred years. You will have to go further west'—he pointed to the sun, then made motions of scalping the man—'and there are many Indians, it is not safe'" (306–307). It is the woman who then voices the attitudes of these pioneers: "She said in English: 'I knew he'd get hisself kilted some day and I wisht I could say I was sorry. You lettin' them run us off, George, ain't that what they want?'" (307). As if to add "diversity" to this dichotomous scene, the surviving man's response reveals that even among these people there are various degrees of respect for the property of others. "'It's their land, Katie.' The man looked apologetically at Luis Gonzaga...." But his response only brings out the racist views of the woman: "[She] pointed a finger at him and screamed, 'That's what they say, and even if it's theirs they're only Mexicans. We be white folks and this is the United States, ain't it? We got the right of it. They kilted an American, you goin' to let that get by?'" (307). We then hear the narrator's voice foreshadowing the future history of this land and the continued plight of the *Mexicanos* in their efforts to maintain possession of their property:

> It was a scene that was to be repeated in variation for many years to come, until an empire of state would rise on land that had scarcely a square yard of it that had not been wet with blood. The fugitive, like the man Tomas had shot; the land greedy who justified their rapaciousness with the word "pioneer" and used it as a blanket to cover their evils—sullying the good word and the constructive men entitled to it; the trash, the "puerco," like George and his sister, squeezed out of a community that refused to support them any longer; the wanderer, fleeing from nothing but himself; the adventurer, his conscience and his scruples long dead. All these, and more, came to Texas like buzzards to a feast.
>
> "Remember the Alamo!" they shouted, and visited the sins of Santa Anna upon all his countrymen, and considered themselves justified in stealing the lands of the Mexicans. Some built themselves a house of righteousness like a snail builds his shell and carries it to him. "The Mexicans are Papists, Catholics who worship idols and pray to a woman they call the Blessed Virgin." They pillaged, and

stole, and insulted, and called themselves a sword of the avenging
God, and shouted their hymns to drown their consciences.

They came on and on, and killed, and were killed. And the earth
took their bodies, dust to dust returning, and sent up its flowers in the
spring, and its gift of grass. And smiled in the sun, and lifted its face
to the rain. (308–309)

As if to add balance, later in the novel we also get a view of Webb's pioneers from the perspective of Susanita's husband, Robert Warrener: "Warrener knew [that the family had been in Texas for 100 years], for Susanita
had told him. And already, he thought now, the men piling into the new
state were asserting their rights as "Americans," wearing the rainbow of the
pioneer as if it were new and theirs alone. Already talking loudly about running all Mexicans across the Rio Grande from this 'our' land" (507).

With the landed Mexican's view of the pioneer juxtaposed to that of
Warrener, the southern aristocrat, we begin to see the importance that class
plays in the struggles for power. The Mexicano elite is thus isolated from
the lower classes over which it previously ruled, while it also falls victim
to the great numbers of lower-class Americans who will soon overpower
the Mexicans. The only ally, it becomes clear, is the high-class American,
who unfortunately makes up but a small fraction of the original settlers
and perhaps some Army personnel coming to Texas, "Texas had too few
Stephen Austins, and did what it could without them" (500). While *Dew on
the Thorn* ends with a foreshadowing of how the property owners will
become servants on their own land, *Caballero* ends forecasting war over
property rights. Though war was over as of February 25, 1848, the new
group coming to Texas constitutes the beginning of a new war with a different face:

War, Texas knew, is a fecund mother whose children spring from her
fullgrown. Want, wrapped in a tattered sheet; Hunger, drooling over
bleached lips; disease, mouth open, hands spotted; contamination,
dipping hot fingers in wells; despair, black and ugly screaming curses;
lust, the vile one, stalking the innocent; misery, babbling senseless
prayers; intolerance, *which coined the words "gringo" and "greaser"* and
impregnated them with contempt; prejudice, the long-lived, driving
new nails in the barrier of racial and religious differences. Revenge,
and Hatred, and Murder, and Greed—ah, Greed!—the four that
never slept.

The war. Yes, the war was over. So said the record.

Texas wrote its history with a scratchy, blotty pen, and called its southern line the "bloody border," and strove for peace inasmuch as its poverty allowed—in a chaos that Time alone could bring to a semblance of order. (500, my emphasis)

In her writing of history, González makes perfectly evident the importance of the labeling device in the creation of the mythical history of the West.

CONCLUSION

Even if Jovita González had never acknowledged the injustices against her people in her academic work or taken a stand against them as a university-educated Mexicana, *Caballero,* had it been published during her time, would have certainly established her as a writer with a voice for her people. What is more difficult to ascertain is whether the Mireleses' labor for the benefit of maintaining the Spanish language in the public schools would have been affected or even stopped by the political scapegoating of the time had she succeeded in publishing her novel. With regard to her university work, one must ask if we would have any of her works today had she not made some concessions to the Anglo male patriarchy of the academy. As we have seen, even with her academic success, she had no success publishing her historical novels during her lifetime. Most sadly, by the time of her death, Jovita González had become a recluse, repeatedly attempting to write her story, only to get stuck, rewriting the same lines she had written before. Apart from a few memories among her former students, she had been almost completely forgotten.

Despite the many years Jovita González had lived distanced from her hometown, her final efforts to write her life are filled with an urgency to re-create and in some ways return to a place that had once been her home. In the early morning hours of the day before she died, Jovita insisted that Isabel Cruz walk her to the nearby Alameda. She was convinced that her brother (already deceased) would be coming for her if she waited there for him. He would be taking her back home as he had promised (Cruz, personal interview, August 2, 1996).

Walter Prescott Webb came up against a tradition of scholarly history writing that lent little if any validity to the stories the old-timers had to tell, stories which in *his* history Webb did include and thus validate. González, on the other hand, listened and captured in her novels the stories of a

"*gente decente*" whose "folklore still abounded in 'secluded communities untouched as yet by civilization,' where people lived in 'pastoral simplicity,' retained their attachment to the land, disliked innovation, distrusted Americans, and refused to speak English" (González, as cited by Montejano: 336).
Webb and González thus shared a sense of urgency for preserving the experiences of their people, for they knew, as did the tellers of the stories, that
their knowledge would also be lost with their passing.

> The frontier days were gone, and old timers and *viejos* sensed that
> they were the last of a distinct generation. The basis of the "horse cul-
> ture" no longer existed as before. There was still talk of branding and
> roundups but, as Webb noted, "the oldster understood that the mean-
> ing of these terms had changed." In the Texas Mexican communities,
> observed González, the once abundant folklore was "fast disappear-
> ing": "the goat herds, the source of nature's lore, are almost a thing
> of the past, the old type of *vaquero* is fast becoming extinct, and the
> younger generation look down with disdain on the old stories and
> traditions of its people." (Montejano 152–155)

The difference is that Webb's history was published and lives on, while
González's was lost and forgotten even by Chicano scholars for over half a
century. Ramón Saldívar has noted that without scholars like Américo
Paredes and Jovita González, "the rest of us might still be wandering in a
barren landscape presented to us so partially by the leading Anglo historians of the day" (1990a). Jovita González reminds us of what a long road it
indeed has been for Mexicanos in Texas to achieve finally their own voice, a
voice uncontrolled by the editorial and patriarchal forces (1990a). Without
her writing, the full complexity of even present-day working-class struggles
in search of "success" as it is defined by the North American culture could
not be fully grasped. Her story of negotiation, the cognitive dissonance of
her psychology, so evident in her writings, informs even present-day views
of aspiring youth in our educational institutions. Chicanos and Chicanas, especially those who are less-assimilated or of the working class, continue to
come up against not only a wall of opposition and pressure to acculturate to
the dominant culture, but also against the views of the Mexican elite and
academic scholars who often set a precedent for accommodation and complicity. Jovita González confronted not only Webb and the attitudes toward
Mexicanos which his type of history confirmed in the minds of the Anglo
academic world, but also the precedent of making deep concessions in ex-

change for "success." Teresa Palomo Acosta's words leave us with what I hope is not the final image of Jovita González; it perhaps explains why the writings of early Chicanas are only now being uncovered: [19] "Thus no harm could come to a man relating tales to a woman diffidently bent over a complex knitting pattern, politely extracting stories, his stories, about *el paisano,* the mockingbird, and the devil on the border." The split in González's intellectual environment, her aspirations, and the climate of the times demanded that she leave her more blatant outcries against both the Anglo and the Mexican patriarchies and elitist/racist views about "her" people to future generations—or to the mostly working-class Chicanas and Chicanos of her time whose sense of *decencia* was not so refined as hers.

4

MARÍA CRISTINA MENA'S ELITE, FERMINA GUERRA'S "FOLK"

The Struggles of Their Distinct and Converging Worlds

The odds were clearly against Tom Radigan when the beautiful Angelina Foley claimed his ranch for her own. She had a Spanish Grant to it, 3,000 cattle and a gang of cutthroats willing to kill for her. Radigan had little more than savvy, determination and right on his side.

—Advertisement for *Radigan*, by Louis L'Amour

 In this chapter I focus on two U.S. women writers of Mexican descent whose perspectives also shed light on some of the complexities of a history obscured by dominative ideology. The early-twentieth-century writer María Cristina Mena, with her short story "The Education of Popo," achieves a multidimensional view of Mexicano culture that contradicts the reiterated, stereotypical picture of Mexicanos still prevailing throughout much of popular U.S. fiction. Though she wrote at a great distance from Webb and his Southwest, she deserves special attention because in her time she was the only author of Mexican descent to be published in well-known literary magazines that had a wide circulation in the United States. She thus more effectively countered the prevailing views of her culture within U.S. literature. Though her story for the most part pictures both the North American Anglo and Mexican elite, her satirical tone undermines the fashionable materialism of a time when these two bordering cultures, in complicity with one another, had no apparent concern for the socially and economically deprived, the poor upon whom the burden of their wealth rested.

Fermina Guerra, like Jovita González, is a folklorist and graduate of the

University of Texas at Austin. Writing from a Texas-Mexican perspective eleven years after Jovita González was to complete her work at UT, she provides a varied and realistic account of ranch life on the South Texas border near and around Laredo. For this reason her work has a particular historical significance, for it pinpoints, in the simplicity of the life portrayed, an apparent lack of materialism among people of the Mexican culture who, through no choice of their own, had recently been made part of the United States. Her characters thus represent a symbolic crossing of the border into their world, which is gradually becoming imbedded within the dominant one.

MARÍA CRISTINA MENA

In *With the Ears of Strangers: The Mexican in American Literature,* Cecil Robinson shows how (as in Webb's history) the cultural diversity of the Mexican has been reduced and flattened by U.S. writers who, according to Robinson, have sacrificed "the reality of man" to the type: "the various types of Mexicans to appear in American writing in different periods," according to Robinson, reveal the psychic needs of the writer who "turned to the Mexican out of a sense of his own deficiency or of the deficiencies of the society in which he grew up. In either case, the Mexican and his culture have been used as compensation." What remains "under the compulsion of a sense of guilt in the name of his own race-proud society," is an oversimplification by the modern American writer of Mexican characters, "in the direction of some stoic or primitive ideal." Further, Robinson writes: "The resultant literary images of the Mexican as one of various types of noble savage, or as the emotionally unhampered, picaresque product of an unsterilized society, or yet as a graceful representative in the New World or the mellower culture of traditional Europe are often as unreal in their overemphasis as the earlier stereotypes of the brutal, dirty, cowardly Mexican of the border chronicles and the first novels of the Southwest" (68).

María Cristina Mena (1893–1965) complicated this dichotomized picture, perhaps even while it was in its formation. She provides opposition to this literary trend and in so doing responds to a dominative history. Mena was born in Mexico City to a "politically powerful and socially prominent" family, and her father "was a partner with several Americans in a variety of businesses during the last two decades of the rule of Porfirio Diaz" (Simmen: 39). She is credited with holding "a unique place in American literature" for being the first "naturalized American from Mexico to write in English and publish in prestigious American magazines" (Simmen: 39). At the age of fourteen, having led a privileged life "educated at an elite convent school 'Hijas de María' (Daughters of Mary), in the Mexican capital, and later at an English boarding school" (Simmen: 39), Mena was sent to live with family in New York because of the Mexican Revolution. There she continued her studies and began to write. According to Simmen, "She was twenty when her first two short stories were published in November of 1913; 'John of God, the Water-Carrier' in *The Century Magazine* and 'The Gold Vanity Set' in *The American Magazine*. By 1916, Mena had published a total of eight stories and one biographical essay. 'John of God' was reprinted in the October 1927 issue of *The Monthly Criterion,* a literary journal published in London and edited by T. S. Eliot. Edward O'Brien selected the work for his volume of *Best Short Stories of 1928"* (39).

Like one of the daughters of the *Caballero,* in 1916 Mena intermarried. She and her Australian playwright and journalist husband, Henry Kellett Chambers, a divorced man twenty-six years her senior, "traveled in literary circles and counted D. H. Lawrence and Aldous Huxley among their friends" (Simmen: 39). Like Ruiz de Burton, the author reveals in her writing a commitment to "promoting more positive images of her culture" (Velásquez-Treviño: 19): "Mena's ideological perspective is revealed in her discussion of the children's novelettes she has written: 'I've written this book—my first juvenile—with "the hand in the heart" as we say in Mexico. It is my small contribution and very large wish for a better understanding by the youth of the United States—my adopted country—of Mexico—the country of my birth'" (Velásquez-Treviño: 19).

Raymund A. Paredes, on the other hand, finds Mena's attempt to portray Mexican culture in a positive light to have "unfortunately tended toward sentimentalism and preciousness." Though he must be given credit for his inclusion of Mena, given the neglect of most male critics to include women of this period, Paredes diminishes Mena's significance to little more than "a talented storyteller," when he notes that the "great decorum" she employs in her stories makes them "seem trivial and condescending," though she occasionally strikes "a blow at the pretensions of Mexico's ruling class, but to little effect; Mena's genteelness simply was incapable of warming the reader's blood" (Raymund Paredes 1982: 49).

Not having had the borderlands experience of resistance or witnessed the occupation of Texas that Américo Paredes both lived and heard about from the elders in his community, Mena's writings do not resist Anglo dominative history in the same direct way that Jovita González's or Américo Paredes's writings do. Her awareness of the derogatory way in which her native culture was being inscribed into the American history of the Southwest is difficult to determine. Yet, intentionally or not, in her portrayal of the Mexican people she does anticipate the Anglo American stereotyping of the Mexican that would later take hold of the American imagination. Her writings show not only the varying class systems within Mexico but also the various ethnic identities of the Mexican people and their views of the world, a layered multiplicity celebrated by Hart Crane: "Mexico is more vast than you can ever realize by looking at a map and more various in its population than any country on earth. Layer on layer of various races and cultures scattered in the million gorges and valleys which make the scenery so plastic and superb" (cited in Robinson, p. 68).[1] What is more, with Mena's concern for "a better understanding by the youth of the United States . . . of Mexico," she unknowingly responds to the influence Walter Prescott Webb would later exert over the minds of children with regard to Mexico and Mexicans with his writing of Texas history textbooks for state adoption, as well as to his influence on future teachers of Texas history (see Chapter 7).

A closer reading of Mena reveals that the "genteelness" Raymund Paredes points to is a distinctively feminine quality and a question of subtlety of language, a subtlety often eclipsed by the direct oppositional stance of writers of and after the Chicano Movement (those R. Paredes refers to as the Quinto Sol writers). Not unlike some of Jovita González's condescending descriptions of the poor, Mena's work reveals a complexity with regard to class identity, as Raymund Paredes notes: "Mena took pride in the aboriginal past of Mexico, and she had real sympathy for the downtrodden Indians, but she could not, for the life of her, resist describing how they 'washed their little brown faces . . . and assumed expressions of astonishing intelligence and zeal'" (49).

"The Education of Popo"

Granted that Mena's writing, specifically the story I discuss here, "The Education of Popo," is far from the "border strife" and in-between existences of later Chicano/a writers, her narrative represents a complex approach to Mexican culture and class differences as well as to racial relationships and attitudes. Gloria Velásquez-Treviño includes this story (among many) in her dissertation and detects in Mena's language an ambivalent attitude about female experience.

Mena's treatment of the social structures or gendered constructions of "the female experience" employ a tongue-in-cheek irony. The social and political situations she exposes in her narratives reflect her critical view of class and gender relationships. Any apparent ambivalence should be attributed to the literary styles of the time—she lets her characters speak, with her own voice somewhat obscured—and to the influence exerted on her by the literary circle within which she moved and by the expectations of the audience she wrote for. While some of her female characters may seem stereotypical, they are nonetheless individual women as she sees them, often women who define themselves through their roles in men's lives. That is Mena's reality. The depiction becomes stereotypical when those are the only women an author allows us to see.

Regarding social, racial, or political relationships, in this story Mena presents a close view of the less troublesome world of the Mexican aristocracy and its courtship, acceptance, and even adoption of U.S. culture by noticeably non-nationalistic Mexicans. In Mena's narrative, we witness the Mexican and U.S. cultures coming together with an apparent disregard for previous national conflicts, and with only a passing mention of the lower classes. Though in her other stories, such as "The Gold Vanity Set" and those mentioned by Raymund Paredes, she portrays the life of the "inditos," their relationship to the Mexican *patrón,* and his relationship to the "americanos," in "The Education of Popo" Mena focuses less on class distinctions and more on the inner workings of the enormously wealthy Arriola family. The family governs a state in Mexico with "its florid magnificence of the Maximilian period" (76). In its eagerness to give "a most favorable impression of Mexican civilization" (68) and in its efforts to receive the Cherrys, an American elite family, into their home, the Arriolas eagerly, and with apparent disregard for the expense, import American goods for the Cherrys' comfort. With exaggerated descriptions of these commodities that *must* be procured, Mena satirizes the excessive wealth and luxury these people enjoy in comparison with other people who literally carry their burdens on their backs. Her criticism is subtly expressed in this manner:

> On the backs of men and beasts were arriving magnificent qualities *requisitioned from afar,* of American canned soups, fish, meats, sweets, hors-d'oeuvres, and nondescripts, ready-to-serve cereals, ready-to-drink cocktails, a great variety of pickles, and much other cheer of American manufacture. . . . Above all, an *imperial* call had gone out

for ice, and precious consignments of that *exotic commodity* were
now being delivered in various stages of dissolution, to be installed
with solicitude in cool places, and kept refreshed with a continual agi-
tation of fans in the hands of *superfluous* servants. By such amiable
extremities it was designed to insure the ladies Cherry against all danger of going hungry or thirsty for lack of conformable ailment or
sufficiently frigid liquids. (69; my emphasis)

We find that all of this care is taken for the Cherrys' comfort in order
to facilitate a mutually profitable business agreement between Governor
Fernando Arriola and Señor Montague Cherry, as he is called in the story:
"The wife and daughter of that admirable Señor Montague Cherry of the
United States, who was manipulating the extension of certain important
concessions in the State of which Don Fernando was governor, and with
whose operations his Excellency found his own private interests to be *pleasantly* involved, their visit was well-timed in a social way, for they would be
present on the occasion of a great ball to be given by the governor" (69; my
emphasis).

"How convenient it all is," Mena seems to be saying. Given her perspective on the Mexican Revolution that was to come, she lightly ridicules the
protected decorum of the Arriolas and the Cherrys. Just as eagerly as the
family imports American goods, it apparently sells Mexican resources to
the United States for personal profit—the very theme Carlos Fuentes was
to explore in *La muerte de Artemio Cruz* (1962) almost half a century later.

Whether it was her intention or not, Mena also exposes the complicity
with which these elite Mexicans, who, perhaps like her father, sell Mexico to
the United States, though she describes these transactions as mere commonplace business deals within the class from which she has emerged. The
world Mena describes is far removed from Américo Paredes's depiction of
Mexican American life in the United States, but both writers show close ties
with Mexico—Paredes through his borderlands upbringing and Mena
through her status as a U.S. citizen of Mexican upbringing. The deprived
Chonita from Paredes's "The Hammon and the Beans," for example (see
Chapter 5), with her one-room shack, her shabby clothes, and her quest for
the "luxuries" she could provide for her family from the scraps she received
from Fort Jones, can be contrasted with both Próspero Arriola and Alicia
Cherry, who have grown up as children of these "ruling" families. Chonita's
parroting of the soldiers' English to impress the privileged children of her
neighborhood is easily paralleled with Próspero's and Alicia's learning of

foreign languages to indicate their status. Though she could not have intended it, Mena's narrative is effective for the sharp contrast it presents to
the figure of poor Chonita standing on a fence shouting, "Give me the
Hammon and the Beans!" so that she too can impress the children who, unlike her, get to go to school. The role that language plays in culture, coupled
with the disparity in social and economic conditions, cannot help but lend
irony to Próspero's and Alicia's learning of the "foreign" language: "And
now Próspero, the only son, aged fourteen, generally known as Popo, blos-
somed suddenly as the man of the hour; for, thanks to divine Providence, he
had been studying English, and could say prettily, although slowly, 'What
o'clock it is?' and 'Please you this,' and 'Please you that,' and doubtless much
more if he were put to it" (69).

The contrast of these writers' distinct ideological views provides a culturally and linguistically complex image of the Mexican culture—a multi-
voiced history—so often missing in the U.S. literature to which Robinson
points. Indeed, the "sentimentalism and preciousness" ascribed to Mena's
prose by Raymund Paredes can indeed be quite differently construed: Mena
achieves a special kind of heteroglossia by weaving phrasings into her text
which read like quoted clichés; these are to be understood as ironic framings
of typical speech patterns which saturate and direct the thoughts of her characters, not as lapses. Her models might well have been Flaubert and Tur-
genev, both of whom were known for their literariness and who would
certainly have been much read among the literary group within which she
circulated.

Though the Arriola family has stressed to Popo that he "comport himself
as a true-born *caballero*" (60), Mena describes Popo's easy discarding of
the Mexican courtship traditions as efforts to impress the beautiful Señorita Cherry. Instead of paying attention to the older Cherry, he entertains
the younger. And when Miss Alicia Cherry "conceived a strong desire to go
down and become merged in that moving coil" of ladies and gentlemen
promenading around the kiosk of the band serenading in the plaza, he accompanies her without an escort:

> When the visitors arrived, he *essayed gallantly* to dedicate himself to
> the service of the elder lady, in accordance with Mexican theories
> of propriety, but found his well-meaning efforts frustrated by the
> younger one, who, *seeing no other young man thereabout,* proceeded
> methodically to attach the governor's *handsome little son* to herself . . .
> but she did beg the privilege, however unprecedented, of *promenading*

with a young gentleman at her side, and showing the inhabitants how
such things were managed in *America—beg pardon, the United States.*
　　So they walked together under the palms, Alicia Cherry and Próspero Arriola, and although the youth's hat was in the air most of the
time in acknowledgment of salutes, he did not really recognize those
familiar and astonished faces, for his head was up somewhere near
the moon, while his legs, in the proud shelter of their first trousers,
were pleasantly afflicted with pins and needles as he moved on tiptoe
beside the blonde Americana, *a page beside a princess.* (70–72, my
emphasis)

There is a subtle irony in the tone here; moreover, the naming of her characters cannot be accidental. Próspero wants to "prosper," and the way to prosper is to learn English and the ways of the Americans and to study at a U.S.
university to which his parents are more than willing to send him.[2]

　　He attaches himself to the "princess," though the Arriolas have a social
status equal to that of the American Cherrys, if not higher. For Alicia, on the
other hand, whose last name connotes virginity or high quality (as in a
cherry car) in idiomatic American English, any Mexican will do, but since
no other young man is immediately available, the fourteen-year-old suffices.
The title of the short story is also ironic as it deals with Popo's education—
but of a different kind. Mena's superficial reverence for the United States,
or perhaps her disillusion with her adopted country, becomes apparent in
her correction of her naming of the country. "America—beg pardon, the
United States" has a tone that is definitely mocking. Mena also criticizes
the Mexicano's disregard for Mexican beauty when faced with the allure of
the white skin and blond hair of the *gringa:*

> Never before had he seen a living woman with hair like daffodils,
> eyes like violets, and a complexion of coral and porcelain. It seemed
> to him that some precious image of the Virgin had been changed into
> a creature of sweet flesh and capricious impulses, animate with a fear-
> less urbanity far beyond the dreams of the dark-eyed, demure, and
> now *despised damsels of his own race.* His delicious bewilderment was
> completed when Miss Cherry, after staring him in the face with
> a frank and inviting smile, turned to her mother, and drawled
> laconically:
> 　　*"He just simply talks with those eyes!"* (71, my emphasis)[3]

What is for Alicia Cherry simply a summer flirtation, pleasing to her vanity, shows itself to be of the utmost seriousness for Popo as he experiences his

first love. The night of the grand ball, Miss Cherry is to dance a specific waltz with Popo, one they had heard during their promenade the night of the *serenata* and which she had promised to him. Days pass, and after much flirtation the night of the ball arrives, but by then the reader knows something the Arriolas do not. Miss Alicia Cherry's youthful appearance has made her a convincing *señorita,* but we learn from her mother, who has felt ignored and slighted by Popo's attentions to her daughter, that Alicia has really been making false pretenses: she has been married and is only recently divorced. She has accompanied her family on this trip in order to recover from her husband's indiscretions and her grief over the separation. With ironic phrases that sound like quotations from a repertory of stereotypes, Mena criticizes Alicia Cherry's, the "confirmed matinée girl's," vanity and materialism, for Alicia "wished that all her woman friends might have seen her at that moment she had on a sweet frock and a perfectly darling hat" (77). Mena is also critical of how Alicia has used Próspero's courting to mend her injured heart, "that they [her friends] might have heard the speech that had just been addressed to her by the leading man. He was a thoughtful juvenile, to be sure, but he had lovely, adoring eyes and delightful passionate tones in his voice; and, anyhow, it was simply delicious to be made love to in a foreign language" (77). Mena not only points out Alicia's vanity and her "use" of Popo but also makes light of Alicia's being drawn into and believing the role she has been playing:

> She was extremely pleased, too, to note that her own heart was going pitapat in a fashion quite uncomfortable and sweet and girly. She wouldn't have missed that sensation for a good deal. What a comfort to a bruised heart to be loved like this! He was calling her his saint. If that Edward could only hear him! Perhaps, after all, she *was* a saint. Yes, she felt that she certainly was, or could be if she tried. Now he was repeating some verses that he had made to her in Spanish. Such musical words! One had to come to the hot countries to discover what emotion was; and as for love-making! How the child had suffered! (77–78)

The night of the ball arrives, and Alicia has her coming out in all her glory, living out in Mexico the fantasy of being the only *señorita* with blond hair. "To be the only blonde at a Mexican ball is to be reconciled for a few hours to the fate of being a woman. Alicia, her full-blown figure habited in the palest of pink, which seemed of the living texture of her skin, with a generous measure of diamonds winking in effective constellations upon her golden head and dazzling bosom, absorbed through every pore the enravished admiration of the beholders, and beneficently poured it forth again in magnetic waves of the happiness with which triumph enhances beauty" (79).

But her ex-husband, Winterbottom, an apparent antithesis for the romantic allure of the "*hot* countries" and also a perfect match for her in vanity and materialism, arrives the night of the ball. As a result, Popo's heart must be broken, not yet by the truth but by the appearance of an American rival: "Mr. Edward P. Winterbottom was one of those fortunate persons who seem to prefigure the ideal toward which their race is striving. A thousand conscientious draftsmen, with the *national ideal in their subconsciousness,* were always hard at work portraying his particular type in various romantic capacities, as those of foot-ball hero, triumphant engineer, 'well-known clubman,' and pleased patron of the latest collar, cigarette, sauce, or mineral water" (79–80; my emphasis).

Mena satirically criticizes the conscious effort on the part of Americans to create some kind of "national ideal" of the American male, through an artificial construction of him as a creature of materialism. Edward Winterbottom is painted as an image of progress and as such represents a foreshadowing of an image which will be reproduced for the U.S. people and then sold to neighboring Latin American countries through modern commercial advertising. Here Mena's criticism is subtle; her innuendo anticipates the criticism of later Chicano and Latin American writers who, over half a century later, would attack directly the materialist fetishism which accompanies the "anesthetizing of consciousness."[4]

The opening of Mena's story emphasizes this importation of American culture. Rather than enjoying what Mexico offers, the Arriolas feel it essential to be more like Americans than Mexicans: Popo abandons the customs of his people to adopt the ways of the Americans; Alicia is only too eager to show how such things as the promenade in the plaza "were managed in America" (72).

In "The Education of Popo" Mena does not become explicit as to how this importation of U.S. materialism eventually trickles down to the lower classes, though she very effectively handles this theme in "The Gold Vanity Set." In this story, a gold vanity set is left behind by a rich American woman. When an *indita* finds it, she applies the makeup in the set to make her husband love her more and beat her less. Petra, the *indita,* fetishizes when she attributes magical qualities to the vanity set. It has made her more beautiful, like an apparition in her husband's eyes, and she therefore offers it up to the Virgin of Guadalupe. Eduardo Galeano's criticism of postmodern Latin America is like Mena's in her earlier writings when he points to the effects of such consumerism on the poor: "Illusions of riches are sold to the poor, and of freedom to the oppressed, dreams of triumph for the defeated and of power for the weak. There is no need to be able to read in order to consume the symbolic justifications for the unequal organization of the world disseminated by television, radio and the cinema" (190–191). Galeano speaks directly of how this consumerism affects our perception of the past and how it facilitates our acceptance of a dominative history. Though speaking of Latin America, he might just as well be speaking of the American Dream, as sold through histories such as Webb's which idealize a special breed of American pioneers who overcome all obstacles and succeed as a result of the inventions of U.S. industrialization:

> The falsification of the past pushes out of sight the true causes of the historical failure of Latin America, where poverty has always fed the prosperity of others: on the small screen or on a big one, the best man wins, and the best is the strongest. Wastefulness, exhibitionism and lack of scruple produce not disgust but admiration; everything can be bought, sold, rented, consumed—not excluding the soul. Magical properties are given to a cigarette, a car, a bottle of whisky or a watch: they provide personality, make you succeed in life, give you happiness. The proliferation of foreign models and heroes goes with the fetishism surrounding products and fashions from the rich countries....
>
> Consciousness of our limitations is not consciousness of impotence: literature, a form of action, has not supernatural powers, but the writer can achieve his measure of magic when he secures the survival, through his work, of people and experiences that have a real value. (192, 196)

Mena's Winterbottom intrudes upon a scene of romantic idealism as the representative of U.S. capitalism and breaks the spell of the Mexican social system into which the Cherrys have become absorbed. Alicia's fling with the infatuated Popo ends abruptly. She disappoints him and pays attention only to her former husband, with whom she dances the intended waltz. The following day, Popo's family is distressed because Popo has been missing all night. Realizing her responsibility for Popo's disappearance and how she had merely played with his infatuation in order to restore her self-confidence, Miss Cherry searches for him in order to make amends. She takes her ex-husband along with her, telling him the whole story of her summer flirtation. Velásquez-Treviño attributes to a "feminist perspective" Mena's revealing the manipulative nature of women's relationships *vis-à-vis* men, in this case, specifically, Miss Cherry's relationship with Winterbottom. She notes that Winterbottom is described as having "an adequate assortment of simple emotions easily predictable by a reasonably clever woman" and how "a long course of such discipline would go far toward generating him as a man and a husband" (Velásquez-Treviño: 57).

Only through Alicia's discourse with her husband as they return to the town do we learn what happens when she finds Popo. What is interesting here is the way Alicia interprets Mexican culture and traditions through cultural customs of her own defining. In this way, Mena's narrative accomplishes a layering of perspectives in a multicultural view; there is no overt expression of struggle, resistance, or even of the hatred so often apparent in Chicano and Anglo American narrative depictions of the "other" culture. The criticism from both sides in Alicia Cherry's observations may lack political profile, but it is certainly candid:

> "One thing I've demonstrated," she continued fretfully, "and that is that the summer flirtation of our happy land simply cannot be acclimated south of the Rio Grande. These people lack the necessary imperturbability of mind, which may be one good reason why they're not permitted to hold hands before the marriage ceremony. To complicate matters, it seems that I'm the first blonde with the slightest claim to respectability that ever *invaded* this part of Mexico, and although the inhabitants have a deluded idea that blue eyes are intensely spiritual, they get exactly the same Adam-and-Eve palpitations from them that we do from the lustrous black orbs of the languishing tropics." (81; my emphasis)

However eager the Arriolas may have been to import American culture through its products, there remain an opposition and resistance to any altering of the basic rules of courtship and ancient Mexican traditions. Mena reveals how this astonishes Alicia Cherry, whose first impression had been one of easy acceptance of the manners of her "superior" culture.

Miss Cherry's views on courtship coincide with some entertained by the American authors whom Cecil Robinson studies. In other sources there appear Mexican women who correspond to what Miss Cherry says about the other blondes whom Mexicans have known, those not as "respectable" as she. Robinson writes:

> When, during the Mexican War, American men in large numbers, many of them from puritanical rural areas, first encountered the women of Mexico, they were both fascinated and much taken aback. "The Missourians," wrote Bernard De Voto, "were shocked by the paint on their faces, their familiarity and easy laughter, and, the truth is by the charm they gave to what had to be considered vice. They showed their breasts and, it was believed, in fact it was soon proved they could be easily possessed—for pay, for kindness, or for mere amenity. An instructed prudery showed itself: sex ought not be decorative."
>
> Yet the situation described by De Voto was the irregular one of war time. For all her intensity, the Mexican woman who is not a professional prostitute does not usually give herself casually. There is the combination of passion and formalism, the marked respect for convention, the sense of propriety, and yet the interest in intrigue. Sex manners vary in Mexico, as elsewhere, according to class and are most complex among the most cultivated people. (86–87)

Mena in her narrative succinctly articulates a cultural fact later analyzed by Robinson: that people, right or wrong, imagine others in other cultures in ways which bring their mirror-images of each other so close as to be in certain respects interchangeable.

Miss Cherry goes on to tell her husband what happened during her talk with Popo (while he had been waiting for her at some distance). After Popo in his anger and resentment had called her "by a name which ought not be applied to any lady in any language" (83), she had explained to him that she had been married to Edward and that she is eleven years older than Popo. She then offers to make amends and "restore his faith in love" (83) by letting him kiss her. Playing up the jealousies of her ex-husband, Alicia tells him she will allow this kiss as they ride searching for him. Popo, being a *caballero,* refuses to act on her offer. He is shocked by the truth and instead tries to persuade Alicia to remarry her husband. Mena's technique of unfolding the action while simultaneously providing the commentary of Alicia and Edward reveals how Popo's actions and words are portrayed and interpreted through the fixed ideas of these two Americans. Rationalizing her actions, Alicia remarks to her ex-husband as they ride back to the Arriolas' place:

> "He had simply worked out my probable actions, just as I had worked out his. Of course he looked like a wild thing, hair on end, eyes like a panther, regular young bandit . . .
>
> ". . . [when] I revealed my exact status as an ex-wife in process of being courted by her divorced husband, his eyes nearly dropped out of his head. You see, they don't play "Tag! You're it!" with marriage down here. That boy actually began to hand me out a line of missionary talk. He thinks I ought to remarry you, Ned."
>
> "He must have splendid instincts after all. So of course you didn't kiss him?"
>
> "Wait a minute. After mentioning that I was eleven years older than he, and that my hair had been an elegant mouse-drab before I started touching it up—"
>
> "Not at all. I liked its color—a very pretty shade of—"
>
> "After that, I told him that he could thank his stars for the education I had given him, in view of the fact that he's going to be sent to college in the U. S. A., and I gave him a few first-rate pointers on the college widow breed." (83)

The question of image versus authenticity resurfaces with Alicia's reference to the dyed blond hair with which Popo had fallen in love, and to the widows probably also passing themselves off as *señoritas* in colleges like the one he is likely to attend. Hearing of Popo's refusal to kiss his ex-wife, Winterbottom comments, "That young fellow is worthy of being an American" (84), at which point the stereotype of the treacherous Mexican also subtly surfaces. To this, Alicia responds:

> "Why, that was his Indian revenge, the little monkey! But he was tempted, Ned."
>
> "Of course he was. If you'd only tempt *me!* O Alicia, you're a saint!"
>
> "That's what Popo called me yesterday, and it was neither more nor less true than what he called me today. I suppose we're all mixtures of one kind and another. And I've discovered, Ned, that it's the healthiest kind of fun to be perfectly frank with—with an old pal. Let's try it that way next time, shall we, dear?" (84)

Whether Mena was aware of the tendency of American writers to attribute animal qualities to Mexican characters or not, this tendency has been the subject of much study, from Cecil Robinson to Felipe Ortego y Gasca, to Arnoldo De León and others. The reference to the stereotypical "bandit" is also too direct to be ignored but must be interpreted as Mena's conscious critique of an American's perceptions of Mexicans, elite or not.

The feminine duality that has been treated in many cultures appears here when Mena has Alicia discover that she is both virgin (saint) and whore and that, like her husband, she is capable of living out both of her selves. In revealing both beings in one Anglo woman, Mena challenges established notions of the Mexican woman as she has been dichotomized. This dichotomized character has been the subject of much analysis among Chicano and Chicana writers of latter generations who have repeatedly examined specific variations of the Virgin of Guadalupe and the Malinche figure in both Mexican and Chicano/a letters. Even more often, later writers have wrestled with the traditional casting of the Mexican American female characters into either virginal roles or as "las otras," as Jovita González would have it, hardly ever allowing for the kind of complexity generally attributed only to male characters. Though Velásquez-Treviño believes that "another predominant image of woman that recurs in Mena's discourse is that of the saint or the virgin," the author does show how they coexist at least in this particular character.

Raymund Paredes attributes Mena's less confrontational style and "charming though artificial creations" to a lack of bravery ("One can also say that a braver, more perceptive writer would have confronted the life of her culture more forcefully") and to Mena's willingness to give to her audience what they wanted, the images they expected, as well as to editorial control: "Undoubtedly, a good part, if not most of this sort of characterization can be attributed to popular taste and editorial control; it has only been in recent years, after all, that Americans have recognized honest expressions of minority consciousness" (51). Yet Mena's writing is no less valuable an artistic, cultural production because it is not like the later Quinto Sol writers whom Paredes upholds as epitomizing Chicano consciousness (and I stress Chicano rather than Chicana), or because it does not fit into the very specific, symbolic *Aztlán* framework. To be sure, having come so early, her writings do not serve *La Causa* directly, yet they are valuable for the texture they present of the subsequently flattened images of the *Mexicano*. The variable relationships enacted between the two cultures reflect delicately shaded differences, class distinctions, and race relations, before "Chicano" writing entered the arena. As to the issues of editorial control and willingness to give an audience what they expect, Mena's response to her presumed audience was little different from the way the Quinto Sol writers responded to what their very specific audience expected of them. How much "bravery" did Quinto Sol writers need to write within literary currents of the Chicano Movement? Mena wrote for a receptive Anglo audience; later Chicano writers wrote for a receptive Chicano one. Raymund Paredes argues: "The careful explication, born of a desire to acquaint Anglo readers with the Mexican culture of the United States, *is generally absent* from the works of Quinto Sol authors. They wrote primarily for an audience that shared their experiences; they felt no need, therefore, to justify their culture" (R. Paredes: 60; my emphasis). The very category of opposition comes into question here. Must "opposition" always be direct conflict such as that found in the folk-based *corrido* tradition or the literature of the Quinto Sol period? Two issues—viewpoint and didacticism—pertain. Mena conducts her narrative through a modulation of viewpoints, Alicia's being the most sharply focused. Mena also does not prescribe for readers a lesson about conflicts, differences, or injustices. In many later Chicano narratives, authorial viewpoint becomes paramount, and a didactic manner, at least as undertone, takes over. Raymund Paredes views this style as "bravery," addressing consciously ideological issues, a style absent from Mena's work. This absence can be attributed to the influence of Mena's upbringing, the ideology of her class background, and the influence of literary currents of the time—and not the lack of "bravery." As with Jovita González's work, much more can be said about the power that an audience's expectations exerted as well as about the editorial control over other writers of those times.

FERMINA GUERRA

Fermina Guerra was also a descendant of the early colonizers of the Rio Grande border. The daughter of Florencio and Josefa Guerra, she was born and reared in Laredo, Texas, where she graduated from the Ursuline academy. In August 1938, she received her B.A. from the University of Texas at Austin with a Teacher's certificate from the Department of Education. She taught in Webb County, Texas, for four consecutive years and later in the primary grades in the Laredo schools. In August of 1941 she received her master's degree also from the University of Texas.

"Rancho Buena Vista,
Its Ways of Life and Traditions"

The selection I discuss here, "Rancho Buena Vista, Its Ways of Life and Traditions" (also published in *Mexican-American Authors*), is taken from Guerra's master's thesis (written eleven years after González wrote hers) and consists of four chapters. The first is on the early history of the Laredo area, the second discusses the ranchos on the arroyo, the third treats the family life at Buena Vista Ranch, and the final chapter is on the ranch year or the holidays and festivities surrounding those holidays. J. Frank Dobie was on Guerra's thesis committee, but his name does not appear as the first signature.[5]

Her very brief writing career expands the notions of femininity that Jovita González had written about her people within the academy as well as in her novels. In a paradoxical way, the history Guerra offers comes closer in style to Webb's version of history writing, for her ranch people are not aristocratic like González's. Her stories resemble those which Webb derived from the history of his people. In her master's thesis she offers a description of the life in and around her family's three thousand acres of ranch lands (at that time relatively small): "Not presuming to domain or wealth," as Guerra points out, her family's ranch "became a social headquarters for the country around it" (19). In recording these events, Guerra gives a history of the Mexicano people of the Laredo area, as reflected in the stories of her people, as they were told over and over again, particularly within her immediate family:

> The traditions pertaining to Buena Vista that have been told over and
> over among the children and grandchildren of Florencio Guerra and
> his wife Josefa Flores, are the kind of traditions to be heard all up
> and down the Border country. Some of them, perhaps a majority of
> them, treat of actual happenings, and are folklore only in that *they are
> traditional and that they are hardly important enough for history*. The
> stories are of Indians, floods, captives, sheepherders, buried treasure,
> violent death, happenings when the bishop came or the wool went to
> town. When a fire burns on a winter night or when it is raining and
> the water in Becerra Creek is high, people at Buena Vista tell and
> hear these traditions of the land. (19; my emphasis)

Fermina Guerra's writing approaches Webb's insofar as it provides a narrative history of the region; she differs in that she includes the Mexican's history along with that of the Anglo. Even so, Webb's writing was called history, whereas Guerra's was called folklore, for she too studied under J. Frank Dobie. But unlike Dobie's quaint, paternalistic portrayal of the Mexicans, Guerra's stories record the hard work and struggles of her people, which can be seen as parallel to those of Webb's pioneering settlers. Most importantly, she situates the history of her people and the development of the Mexican ranching industry within the historical events in the United States and worldwide conflicts that may have concerned the United States but to which people were still oblivious in their existing relative autonomy in this part of the world, which she describes as "scores of Mexican ranches between the Nueces and the Rio Grande, in the brush country of Texas— and also in the Border country of Mexico" (19).

> After the Civil War broke out and the Southern ports were block-
> aded, the only outlet for cotton was through Mexico. One of the
> cotton roads from San Antonio to the Rio Grande was hacked out
> through the brush six miles north of La Becerra Ranch. The open-
> ing through the brush, now grass-covered, and the marks that the
> wide iron tires of the ox carts left on flint rocks in their path can yet
> be seen. While the guns of war thundered far away and ox carts
> rumbled across the Becerra, Don Justo Guerra, his wife, and their
> sons saw their herds increase. Ranching was the sole occupation of
> the country, and for most of these Border ranchers the war was as far
> away as the operations of Bismarck in Germany. (18)

Guerra does not romanticize or mystify the story of her people, nor does she invent dehumanized enemies to add drama, as does Webb when writing of his people. With her matter-of-fact telling, she makes it a point to show how "the ranchmen kept the peace among themselves; the struggle with Nature occupied their chief energies," as when she mentions only in passing the names of the ranchers erecting the first fence: "The first fence went up in 1891. Don Florencio's son, Donato, used to go out of his way before and after school to watch the fence-building operations being carried on by the Callaghan Ranch hands, who were erecting a fence between Buena Vista Ranch and theirs" (20). The motivation behind the building of a fence by the Callaghans, a Mexican family with a non-Spanish last name, as is common in South Texas, seems unimportant as she imbeds their motivation and identity within the foregrounded actions of Don Florencio's son and the fence-building event itself.

As with Webb's people, "Ever-present in the minds of ranch people is the question of water," and Guerra goes on to present a history of how these people dealt with its shortages as well as its torrents, specifically the three occasions in the history of the Buena Vista Ranch when La Becerra Creek, because of too much rain or flooding, had been "half a mile wide—in 1878, 1903, and 1937" (20). Unlike González in "Among my People" and Webb, Guerra makes the lives and struggles of women just as important as those of men. In the selection "High Water" in her description of the flood of 1878, she includes the actions of the women along with those of the men when the water from the creek continues to rise in the pouring rain. Don Justo, the apparent patriarch, fears nothing when the rest of his family grows frightened, something he later regrets:

> A young matron, wife of Don Carmen, holding her child in her arms, told her husband to take her to higher ground. She feared remaining in the house another night with that constantly rising water. Gladly enough, he complied. Before leaving, he begged his aged father and mother to accompany him, but they laughed. "You will get all wet for nothing," they said. "We have a roof over our heads. What if there is a little water in the house?"
>
> But the young mother set out for the hill to the east. Before she reached it, she was obliged to swim to save herself and child, her husband aiding her. The rain was still pouring so hard that they got lost in the brush, but they went on eastward.
>
> Eventually they found themselves on a well-known hill. Don Florencio's ranch was just a mile to the northwest. The mother asked her husband to go down there and ask for some dry clothing for the baby, as the night was cold and it was still raining hard. Willingly enough, Don Carmen set out. (20)

Don Florencio, hearing of the flood from his brother, Don Carmen, sets out in search of his parents. He finds Don Justo and his wife perched on the roof of their house. Because "like most ranchmen of his time, Don Florencio could not swim" (21), and he could not convince his horse to cross the "raging torrent between him and them," he had to wait for the water to begin to recede on the next day before saving "the exhausted old people from their predicament" (21). Not only are the actions of a young woman included here, but her judgment is shown to be better than that of old Don Justo, whose experience is more ample. This nexus of events leaves one wondering if Webb would really have been so hard pressed to identify scenes in which women were major participants in local history. The image of this woman swimming for her life and that of her child in the flood stands in sharp contrast to the picture Webb presents of the women on a similar terrain as that of South Texas (which he includes in his definition of the Great Plains): "The wind, the sand, the drought, the unmitigated sun, and the boundless expanse of a horizon on which danced fantastic images conjured up by the mirages, seemed to overwhelm the women with a sense of desolation, insecurity, and futility, which they did not feel when surrounded with hills and green trees. Who can tell us how the Great Plains affected women, and why?" (506).

Guerra's portrayal of brave, struggling women does not end with Don Carmen's wife. In the selection *"La Cautiva,"* Guerra depicts the life of Antonia Hinojosa, the captive. Antonia is captured by Indians from across the border one day as she is washing clothes by a creek with her infant son in the Mexican state of Chihuahua. They cut off her son's ears and leave him by the creek bank but take her. After living among the Indians for several years and becoming the wife of a brave, she gives birth to a daughter, Lola. But, we are told, "she longed to escape." Antonia is separated from her daughter during a battle between tribes, but her grieving husband reveals to his daughter the Spanish name of her mother, "and urged her to seek her if anything ever happened to him" (24). When Lola's father is killed in a fight with another brave, Lola escapes and grows up among white people:

> She never ceased searching for her mother, but it was many years before she found her.
>
> Meanwhile, the mother, Antonia, had been released by the Indians because the United States Government made them give up all their captives. She came to La Becerra Creek and took up a homestead. She lived alone and often had not even a laborer to help her. (24)

Lola finally hears of her mother while she is living in Austin, goes in search of her, and finds her on her ranch, where they live together for a few years. Several years pass after Lola has moved back to Austin. Now sixty years old, she hears that her mother has fallen ill. On her way back to her mother's ranch, she hears from nearby ranchers that her mother, who was one hundred five years old, "did not live till her daughter arrived": "The shock was too great for the aged traveler; she was unable to continue her journey. Soon she herself died, and the two are buried side by side on the ranch of La Cautiva" (24). Certainly, racial relations between American Indians and Mexicans are more realistically drawn here than in Webb's history, with his dramatic rendering of the "red Knights of the prairie" (1931: 68).

From this story of adventure of two women, we turn to the classic western themes of cowboys and Indians in two stories entitled "Indians" and "Tío Pedro and the Rangers." "Indians" tells of one isolated incident among Indians who were probably from reservations where, as Guerra informs us, they had been "gathered" by the U.S. Government: "but it was customary to allow a few at a time to leave the reservations for the purpose of hunting. These would band together at some distance from the reservations and make forays to the south, where there were no soldiers to stop them" (22). In about 1877, a band approaches Don Carmen and Don Florencio on the range. As Guerra informs us, "The Indians came, though, chiefly to steal horses. They generally killed only in case of resistance. Don Florencio and his brother had worked too hard, in getting their horses, to stand idly by while the Indians drove them away" (22). There is a brief battle in which a "volley of arrows and several pistols" are fired. The horses are startled into flight and head for the Buena Vista ranch house. The Indians come across Marcos, the *pastor* (goat herder), and kill him with an arrow when he quarrels with them. Guerra ends the narrative without judgment but with a simple reporting of events, even when it is one of her people that has been killed:

> That visit was the last that the Indians made to Buena Vista Ranch.
> Although the Indians did have firearms at this time, they used arrows on many occasions. They had used both pistols and arrows in the encounter earlier in the day, but on passing by the ranch, they killed Marcos with an arrow. They saw no need of wasting their ammunition. (23)

"Tío Pedro and the Rangers" tells of "a peaceful man with a wife and two children" who one day shoots a Mexican thief who had stolen some of his horses as he was being fired upon. Feeling remorse for what he has done, Tío Pedro turns himself in to the authorities for trial. He is cleared and returns to his ranch and takes "up his peaceful life again." The real trouble begins when two Texas Rangers present themselves at the Buena Vista Ranch asking for "don Pedro Fulano, who had killed a horse thief in defense of his rights."

> Don Florencio asked why the Rangers were seeking him. They laughingly replied that they had never seen a Mexican brave enough to stand up for his rights and would like to set eyes on one. As they were passing through the country on their rounds, this seemed a good opportunity to do so.
>
> The tale did not ring true to Don Florencio. It was about dinner time; so he asked the strangers to remain for the meal, offering to take them afterward. Much to his surprise, they stayed and chatted in a friendly way over the meal. (25)

In the meantime, Don Florencio, not trusting the Rangers, asks his son to ride to Tío Pedro's and give him the message about the two Rangers.

When Tío Pedro receives the message, "[the] tales he had heard of the 'rinches' made him fear that they would pay little attention to the laws of the country if they had inclinations otherwise" (26). Knowing that once the Rangers got a hold of him, he would "stand no chance of escaping," he saddles his horse and rides to Old Mexico. From this safe haven, he writes to his family asking them to "sell the property and join him." Guerra ends the story thus: "This they did, and crumbling walls now attest to the terror of the 'rinches' that lived in the hearts of even honest men." In this one brief tale, with its deep retrospect, for it explains the origins of the existing crumbling walls, we have a central theme upon which Américo Paredes and historians like Acuña and De León would build their work—the loss of property, the denigration of the Texas Mexican, and the history of conflict between Anglos and Mexicans in Texas. Yet so little has been said or written about Fermina Guerra. Guerra's writings (however few they may have been) remain a tribute to the honesty with which she recorded the events of her isolated South Texas and the people whose way of life would soon be erased forever by Anglo occupation, investment, and commercialized farming. Unlike Jovita González, Fermina Guerra, as far as we know, did not write very much, perhaps because of lack of encouragement or because she was not so inclined, though her rich narratives speak otherwise. She also did not become president of the Texas Folklore Society as González did, perhaps because she did not sufficiently reinforce the folkloric views of Mexicans made popular by Webb and Dobie. Even so, all of these efforts can be looked upon as a recovering of a lost history that gave rise to Chicano literature and responded to the rhetoric of dominance.

○ ○ ○

Both María Cristina Mena and Fermina Guerra challenge commonly held notions about their people and thus resist the sacrificing of their people's reality to stereotypes such as those Cecil Robinson discerns. They both, in distinctive ways, have the power to change attitudes and values that were preserved in Webb's history, and they did so long before such a challenge became legitimized through revisionist history. Their portrayals of characters and events also illuminate their society's own values and struggles from within. They are true voices, articulate intelligences writing the "banished history" of their people.

5
AMÉRICO PAREDES'S NARRATIVES OF RESISTANCE
Property, Labor, Education, Gender, and Class Relations

> *The word Mexican had for so long been a symbol of hatred and loathing that to most Anglotexans it had become a hateful and loathsome word. In Spanish Mexicano has a full and prideful sound. The mouth opens on the full vowels and the voice acquires a certain dignity in saying mexicano. But in English it is much different. The lower lip pushes up and the upper lip curls contemptuously. The pursed lips go "m-m-m." Then they part with a smacking, barking sound, "M-m-mexsican!" Who doesn't understand will think he's being cursed at. It is a word that can be pronounced without opening your mouth at all, through clenched teeth. So the kindly Angloamerican uses Latin American to avoid giving offense.*
>
> —PAREDES, GEORGE WASHINGTON GÓMEZ

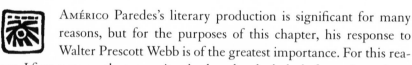 AMÉRICO Paredes's literary production is significant for many reasons, but for the purposes of this chapter, his response to Walter Prescott Webb is of the greatest importance. For this reason, I first compare the two writers' cultural and scholarly formation as it relates to their literary interpretations of history to draw parallels between their very distinct cultural productions. Second, I point to how the property, labor, education, and gender relations so effectively dramatized in Paredes's various literary works become a single narrative construction of resistance against Webb's history.

At the same time that Webb was engaged in writing histories about what he perceived as his people's struggles in the Southwest, Paredes was creating a narrative in both his poetry and fiction that specifically became a direct response to this rhetoric of dominance. During the first half of the twentieth century, many Mexicanos and Mexicanas were privately and collectively engaged in resistance efforts against the ever increasing Anglo domination of South Texas. They were essentially engaged in a struggle to live out their lives with dignity while at the same time maintaining their cultural values. The story Paredes provides through his fiction and poetry became a literary statement of protest against the generally accepted ideological views of the Mexicano people of the Southwest. Paredes was born in 1915 in the border town of Brownsville, Texas, the very year that, according to Paredes's own description of the seditionist activity then rampant, "along the Lower Border that same year . . . 'bands of Border men under the leadership of Aniceto Pizaña and Luis de la Rosa raided as far north as the King Ranch, burning ranches, derailing trains, killing American civilians, and attacking U.S. army detachments'" (1976: 32–33). Today, he is considered one of the foremost ethnographers, literary critics, and social historians of his time, and in fact, by some, the dean of American folklore. Presently he is Professor Emeritus of English and Anthropology at the University of Texas at Austin.

Growing up during the 1920s and 1930s, he witnessed a period of significant transition of economic and political power in South Texas. Also a product of his environment, Paredes recounts in his narratives what he witnessed for himself as well as what he heard recounted by the *viejos,* the elders, of his community. On numerous occasions, Paredes has spoken of how it was the *viejos,* and the oral tradition they kept alive, that provided and preserved what is now the subject of serious scholarship: "I have absorbed the history and culture of our people from the 'viejos,' guided [by] their oral narratives, their songs and anecdotes and by a bitter need to use all the things I have learned from [them] to combat the defamatory picture given to us by Anglo historians and 'raconteurs'" (1990b).[1]

Likewise, Webb continually referred to his early childhood experiences as having been the catalyst for not only his perception of Southwest history but also his particular style of writing. Jacques Barzun has noted that Webb often stated that "he was writing history as [he] saw it from Texas, not from some center of learning" (Barzun: 12). That contact with his environment and the authenticity it is said to have lent his work added much to Webb's reputation as a unique scholar. "Webb was sure that his preparation had begun at the age of four, when he heard tales of Indian raids and massacres and observed, albeit unconsciously, the climate and ways of life" (Barzun: 12). In the preface to *The Great Plains,* Webb comments on his personal experience in relation to his study and writing of history: "In childhood my father and mother gave me a thorough course in Plains life by the direct method, one that enabled me to understand much that I read and see beyond some of it."

Paredes, with his own background of experience, brings the Webb project into question along the four parameters of property, education, labor, and finally gender and class relations, upon which the first three converge. While Webb all but eliminates Mexicanos from the history of the Southwest, Paredes inscribes them into that very history by means of his historical narrative; while Webb's discourse lends credence to the myth that the land is the birthright of every hardworking Anglo pioneer, Paredes focuses on what means were used to appropriate the land; while Webb glorifies the Texas Rangers, Paredes shows them to be the instruments of cruelty and injustice, usurpers of land rights. But there exists another very important difference between these two literati historians. Unlike Webb, Paredes was not writing for a very receptive audience, nor telling them what they wanted to hear. The reading audience of his time was not willing to applaud his efforts nor to receive his new style of writing history. After writing his classic *With His Pistol in His Hand: A Border Ballad and Its Hero* (1958), Américo Paredes was threatened by a former Texas Ranger who wanted to "pistol whip the sonofabitch who wrote that book." While Webb rose to a position of authority and power at the University of Texas at Austin, Paredes was criticized for his scholarship, was denied faculty salary raises, and was initially refused publication of his pioneering work unless he removed all negative commentary regarding the Texas Rangers and Webb. Despite this discouragement from the administration of the University of Texas and the absence of a receptive audience like the one Webb had enjoyed, Paredes continued to record what he had observed around him, more specifically what he saw happening to his people in relation to dominant socioeconomic and political systems of the past.

Most often Webb's most acclaimed contribution, his unique style of history writing, is ascribed to his having been brought up on the frontier. His biographers frequently point to his particular style of writing history, emphasizing that his view stood in contrast to the highly academic and scholarly style prevailing during his time, perhaps even the approach to history of "hyper-empiricists" like Fred Shannon.[2] Many of his biographers have attributed Webb's style to his background and formation and to his close identification of himself with the pioneers he wrote about and admired. He acknowledged that the "only pioneering left was of the intellectual sort":

Webb was maturing intellectually as well as professionally. During
his research on the Texas Rangers, he became more aware of the
impact of the environment on the people who lived on the land, or—
in the case of pioneers on the Great Plains—who moved onto it.
More important, he was gaining a sense of himself, or what he should
be about in his career. "It was about this time that I became reconciled to the fact that I had grown up on the frontier and that I could
not rub off the evidence" he later wrote. (Kingston: 74)

Américo Paredes's spirit of resistance and his "speaking to power" may
well have stemmed from the spirit of the borderlands. His experience of
growing up in a border culture of conflict may have brought about the particularly rare type of scholarship that not only goes against the current but
challenges old notions while they still prevail. "Since at the border of all discourse we often find conflict, such an intellectual [as Paredes] does not hesi-
tate to speak truth to power, to address an intelligent, learned discourse to
political questions" (Limón 1987).

Because of his distinction in his many careers in music, folklore, literature, anthropology, history, and culture, Américo Paredes was awarded the
Order of the *Aguila Azteca,* the highest honor Mexico bestows on foreign-
born citizens. On November 20, 1990, when accepting the distinction, Paredes spoke to power once again as he reminded representatives of the Mexican government that Chicanos have been around since 1848 and have since
then very much needed the support of the intellectuals from a Mexico which
has more often than not failed to speak up on the behalf of its forgotten children: "For the better part of this period of almost a century and a half, we
Mexican Americans have been the object of scorn, of social and economic
discrimination—of abuses that sometimes have culminated in legally sanctioned murder," he said. He cited as an example the case of Antonio Rodríguez, who was burned alive near Rock Springs, Texas, on November 4,
1910. Official protest from the Mexican government and public demonstra-
tions "had little effect, perhaps because we Mexican Americans have lacked,
until very recent times, the moral support of Mexican intellectuals. That is
something we have rarely had." Here we see Paredes critically identifying
another official history—that of the Mexican intelligentsia—which, like
Webb, also excluded the U.S. Mexicano. Paredes's words recalled to the audience how the Chicano/a has been trapped "between two worlds," both

projecting disparaging attitudes: "During the second decade of the past century, while the rural police of the State of Texas was butchering hundreds of defenseless Mexican peasants in South Texas, José Vasconcelos was busy branding us as *pochos*. Yet it was the *pochos* in Texas who gave Vasconcelos shelter, saving his life, when the political party to which he belonged fell apart, forcing him to flee to the United States. Even then, when told about what was happening farther downriver, Vasconcelos showed no interest" (1990b).

Paredes took an opportunity to present a history of a people's struggles not as a result of the harsh environment, as Webb represented his pioneers, but as a direct result of actions based on the type of ideology of supremacy that Webb's history perpetuated. He recounted for the audience the atrocities committed against Mexican American teenagers in 1943, in Los Angeles, California, during the so-called "Pachuco or Zoot-Suit Riots": "Hundreds of members of the U.S. armed forces, assisted by the Los Angeles police, invaded the barrios, savagely beating not only those teenagers wearing the *pachuco* costume but every dark-skinned boy they happened upon." Citing from Octavio Paz, Paredes effectively demonstrated the complexity of the Mexicano struggle in the southwestern United States and the absence of the voice of protest from Mexico's intelligentsia about such atrocities: "While Anglo American critics such as Carey McWilliams and Eleanor Roosevelt were not lacking, these violent scenes also had their Mexican commentator, another intellectual. Octavio Paz tells us: 'The pachuco is a clown—impassive and sinister—who seeks not to make one laugh but to terrify. His sadistic attitude goes hand-in-hand with a wish for self-humiliation . . . He seeks, he attracts persecution and disorder'" (Octavio Paz, *The Labyrinth of Solitude,* quoted in Paredes 1990b).

Paredes noted that "one could very well think that a member of the Los Angeles Police Department had written those lines." We might add that Webb could have written those lines as well. "[Yet] this 'impassive and sinister' *pachuco* was an essential stepping stone for the appearance of the 'Chicano' among Mexican American youth, when at last they sound their cry of liberation in the *Movimiento Chicano,*" Paredes added.[3] With the Chicano Movement came forays into new fields of inquiry like those that Paredes had pioneered and mapped out before such a movement came into being. A newly formed audience receptive to Paredes's scholarly as well as literary writings could now lend him the kind of support Webb had enjoyed.

My concern in this chapter is to discuss those of Américo Paredes's literary works which specifically respond to the dominative, ideologically tainted histories of the Southwest. By adding a new perspective, they effectively challenge some of the foregrounded stereotypes and misinformation perpetuated by this dominant history. Américo Paredes's literary works portray "fictionally" a real world and expose the bearing that Webbian histories have on issues of property, labor, and the "education" of the Chicano community. They show how such histories legitimized a particular type of labor force that was sorely needed for the building of the great Southwest. They indicate the conditions in which the dispossession of the Chicano occurred and by which the power and land control of the Anglo occupier were maintained.

Classical and traditional ideas regarding property hold true for the historical moment depicted here. As J. G. A. Pocock argues in his *Virtue, Commerce and History,* regarding these ideas as they came into question in eighteenth-century England: "The citizen possessed property in order to be autonomous and autonomy was necessary for him to develop virtue or goodness as an actor within the political, social and natural realm or order. He did not possess it in order to engage in trade, exchange or profit; indeed these activities were hardly compatible with the activity of citizenship" (1985: 103).

Also with regard to the rights of eighteenth-century English citizens, E. P. Thompson in *The Making of the English Working Class* focuses on how a citizen's rights were dependent on his possession of property, for "without a fixed estate in [the] kingdom, he hath no right" (1966: 23). Regardless of whether he had fought for the liberty of the state, the Texas Mexican, like the eighteenth-century Englishman "without a permanent fixed interest in this kingdom," could no longer be perceived as a significant member of, and important and rightful contributor to, the new society under construction.

David Montejano, writing more specifically about South Texas landownership in relation to education, notes the clear relationship of illiteracy rates to dispossession of land: "The relationship between Mexican landownership and education is suggested by the 'illiteracy' rates of 'native whites' and Mexicans, a 1930 Census statistic. The distribution of Mexican illiteracy in Mexican and Anglo counties . . . reveals a clear pattern: where Mexicans own land, there was less Mexican illiteracy; where Mexicans were landless, their illiteracy rates were high" (248–249).

Texas Mexicans were forced into an economic, political, and cultural struggle after suffering conquest as a result of the U. S. War with Mexico.

Two generations after this historical moment, a moment hardly accounted for in Webb's history, Texas Mexicans suffered defeat once again after the failed attempts of *los sediciosos* [the seditionists], who rose up in arms to try to take back control of the land. Montejano describes this period in history: "In the context of this ranch-farm struggle occurred one of the most dramatic episodes in the history of the Southwest, the armed insurrection of Texas Mexicans and its brutal suppression by Texas Rangers. The conflict turned the Valley into a virtual war zone during 1915–1917" (116). The events surrounding this conflict were seen by the general public as mere "bandit activity" and generally have been viewed as such by histories such as Webb's; however, as Montejano also notes, they were the direct result of how Texas Mexicans were treated:

> Most U.S. military observers stationed in Texas recognized that a basic condition making for the rebellion was the prejudice and contempt that Mexicans in the region were subjected to. The dire and pressing situation of the Texas Mexican was clear. The sense of urgency appears in various pieces of evidence: in the call to not sell the land; in the bitterness of the old elite; in the displacement of *rancheros, vaqueros,* tenants, and artisans; in the racism of the newcomers; and in vigilante lynchings and police executions. As in many revolutionary situations, vengeance for specific wrongs (usually the killing of a relative) rather than commitment to a radical ideology was the prime catalyst behind the Texas Mexican insurrection. (118)

Paredes's historical narratives, written long before such revisionist histories as Montejano's were to make their appearance, had already inscribed into the history of the Texas Mexican this "sense of urgency," the bitterness and resentment, the displacement, the racism, the lynchings, and the "police executions." Montejano describes such practices:

> Executions and lynchings of Mexicans became so commonplace the *San Antonio Express* (September 11, 1915) reported that the "finding of dead bodies of Mexicans, suspected for various reasons of being connected with the troubles, has reached a point where it creates little or no interest. It is only when a raid is reported, or an American is killed that the ire of the people is aroused." A few days after this report, the *Express* (September 15) described the typical manner in which executions were carried out: "Three Mexicans among six prisoners taken on suspicion after the Los Indios fight yesterday were killed today

near San Benito. It was stated that they escaped from the San Benito jail during the night, and that their bodies were found some distance from town today with bullet holes in their backs." Executions of "escaped" suspects were not the only evidence of Anglo retribution. Posses burned homes of suspected raiders and sympathizers, disarmed all Mexicans, and forced them to move into towns where they could be better controlled. (122)

According to Paredes, this form of execution was a common practice at the time.[4] The Rangers would simply petition to take a prisoner to a county jail. Encoded into the order to transport the prisoner was the execution order: "Take the prisoner to the X county jail and be back in an hour," for example, really meant "Shoot the prisoner as he tries to 'escape,'" as the county jail required more than an hour's traveling time (conversations with Paredes, 1994). This is the backdrop for Paredes's narrative, particularly as it is dramatically depicted in his novel regarding Gumersindo's murder, which is discussed later in this chapter.

From the point of view of Anglo colonialism, internal cultural diversity on the borderlands had been eliminated among Texas Mexicanos. For the Anglo, no longer could there be such a person as a "proud Mexican and loyal Tejano" as Mexican leaders like Juan Seguin had once thought they could be (Montejano: 26). The "good Mexican/bad Mexican dichotomy" from the Anglo point of view disappeared by means of the stereotyping that usually accompanies conquest and colonialization. What is more, all Mexicanos are in danger, making impossible the integration of most Texas Mexicans into the emerging economic system. Through Paredes's narrative we see in "fictional" narrative terms how the Mexicanos' relationship to the new socioeconomic world in which they gradually find themselves becomes a dependent one. Their new assignment to, for the most part, menial and servile roles in turn guarantees Anglo domination. Under the Anglo colonialist domination, Mexicanos' identity, values, language, traditions, and even their freedom to claim their true ethnic origin are threatened. Narrative in this case becomes an instance of ideological critique. We see *how* a dependent, subservient relationship once established by the repressive state apparatus is maintained by the ideological state apparatus in a manner set forth by Althusser in his essay, "Ideology and Ideological State Apparatuses":

Remember that in Marxist theory, the State Apparatus (SA) contains: the Government, the Administration, the Army, the Police, the

Courts, the Prisons, etc., which constitute what I shall in the future
call the Repressive State Apparatus. Repressive suggests that the State
Apparatus in question "functions by violence"—at least ultimately
(since repression, e.g., administrative repression, may take non-
physical forms).

I shall call Ideological State Apparatuses a certain number of realities which present themselves to the immediate observer in the form
of distinct and specialized institutions. (1969/1971: 142–143)

As he develops his distinction of the two apparatuses, Althusser lists several
of these institutions; the schools—scrutinized closely by Paredes—hold a
prominent position as the church once did, because in the schools, children
spend six to eight hours a day during their most formative years: "the Ideological State Apparatuses function massively and predominantly *by ideology,*
but they also function secondarily by repression, even if ultimately, but only
ultimately, this is very attenuated and concealed, even symbolic. (There is no
such thing as a purely ideological apparatus.) Thus Schools and Churches
use suitable methods of punishment, expulsion, selection, etc., to 'discipline'
not only their shepherds, but also their flocks. The same is true of the Family. . . . The same is true of the cultural IS Apparatus (censorship, among
other things), etc." (1969/1971: 145).

Althusser's theory allows little room for the kind of resistance dramatized in the narratives examined in this chapter and the ones that follow. Still, Althusser's model is useful when examining how Paredes's narratives give rise to many historical questions that Webb's history fails to
consider: With their place and position removed through all forms of repression and injustice, what remains for Mexicanos? How will they re-
build their place and maintain their culture and survive in this new and
emerging sociopolitical system? Most important, for the study of Paredes's narratives as a conscious critique of cultural hegemony, there remains
the question of what forces, apparatuses, state institutions, and practices
were established to assure that *Mexicanos* would not reclaim possession—
however symbolically—of the place that was once theirs. What conditions
would obstruct the building of a place for themselves in this new society, if
that place is even possible?[5] Answers to these questions lie not in Webb's
story nor in any histories following his tradition, but to a great extent in
Paredes's narratives. In fact, throughout his early writing, Paredes gives

voice to experiences of characters who had never been written into Webb's story. Américo Paredes's narratives supply the text missing from Anglo histories: the text tells of the struggles of Mexicanos.

THE POETRY OF AMÉRICO PAREDES

Though not well known as a poet until recently, Américo Paredes has been writing poetry since the age of fourteen. In 1989 he referred to his poetry as "the scribblings of a 'proto-Chicano' of a half-century ago," as "no garden of verses . . . but more like an overgrown clearing in the chaparral, with more burrs and thistles than flowers" (1991: 10–11). The theme of dispossession, with the resulting losses of social and political position and of rights as a member of society, emerged early in Paredes's poetry:

> *A cit'zen of Texas they say that he ees,*
> *But then, why they call him the Mexican Grease?*
> *Soft talk and hard action, he can't understan'.*
> *The Mexico-Texan he no gotta lan'*

(1935: "THE MEXICO-TEXAN")

As Paredes notes in the 1991 publication of this poem in *Between Two Worlds* (note 2), this poem is "perhaps the best known of [his] efforts at versifying" (139). He states that he originally composed this poem in the spring of 1934, "while walking the 21 blocks home from [high] school one afternoon," but eventually as a second, written version, it "became current in manuscript form in south Texas, was used in political campaigns, was reprinted a few times as anonymous, and entered oral tradition locally" (139).

Also printed in *Between Two Worlds* is another "story" of displacement where the destiny speaks to the persona created by this new situation. As Paredes's notes to the text indicate, the poem *"Alma pocha"* was written on occasion of the Texas Centennial celebrations. On this occasion, *La Prensa* of San Antonio, a Mexican American newspaper which had on occasion published Paredes's verses, "declined to print it" (p. 139, footnote 4). This story, told in verse, is about the defeated soul of the Mexicano who has suffered defending the toil of his people, *"el sudor derramado,"* and is now a stranger in his own land. He sees his father shot down, his brother lynched, and everything he once felt an important part of himself—the fields, the skies, the birds, and flowers—are now being enjoyed by the invading stranger. He is haunted always by a history that has made the name of Santa Anna the shame of every Mexican. Destiny's mouth is made despicable when it speaks of the Texas (Texan's) journey:

> Alma pocha
> ensangrentada,
> la sufrida,
> la olvidada,
> la rebelde sin espada;
> alma pocha
> salpicada
> de tragedia y humorada,
> alma pocha.
> En tu propio terruño serás extranjero
> por la ley del fusil y la ley del acero;
> y verás a tu padre morir balaceado
> por haber defendido el sudor derramado;
> verás a tu hermano colgado de un leño
> por el crimen mortal de haber sido trigueño.
> Y si vives, acaso, será sin orgullo,
> con recuerdos amargos de todo lo tuyo;
> tus campos, tus cielos, tus aves, tus flores
> serán el deleite de los invasores;
> para ellos su fruto dará la simiente
> donde fueras el amo serás el sirviente
> por la ley del fusil y la ley del acero.
> De este modo
> habló el destino
> en la jornada tejana
> ¡y la boca se envilece
> con el nombre de Santa Anna!
> Alma pocha
> vas llorando
> la verguenza mexicana.
> Alma pocha,
> alma noble y duradera,
> la que sufre,
> la que espera.

> 1936 (35–36)

[Soul of the pocho
the bloodied one,
that which has suffered
and been forgotten,
rebel without a sword;
soul of the pocho
splashed
with tragedy and tempered,
soul of the pocho.
In your own native soil you shall be a stranger
by the law of the gun and the blade;
and you shall see your father die, riddled with bullets
for having defended his poured out sweat;
you shall see your brother hanging from a tree branch
for the mortal crime of having been brown-skinned.
And if by chance you live it shall be without pride,
but with bitter memories of all that was yours;
your fields, your skies, your birds and flowers
shall be the delight of the invaders;
for them the seed will give its fruit;
where you would have been master, you shall be a servant
by the law of the gun and the blade.
In this way
did destiny speak
while on its Texas journey
and the mouth becomes despicable
with the name of Santa Anna!
Soul of the pocho
you go crying out
the Mexican shame.
Soul of the pocho
noble and lasting soul,
one that suffers,
one that waits.]

(MY TRANSLATION)

GEORGE WASHINGTON GÓMEZ,
A MEXICOTEXAN NOVEL

Paredes's poetry tells what Webb's history ignores—the economic, political, and cultural struggles forced upon Texas Mexicans. Paredes's *George Washington Gómez, A Mexicotexan Novel* more elaborately dramatizes these same issues, allowing us to view them more closely. The first chapter presents the Seditionist uprising and the period of strife into which the author himself was born. Paredes wrote the novel between 1936, when he had just graduated from junior college, and 1940, when World War II took him to the Far East, where he remained for ten years. While writing the novel, he was engaged in his studies, journalism and music. It remained in manuscript form until 1990, when it was published for the first time by Arte Público Press (University of Houston). Why the half-century hiatus? During his many talks to various audiences at the University of Texas at Austin, Paredes has spoken of the discouragement he experienced at the time as a Chicano writer; he received rapid rejections from publishers or simply negative reactions due to the protest component in his writings. Given this novel's treatment of the Texas Rangers and of folklorist J. Frank Dobie, Webb's colleague and ebullient ally, Paredes had little hope that this novel would ever be published. Still, well before his other writings were to become known, the unpublished *George Washington Gómez* had already responded extensively to the prevailing view of the Mexicano, at a time when transformation of the social and political order was still fresh.[6]

George Washington Gómez is set in early South Texas, and its narrative spans most of the first half of the twentieth century. The first chapter depicts the loss of Mexican-owned land to Anglo colonialists aided by the absolute "authority" of the Texas Rangers, or *rinches,* and the last stand of the *sediciosos* as well as their final defeat. With the loss of their property came the loss of Mexican autonomy. More specifically, Paredes shows how after the U.S.-Mexican War and especially after the failure of the *Plan de San Diego,* all Mexicanos were considered enemies of the state by the dominant culture; nonetheless, the novel effectively portrays the diversity that exists within that population of south Texas people who still call themselves Mexicanos.

Part 1 of the novel, "*Los Sediciosos*" (The Seditionists), shows the birth of the supposed "leader of his people," George Washington (Guálinto) Gómez, the death of his father, Gumersindo, at the hands of the *rinches,* and the promise made him by Feliciano García, Guálinto's uncle.[7] Not wanting his son to grow up with hatred in his heart, Gumersindo's dying wish is that Guálinto never be told how his father died. Feliciano reluctantly gives his word. This silence symbolically comes to represent the banishment of a history and with it Guálinto's true identity along with that of many other Mexican American children. Feliciano's silence also foretells the failure of the final Seditionist uprising, the flight of one of its leaders into Mexico, and even comes to symbolize the displacement and silent suffering of the oppressed.

Part 2 begins with Feliciano's arrival and new start in the city of Jonesville-on-the-Grande, in reality Brownsville, Texas. In Jonesville-on-the-Grande, amid Feliciano's struggles to gain economic security for his family, Paredes introduces a variety of characters from various social and economic classes and historical backgrounds within one distinctive South Texas Mexicano community. We meet the wealthy Osunas, Mexicano elite property owners who conveniently identify themselves as "Spanish"; a prosperous Mexican lawyer, López-Anguera; and Guálinto's teacher, Miss Cornelia, the only Mexican American school teacher. Along with Filomeno Menchaca, a professional killer until he is quite literally "fired," these are the professionals in the novel.

From the merchant class come the Rodríguezes, grocery store owners, as well as various neighbors of the Mexican community; lower on the social ladder is Juan, who helps Feliciano on his small farm, and Doña Tina, a barmaid. One of the most important figures in the Anglo community is Judge Norris, who runs the political machinery and helps Feliciano rise to a prominent position in his community; there are soldiers from Fort Brown, some vigilante/*rinche* types, the school administrators, and various social and economic class levels represented among the school children and teachers of both cultures.

Having secured safety and economic support for his family, Feliciano begins to learn to "work" the political and social system that surrounds him. He begins as a bartender at the *Danubio Azul* and soon makes himself very useful to Judge Norris, whose political advantage depends on getting the Mexican vote.

Part 3, "Dear Old Gringo School Days," shifts the focus to Guálinto's conflicts within the Anglo-dominated school system. As his struggles to accommodate himself come into closer view from the perspective of his Mexican world, the novel traverses time through the Great Depression years (Part 4, "*La Chilla*") up to his high-school graduation and ends at the onset of World War II. The last segment of the novel, Part 5, "Leader of His People," takes place in 1939 or 1940, one year before the United States officially entered the war. It depicts Guálinto's return to his community after a long absence; he has become a lawyer and is now a first lieutenant in the U.S. Army working in counter-intelligence. His job is to spy on the border Mexicans and to watch for sabotage and infiltration by German or Japanese agents.

The history Paredes's narrative provides becomes evident when the events he describes correlate perfectly with the historical accounts written later by revisionist historians such as David Montejano. When Feliciano discusses Gumersindo's murder with another character, it is explained away as having been the result of a so-called attempted escape: "It was the city judge, without a doubt, you remember how it happened to Muñiz. The judge signs a paper authorizing the rinches to take the prisoner from San Pedrito to the Jonesville jail. Two miles is about as far as they go" (23).

In this novel, as in Paredes's early works, we see the end result for many Mexicanos in Texas whose choices became limited with Anglo occupation. But in ideological terms, once the constant vigilance of the *rinches* or the Army is no longer necessary for maintaining the new social order, institutions take their place to guarantee the continuance of a system of domination. For this system of domination to be upheld and perpetuate itself, labor power must be ensured. That labor power is supplied by the now subjugated Mexican with his "submission to the rules of the established order" which in turn "provide[s] for the domination of the ruling class 'in words'" (Althusser 1969/1971: 132–133). As Althusser has also noted, "it is not enough to ensure for labour power the material conditions of its reproduction if it is to be reproduced as labour power" (1969/1971: 131). In other words, if one draws upon Lacanian theory of the subject and his "imagined relationship to the real conditions of his existence," here, ideology imposes illusion. Althusser believes that the way we imagine our relationship to the real conditions of our existence in fact *becomes reality* for us, because that is the reality by which we live, whether it be true or not. Through this analysis, Althusser makes more evident the coexistence of competing truths. He goes on to point out how material conditions for labor alone are not sufficient. In other words, the people and machinery and the skills are not all that is necessary in order for labor power to perpetuate itself and uphold the conditions of the surrounding world. The labor power not only has to be "skilled," possess the know-how, but also to possess (in this case) the "acquired" attitudes to (this kind of) work, that which is already scripted for it. Given the history of the Texas Mexicans, dispossessed of a land they once owned, forced into servile, humiliating roles to survive, this "acquired" attitude becomes all important. How would the proper attitudes toward work and this new place in the labor force be acquired, and, more importantly, how would they be reproduced?

A transformation occurs within the novel in the hierarchical external social, political, and economic relationships, and also in the minds of the Texas Mexicans who acquire attitudes that facilitate their functioning subordinately as members within the more powerful, dominant, Anglo community. However true Paredes's novel is to existing conditions, within this region of South Texas there existed from county to county, and even from town to town in some cases, different degrees of Anglo control and dominance. What relationship this variation of control had to illiteracy (in most cases, a term synonymous with formal education) has been well documented.[8]

In some towns, however, the Mexicans had a relative advantage. Brownsville, for example, was never really segregated. In fact, to some extent and due partially to different class systems, Mexicanos have always exercised a degree of input in the political systems, as Paredes shows in his novel. During various conversations with the author, he has referred to an incident in the Port of Brownsville which dramatically points to the distinctions emphasized by either class or race among some South Texas Mexicano communities. He tells of an incident in which a businessman from "somewhere in the South" established a road house/beer joint but refused to serve Mexicans. As a result, a group of middle-class Mexicans "trashed the place. The owner got the message and left town." Also because of class distinctions, the Raza Unida party activists were later not successful in gaining support in some of these Valley towns. As Paredes points out, Brownsville's already well-established middle class defined them as *pelados,* low-class Mexicans, who were up to no good. Yet discrimination strictly on the basis of being Mexican, in other words on the basis of race, would not be tolerated (personal interview, March 4, 1995).

On the other hand, in neighboring Harlingen (Harlanburg in the novel), a business owner could get away with racial discrimination because Harlingen was strictly segregated for many generations. In fact, to this day it is generally considered an Anglo town. In the novel we see an example of this segregation when Guálinto and three other Mexican high school seniors, the only Mexicans in their class, are refused entrance into "La Casa Mexicana," a nightclub in Harlanburg where the class celebrates its graduation. The novel depicts in striking ways the struggles of the Mexicano/a to regain some socioeconomic position through education and the reacquisition of property, as is the case with Feliciano. Meantime, Feliciano's nephew, Guálinto, and his two nieces have begun their education in a public school system set up to ensure Anglo domination.

The transition whereby the repressive state apparatus is replaced by an ideological one (Althusser's ISA) is described in minute detail in Paredes's account of an educational system established in South Texas which remained intact for many generations. What this novel also shows, with crystalline clarity, is the process by which a whole new class of subordinates (with proper attitudes secured) came to be shaped, if not by policy, then by a design that works by random selection. *George Washington Gómez* is a fictionalized yet nonfictitious narratization of this process. According to Althusser's analysis, without production, the ruling class ideology has nothing over which to rule. His ISA essay posits a necessary condition of production—"the reproduction of the conditions of production." Althusser points to what Marx had already stated, that "every child knows that a social formation which did not reproduce the conditions of production at the same time as it produced would not last a year. The ultimate condition of production is therefore the reproduction of the conditions of production" (1969/1971: 127). In other words, the labor force must be continually reproduced along with the proper attitudes and know-how. Children of laborers climbing out of that social status to become part of the dominating class (those who operate either the ideological or the repressive state apparatuses) would not be beneficial in a land so rich in production potential but so short on labor force.

If we look at the educational system described in *George Washington Gómez,* we see a state institution which systematically serves to secure the established hierarchical system set in place by a ruling class and by that class's reproduction of its conditions of production, its "Labour Power" (Althusser 1969/1971: 130). The ruling class ideology is reflected in the hierarchical system, with Texas Mexicans continuing to occupy, for the most part, the lower stratum both ideologically (in their minds) and externally as cheap labor in the visible socioeconomic nexus. Other significant factors perpetuated a hierarchical class system. Mexican Americans increasingly constituted the lower stratum while Anglos made up the higher classes.[9] Regardless of whether he once was a *ranchero* landowner, of the merchant class, or a peon, the Texas Mexican, displaced as he was, would oftentimes have little choice but to join the laboring class.

The Texas school system Paredes describes in Part 3, "Dear Old Gringo School Days," is not fiction. This system is described as it operated during Paredes's upbringing and as it remained long after the desegregation law of 1954 was passed. Mexicanos were not expected to go beyond the sixth grade, and in many communities of Texas they were not allowed to do so. As one real-life example, Sapopita Dávila de Aguirre (1919–1984) during the early forties challenged the Luling school district's policy of not allowing Texas Mexican children to go beyond the sixth grade. With the full support of her parents and family, she asked the principal of the high school to allow her to attend the all-Anglo school despite segregation. After several meetings took place to discuss the matter, the principal's answer according to her brother was that "they couldn't build a high school for just one Mexican"; therefore, she would have to attend the Anglo high school. Other Mexicanos and Mexicanas soon followed. Aguirre became the first Mexicana to graduate from Luling High School (personal interview with Mike Dávila, February 1995).[10]

Another real-life example of the discouragement faced by Mexicanos in the Southwest is perhaps best provided by the author himself. On the occasion of a talk he gave at Southwest Texas State University in San Marcos, on March 24, 1994, Paredes remarked on some of his own experiences in his struggle to further his education:

> It was in 1936 that I graduated from junior college in my hometown of Brownsville, Texas. We were a sizable graduating class. And we made history, I think. Three of us were of Mexican descent.
>
> We three had great dreams, dreams which were not realized. One of us wanted to be an engineer, another a CPA. My dreams were the wildest of all. I wanted to get a Ph.D. and teach at a university. I said as much to my English teacher, when she asked me what I intended to do after graduation. She told me, "Mr. Paredes, you have a facility with words. Why don't you apply for a position with the local newspaper?"
>
> Many years later, I read about a Black activist (Malcolm X, I believe), who became a radical after one of his teachers squelched his ambition to be a lawyer by telling him that such a career was not for people like him. I have a pretty good idea how he felt.

My teacher's remarks did not make a radical out of me. I already
was one, according to the standards of the time, at least. But her
words left a thorn in my side, so to speak. And when, twenty years
later, I did get a doctorate, it gave me some satisfaction that I obtained
it in English. But Miss Hyman (that was her name) was a good
prophet. Or employment adviser, if you will. After graduation I
drove a truck for a few months, and then I got a better job—with
the local newspaper.

The years have given me a different perspective on Miss Hyman.
Perhaps she was not discouraging or belittling me. She may have been
advising me to be realistic, to look at the world as it really was. In
1936 we were still in the depths of the Great Depression. Jobs were
hard to come by. Only through a series of minor but lucky happen-
stances had I been able to attend junior college. There were no scholarships in those days for "Latins," as we were called. Even in the
1950's, when I came to U.T., there were no scholarships for which
Texas Mexicans were eligible. On the other hand, by the time I
finished junior college, I already had some newspaper experience. So
it appears that in 1936 college was not for people like me, while newspaper work was.

Another form of discouragement was strongly present in the job force.
Though Brownsville was not a segregated town, Paredes recalls how as a
cub reporter working for the *Brownsville Herald* he earned $10.00 a week,
and later as a proofreader he earned $11.40 a week proofreading in both
Spanish and English. Yet an Anglo woman during this same period of time
earned $35.00 a week. "It was thought that Mexicans needed less money to
live on" (personal interview, March 4, 1995).

Despite these real-life examples, it is through his "fiction" that Paredes writes a history. His artistic depictions, inspired by his own real-life
struggles and those of others like him, directly answer Webb's claims that
a culturally specific, Anglo pioneer hero struggled on the harsh terrain of
the Great Plains. Showing how the Anglo's "survival" or overcoming of
"obstacles" caused a diversity of parallel and multileveled struggles, Paredes reveals the costs of their "success," costs borne by a conquered and
colonized population of people whose presence preceded that of the "American" pioneer of the West. The novel thus becomes just as "real" in a scientific, historical sense as Webb's mythopoetic history. Paredes openly voices
his own set of biases, but in so doing, he adds dimension to a flattened

picture by recalling and thus constructing the history of his own people's struggles.

Analyzing *George Washington Gómez* in this way requires that the reader be able to contrast some of the fictional Texas Mexican characters in order to note their varied and diverse perspectives regarding the new and changing Anglo colonial world surrounding them. Unlike histories written about and for the victors, which for the most part set up one cultural unit in conflict with another, Paredes's fiction captures the variety of characters and their responses to the new social and political order.

From the start, two characters are strikingly different in their view of their relationship to the Anglo American society—Gumersindo, Guálinto's father, and Feliciano, the uncle who helps raise him after Gumersindo is murdered. Feliciano's view of the Anglo as invader and enemy sharply contrasts with Gumersindo's view of him as benefactor. Well-meaning Anglos like Doc Berry at this point in time are more likely to see Gumersindo as a "good Mexican" as he describes him to a ranger: "'He's a good Mexican,' Doc said. 'I can vouch for him.' 'He's okay if you say so, Doc,' MacDougal answered. 'But it's getting kinda hard these days to tell the good ones from the bad ones. Can't take any chances these days. But he's all right if you say so.'" (12). Gumersindo finds it difficult to agree with Feliciano's resentment of the Anglo. He is a visitor/opportunist on the "gringo's land," as he explains to Feliciano when he says, "After all, it's their country" (20). As a result of this perspective he is willing and able to *hacerse al ambiente,* mold himself according to his surroundings in order to gain from it and its inherent systems an economic advantage. Gumersindo feels safe knowing that the Anglos distinguish him from the others when they identify him as a "good Mexican."

Feliciano, on the other hand, knows Gumersindo's view to be false and naive. He is well aware that a Mexican is a Mexican as far as the Anglo is concerned, and that Gumersindo is in as much danger as any of the rest of them. His light complexion notwithstanding, Gumersindo is subject to dispossession of his property, a violation of his rights; moreover, he could be murdered by the Texas Rangers or by vigilante groups posing as authorities, just like any other Mexican. When the Rangers learn that his brother-in-law is Lupe, a seditionist leader, Gumersindo is arrested, questioned, and in an apparent attempt to escape, is shot: "Two miles is about as far as they go" (23). The order had been given for an execution that would be disguised as an escape attempt. The very word "Mexican," as Paredes describes the situation, had became such "a symbol of hatred and loathing that to most Anglotexans it had become a hateful and loathsome word" (118). Had Gumersindo not been of the working class, he might have saved himself a lot of trouble by identifying himself as "Spanish" instead of Mexican or by being more complicit with the Anglo establishing order, as did the upper-class, propertied family, the Osunas, whom we meet later in the narrative. Through Gumersindo, Paredes shows us divisions within the Mexicano working class, further complicating Webb's better-known images.

Feliciano, on the other hand, represents Mexicanos who formed part of the resistance, either overtly or by maintaining their identity and culture despite the hostile surroundings. After the defeat of the *sediciosos,* Feliciano must go to great lengths to maintain even inner resistance, making accommodations to preserve his life and that of his family. At the close of Part 1, a once proud, independent *ranchero,* and a member of the resistance, has taken on the *persona* of a humble peasant farmer in order to hide his past but also because that is the status to which he is indeed reduced (32). Once he has arrived at Jonesville-on-the-Grande, tending a bar at the *Danubio Azul,* Feliciano finds it difficult to accommodate to the lightheartedness with which he must serve the Anglo soldiers. As far as he is concerned, it is their job "to shoot people like [him]" (43).

Despite the difficulties of his new class identity, Feliciano can at least superficially and momentarily humble himself in this external world for the sake of the security and future of his family. On the other hand, his determination to use cash rather than credit to purchase a good part of his "Place," the house and land that he eventually fully possesses, negotiates some of the outer humility that he must, for convention's sake, display. In this way, Feliciano manages to maintain his dignity as he gradually incorporates himself into the capitalist system and learns to manipulate it for his own sake. Aided by Judge Norris, his mother's savings, and his political imagination and cultural know-how, Feliciano combines the old and the new to achieve his success. So successful is Feliciano that the humble peasant farmer who presented himself at Jonesville-on-the-Grande six years earlier is recognized as "Don Feliciano," the impressive figure wearing a suit, shiny boots, and a Stetson hat, when he registers Guálinto for school (108–109).

Paredes's sense of the social historicity of the individual imbues his narrative with its historical texture as a scene of structural transformations and emergent events develops. Feliciano's life becomes an exercise in forming new relationships with a new ruling ideology. He thus learns to manipulate the system for his own benefit and perhaps even to wear a different public face in order to fulfill hopes dreamed long before the Anglo occupation. In so doing, he adopts Gumersindo's dream of a new land. Fulfilling that dream requires money, education, hard work, and cunning:

> Feliciano endeavored to make as much money as he could, by all means possible, in order *to realize Gumersindo's dream* because he knew that dreams are more likely to come true if one has money. There were many factors in Feliciano's increasing prosperity—hard work, luck, Judge Norris and the Blue Party, Santos de la Vega. *That and his mother's fierce determination to regain for her children something of what had been lost to her grandparents when the Gringos came.* Her parents had only dim memories of their own as to what life was like before the Delta became part of Texas, but they passed their parents' memories down to her generation. That was why her children had learned to read, write and figure at the escuelita in San Pedrito and why *she had saved what little money she could throughout her life, a nickel or a quarter at a time.* (155, my emphasis)

Feliciano eventually reestablishes relative autonomy with a place for himself. He owns once again a bit of land that he can work and by which he can help his nephew continue his education. Apart from his disappointment with Guálinto (which will be discussed later in this chapter), *his* is a happy story. This second part of his life is indeed an American success story. Like Webb's pioneers, Feliciano adapts, not to a new and difficult terrain, but to the new ruling order over his homeland. It is important, however, to note that Feliciano's outlook is different from the start. In effect, despite his adaptations, Feliciano is not a product of this new ruling ideology.

Feliciano's view of the world and his imagined relationship to that world had been fully formed before full transition of power was complete, before defeat was accepted. Shrewd enough to compromise just enough to manipulate this new system to his advantage, Feliciano consciously draws from both worlds. Now an owner of his own grocery store, Feliciano, out of necessity, develops the fluidity with which to move in and out of two worlds. Shortly before the Great Depression in the United States, but after the Revolution in Mexico, he takes advantage of his connection with Mexico through an old friend of the Seditionist Movement, *El Negro,* who had fled to Mexico to save himself from the "rinches." Having served the Mexican Revolution, *El Negro* reappears as Don Santos de la Vega, a member of the newly formed, "respectable" establishment. Feliciano enters into a profitable business arrangement with him, smuggling U.S. goods into Mexico. In Mexico he makes use of de la Vega's political clout, while in the United States he capitalizes on, but never completely trusts, this new world that surrounds him. In order to establish credit, he does as Judge Norris recommends and puts money in the gringo banks, but he reserves all that he can outside that system of credit. *El Negro* advises him:

> "Whatever you make, change it into gold coins and put them away. Gold and land, they're the only things that stay with you, the only real wealth in the world."
> "That also is my thinking, but I had to put money in the bank, open an account as they call it, so I could borrow money to lease El Danubio Azul and stock the store. I'm sunk in debt up to my ears right now, but I'm paying it back."
> "Did you put all your money in the bank?"
> "No I kept out what I could."
> "I didn't think you would risk it all in a Gringo bank." (81)

Having saved some money, as his mother also had, in the traditional Mexican way, "La Chilla," the Great Depression Paredes describes in Part 4, does not drive him into total bankruptcy as it did so many others whose single world knowledge became their trap. Notwithstanding Feliciano's "success," it is the exception rather than the norm.

A few other characters reveal the diversity of outcomes resulting from the transition to Anglo-dominated society. Some are universal types who for some reason or other have fallen into patterns of behavior reflecting both stereotyped images and actual attitudes. "El Colorado" is one of Guálinto's schoolmates, and he is significant for the contrast he presents to Guálinto in his own struggles to obtain an education. Whereas Guálinto, as presumed leader of his people, has extensive family support, "El Colorado's" father returns home at night often drunk and beats his wife and children. His way of life and his relationship with his wife manifest a pessimistic worldview reflected in the recurrent themes of some of the old Mexican songs and stories with which, as a musicologist, Paredes was familiar. An example is a song that is still very popular in its endless renditions and new interpretations into the popular *Tejano* music danced to today. As if in celebration, the song throws to the wind all day-to-day concerns about securing a living and some material gain or stability:

> *El día que yo me muera, no voy a llevarme nada.*
> *Hay que darle gusto al gusto, La vida pronto se acaba . . .*
> *Lo que pasó en este mundo, nomás el recuerdo queda . . .*
> *Ya muerto, voy a llevarme nomás un puño de tierra . . .*
> *("El Camino a Comila" or "Un puño de tierra")*

> *[The day that I die, I won't be taking anything with me.*
> *One must give to pleasures all that one has;*
> *life comes to an end very quickly . . .*
> *Whatever happened in this world, only the memory remains . . .*
> *Once dead, all I will be taking with me is a handful of dirt . . .]*

(MY TRANSLATION)

The popularity of this recurring theme to this day among Chicanos could be explained as the voice of the dispossessed expressing the futility of resisting colonization. The song could still be said to voice refusal and rejection of a new, imposed ideology with no real positive alternative in sight. It represents an almost ironic sense of defeat, yet not total submission. The *persona* steps outside the systems of political and social control into the realm of the metaphysical world to resist all institutions of this world that would trap the spirit. As an unfortunate "alternative form of consciousness," this attitude characterizes those who *se han hechado a la perdición,* those who find themselves permanently excluded from any opportunities for a better life, such as Feliciano's. Shunning materialism, they give themselves over to a life of perdition.

Paredes's depiction of "El Colorado's" father's attitude toward a life without hope links the suppression of the South Texas rebellion with its far-reaching effects. This dramatization of the creation and existence of a particular "unconscious" is a direct contradiction to the American dream mythology that Webb's work promotes. Whatever Paredes's biases may be, his fiction is "truer" than some other forms of history; making no pretensions to objectivity, it is thus free to be emotionally and imaginatively true. The question of "authorial perspective" must also be taken into account. First of all, in the novel a reader allows for the portrayal of life to develop according to the author's and/or characters' perspectives. Secondly, the historians' portrayal makes a truth claim (as if it enjoyed objective validity transcending the fictional perspectives); yet in effect, once the reader has seen through Webb's rhetorical strategies, his portrayal is seen to be partial, whereas the fiction of other voices, variable perspectives, in the novel, imparts a stronger sense that the conditions described are described truly.

Paredes's novel, through its narrative, places before our eyes three prominent issues: the issues of property, labor, and education as well as the resulting gender and class relations. The novel foregrounds the public educational system, as a state apparatus that can actually obstruct the Mexicanos' attempts to reclaim their place, showing how, in Althusserian terms, "the ideology of the ruling class does not become the ruling ideology by the grace of God, nor even by virtue of the seizure of State power alone, [but] by the installation of the Ideological State Apparatuses" (1969/1971: 185). The ISA creates this "unconscious" and then utilizes it to perpetuate a class of people who, unlike Feliciano, do not aspire to a better life. This demotivation is due to the imagined relationship subjugated selves have to the real conditions of their existence, that is, to a society that will always marginalize them, one that will give them some hope within the framework of their usefulness as laborers, only to stomp them back into their place should they aspire to more—or, what is worse, wear out their usefulness. The novel narrates *how* this has occurred and how none of it has come about simply "by the grace of God." The ruling class ideology that feigns freedom and opportunity for all, yet keeps certain classes of people "in their place" is a phenomenon that can be seen taking place in the novel during the very time of transition to a new social and economic order.

Althusser effectively defines the unconscious as it exists in all humans as an effect of the humanization of a biological creature that has survived the process: Though "some [of these humans], the majority, have emerged more or less unscathed—or at least, give this out to be the case; many of these veterans bear the marks throughout their lives; some will die from the fight" (1964/1971: 205). This unconscious factor becomes significant for an interpretation of Paredes's narratives of protest, for, as Stuart Hall points out, we can now "put on the agenda the whole neglected issue of how ideology becomes internalized, how we come to speak 'spontaneously,' within the limits of the categories of thought which exist outside us and which can more accurately be said to think us" (1986: 31). Characters such as "El Colorado's" father are definitely not among the Althusserian survivors; nevertheless, they do function in a limited way with an internalized ideology. They have internalized a sense of worthlessness, and life is worthless for them as long as there is no point to their resistance and no positive outlet separate from that which is under the control of the ruling ideology. From another stand-point, he is merely a drunk and an abuser.

Yet characters such as Guálinto, who in the end would seem to have achieved great success within the United States via its public education system, have "survived" at the cost of their identity. Though Guálinto is in many ways diametrically opposed to characters such as "El Colorado's" fa-ther, he is not among the majority who have emerged "unscathed"; eventu-ally, as an interpellated subject, he comes to speak "spontaneously," within limits taught to him and maintained by the Ideological State Apparatus. Just as Althusser's study of psychoanalytic processes becomes relevant to the un-derstanding of how state institutions work to inscribe themselves upon their subjects, Paredes describes a parallel process taking place in a specific com-munity; he illuminates how present-day ideological systems work to social-ize their subjects. Several characters, events, and community institutions contribute to Guálinto's socialization.

The Rodríguez family are store owners who employ the adolescent Guálinto during the Depression years. They capitalize on the misfortunes of others, paying low wages and selling overpriced goods. Exploiting their own community, these Texas Mexicans of the merchant class have what Paredes describes as a dual personality. Survival takes various forms during the Depression years, with the "people divided into two categories: poor Mexicans and rich Spaniards. So while rich Negroes often help poor Ne-groes and rich Jews help poor Jews, the Texas Mexican has to shift for him-self" (195–196).

Paredes's narrative shows that all these possibilities exist as a result of ef-forts of the displaced Texas Mexicans to reestablish themselves, to make for themselves a place in this newly formed socioeconomic environment. In-cluded are the actual casualties in this "war humanity pretends it has never declared" (Althusser 1964/1971: 205). In Part 2, Filomeno Menchaca is mur-dered in front of Guálinto's eyes. The subsequent "investigation" into the murder makes apparent that this is a police execution:

> Meno looked up the street where two men were walking toward them. "Some friends of mine," he said and moved down along the fence to meet them at the gate. "*Qui'ubo, muchachos,*" he said with a grin.
>
> One of the pair smiled a frank, engaging smile. "Nothing new, Filomeno. How's things with you?" Still smiling he pulled a gun from under his coat and fired. (55)

Filomeno Menchaca had become a marked man and his murder was sanctioned by the law: when the Anglo authorities arrive, they allow the men who killed him, still "in plain sight," to walk away, to the dismay of the bystanders:

> "Don't touch him," the old man said. "We must leave everything as it is for the law. You over there, don't kick up the dirt. The law won't like it if you rub out any signs. . . ."
>
> The young man with the pad and pencil pointed at the two men in the distance. The policemen glanced idly in that direction and turned to enter the gate. Again the young one pointed, and he said something Guálinto did not understand. The older of the other two answered, and he sounded annoyed. By now the crowd had begun to gather around the policemen. The faces were animated, expectant. Even professional killers can be likable, and Filomeno Menchaca had many friends in the "barrio." With a kind of repressed excitement the crowd glanced now at the officers, now at the distant figures. Men began telling each other just loud enough so the law could hear, "*Esos son*. That's them. They can still catch them." The killers were growing smaller and smaller in the distance. (57)

Filomeno Menchaca, though a known killer, had been allowed to live comfortably within his community as long as he was useful and until he transgressed the bounds set for him. Having become a liability for the bosses, he is murdered with impunity and in broad daylight for everyone to see. Such execution-style murders have their role in a subjugated society. A few Filomeno Menchacas now and then are made examples for the benefit of other possible transgressors. But the other message that comes across even more offensively to those who place faith in the system by which they sincerely try to abide and make a livelihood is that the law does not exist for "their" protection. The law can be altered depending on the circumstances and depending on *whose* civil rights have been violated.

Paredes thus not only recreates for us a police execution but also dramatizes the breaking down of a community's faith in "justice for all" when its members witness the selective enforcement of the law. The murderers "get away." At the same time, Menchaca's murder provides for the perpetuation of this oppressive system. It provides a useful opportunity to teach the younger Anglo lawman how the system works for them and that he is better off just going along with it:

The elder of the two policemen was annoyed. It was more than apparent in his voice when he addressed the young man. The young man talked back and the policeman spoke sharply and with finality. Then he turned to the crowd, *"Vamoose,"* he shouted. *"Vamoose pa' la casa."*

The law opened the gate and walked in while the crowd dispersed slowly and with many backward looks. Little groups of three or four straggled off in different directions, muttering and glancing at the officers and at the empty distance into which the two killers had disappeared. Angry accusing looks were directed at the men of the law, who either did not notice them or did not care. After the crowd was gone they just stood around. They did not look for signs or anything like the old man had said they would. They just looked at the body. The oldest stepped over and stirred the body with the toe of his boot. He gave it a little kick and said something which made the red-faced one laugh. *The young one did not laugh.* After a while they moved away from the body and started talking to each other. They passed cigarettes around and smoked. *Even the young one was laughing by this time.* (57–58, my emphasis)

Guálinto witnesses at a young age the swift "justice" applied to transgressors, but with no historical contextualization from which to draw conclusions, his process of finding a "place" in this society, his reeducation within it, is more complicated than Feliciano's. With the transition in the social order complete, Guálinto will be a product of that new order. Ignorant of the circumstances of his father's death and unaware of Feliciano's resistance days, he has no reason to question institutions of this society, the only one he will experience. In his unconscious, within his own psychological or imagined relationship to the real conditions of his existence, his is a divided self. While he passionately challenges the negative way in which his teachers present the Texas Mexican's role in Texas history, he is in love with learning. Because of his light complexion, he could "pass" for "Spanish" instead of Mexican at the door of *La Casa Mexicana* in Harlanburg, where his senior class has planned its graduation celebration. Yet he still refuses the admittance offered to him because his three more obviously Mexican classmates are refused entrance.

Guálinto's conflicting selves present themselves throughout his formative years and continue to haunt his subconscious even as an adult. As a child, his occasional daydreams and the old men's stories he listens to at night on his front porch provide only momentary departures from what constitutes the "real" world around him. Regardless of how he perceives his fit into that world, into the hierarchical system that surrounds him, the questions set before us by the dramatization of Guálinto's character formation concern the reeducation of a newly formed culturally specific people—the Mexican Americans. This reeducation for the most part takes place in the schools Guálinto attends.

Paredes devotes a large portion of the narrative to describing Guálinto's "education" and to tying its significance to the conditions, struggles, and formation of his characters. The Anglo-dominated world is the only one Guálinto will aspire to be included in as a full member and participant. He is thus a product of that world and its institutions, yet he attends its public school with the ideas and expectations of education shaped by his culture and class identity, what his parents and grandparents meant by "education." The meaning of *preparación* for Guálinto is tied to the elevated Old World ideal associated with people of worth and promise. It is also the only means by which to regain that place for himself and others like him. That is why his grandmother had believed it important for her children to learn "to read, write and figure at the *escuelita* in San Pedrito [as well as save] what little money she could throughout her life" (155). So significant is the education of the man of the family and future leader of his people that it is Feliciano and not María who registers Guálinto for school: "But Guálinto was a boy and Feliciano decided he should be registered by a man. . . . [María] prepared her son for his long-awaited first step on the road to an education, which would make him a great man some day" (107).

The narrative offers an example of the prestige enjoyed by educated persons through the community's reaction to *el Licenciado,* Santiago López-Anguera. Although in this case the *Licenciado* happens to be the only person in the neighborhood who owns an automobile, being "educated" in this Old World sense does not require the material gain education is expected to bring in capitalist systems. In other words, a *persona bien preparada* in the traditional Mexican culture signifies a privileged status merely because of the value placed on learning, not necessarily because of any material gains that may come from that education commodified. The difference between consciousness and material fetishes begins to present conflicts for Guálinto, who learns to associate "things" with the privilege enjoyed by the non-Mexicans of his society. The conflicting relational selves are created in the schoolroom environment and grow within him as he approaches puberty, caught between two worlds and two identities, "hating the Gringo one moment with an unreasoning hatred, admiring his literature, his music, his material goods the next. Loving the Mexican with a blind fierceness, then almost despising him for his slow progress in the world" (150).

The status enjoyed in the inner society of the school by his first love, MaElena, daughter of the wealthy Osuna family, for instance, has very little to do with her intelligence or education. Her family has property as well as *cuartos,* some miserable rooms they rent to the very poorest of the Mexicanos whose helplessness they exploit. Increasingly conscious of his relative poverty, Guálinto, through his education, becomes ashamed of the home which Feliciano views with pride. As he is dropped off by his friends, Guálinto walks past his home to avoid letting MaElena know where he lives, just as Feliciano sits on the porch, content and even proud of his progress and the material signs of his prosperity: "Once he had lived in what in retrospect seemed unbelievable poverty. Now he felt well-to-do, if not rich. He had read by the light of a candle, whenever he was not too tired to read at all. His nephew had his own little room with a study table and an electric light" (156). Feliciano's former poverty had not excluded learning altogether, but Guálinto's formal learning makes him ashamed of his (relative) poverty. Feliciano's pride, as opposed to his nephew's shame and the horror he sees in Guálinto's face at the prospect of his peddling fruit during *La Chilla,* make Feliciano aware that while his nephew has been acquiring an "education," he has also been learning a new set of values. "They have been teaching you strange things in that Gringo school. Honest work is not shameful, even peddling in the street," Feliciano says to Guálinto when he realizes "all" that the school system has taught his nephew (192). For Guálinto, honest work is no longer in itself honorable if the material gain is not immediately apparent. Guálinto's learning has brought the value systems of his conflicting worlds into sharp contrast with one another, and he begins to feel the pressure to alter his identity for the sake of the dominant culture's standards.

As a child, Guálinto, the presumed "leader of his people" and favored son for whom this "education" is essential, is not equipped to withstand the socializing forces disguised as education, those forces that denigrate rather than validate the learning he brings to the school from his family and community. These forces are diametrically opposed to their ostensible purpose, to what Guálinto has gone to school expecting. The day of his initial school registration, "his mind was already forming scenes in the unknown setting of Miss Cornelia's classroom, scenes where Guálinto was the central figure while Miss Cornelia looked on approvingly" (111). The reality for him and for many other children of the Texas Mexicans turns out quite otherwise. His exaggerated expectations make his disappointment in the face of repeated punishment, and real humiliations he suffers at the hands of the cruel and sadistic Miss Cornelia, that much more traumatic to his identity. The workings of this particular ISA negatively shape his "imagined relationship to the real conditions of his existence." He and others like him are labeled as the "lower" ones when they are placed in low first and second grade. In Guálinto's case, this objective constraint is made more pronounced in his subjective experience because he is quick to learn, a person of superior intelligence, and has a "white" exterior.[11] Guálinto is more vulnerable than his uncle not only because of his youth but also because he cannot understand, as Feliciano does, the social, economic, and political world in which he moves. Unlike Feliciano, he is not yet equipped to work with or even around the dominant culture without trading precious values in exchange for success.

Significant is Guálinto's ignorance of the circumstances of his father's death. His formal education has not taught him how to deal with false representation. In contrast, Feliciano has been aware of it from the very beginning of Anglo colonization as he had lived it and come to know of it through his mother's own retelling of history. Guálinto has had only inklings of how an oppressive system works, as when he witnesses the Menchaca murder, which according to some was due to the fact that the victim "knew too much about a lot of things" (53). Guálinto cannot see the connection between his discouragement in primary school, his penalty for knowing more than a good Mexican should, and Menchaca's murder. Being a child, he cannot see that the disqualification of the learning he brings from his family and community (as when Miss Cornelia humiliates him for including the letters from the Spanish alphabet in one of his first writing assignments) is part and parcel of the subjugation of his "self," and in fact represents the reeducation of the colonized mind as near as it may be to that in a democratic system. Never does it enter his head that the educational system to which he entrusts himself is a key to leadership primarily for others, not for those like himself who are designated to be left behind in order to "reproduce the existing relations of production" (Althusser 1969/1971: 128).[12]

Guálinto emerges out of public school with a self-image that is confused and contradictory. Negative effects on the children's self-image result from the "not-quite-so-natural selection" (117) to which Paredes ironically refers: "In larger communities Mexican children were offered an English-language education in elementary schools built especially for them—separate but unequal" (116). The narrative describes the results of the special arrangements made to accommodate the Mexican children in offering them the education they are entitled to under a democratic state: "So the double-class arrangement seemed the only alternative. At all events, more than half of the low-firsters dropped out after their first year of school and considerably less than half of the second graders made it into the third grade. It was a process of not-quite-so-natural selection, and it did wonders for the school budget" (117).

With this attack on social Darwinism Américo Paredes opens our eyes to both the surface and internal effects of a school system that still exists and continues to perpetuate itself. Paredes strikes a central nerve, still raw, so that his "fiction" articulates a still prevalent paradigm.[13] If the Texas-Mexican cannot adapt to the new social order as Webb's pioneers did to their new and harsh environment, they are simply not fit for survival.

> The Mexicotexan knows about the Alamo, he is reminded of it often enough. Texas history is a cross that he must bear. In the written tests, if he expects to pass the course, he must put down in writing what he violently misbelieves. And often certain passages in the history text-book become subjects of discussion.
> "Isn't it horrible what the Mexicans did at the Alamo and Goliad?"
> "Why are they so treacherous and bloody? And cowards too."
> (149)

Although like Guálinto, many children of the Texas Mexicans did not go to school expecting their teachers or the process of learning to be instruments of their people's oppression, it is easy to see from Guálinto's ill treatment how his teacher and the school system that condones her treatment of the "Latin children" could become the primary oppressors in these children's lives. Even though Guálinto is from the start considered exceptional, his destiny anticipated by his family's expectations, his "place" within the class-structured modes of production already awaits. His "not-quite-so-natural" destiny is prescribed by this system which disguises itself as "opportunity." The system teaches him to feel inferior and know "his place." The newer the experience, the more painful it is; the greater the illusion of something better, the greater the disillusion. Once that "ruling ideology" is thoroughly inscribed in the minds of Guálinto and his schoolmates (133), their submission to the rules of the established order, a reproduction of workers' submission to that ruling ideology, is inevitable. With this accomplished, labor power and proper attitudes are assured, for as Althusser points out, "it is in the forms and under the forms of ideological subjugation that provision is made for the reproduction of the skills of labour power" (133). For Guálinto and others like him whose aspirations exceed family and cultural loyalties, the only escape comes in the choice to shed their former identity as Mexicanos, in touch with their traditions, language, cultural values, and, most importantly, their sense of their past— *their* history.

The way the system "works" is reflected in the fact that of all the Mexicano children who began school as Guálinto did, only four remain in the senior class (not counting MaElena Osuna, as she is "Spanish"). Guálinto's "survival" has both privileged him and segregated him from those for whom he would be a leader. His survival has made it a necessary condition that he adopt some of the attitudes of the oppressor already much a part of him. As an interpellated self, it is that much more difficult for him to oppose the dominant views already fixed within him.

By the time of his graduation, as Guálinto is about to receive the grand prize, the multiprismatic characteristics of his personality are already very much diminished, foreshadowing what Guálinto will become by the novel's end. He has succeeded in earning his high school diploma, but at a high cost and thanks to advantages many Mexicanos are unlikely to possess. His family's perception of him as a presumed leader has much to do with his success in school, but he is shamed because of his culture and family. Guálinto is glad his mother and uncle have not embarrassed him by attending his graduation, for the schoolbooks have taught him how parents should look and act, and his own do not match the image. Finally, he must listen, though he does so with contempt, to the acclaimed "historian" (in reality, J. Frank Dobie) who makes disparaging remarks about his people. In this way, the prize he has worked so hard to achieve becomes loaded with equivocation. How Guálinto comes to see himself in relation to his people is predicable and explains the "surprise" ending of the novel. He has earned what the world around him prescribes as a condition to "success," but that winning comes at the high cost of his sometimes feigned, sometimes sincere acceptance of his "imagined relationship to the real conditions of his existence," which in the end signifies a symbolic betrayal of his people. Paredes's narrative responds with its complexity of characters and multileveled perspectives to the unidimensional story that Webb presents in his story of the Great Plains.

The author omits Guálinto's university education; in Part 5 we find him as an adult, married to an Anglo woman. Apparently, the process of cultural assimilation was completed during his college years. He returns to his home town as an agent for the government; apart from superficial social exchanges, he will have nothing to do with his former classmates, whose exclusion from their graduation celebration he had once protested. These former friends are now political activists engaged in reform, but he will have nothing to do with their efforts.

In an interview (August 17, 1992) Paredes explained why he omitted Guálinto's university education: "When I stopped writing that novel, I was still in the process of writing Part 5, which was supposed to be a bridging chapter to what would later follow. I intended to bring him back and have him set up law practice in Jonesville-on-the-Grande and discover that Frank Dell, his father-in-law, was one of the Rangers who had killed his father — he would have to confront this." Paredes also explained Guálinto's apparent complete assimilation:

> It was what I saw at the time. This was before there was any Chicano movement. The LULACS were trying to teach their children not to speak Spanish. They had a law passed saying that Mexicanos were white, which didn't help us with the issue of segregation in the schools. Then they could have schools that were half black and half Mexican, the "whites" still segregated. The trend was toward assimilation. I wanted to send Guálinto to UT, but I couldn't go there with him. I had never set foot on the UT campus. Then the War came about as I was still writing Part 5. I rewrote this last part before I left for the Army.
>
> When Rolando Hinojosa agreed to write an introduction to the book (to be published in 1990), I talked to him over the phone and said that the novel *no está acabada* (it's not finished), but he understood that it was in rough draft form. The truth was that it had been worked and rewritten before I left Brownsville.

By gaining a higher education, Guálinto has tried to circumscribe a place for himself in a society within which he will become leader of his people; but in that process he has become not their leader but rather a sign and symbol of what they must reject and even despise if they are to hold true to their political views and cultural identity. We see this in one of the final episodes of the novel, with his former classmate's, Elodia's, response to Guálinto when he upholds the status quo during their political meeting. "'Ge-or-ge,' she called in an exaggerated Gringo accent. He looked back. Tears were running down her rigid, expressionless face. 'Cabrón!' she said. 'Vendido sanavabiche!'" (294).

Even as one who has "sold out," Guálinto is not, however, an "unscathed" survivor of that war "humanity pretends it has never declared" (Althusser 1964/1971: 205). He has survived systems at work in the educational sphere which persist in circumscribing a place and identity for him and for his people, but in doing so he comes to consider his former school friends "a bunch of clowns playing at politics" (300). If they are to "make something of themselves," he tells his uncle, they must do as he has done and "get out of this filthy Delta, as far away as they can, and get rid of their Mexican Greaser attitudes." The process of Guálinto's reeducation, as a subject of the new order, is now complete. It was initiated in the public school system where his dual selves first conflicted and became problematic. His reeducation continues through his university training.

Guálinto's conflicted selves, brought about by an absence of family history, a biased view of Texas history, and a method of teaching which Webb decisively influenced, is not quite resolved within him even later, as an adult. The recurrent, disturbing dreams he experiences during his married life reenact and revise old conflicts and resistance efforts by Texas Mexicans against the U.S. Army and Navy:

> He would imagine he was living in his great-grandfather's time, when the Americans first began to encroach on the northern provinces of the new Republic of Mexico. Reacting against the central government's inefficiency and corruption, he would organize *rancheros* into a fighting militia and train them by using them to exterminate the Comanches. Then, with the aid of generals like Urrea, he would extend his influence to the Mexican army. He would discover the revolver before Samuel Colt, as well as the hand grenade and a modern style of portable mortar. In his daydreams he built a modern arms factory at Laredo, doing it all in great detail, until he had an enormous, well-trained army that included Irishmen and escaped American Negro slaves. Finally, he would defeat not only the army of the United States but its navy as well. He would reconquer all the territory west of the Mississippi River and recover Florida as well. (282)

Just as the daydreams of his boyhood had relieved the bitterness and frustration of his boyhood, these dreams play out a subconscious struggle against what he has become. They also indicate that his struggle to survive is not quite over. From Paredes's own account (see personal interview, August 17, 1992), we find that this is not the end of the story, only perhaps a significant phase in the life of Guálinto, yet it *is* the end in the novel and, in many cases, the real-life ending. Althusser's analysis has a direct bearing on the interpretation of George W. Gómez's dreams. Althusser reminds us that Lacan recognized that just like slips, failures, jokes, and symptoms, "dreams themselves, became 'signifiers,' inscribed in the chain of an unconscious discourse, doubling silently, i.e., deafeningly, in misrecognition of 'repression,' the chain of the human subject's verbal discourse" (1964/1971: 207–208). The recurring dreams reveal that Guálinto's assimilation has not occurred without a great deal of repression. Thus, unlike Webb's histories, Paredes's narrative reveals the degree of complexity in struggles that take place within *all* peoples. Those struggles take different forms depending on whether access to sites of power is perceived as being shut off or opened during the times of transition. Along the parameters of property, education, labor, and class struggle, Paredes's narrative becomes an illuminating history that penetrates surface phenomena to expose a deeper patterning in relationships which have perpetuated themselves into our own time.

"THE HAMMON AND THE BEANS"

The same episodes from South Texas history that give rise to Paredes's novel come to life in his short story "The Hammon and the Beans" (1963, reprinted 1971). The results of this episode in the history of the U.S. War with Mexico, the 1910 Mexican Revolution, and the Seditionist uprising are viewed close up through the depiction of the life led by Chonita, one of Paredes's most significant female characters. Chonita is a little girl from the narrator's neighborhood. She brings scraps of food to her family that are left from the soldiers' meals at Fort Jones, where the soldiers who maintain control of the border "troubles" are stationed. Paredes's sharp irony makes it clear where the Mexican's "place" is situated in the new order, as Chonita watches the soldiers eat (her nose pressed against the screens) before gathering the scraps of food she is allowed to take home. The author also provides the reader with some historical background: "[Chonita's father] was a laborer. Ever since the end of the border troubles there had been a development boom in the Valley, and Chonita's father was getting his share of the good times. Clearing brush and building irrigation ditches he sometimes pulled down as much as six dollars a week. He drank a good deal of it up, it was true. But corn was just a few cents a bushel in those days. He was the breadwinner, you might say, while Chonita furnished the luxuries" (276).

The spiritual and material conditions of these people is expressed by the doctor who attends to both the narrator and Chonita as they suffer from the symptoms of the illness brought about by the same fever. The narrator survives, but Chonita has not the strength to resist. Frustrated by his failure to save Chonita, the doctor lashes out at the conditions of her life as he comments to the narrator's father: "You know what? . . . In classical times they did things better. Take Troy, for instance. After they stormed the city they grabbed the babies by the heels and dashed them against the wall. That was more humane" (278). Class differences within the Mexicano population of South Texas once again emerge. The doctor and the narrator's family have it within their power to alleviate Chonita's poverty. She lives in a shack owned by the narrator's family. Chonita's mother repays the narrator's family by doing their laundry. Rather than letting Chonita's family live there for free, these White Mexicans, like the Osunas in *George Washington Gómez,* exploit their own people and then use their narrow interpretation of the conditions of the poor for their own polemics.

Paredes exposes specific struggles within the history of his people. His little Chonita, despite her poverty, is the first of his female characters to try to negotiate, through learning and language, between her oppression and the powerful presence of Fort Jones, with all the privilege it represents. Ramón Saldívar comments on Chonita's most memorable epiphany, as it is recounted for us by the narrator of the story—her act of standing on top of an alley fence in her tattered clothes shouting, "Give me the hammon and the beans!" Showing the neighborhood children that she has learned from the soldiers the "foreign language," she transmits to them her learning of the new language and with it an aspiration to discover what this new world is all about, a world that has fed her and her family humiliating scraps of food: "Chonita, who probably does not attend the American school, speaks no English, but mimics with creditable accuracy the sounds of the soldiers' calls across their food-laden tables. (In Spanish, 'ham' is *'jamón,'* close enough for Chonita's purposes.) Her mimicry and her daring are the instruments of her poetry. The other children—the narrator's friends, middle-class children who learn English at the American school—egg her on by pretending that Chonita 'could talk English better than the teachers at the grammar school'" (Saldívar 1990b: 53).

As victim of a disease called poverty, Chonita dies, but her spirit remains alive in the heart of the surviving little boy narrator who enjoys the comforts and security of his own home. The doctor, a member of the Mexican intelligentsia before the Revolution of 1910 required him to flee Mexico, describes with disapproval the ways of the lower-class Mexicanos that he has observed in Chonita's family: "'They're like animals,' the doctor was saying. He turned round suddenly and his eyes glistened in the light. 'Do you know what that brute of a father was doing when I left? He was laughing! Drinking and laughing with his friends'" (277). This is reminiscent of "El Colorado's" father from *George Washington Gómez,* who also, with seeming hopelessness, drinks his life away. With her passing, we also find out that Chonita's natural father's death had been the direct result of the South Texas border troubles. He was unfortunate enough to have been a Mexican working at the site of the Olmito train derailment, another actual episode during this same period in history:[14] "'This is the woman's second husband,' my father explained. 'First one died before the girl was born, shot and hanged from a mesquite limb. He was working too close to the tracks when the Olmito train was derailed'" (278). Yet even with a washerwoman mother, one father lynched, and her other father drinking and laughing in the face of her death, Chonita's spirit prevails in the heart of the adult narrator: "In later years I thought of [Chonita] a lot, especially during the thirties when I was growing up. Those years would have been just made for her. Many's the time I have seen her in my mind's eye, in the picket lines demanding not bread, not cake, but the hammon and the beans" (277).

According to Paredes, Chonita could have become an Emma Tenayuca; inspired by such women struggling to exercise their civil rights in their fight for better working conditions, Paredes created Chonita.[15] The reader of today knows that in every poor neighborhood there still lives a Chonita. With propositions like California's 187, more Chonitas will exist than ever before as a permanent underclass once again becomes fixed into the American Dream experience. One can only hope that her spirit will resist poverty and the lack of education and health care even when these factors continue to crush her physical being.

Property loss, with its threat to human dignity, is set forth in Paredes's short story; he also brings to light the contradictions that are created within an educational system controlled by the oppressor yet still enjoyed by those more privileged than Chonita. The way this system produces conflicts of loyalty and patriotism among its participants is effectively dramatized through a description of the conflicting divided selves of the narrator and his classmates:

> At six the flag came down, and we went to watch through the high wire fence that divided the post from the town. Sometimes we joined in the ceremony, standing at salute until the sound of the cannon made us jump. That must have been when we had just studied about George Washington in school, or recited "The Song of Marion's Men" about Marion the Fox and the British cavalry that chased him up and down the broad Santee. But at other times we stuck out our tongues and jeered at the soldiers. Perhaps the night before we had hung at the edges of a group of old men and listened to tales about Aniceto Pizaña and the *border troubles,* as the local paper still called them when it referred to them gingerly in passing.
>
> It was because of the border troubles, ten years or so before, that the soldiers had come back to old Fort Jones. But we did not hate them for that; we admired them even, at least sometimes. But when we were thinking about the border troubles instead of Marion the Fox we hooted them and the flag they were lowering, *which for the moment was theirs alone,* just as we would have jeered an opposing ball team, in a friendly sort of way. (274–275: my emphasis).

Here too, the conflicts explicitly drawn for us in Paredes's novel are more succinctly dramatized. Yet in the mind of this narrator Chonita becomes the spirit left alive and untouched by the harshness of her circumstances. We are thus left with the sense that the narrator, despite his privilege, will not forget her as a symbol of his people left behind as a part of the laboring class essential to the new social order.

THE WOMEN IN
AMÉRICO PAREDES'S NARRATIVES

Paredes's narratives, specifically "The Hammon and the Beans" and *George Washington Gómez,* include an entire spectrum of women in various degrees of self-fulfillment, many as full participants in the world around them. These characters add to the multiplicity of possibilities that counter the flattened version of Southwest history, where Webb presents women as weak and unable to cope with the harshness of the Plains. With the diversity that Paredes captures, he responds not only to Webb's history but the concept of a unified Chicano community, as Chicana feminists were to do later with their challenging publications of the 1970s to the present.

In *George Washington Gómez,* one of the first images of women that we find is that of the survivor, "toothless and wrinkled, like a prophecy" (15), Guálinto's grandmother, the matriarch and economizer. As noted earlier, it was her inability to say "Washington" that resulted in her new grandson being called *Guálinto.* This name stays with him throughout most of the novel and in effect makes her existence ever present until he discards the past, changing his name to George G. Gómez—and with it his identity. The grandmother's transmitting of the stories of the past, the lost history of Mexicanos gives Feliciano a strong sense of self and the fighting spirit and the cunning with which to help himself and his family survive the final tran-____ ____power into the hands of the Anglos. It is also the grandmother's sav-____ ____ and dimes here and there, that aids Feliciano's financial ____ the Great Depression, and the eventual recovery of ____ropertied class of South Texas.

____it Paredes character, María, Guálinto's mother, repre-____ *decente, mujer sufrida* (suffering woman). She never re-____usband's murder, though she has potential suitors. With ____ncreasingly rigid in her ways and in her possessiveness of ____other. She lives a restricted life within the most rigid self-imposed bou____ s and dictates of her culture and class identity. With these restrictions for herself comes an intolerance for transgressions in others, as when she severely beats Maruca, her daughter, for having become pregnant outside of marriage. Her daughter's shame places Maruca, in María's eyes, in the category of whore rather than the saintly woman she has tried to be. María is incapable of understanding any fluidity between cultural norms and practices. María also upholds the traditional male hierarchy against the outside world, though in effect she holds the power within her own family. Paredes's narrative shows how she promotes her son's education, yet she shows no understanding of her younger daughter's, Carmen's, intelligence or her ambition for learning. Instead, Carmen must drop out of school and stay home to care for María when she breaks her leg. María is closed-minded in her female perceptions, making herself and those around her more miserable for the lack of options she allows herself.

In Paredes's novel the recurrent theme of the virgin/whore dichotomy first emerges when Feliciano, upon his arrival at Jonesville-on-the-Grande, not wanting to take María, a *mujer decente,* anywhere near the *cantina,* where he is to apply for a job, unknowingly leaves her in the care of Doña Tina, who ironically turns out to be a woman called *La Alazana,* a *cantinera* or barmaid/prostitute. Because Doña Tina has acted with propriety, offering them coffee and rest from their long trip, Feliciano has no reason to suspect that she is not a decent, virgin-like woman. We see how Paredes, through the voice of Feliciano, deconstructs this dichotomy when, upon his discovering the truth, he says, "There are different ways of being good." But he hesitates to reveal the truth to María, knowing that she would not want it known that she has accepted the hospitality of such a woman: "As he slowly led the mule down the street, Feliciano thought that sooner or later he would have to tell María who Doña Tina was. But that could wait" (38).

Finally there is Elodia, the firebrand of a woman from the Rio Grande City area of South Texas, the one who foreshadows the fighting Chicana of the Chicano Movement. She is, according to the author, the only character he takes almost completely from the reality of his own high school days. Though he didn't know her very well, she left a strong impression (personal interview, March 4, 1995). As a student she is the defender of her people against the dominative history taught in the schools, and as an adult she becomes an activist working to reform the political system that has kept her people oppressed. She appears in this role in the community when George returns to South Texas after he completes his university education and is on assignment with the federal government.

When asked what inspired his portrayals of strong, resilient women, Paredes responded with the following anecdote about his Aunt Pilar, who lived during the time Webb's portrayal of Anglo pioneers was taking hold of the American imagination:

> Years ago when I was small, my mother would often talk about my
> father's sister, Tía Pilar. She would tell my younger sister, "Te pareces
> a tu Tía Pilar," you remind me of your Tía Pilar. You see, my Tía
> Pilar was a very aggressive woman. My mother would tell us a story
> of how she was a crack shot with a Winchester rifle. According to the
> history, the only time my Tía Pilar missed her target was when a
> mule got in the way, and that was fortunate because Tía Pilar had no
> intention of shooting the mule. She was shooting at her son-in-law.
> Why, you ask? Because he had beaten her daughter and she for one

was not going to put up with that type of behavior. Both families became involved in a dispute over who would pay for the mule. Tía Pilar's family paid for the mule, and her son-in-law never beat his wife again. (remarks made at Southwest Texas State University, San Marcos, March 24, 1994)

CONCLUSION

Both Webb and Paredes draw from living memory for the strength and uniqueness with which they infuse their historical narratives. While Webb's history is imbued with romantic, literary features, Paredes's narrative is definitively marked with the very spirit of struggle and survival that Webb attributes to his pioneers. Webb's simplistic hero/villain story is countered by Paredes's resistant stance on multiple layers against the dominant word of a tainted history for the benefit of a dominant society. Along the lines of property, labor, education, gender, and class struggles, Américo Paredes recovers through narrative the banished history of a decent people. He thus provides a powerful response to the rhetoric of dominance which continues to inspire present-day writers, two of whose works we will examine in the following chapters.

6

MEDIA REPORTAGE AS "HISTORY-IN-THE-MAKING"

Two Short Stories by Helena María Viramontes

Twenty years after a Dallas police officer abruptly ended his life, the ghost of a Latino youth still haunts Dallas. On July 24, 1973, a Dallas police officer shot 12-year old Santos Rodriguez point blank in the head while the boy sat hand-cuffed in a police car.

In the name of conducting a war on drugs and gangs, the Latino community is being subjected to a reign of terror. . . . Most people do not know this because the national media only sees the problem within a black/white context. As proof, activists cite the spring 1992 uprising in Los Angeles: Police reports indicate that the majority of participants, arrestees and victims were Latinos. Yet the national media generally projected it as a Black/ White/Korean confrontation.

—Roberto Rodríguez, "Abuse in the Barrio, Still"

In this chapter I examine two short stories, "The Cariboo Cafe" and "Neighbors," in relation to present-day media reports or what could be construed as history-in-the-making. They are written by a contemporary woman writer, Helena María Viramontes, and come from her collection of short stories entitled *The Moths and Other Stories* (Arte Público, 1985); the stories in this slim volume have been included in over fifty anthologies. The volume has been reissued in a second edition, with close to twenty thousand copies sold.

After publication of her novel, *Under the Feet of Jesus,* in 1995, the Longwood Foundation bestowed upon Viramontes the John Dos Passos Prize for Literature, honoring her "for her use of places and characters that are distinctly American, yet are not usual or stereotypical in American fiction; the amazing variety and experimentalism of her individual works of fiction;

and above all, the stunning unity of each work, with word and idea, image, symbol and theme all woven into seamless whole." Her work has been translated into Hindi, Spanish, and German. Presently, she teaches at Cornell University in the Creative Writing Program. Of this experience she has stated, "Ithaca, New York is a long journey from First Street, East Los Angeles where I grew up, but the love and anger of family and of community are the very sources that inform and inspire my work" (biographical material provided by Viramontes to the author).

Viramontes responds to a recurring of the rhetoric of a dominative history into the later twentieth century by dramatizing the complexity of contemporary issues such as immigration and neighborhood violence that could be "flattened" in the future by Webbian histories. She thus succeeds in breaking up the prescribed, stereotyped notions that make for a facile ordering of reality. In this way, we see in these two stories a further though perhaps quite distinctive form of resistance to a new historiographic mode. The events can be placed in a context of media news coverage, which has become a kind of "history-in-the-making," where history is manifest according to the location of the cameras. Within the narrative "fiction" of these two stories, as is often the case in real life, "criminals" are tried and convicted before any investigative or judicial process can take place. The stories depict what would otherwise be an everyday account of inner-city violence typically reported on any news day. The writer's task here becomes to uncover the real particulars underneath accounts of events provided by media, manipulative or not, which work in the service of a dominant ideology. The complex and subtle reality of the individual threatened by media distortions is at stake.

The distortions of some present-day media coverage can be compared with those of histories such as Webb's. In his day, the promotion or institutionalization of a certain kind of history had a similar effect on readers: a warping, in the name of true representation. To a certain extent, the history being banished before our own eyes through these channels can also be recuperated through narrative fiction. Both "traditional" Hispanic woman protagonists in Viramontes's two stories are coming from an older world in which the rules for womanhood were defined for them in a way that no longer fits their reality. Viramontes, a contemporary Chicana writer, now gives an account of the unfortunate effects of a failing economy and alienation on these women. First, though, some theoretical considerations should be taken into account, insofar as the contemporary historic situation, as narrated in "The Cariboo Cafe" and "Neighbors," does involve issues tackled by cultural theorists.

First, I inquire how public language can be modeled to project what is true and false at the same time. Secondly, I explore *labeling* once again as a specific linguistic device frequently used rhetorically and with reiteration in history texts as well as current reportage. This practice of flattening or collapsing an event by removing it from any fuller contextualization occurs in current media reports. By examining two of Viramontes's fictional narratives I hope to show how a gradual unfolding of the variability and multiplicity of an event presented in fictional narrative (but not allowable in history) can bring reality home, full and fresh, to the reader, and thus challenge the rhetoric of dominance.

These complex matters have a deep background. Most especially, I need to acknowledge Raymond Williams's discussion of the "sign"—which relates to "labeling" in his *Marxism and Literature* (1977). Williams argues that the important medieval concept of the sign, Latin *signum,* a mark or token, which "has been so remarkably readopted in modern linguistic thought," is intrinsically a concept based on a distinction between "language" and "reality" (23). After tracing the development of notions such as "naming," "a priori," and the central activity of language in the process of making a society and understanding it, Williams arrives at the Marxist idea of "language as practical consciousness" (29). In other words, language constitutes the "practical, constitutive activity" and often works reductively. It is necessary to recognize this reductive character of the linguistic sign, just as we recognize that news reports shrink the events they relate.

Before Williams, Volosinov (widely recognized as Bakhtin's pen-name), in his study of words as semiotic signs, had credited the word with being preeminently "the material of behavioral communication," though he also states that "there is no really adequate verbal substitute for the simplest gesture of human behavior. To deny this would lead to the most banal rationalism and simplisticism" (14–15). Invoking *The German Ideology,* the thinking of Vico and Herder, and expatiating on Volosinov's writings, Williams argues: "In reflexive theories of language, whether positivist kinds of materialism, or such theories as psychological behaviourism, all 'signs' are in effect reduced to 'signals' within the simple models of 'object' and 'consciousness' or 'stimulus' and 'response.' Meanings are created by (repeated) recognition of what are then in effect 'signals': of the properties of an object or the character of a stimulus. 'Consciousness' and 'response' then 'contain' (for this is what meaning now is) those properties or that character" (38).

It is acknowledged that imaginative stories, like news reporting, dilate or contract events they relate, according to the narrator's judgment. Of course it must also be acknowledged that all stories can be reduced to basic plot lines, whereas in journalistic writing, only the events would be reported, and that the reverse is also true, with all news items having the capacity for being turned into fuller accounts through fictional narrative. In order to investigate the question of differences between modes of reporting reality and thus defining it, I will be discussing two imaginative stories for their bearing on their reducibility to news items. This will enable us to see that abbreviation in news reporting tends to drain essential values out of the scene being reported. Though we can agree that there is "no really adequate verbal substitute for the simplest gesture of human behavior," the narratives in question entail an amplitude and structuredness of perspective which subvert the ideologically slanted report and open a reader's heart and mind to the "great variety of the world," as well as to human intimacies.

"THE CARIBOO CAFE"

Upon reading Helena María Viramontes's "The Cariboo Cafe," we are exposed to a number of consciousnesses and given an abundant sense of engagement with social reality. By breaking up the "falsely unified view" and introducing the "variety of the world" into an inner city, where the lives of Anglos, Mexicano undocumented workers, and Central American refugees come together within a tightly closed setting, Viramontes recovers the human complexity of a scene which would otherwise be banished from the varied history of the people of the Southwest.[1] One illuminated consciousness (which Bakhtin refers to as language itself) reveals itself and in so doing presents the reader with a backdrop against which single consciousnesses can be successively projected, filling out what becomes flattened or collapsed by the usual reporting of events through media as well as through a certain type of history writing. In this way we see again how reality is defined by those in a position of authority to define it.[2]

"The Cariboo Cafe," as narrative, resists at least one major aspect of a dominative history, the leveling out of consciousness through labeling. Viramontes accomplishes this through her narrative's rejection of the possibility of any clear-cut dichotomies and the achievement of a multiperspectival view of events from within the consciousness of the participants. Consequently, the narrative thread becomes complicated and facilitates what is in essence a historical understanding that stands in direct opposition to public history as Fielding saw it, or what would be in Bakhtinian terms the unified official language. In Viramontes there is a rigid and ruthless externality, and yet the greatest degree of multiplicity is achieved through the convergence and "social intercourse" of the various voices, and distinct social languages are heard, even within one national language, each carrying with it a distinct worldview, as they interact during a historical moment "chronotoped" in time and space.

If the events narrated in this story were to be narrated in a newspaper or on a TV news program, they might read like this:

> *Illegal Alien Kidnapper Killed by Police in Rescue Attempt*
> Two children were rescued today from the grasp of an illegal alien whose identity has not yet been disclosed. Cariboo Cafe owner [name] called police to report that the two children whose pictures appeared on our news program late last night had been in his cafe in the company of a strange-looking woman. Though apparently unhurt, the children were in obvious danger. Today when the woman appeared again in his cafe, [name] called police, and rescue efforts succeeded in freeing the children. Officers report that the woman became violent, resisted arrest and threw a pot of hot coffee at an officer's face. She was shot once in the head, and the children were returned to their parents unharmed.

Stuart Hall's "Encoding/decoding" in his *Culture, Media, Language,* shows how mass communication conceptualizes the process of communication in terms of a circuit or loop, taking into account the sender/message/receiver model, which has been criticized for its linearity. He goes on to show how faulty this model is when trying to communicate an event: "A 'raw' historical event cannot, *in that form,* be transmitted by, say, a television newscast. Events can only be signified within the aural-visual forms of the televisual discourse. In the moment when a historical event passes under the sign of discourse, it is subject to all the complex formal 'rules' by which language signifies. To put it paradoxically, the event must become a 'story' before it can become a *communicative event*" (129).

The "story" as told by this supposed report, an invention of mine, is also an "accurate representation" of events as they occur in Viramontes's short story. But it is through the empathetic fiction, the story I am about to summarize, that a greater conceptualization of reality is recovered. This conceptualization is not specifically constituted by the events related in either the story or the news item, but by including "the great variety of the world." The story is about the way in which each event, taken from within its own context within the consciousness of each actor, can uncover a kind of truth, so often marred and banished from the factual, even historical narratives that we accept as true. This uncovering is in effect what results not from the dialogue of different languages, each carrying with it a different worldview, as Bakhtin would have it; instead, the literal consciousnesses come together in the same moment in time, in the same narrative, and articulate how it is that these events came to take place singularly in the perspective of each participant.[3]

The story opens as follows: "They arrived in the secrecy of night, as displaced people often do, stopping over for a week, a month, eventually staying a lifetime. The plan was simple. Mother would work too until they saved enough to move into a finer future where the toilet was one's own and the children needn't be frightened" (61). From the moment we read "Mother would work . . ." we become aware that the narrator is a child, now grown up enough to relate the narrative. Already the narrative unfolds into a dual perspective of an adult retrospectively relating a childhood experience (through a child's eyes), looking back to put the chain of events as well as her parents' vision together. At least this is what we are thinking until we read the next line, which begins, "In the meantime, they played in the back alleys, among the broken glass, wise to the ways of the streets" (61). Now we know there is a third perspective to be taken into account—the perspective of a more distanced third-person omniscient narrator, who enters the mind of the character named Sonya, one of eight characters already introduced to us within the first two paragraphs. There is the mother; the father, who has warned against the police, or the "polie," who are really "La Migra" in disguise; there is the neighbor who "paced up and down the hallways talking to himself"; there is Mrs. Avila, who takes care of Macky, Sonya's younger brother; and there is Lalo, who has "wrestled [Sonya] down so that he could see her underwear" and in the process caused her to lose her key to their apartment. Already the fact that the children must beware of the police contradicts a sign of police as protector and a person to whom one goes for help. In this case an encounter with the police, even for these lost children, is the worst of all fates, for they would then be all sent back to Tijuana, as her Popi has warned.

Entering Sonya's mind, we discover that she and Macky must stay in their apartment after school, avoiding contact with all other people, until her parents return from work. Having lost her key and her way back to Mrs. Avila's house, confusion follows as Sonya becomes disoriented amidst the traffic and busy streets of her neighborhood, where she witnesses the arrest of her classmate's father. She hides and runs from the police and finally decides to head for the "zero zero place," the Cariboo Cafe, where "at least . . . the shadows will be gone" (64).

The second part of the story is told through the perspective of the Cariboo Cafe owner/cook as he talks to a buddy or a customer we assume is present but whose responses we never hear. In addition to this shift in perspective, the reader experiences a temporal shift. We have advanced into a future well beyond the moment in which an incident central to the story has occurred. The Cariboo Cafe owner offers, through his many and repeated explanations and rationalizations, his justification for having called the police. We learn that because of this act, which involves "a crazy lady and the two kids that started all the trouble," the community now ostracizes him and no longer frequents his cafe: "That's the trouble. It never pays to be honest. I tried scrubbing the stains off the floor, so that my customers won't be reminded of what happened. But they keep walking as if my cafe ain't fit for lepers. And that's the thanks I get for being a fair guy" (64). His initial narration offers the reader an extension of the events in Part 1 which have left the little girl, Sonya, wandering about lost, in hopes of arriving at the Cafe.

We learn in this section that the Cariboo Cafe owner's wife, Nell, has left him, that his son was killed in Vietnam, and that he considers himself tolerant of the undesirables in the community. The first night that "the crazy lady with the two kids" comes in, he sees a news report identifying the same two children as kidnap victims. Recognizing their faces, he decides he should call the police despite his dislike and distrust of them, but he waits for the next day. The next day his friend and regular customer, Paulie, overdoses in his restroom, and the police harass him as a suspected drug peddler.

Later that same day during an INS raid, he signals toward the restroom, where three "illegals," also regulars who work in a nearby garment warehouse, are hiding from *la migra*. He is troubled by the accusing look one of the undocumented workers had given him as they were all taken away: she "looked silly in handcuffs on account of she's old enough to be my grandma's grandma." There is a contradiction in the image of the old undocumented woman worker in handcuffs being arrested like a common criminal. This distorted image, which he cannot forget, disturbs his idea of what his grandmother signified; his grandmother would never have been arrested for the criminal act of running from hunger and poverty into another country to find work.

At the end of this day, in walks the same "crazy" woman with the two kids, and Part 2 comes to a close. He who would like to be the good citizen and property owner, we learn, is also distrustful of the police. But the real irony of the conditions of his existence lies in the fact that this man, even if he is just an everyday Joe turned hero, has more in common with the "crazy" woman than any other character in the story. They have both lost their sons as a result of a U.S supported "anti-communist" war; they are both victimized by their environment, and they both are now lost, no longer knowing what is right or which way to turn. They both latch on to some well-instilled notion from out of the past in order to go forward. As we shall see, he clings to the idea that "Children gotta be with their parents, family gotta be together," and catastrophically so does she.

In Part 3 we get inside the head of the "crazy" woman and go back in time to the night when she and the two lost children meet, and then we go back further into the events in her life before she left Nicaragua (we can assume), the place that could no longer be her home. As she removes the lice from Macky's head, she reminisces about her five-year-old son, Geraldo, whom she now confuses with Macky. Geraldo had become one of the many *desaparecidos* when she sent him out one day to buy her a mango. From what she can gather, he may have been passing out propaganda leaflets for the *Contras* when he was arrested. All her inquiries and pleadings do no good. Her recollections reveal that the site of struggle for this woman has not been situated in the streets but in her home, which, without Geraldo, can no longer be her home. The guilt she suffers and her grief have begun to distort her mind as she remembers how she had felt in the chaotic world of her home country before her nephew Tavo had sent her the bus fare to Juárez. In fact, the woman has now become completely disoriented, as compared with the character portrayed earlier. Disorientation has now become her central experience, as the older system of the woman's ample world, her home, her village, no longer offers any points of reference:

These four walls are no longer my house, the earth beneath it, no longer my home. Weeds have replaced all good crops. The irrigation ditches are clodded with bodies. No matter where we turn, there are

rumors facing us and we try to live as best we can, under the rule of
men who rape women, then rip their fetuses from their bellies. Is this
our home? Is this our country? I ask Maria. Don't these men have
mothers, lovers, babies, sisters? Don't they see what they are doing?
Later, Maria says, these men are babes farted out of the Devil's ass.
We check to make sure no one has heard her say this. (71)

The chaos and destruction she has come out of is reflected in the numerous
contradictions within the language itself, with "bodies clodding irrigation
ditches" where water should be flowing. Another contradiction of the signs
we associate with political struggle lies in the fact that whatever sanctuary
the home once offered or whatever immunity or protection women and
children once enjoyed within the site of political struggle has also been violated.[4] Yet Viramontes's own characterization of the woman simply as victim of the chaotic world she lives in is also to be called into question, as
is Yvonne Yarbro-Bejarano's reference to Viramontes's work as addressing
"the plight of women suffering under repressive regimes which rob them of
their children."[5]

Some knowledge of the background here will enrich a reader's response:
the Mothers of Matecalpa is an organization of women in Nicaragua, mothers who have lost at least one child during the political struggles of the 1970s
and 1980s, when President Reagan made Nicaragua the number-one priority of his foreign policy. At the time of this writing, this organization had
grown from six hundred to six thousand women and constituted a national
movement. These women organized to work the land, to offer aid in the
form of food and clothing to the poor, and to offer solidarity for women who
have lost children, husbands, fathers, or brothers during the political strife.
Though the government and the returning politically exiled landowners
continued to thwart their efforts through taxation of even donated food and
clothing and the destruction of their crops, they continued their struggles
under the leadership of women like Esperanza de Cabrera and the Instituto
Juan Veinti-tres.[6] In this light, I suspect that Viramontes's description of the
woman in "The Cariboo Cafe," in passages such as the following, narrated
from the woman's perspective, conforms to some degree to commonplace
images or stereotypes of victimized peasant women. This woman is "alien-
ated," away from any support system from which she could perhaps have
drawn strength: "Today I felt like killing myself, Lord. But I am too much

of a coward. I am a washer woman, Lord. My mother was one, and hers too. We have lived as best we can, washing other people's laundry, rinsing off other people's dirt until our hands crust and chap. When my son wanted to hold my hand, I held soap instead. When he wanted to play, my feet were in pools of water. It takes such little courage, being a washer woman. Give me strength, Lord" (70). Certainly one must contrast Viramontes's description of a woman driven to desperation at the horrible death of her son with the very strong and very sane Mothers of Matecalpa's response to crisis in the actual, present-day Nicaragua.[7] Viramontes here captures both sides of the spectrum in one character.

As the story continues, we learn that the woman has rushed out into the middle of a busy street to save Macky from being run over by the cars and believes in her delusion that Geraldo has been given to her a second time and that she now has another chance to take better care of him. She will never lose him again to the authorities. She takes good care of Macky. She buys him a meal at the cafe, bathes him, gives him her bed in which to sleep, all the while ignoring the little girl, his older sister. Sonya doesn't exist for her because she doesn't fit into her illusion of having found her lost son, any more than this aspect of the story is any part of what the media will offer to a public who will only see what is pictured for them and what conforms to their ideas of verisimilitude.

When the mother makes her second visit to the cafe, the owner is quite taken by how much younger the woman looks, "almost beautiful," he notes. The little boy is also transformed, looking cleaner and better taken care of. The owner wrestles with his conscience, for by this time he has already called the police and wonders if he has done the right thing. He wishes that his wife were still with him because she would know the right thing to do. When the police enter, the woman is determined not to let go of Geraldo/Macky's hand. In her mind, they are the "authorities" who once before had taken her Geraldo away. She resists, refusing to let herself be intimidated or frightened when they point their guns at her face, while she remembers that her son had "[f]or years . . . cried and she could hear him day and night. Screaming, and howling, sobbing, shriveling and crying because he is only five years old, and all she wanted was a mango" (74). She clutches Macky close to her body, wanting "to conceal him in her body again, return him to her belly so they will not castrate him and hang his small, blue penis on her door" (74). The focus in this final scene is almost entirely on her consciousness; we have caught only glimpses of the other characters in the story. Briefly, we have seen the Cariboo Cafe owner nervous and perspiring; we witness his outer shell breaking down for the first time since we have known him: "Aw, fuck, he says, in a fog of smoke his eyes burning tears. He can't believe it, but he's crying. For the first time since JoJo's death, he's crying. He becomes angry at the lady for returning. At JoJo. At Nell for leaving him. He wishes Nell here, but doesn't know where she's at or what part of Vietnam JoJo is all crumbled up in. Children gotta be with their parents, family gotta be together, he thinks . . ." (73).

We know that people are gathering outside the cafe to watch and that one police officer is telling her to let go of Macky as he "pushes the gun barrel to her face" (74). Slowly the perspective closes in and we witness her death only from within her own consciousness. Here, she is not being passive. As she challenges the authorities whom she has had her fill of, the resistance or political activism can be seen along a personal/social spectrum. When her resistance becomes violent, we read her thinking: " . . . then I hear something crunching like broken glass against my forehead and I am blinded by the liquid darkness. But I hold onto his hand. That I can feel, you see, I'll never let go. Because we are going home. My son and I" (75).

What is for the "crazy" woman a reclaiming of her son and a recovering of her home, and what is for the Cariboo Cafe owner also a reencounter with the painful past, subverts any reader's perception of events as they would be flattened out by the collapsing effects of catchwords of reportage. Stuart Hall in his chapter "The Social Production of News" in *Policing the Crisis: Mugging, the State, and Law and Order* discusses what I see as the collapsing or abbreviating of events into news reporting as a third aspect of "a complex process which begins with a systematic sorting and selecting of events according to a socially constructed set of categories" (53):

> The third aspect—the moment of the construction of the news story itself—is equally important, if less obvious. This involves the presentation of the item to its assumed audience, in terms which, as far as the presenters of the item can judge, will make it comprehensible to that audience. If the world is not to be represented as a jumble of random and chaotic events, then they must be identified (i.e. named, defined, related to other events known to the audience) and assigned to a social context (i.e. placed within a frame of meanings familiar to the audience). This process—identification and contextualization—

is one of the most important through which events are "made to mean" by the media. An event only "makes sense" if it can be located within a range of known social and cultural identifications. (1978: 54)

Likewise in "The Cariboo Cafe," the characters and events even within the narrative are labeled through a naming device so commonly employed within very specific ideological frameworks. The woman is an "illegal alien," already a criminal by her very presence, already an undesirable because of the burden these workers supposedly present to society. The Cariboo Cafe owner is counterposed as her opposite, not as a hardened man full of contradictions and constraints due to the stark reality he faces on a day-to-day basis, but the upstanding citizen, a believer in democracy and "justice, for all." The children are labeled as the woman's victims rather than the victims of the learned fear projected upon them by the circumstances of their inner-city world. Foregrounded is their fear of the police, their would-be rescuers, and not the woman, the villainess/kidnapper. The only true perceiver of this complexity can be the reader of the narrative, a fiction. Only within this fiction is the action articulated for the reader, spelled out nakedly in all its implications.

One might ask what a story about a Central American exile or refugee has to do with Chicanos and Chicanas relative to Webb. The alienation of the woman in "The Cariboo Cafe" and the quick "effective" way in which she, as "the other" is disposed of by the police is the dramatized culmination of an attitude sanctioned by a particular type of history, one that has perpetuated certain attitudes against those who did not fit within a narrow description of what is "American." Those attitudes have a tendency to reappear. They allow scant tolerance for or acknowledgment of the struggles of "the other," resulting in ideological motives that facilitate dehumanization and violent suppression. Viramontes pictures people similarly dehumanized and thus victimized through the power of rhetoric, the catchwords of dominance. These signs are particularly relevant today as we see a reemergence of the particular rhetoric used to pass laws denying immigrant children the right to a decent life and promote the establishment of a permanent underclass. The author's fictional, narrative representation of reality is resistant to the flattening effects that media language continues to have on her people. Through fiction, she creatively fills out the picture of the types of struggles not taken into account by anti-immigration propaganda. Through the power of imagination, Viramontes's work combats, or at least offers a greater comprehension of, "the great variety of the world" against the grain of linguistic devices employed to present a tainted though believable perception of history.

"NEIGHBORS"

In "Neighbors" Viramontes again depicts the alienating effects of displacement, but here she comes closer to the lives of the Chicano people of the Southwest. "Neighbors" zooms into a neighborhood where, apparently, mostly Chicanos live. The story is about neighborhood violence and the effects of aging on two particular characters, Aura and Fierro, whose worlds have essentially disappeared. Aura and Fierro are like the old-timers upon whose stories some historians and anthropologists have relied. They could be the elders of any community, respected for their years of learning and for their ability to pass on the history of their people. In this case, however, Aura and Fierro have no audience for their stories of past struggles. Instead, they face defeat and the resignation of their community. Their immediate surroundings offer no validation for their past existences or value systems. The transition taking place before our eyes in Paredes's *George Washington Gómez,* like past challenges and changes which Webb validates through his history, are here negatively completed. The economy gives no hope. Aura and Fierro witness a community turning upon itself. The characters in this story, as in "The Cariboo Cafe," seem stuck in the inner-city hopelessness of a failing economy with no more frontiers left to challenge and no more common enemy to fight, except of course for the enemies they create amongst themselves. For them there no longer exists a communal, village, or even nationalistic struggle. The rules of Aura and Fierro's former world no longer apply, as they are constantly assaulted by the new ways of their violent and alienating environment. The story begins:

> Aura Rodríguez always stayed within her perimeters, both personal
> and otherwise, and expected the same of her neighbors. She was
> quite aware that the neighborhood had slowly metamorphosed into a
> graveyard. People of her age died off only to leave their grandchildren
> with little knowledge of struggle. As a result, the children gathered
> near her home in small groups to drink, to lose themselves in the
> abyss of defeat, to find temporary solace among each other. She
> shared the same streets and corner stores and midnights with these

tough-minded young men who threw empty beer cans into her yard;
but once within her own solitude, surrounded by a tall wrought-iron
fence, she belonged to a different time. (102)

The struggle is what is important to the seventy-three-year-old Aura, but
the young people who surround her know nothing of what she and her generation lived. All they know or will ever know is a sense of defeat that has
no history. Because they know nothing of the struggles, they have no sense
of the origins of their defeat, or how they have gotten to the place their present world assigns them. The past for them is unaccounted for. The aged
Aura is not even regarded and much less respected by these young people as
an elder, as someone of her age would have been in her own time. Somehow,
the old ways have been lost, along with an accounting for the struggles. Later in the story we are introduced to the second elder, Don Fierro. He lives
in the world of his thoughts, and it is through those thoughts that we learn
that the whole community had been moved to this section of town because
a freeway had been built. This old man, whose only son had been stabbed to
death several years back, cannot walk the streets of his present neighborhood without recollecting his old world:

> He heard the sirens again, the swift traffic whirling by beneath him.
> He was suddenly amazed how things had changed and how easy it
> would be to forget that there were once quiet hills here, hills that he
> roamed in until they were flattened into vacant lots where dirt paths
> became streets and houses became homes. Then the government let-
> ter arrived and everyone was forced to uproot, one by one, leaving
> behind rows and rows of wooden houses that creaked with swollen
> age. He remembered realizing, as he watched the carelessness with
> which the company men tore into the shabby homes with clawing
> efficiency, that it was easy for them to demolish some twenty, thirty,
> forty years of memories within a matter of months. As if that weren't
> enough, huge pits were dug up to make sure that no roots were left.
> The endless freeway paved over his sacred ruins, his secrets, his
> graves, his fertile soil in which all memories seeded and waited for
> the right time to flower, and he could do nothing.
>   He could stand right where he was standing now and say to him-
> self, here was where the Paramount Theater stood, and over there
> I bought snow cones for the kids, here was where Chuy was stabbed,
> over there the citrus orchards grew. (106)

The loss is of more than just space; with the "uprooting," the old ways have also become lost for him, and there is no more hope that new seeds will be planted. His memories take the shape of pastoral metaphors. All is open land; the hills where seeds were planted on fertile soil and where graves were made into sacred ruins no longer remain. Even the roots are gone. Fierro is thought "strangely touched" by everyone in the neighborhood. Again, as we have seen in the narratives of González and Paredes, there reappears in Chicano letters the theme of a lost time and place, a lament for the loss of the old traditional ways in the name of "progress" and an overriding suspicion and even inadaptability to the new.

Now, more than "his fear of death or of not receiving his social security check," he fears "that he would forget so much that he would not know whether it was like that in the first place, or whether he had made it up, or whether he had made it up so well that he began to believe it was true" (106). The absence of a history for him is agony, for without his memory or his existence, all is lost. Instead of being intensely aware and confronting the changes as does Aura, his counterpart, Fierro chooses to live mostly in the past and with the ambiguity that it brings him.

One day a very strange barefoot and foul-smelling woman appears asking for Macario Fierro de Ortega. Appearing to be someone from out of his past, she moves in with Fierro and takes care of him during his last days. As Fierro recedes more and more into the past, Aura comes into an increasingly direct and brutal confrontation with her present. Her memories make that present all the more painful. She remembers attending the baptism of Ruben, the leader of the Bixby Boys, who now humiliates her with his disrespectful remarks. This group of young men who congregate next to her home augment the frustration and anger she already suffers from her increasing decrepitude and inability to "get some kindness from [her] neighbors" (108). In her anger she calls the police on the Bixby Boys for playing loud music and throwing empty beer cans into her garden, the one remaining passion in her life: "Her feeling of revenge had overcome her pain momentarily, but when the police arrived, she fully realized her mistake. The five cars zeroed in on their target, halting like tanks in a cartoon. The police jumped out in military formation, ready for combat. The neighbors began emerging from behind their doors and fences to watch the red lights flashing against the policemen's batons" (108). One of the boys momentarily escapes arrest and runs through her garden to her door and pleads with her to let him in. The police, having been provided the pretext they need to justify their brutality, are overly violent with the group of boys.

Aura has crossed an unspoken yet clearly demarcated line, and the Bixby Boys' final words to her as they are being taken away are, "'We'll get you,' . . . 'You'll see'" (109). Aura's calling of the police had broken a silent neighborhood code. She had invited the unwanted oppressors into the neighborhood and provided the justification they needed to abuse the boys. However justified she may have been in calling them, her violation of the neighborhood by this means signifies that she can no longer expect any protection from its members. Knowing this, she becomes increasingly paranoid, receiving threatening phone calls from the Bixby Boys. They take their revenge upon her by destroying her garden, spraying her home with graffiti, and writing vulgarities with excrement on her walls and windows. She resolves to defend herself: "She would have to take care of herself. She was marked, proof to other neighbors that indeed the 'BIXBY BOYS RULE,' as they had sprayed the neighborhood in huge bold letters. *NO.* She refused to be their sacrificial lamb. She shook her head as she got a candlestick out of the linen closet. She pushed the kitchen table aside, grunting under its weight, then rolled up the carpet. She lit the candlestick and opened the cellar door because she refused to be helpless" (112).

The scene in which she descends into her cellar in search of an old gun she had stored there is particularly telling: "She dug her hands into the box, groping, feeling beneath the objects, kitchen utensils, books, photographs, *but found nothing*" (112; my emphasis). Nothing from her past or her memories can help her face her present struggle of alienation from her neighborhood. We learn that her past life was a rough one where, like Webb's pioneers, she had to learn to fight for her survival against the forces of nature: "The summer of the rattlers. The Vizcano desert was far away, yet she could almost feel the rattlers coiled up under the brittle bushes waiting for her. As a child she was frightened by their domination of the desert" (117). In the cellar she eventually finds the gun. She sits prepared to fire as she waits for the final moment of confrontation. In her exhaustion, her mind travels into past moments with her grandfather, who had taught her "how to kill [rattlers] if necessary." Her memories of the slickness of the rattlers and "their instinct to survive" mix in her mind with her present fear of the Bixby Boys, and in her sleepiness she becomes incapable of distinguishing the past fear from the present: "Her eyes grew heavy with sleep but she refused to close them, for the rattlers were out there. Somewhere" (117–118).

In the meantime, her neighbor, Fierro, and his mysterious woman friend have been enjoying music together, sharing meals and old times, when he is suddenly struck down by an apparent heart attack or stroke. His friend runs toward the porch of Aura's house searching for help and begins pounding on Aura's door just as the escaped Bixby Boy had done days before. Aura is woken out of her sleep into the anticipation of an attack from one of the Boys. The last lines of the story read: "Someone was on her porch and she prayed to be left alone. She held the gun high with both hands, squeezing, tightly squeezing it as she aimed at the door" (118).

Were this story to be reduced to a present-day news item, it would more than likely simply read as yet one more incident of barrio violence. Viramontes fills out what would have to be omitted for reasons of economy or absence of understanding, probably both. The "point of view" would be that of the outsider with one language and one organized system speaking for and labeling the lives within which Viramontes has allowed us to view lifelike characters speaking for themselves. As in "The Cariboo Cafe," "language as practical consciousness" would label Fierro's friend "strange" or "the victim"; Aura would be senile and aged; Fierro would simply be dead. The dehumanization and lack of history projected upon these characters due to their changed worlds, their displacement and violent surroundings, would be further advanced by a reportage of events in a stereotypical frame of reference, probably stigmatizing these people for their "history of violence."

o o o

Through the power of imagination, Viramontes's "The Cariboo Cafe" and "Neighbors" fill out the stereotyped contextualizations with "an accumulative view" (Braudy 120–121). In so doing these narratives challenge a rhetoric of dominance upon which ideologically tainted reporting can be mounted. In these stories a narrative imagination has recovered episodes in a history which would ordinarily have been made to seem inscrutable but acceptable according to criteria in which the catchwords of dominance congeal.

7

THE TEXAS HISTORY
OF BEATRIZ DE LA GARZA'S
NARRATIVES

Sustaining Women, Hispanic Heroes,
and a Sense of Place

> *The actual physical borderland that I'm dealing with in this book*
> *is the Texas–U.S. Southwest/Mexican border. The psychological*
> *borderlands, the sexual borderlands and the spiritual borderlands*
> *are not particular to the Southwest. In fact, the borderlands are*
> *physically present wherever two or more cultures edge each*
> *other, where people of different races occupy the same territory,*
> *where under, lower, middle, and upper classes touch, here the*
> *space between two individuals shrinks with intimacy.*
>
> —GLORIA ANZALDÚA, *Borderlands/La Frontera*

 BEATRIZ de la Garza was born in 1943 in Ciudad Guerrero, Tamaulipas, Mexico. This Spanish colonial settlement, formerly known as Revilla, was founded in 1750 and provides the setting for several of her short stories. The fluidity that marks the borderlands notion of "place" takes on a literal meaning when De la Garza recounts how even after 1848 her ancestors "purchased thousands of acres from the State of Texas and from the railroads, and in the 1860s, according to family history, moved north across the river to establish a ranching compound, bringing with them ten thousand head of sheep" (1995a). Orphaned at a young age, De la Garza's grandmother relocated to Mexico just on the other side of the river, where she married and raised her own family. After they, too, were orphaned in early childhood, De la Garza and her sister lived with their aunts in Mexico. However, when the joint U.S. and Mexican construction of the Falcón Dam and International Reservoir on the Rio Grande below Zapata was completed, De la Garza's birthplace was flooded and she was forced to join her cousins across the river in the United States while her sister remained in Mexico. De la Garza enrolled in school in Laredo without knowing any English, though she had already begun writing short tales and poems in Spanish. Early on she showed signs of literary talent. As her English progressed she began writing in English and, while in high school, she won awards for her short stories from *Seventeen* magazine in two consecutive years. Later she received a scholarship from the *Corpus Christi Caller Times* to attend the University of Texas at Austin, where she studied journalism and creative writing. During her senior year at UT, she won first place in the undergraduate short-story contest and was published in "Corral," the English Department's literary magazine. De la Garza holds several degrees from the University of Texas at Austin: a B.A. with honors in history and Spanish, an M.A. and Ph.D. in Spanish, and a law degree. She served on the Board of the Austin Independent School District from 1988 to 1994, including two years as president.

The stories examined in this chapter come from her first published collection of short stories, *The Candy Vendor's Boy and Other Stories* (1994, Arte Público Press). Her novel for young adults, *Pillars of Gold and Silver,* is scheduled for publication in 1997. She is presently at work on a novel, *Only the Stones Remain,* which focuses on the destruction of her birthplace, Revilla, from the point of view of one protagonist, and will be followed by a collection of short, interrelated stories, *The Walls of the Temple,* which explores the same topic from multiple perspectives.

De la Garza's writing is imbued with a sense of loss of place and an urgent need for location, a quality perhaps derived from her ancient Revilla, which refuses to let itself be forgotten. Like a scene of magical realism right out of a Latin American novel, the author's birthplace, Guerrero Viejo or Antigua Revilla, continues to assert its presence along the border as it does in her writings. For many years now this old town periodically emerges from beneath the waters of Falcón Lake as the tops of the church, the school, and the kiosk are resurrected when the lake level is low. The author explains: "And when the waters recede, the church even 40 years later, is still standing. If it is only short of miraculous that the church has survived so many years, abandoned and submerged, it is also amazing that after so much time, Guerrero Viejo has not been forgotten. It has instead taken on a life of its own" (1995b: 14). So far, attempts to raise sufficient funds for its restoration have failed, though the history of which this site speaks is being recovered through the stories its native daughter has to tell.[1] Perhaps it is out of this loss of her birthplace that the writer feels even more compelled to restore through literature a symbolic place that speaks through time of its people's response to a rhetoric of dominance that diminished their existence.

De la Garza's life provides us with an example of a writer, scholar, and activist whose primary work has been done outside the university academy. Like the earlier writers examined so far, De la Garza explores many complex aspects of the dialectics of negotiation over class and identity, traditional values, the history of conflict over property, racial misunderstanding, sacrifice, compromise, and public school education. Her narratives recall through fiction the struggles of people who do not yield to flattened concepts but instead demonstrate the complications of crossing geographic as well as social-class and gender-constructed lines.

Like the women in Gabriel García Márquez's *Cien años de soledad,* Nellie Campobello's *Las manos de mi madre (My Mother's Hands),* and *Cartucho,* or even the more recent Mexican bestseller, Laura Esquivel's *Como agua para chocolate,* the women in De la Garza's short stories struggle in their environments in such ways that their lives take on historical dimensions. With few exceptions, such as Américo Paredes and Ernesto Galarza, many Chicano writers have produced literary works which are almost completely male centered, focused on the young man's struggles with his world as he comes into his manhood, on war experience and readjustment to communal life, or on what his very important destiny might be, while his sisters and his mother are relegated to very specific, narrowly defined roles, often just filling in the background of main plot lines. Such narrow images of women in both "American" and Chicano literature have made it necessary for historians like Sarah Deutsch to adjust their view of Hispanic women in relation to the men of their community: "It quickly became apparent that I would have to uncover the history not simply of the women, but of the whole group, and as I conducted my research, the impossibility of making sense of one sex's history without that of the other also became apparent" (Deutsch: 307). De la Garza's narratives restore to U.S. literature a feminine figure of long-standing presence in Latin American letters, one whose struggles are contextualized and made interdependent with those of her male counterparts.

In this chapter I closely examine three of Beatriz de la Garza's short stories, "Temporary Residents," "The Candy Vendor's Boy," and "The Kid from the Alamo." Several other stories in the same collection are worth noting briefly for their handling of similar themes. "Pilgrimage" dramatizes an ongoing dialogue between two women from Mexico who ride the bus to and from their jobs as domestic workers in an unnamed city in Texas. Through their direct speech, the reader learns of their reasons for being in the United States, the much-needed labor they provide, and their strengths and struggles. The story provides an intimate and humane look at the "scapegoats" of legislation such as California's Proposition 187 or the so-called welfare reform.

"Margarita," the protagonist of another story, is a Mexican American student from South Texas attending the University of Texas at Austin during the early 1960s. In an attempt to integrate herself into the dominant society that considers her socially inferior, she calls herself "Margo." She "had always hated the time and place in which she was born" and all that is associated with it: "to live in Texas in 1964, in the shadow of the Alamo—both the building and the movie—as a Mexican, that was to be one of fortune's stepchildren" (167). Her first romance ends in disappointment when her Anglo boyfriend informs her that he could never take her home to meet his mother. On the other hand, coming to terms with her identity forces her to gain a new respect for her South Texas roots, as Margarita eventually draws strength from them to face a world hostile to Mexicans.

In "Agnus Dei" we have the story of a man from the barrio who with the help of his community has completed his studies and become a pharmacist. In his attempt to "give back to his community," he has moved his family back home to the barrio, but when his son is killed by a car, he blames himself for his noble but impractical ideas. On the other hand, his wife, as he comes to find out after much solitary grieving, is very grateful for the love and compassion they receive from lifelong friends and neighbors, and she wonders how they could have endured the torture of their loss without a firm grounding in their community.

In "Pillars of Gold and Silver" a young teacher's attempts to teach according to public school "standards" come in conflict with the urgings of her repressed memory. Frustrated with her failure to reach a student with limited English linguistic abilities, Miss Mills reaches back from her present position of security within the establishment to the years of her childhood spent with her grandmother in a small town in northern Mexico. Drawing from her own childhood memories in Guerrero Viejo, the author depicts her protagonist's travel back through time to a remote land in her distant memory. This memory provides the key element to establishing a common ground with her student, to whom she can finally offer genuine understanding. For Miss Mills, however, there still remains a question of a lost place as she reflects upon the significance it once had for her identity: "I turned my face away from them all, away from that world that I came to be ashamed of, ashamed not only of it because it seemed so foreign, but ashamed of myself, too, for having once been happy there. I never went back. And now I do not know where I belong" (139). These themes of stored memory and loss of place in relation to education are further explored from the perspective of a young narrator in the author's forthcoming novel by the same title.

"TEMPORARY RESIDENTS"

Through storytelling De la Garza portrays historical events which are usually absent from the dominant history of the United States but which relate specifically to present-day experiences. The short story "Temporary Residents," like Ernesto Galarza's autobiographical work, *Barrio Boy,* is a poignant account of immigration enforced by the Mexican Revolution of 1910. For the most part, immigration from Mexico resulted from the repressive policies which caused widespread unrest under the Porfirio Díaz regime. In the United States, the Chinese Exclusion Act of 1882 and the "Gentlemen's Agreement" with Japan in 1907 had virtually shut off Asian immigration, creating a labor vacuum (Moquin and Van Doren: 331). Mexican immigrants and Mexican Americans provided a badly needed supply of labor to the United States, given its rapid expansion into the Western territories: "Mexican nationals and Mexican Americans constituted 80 percent of the work force in agriculture, 90 percent of the workers on Western railroads, and 60 percent of the labor force in the mines. This is in addition to the sizable numbers who gravitated to the industrial centers of the North or who followed the agricultural seasons in other parts of the nation" (Moquin and Van Doren: 331).

For the most part, Mexican immigrants to the United States have been looked upon as a people from very poor backgrounds—miners, for example—who were recruited for their skilled labor, or a people in search of economic opportunity. But during this great migration, many of Mexico's upper middle class and its intelligentsia also took refuge in cities throughout the American Southwest. As *La Prensa* and other Spanish-language newspapers of the time would indicate, in San Antonio many of these new arrivals attempted at first to maintain their former status and living conditions, but because of established patterns and their economic decline, many were soon forced to join the masses of laborers comprised mostly of native

Texas Mexicans or the dispossessed, who had steadily flowed into the United States from Mexico since before the turn of the century.

"Temporary Residents" recovers the social and economic history of an upper-middle-class people, in many cases political refugees, who established themselves in San Antonio as a result of war. Their adjustment to loss of privilege, status, and economic security and their evolving relationship with the established laboring and merchant classes of Mexican Americans in San Antonio during this period of time is a central theme of this story. "*Estamos de paso*" (we are just passing through), the newly arrived are often heard to say, even when for generations they have been integrating themselves into the older Mexican American community of San Antonio, which was established in 1718. This is their story, but it is also the story of one woman's strength and her initial resistance and eventual resignation to loss, and of her acceptance of the fact that she will never go back to her former life.

Adela, the protagonist, tries her best to keep up the appearance of some dignity, despite their economic losses, primarily for the sake of her father. Don Luis, who had "always been fortunate in having women around him who have cushioned life's blows before they reached him" (37), suffers from occasional guilt for having brought his family into such conditions with his political missteps. He clings to the old ways despite changed circumstances and looks the other way when his daughters and grandchild do fine needle-work at home for pay: "The question of a job had been a delicate one from the very first. Don Luis would have been horrified at the thought of his daughters hiring themselves out as employees to anybody. He, himself, was already in his sixties, and what could he do? The chief expertise of this dis-placed former man of property was a knowledge of the social graces re-quired of a gentleman" (41).

With regard to the history of the West, Sarah Deutsch contends that very specific assigned roles led to facile conclusions regarding the subordinate place of Hispanic women on the U.S. southwestern frontier. The complexi-ties of the family and thus the "nuances regarding their status, even within the realm of the family," came to be ignored and disregarded (42).[2] This story offers us some of that missing insight into women's complex negotia-tion of their roles within the family, the workplace, and society. Adela's prospects of being married in Mexico were terminated with the Revolution, yet she is a mother defined by the responsibility she takes for raising her sis-ter's orphaned child, Luisita. In terms of production, it is the male who has been historically granted the role of breadwinner, while the woman has been strictly confined to family cares. But finding that the family is close to destitution, Adela takes on an additional role when she is forced to find work outside their home. As she adapts to her new life as a worker in a garment factory, the family's former prosperity and privileged way of life slowly become fading memories for her.

In the absence of Mexican American women in historical literature and the general failure of historians to accurately depict Chicanas, "except as over-generalized and stereotyped images of submissive, cloistered, and powerless women" (Deutsch 1987: 42), De la Garza shows how the lives and gender roles of its displaced inhabitants eventually could be accommodated to the new environment. Despite the ways in which different notions of class identity determine different constructions of femininity and masculinity, it was necessity rather than gender, as Deutsch notes, that determined what work women would do: "But even the basic outlines of acceptable women's work had always depended more on the composition of the family than on sexual norms" (1987: 54). In this case Adela, the second but stronger daughter, must take on the role of sole provider.

Beatriz de la Garza's portrayal of a woman resourceful in the face of destitution parallels Deutsch's account of women's economy of production and exchange on the frontier, a feature which has remained invisible to historians: "It is highly significant that in the 1910 census for Rio Arriba County, whereas male or Anglo female enumerators listed ten females with occupations for every one hundred males in communities they covered, Sophie Archuleta, a public school teacher in Truchas whose father was a general farmer, whose mother was a seamstress, and whose sister and brother performed labor on the home farm, listed seventy-nine females with occupations for every one hundred males. To Hispanic women, their own work was highly visible and, in terms of value, on a par with that of the men" (Deutsch 1987: 54). This discrepancy between self-estimation with regard to the value of women's work and the supposedly "objective" reporting of the Census parallels the gap between, on the one hand, a social historian and a short story writer who rely on personal narrative and, on the other hand, the sources that Webb relies on for his opinion that the Great Plains were indeed no place for a woman. Also important here are questions regarding the value of work in the home as opposed to the land and the landscape. A fuller and more vivid picture comes to the fore in De la Garza's narrative account of how Adela's hard work on her sewing machine in a garment factory became the sole source for the family income. The author places Adela's industry and common sense on a par with any man's experience of job seeking in the United States. However imbued her hard work is with an exclusively feminine quality, it is no less valuable, for it supports the family and enables all to retain some semblance of their former dignity. Her various roles, within the family as well as within the community, are spelled out.

When the family first arrived in San Antonio they had lived in what was then the best hotel in San Antonio, the Menger Hotel, but Adela had convinced Don Luis to move to a boarding house. As their finances dwindle even further, Adela finds the family a small house, which Don Luis, in his former state, would have called a "jacal," a shack. Ten years pass, and they remain in the same four-room house with the sagging porch. Most of the people in the neighborhood are laborers, with the exception of a few small-business owners, who live in the second story of the building that houses their stores.

Class questions also come sharply into focus, in terms not only of the family's living conditions but also the educational opportunities and social interaction that results. The Academia Hidalgo had been founded by the Mexican exiles so that their children could continue their studies in Spanish while they waited for conditions to stabilize in Mexico, but it soon becomes a struggle for some of these former middle- and upper-class parents to pay even a modest tuition. "The children of the poor fared no better than their parents: schooling was out of the question for them. The truly rich always made provisions ahead of time for living abroad and did not have to pinch pennies to pay for tuition, as Luisita's family had done" (40).

In describing how the Navas, despite their poverty, enjoy occasional diversions similar to those of their former life, De la Garza offers the reader a glimpse of the social life that the exiles try to recreate for themselves in a city where "much of Mexico still remained" in the customs and the names of the people. This does much to console the exiles into thinking that "they were not in a foreign country after all" (44). As in the novels of Jovita González, we enter the culture and social life that was lost to the exiles but which the Mireleses tried to recreate through their roles as educators within the San Felipe School District and later in Corpus Christi. In "Temporary Residents" these occasional cultural events provided temporary relief from the harsh circumstances of their lives:

On a few special occasions, they even convinced Don Luis to take
them all to the Teatro Nacional to watch a touring company from
Mexico City present a *zarzuela*—for he was very fond of musical
theater—or see a play by one of the better known nineteenth-century
Spanish dramatists, who were his favorites. He would agree to go to
these functions saying that he did it only to provide them with an
escort, but he enjoyed himself at these events more than any of them.
He was in his element here, at a theater or a salon, exchanging bows
with the leading members of the Mexican colony, whom he did not
see otherwise.

At the Casino Mexicano, too, which he was too poor to join, he
was happy. Although they were not members, they sometimes went
to the Casino as guests, particularly for Independence Day in September. For him, though, the poetry readings and the musical recit-
als were not the main attraction of these soirees. It was, rather, the
opportunity to put on his best black suit, his silver-striped tie and the
diamond stick pin that otherwise reposed in its velvet case among his
handkerchiefs. (De la Garza 1994: 49)

But back in the reality of their own neighborhood and given their class
consciousness, the Nava family members try at first not to associate too
much with their neighbors. Luisita, especially, is kept aloof from the other
children. She is sent to an "Academia" instead of the "Mexican School" that
the neighborhood children attend a few blocks away. But as the narrative
voice points out, interactions and interdependence are hard to avoid, and
"class distinctions did not preclude courtesy" (45). In other words, persons
who are *bien educados* (of good breeding) show their class background by
being cordial to everyone regardless of class, family origins, or material
wealth. This being the case, the barriers between the Navas and their neighbors eventually break down so thoroughly that, through the years, Luisita,
grown to a young woman, falls in love with Fernando, a native Texas Mexican. Because his family owns a business in the neighborhood, proof that he
can provide a future for his family, he is considered a good match by Texas
Mexican standards. Even so, Adela worries that her niece will become "like
them," and she cannot help but think of what Luisita's possibilities might
have been in their old home in Saltillo: "It was not that Fernando was not a
good boy; he was a sober, hardworking young man and a good son, and very
fond of Luisita. It was—and she would hate herself for the thought—that

he was not of her class. 'Forget those notions' she would tell herself, 'we are all the same here now.' But she did not really believe it, not yet. She knew that her father never would" (50).

Also in similar fashion to Jovita González's detailed exposure of the customs and traditions relating to courtship and marriage, De la Garza describes how despite poverty Adela sees to it that Luisita's hand in marriage be formally asked for and that consent be given by the patriarch. Despite the uneven match between Fernando and Luisita in terms of class consciousness or of property (had the Navas retained their holdings in Mexico), the Medinas, who are better off financially, make the traditional, formal visit. As the Medinas ask for Luisita's hand in marriage to their son, Adela sits nervously "praying that [her father] will not utter some careless disparaging remark. Will he say that it is out of the question, the two families are of such unequal stature, reminding them of his properties and pedigree?" (36). Instead, Don Luis surprises Adela with his quiet acquiescence and defers to his daughter, who will give the reply traditionally reserved for the patriarch: "My daughter knows my thoughts on this matter" (36). The author's description brings to light more traditional customs such as the bride's trousseau, the dishes and linens, the embroidery, the wedding quilt, and preparations for the wedding ceremony and receptions. Despite nostalgic memories of a previous splendor in which Luisita might have married, the Nava family's resistance and their apprehensions about blending into the preestablished Texas Mexican community break down further in the process. On the occasion of this wedding, the meeting of the two elders of the Nava and Medina households comes to mark out a common ground that rejoins two previously connected cultures—one representing the Texas Mexican community, whose memory of declining status is now fading, and the one of the newcomers, whose indignation about what it means to be a Mexican in Texas is painfully fresh: "From the kitchen door Adela sees that Luisita is leading her grandfather to the other end of the table and hurries after them with the frank purpose of eavesdropping on the introduction. Luisita is saying, 'Papá Luisito, this is Fernando's . . . ' she pauses, blushing, 'my husband's great-grandfather, Don Domingo Rodríguez. He was born in one of the houses close to the river and remembers what San Antonio was like even before the Anglo-Americans came'" (57).

Grandfather Nava's words indicate his resignation to his family's new "place," both symbolic and real, where to be a Mexican in the eyes of the dominant culture holds little of the former dignity with which he could live in Saltillo. His assent to time passed and the formulaic offering of his home—"Yes . . . we came from far away, but that was a long time ago. We live in San Antonio now. This is our home . . . and yours"—signals to Adela, who has been feeling "like the lone mourner after everyone has forgotten a death," that "Perhaps it is time for her to forget as well" (59).

Central throughout this story is the woman's movement in and about the business of adjusting to a reconfiguration of gender roles while she is the provider. De la Garza also records an entire generation's crossing of the border and of class lines; its adaptation to behavior patterns that are defined by working-class struggles. Albert Camarillo has pointed out that "much of the early work in Chicano studies depicted the Chicano community very narrowly—as working-class, racially distinctive, and dominated by men" (Winkler 1990: A6–10), but De la Garza reveals the diversification of gender roles within the Mexicano community of the Southwest. Here De la Garza positions herself in the tradition of the other writers here under review: old and newly arrived Texas Mexicanos emerge as in Américo Paredes's characters Feliciano and Gumersindo of the novel *George Washington Gómez,* with rituals and traditions such as those Jovita González preserves, and with accommodation to new ways and a different citizenship as in the writings of Fermina Guerra.

"THE CANDY VENDOR'S BOY"

The adjustment of exiles from Mexico to their new positions in U.S. society has faded from the scene in De la Garza's title story, "The Candy Vendor's Boy." Here she depicts the poverty suffered by many of the older, previously established Texas Mexicans in Austin during the World War I era. This story brings into focus the barrio of the state's capital city, and it differs from better-known portrayals of "typical American" life. Grounding her descriptions in newspaper accounts of actual events and conditions of the times, De la Garza takes us at once into the unusual snowstorm that ushered in the New Year of 1918. Danny Aramberri's walk through the snow toward the city dump by the river, where once the poor Mexicanos lived, and up to the steps of the shanty home of his own family, brings the reader face-to-face with a World War I Texas Mexican soldier's experience of the impossibility of coming home. The writer effectively juxtaposes her character's experience of driving supply trucks to the front lines in France for the 141st

Infantry Regiment and his return to the dismal yet familiar scene which fills him with regret about his family's poverty and ignorance:

> He climbed the worn stone steps that were embedded into the creek bank and that led to the sagging front porch. . . . Before knocking, he paused for a minute to look inside through the front window, the only one with glass.
>
> A lighted kerosene lamp rested on the kitchen table, flickering fitfully, and showed several figures sitting immobile around the table. (10)

Despite the familiar warm aroma of the New Year *buñuelos* as well as the familiar stench of the nearby city dump by the river where his parents live (now known as Town Lake), the transformation that has occurred within Danny makes itself known through the claustrophobia he now feels in "the closeness of his parents' house." This claustrophobia comes to symbolize the oppressive and limiting identity to which he has returned—the son of the man with the broken back who carves out a living selling Mexican candy and *tamales* on the streets of early-twentieth-century Austin. This story rings true, with its universal theme, the disillusion suffered by many even today who have moved away from their communities and, despite accomplishments, return home only to find themselves reduced to the earlier construction of their "identity" by their hometown inhabitants.

The experience of a Mexican American in those times, who can no longer find his sense of place even in *his home*, is that of alienation. In "The Candy Vendor's Boy" it is dramatized by the scene in which Danny self-consciously takes part in the social life of the middle class from which he would most definitely have been excluded had it not been for war and the light-skinned, handsome figure he now presents in his military uniform. Encouraged by a friend to attend a *thé dansant* at the Knights of Columbus Hall downtown, he is at first filled with doubt and apprehension. In his attempts to integrate himself, he dances and even plays the violin at this dance for soldiers hosted by respectable "American ladies." Because he is admired and viewed only in terms of the service he is giving to his country, Danny begins to feel at ease. But this departure from his past is only momentary, for the searing memories of the scorn to which Danny was subjected by the well-to-do children of his childhood are forced back upon him. He discovers that there is no escape from his former identity as "the candy vendor's boy." Whether in school or during the days when he helped his father sell candy on the Ave-

nue and Pecan Street, he was a person with whom these children had nothing to do; they had cautioned others, too, against buying candy from the
dirty Mexicans who "burrowed around the dump for food" (26).

Cultural misunderstanding resulting in Danny's humiliation is effectively dramatized through the patronizing comments a well-meaning,
prominent Anglo doctor makes about Danny's father and his hard work
despite his infirmity. The red-headed, blue-eyed, young and fashionable
woman, who had just moments before been dancing with this handsome
young man who captivated her attention, is no longer interested and even
shuns his company. The disguise is removed, and Danny leaves the Knights
of Columbus Hall as if suddenly awakened from the momentary illusion of
having shed his identity as a poor Mexican in the eyes of the dominant culture. From the steps of the Capitol building, he looks out onto the avenue
down to the river: "It was white all the way to the river. He could not see it
from where he stood, but he knew that the refuse dump was also there by
the river" (27). Danny's own disguise inside the soldier's uniform is symbolized by the temporarily snow-covered river: "It, too, was decently disguised
by the snow today, but he knew that the thaw would soon set in, perhaps as
early as tomorrow, and then the putrefaction would resume" (27). Danny
realizes that his service to his country is only a state of temporary honor. It
will also thaw, but his class, race, and ethnic identity are permanent. He re-
signs himself: "No matter. Tomorrow he would be gone. There was the
Army, the war, the world, perhaps death too, but out there at least the odds
had not been fixed yet" (27). "Out there" may bring a release from the former indignities of a caste system, but the loss of place, he realizes, is the very
high price he must pay for an equal chance.

HÉROES HISPANOS

As an example of how fiction can recover history, the title story calls attention to a void in the record of Mexican Americans in the military. There exists no accurate record of how many Mexican Americans served the United
States in World War I, though some of the acts of its heroes are sketchily
documented in a 1988 U.S. Department of Defense publication, *Hispanics
in America's Defense*. From this document we know, for example, that during World War I nineteen-year-old Nicolas Lucero, from Albuquerque, received the French Croix de Guerre "for destroying two German machine
gun emplacements and for keeping a constant fire on the enemy positions
for over three hours" (25). We also know that a Private Marcelino Serna was

awarded the Distinguished Service Cross for extraordinary front-line battle conduct on the French-German border on September 12, 1918, after the U.S. First Army launched an offensive through the St. Mihiel salient. For later actions, he was awarded the French Croix de Guerre, the Victory Medal with three bars, and the Purple Heart twice. Some of the "fixed odds" become apparent even in the military, where the urgency of war did bring a modicum of social leveling: "Although seemingly eligible for the U.S. Medal of Honor, [Serna] was told by an officer that to be so honored one had to be of a higher rank than a "buck" private, and that he could not be advanced to a higher grade because he could not read or write English well enough to sign reports" (25).

Issues of immigration also come to bear on recoverable history, for along with the forgotten heroes of U.S. history are the many Mexican nationals who quickly and conveniently became U.S. citizens when they were needed on the battlefield, not to mention the airmen borrowed from Mexico who helped build up U.S. air power when it was badly needed. Questions of negotiation of identity are sharply drawn here with the story of a true-to-life hero who could well be De la Garza's fictional Danny Aramberri. Medal of Honor recipient David Barkley Cantú was born in 1899 in Laredo and died on the Meuse River in France on November 9, 1918. David Barkley was awarded his Citation posthumously for risking his life above and beyond the call of duty. He volunteered to swim the icy, dangerous Meuse River to ascertain the enemy's location. He and another volunteer swam the river, crawled 400 yards behind enemy lines, and made maps of the locations of enemy artillery units. As the two men were returning to the river, the Germans discovered them and opened fire. They made it into the water. However, once in the river, Barkley was overcome by cramps and drowned. His partner was able to return safely and relay the information and maps, enabling their unit to launch a successful attack against the enemy (U.S. Dept. of Defense: 51). Added to the tragic nature of this story is this soldier's suppression of his Mexican American identity: David Barkley kept his Mexican heritage a secret. Although he was recognized as the Army's first Hispanic Medal of Honor recipient in a special ceremony on September 16, 1989, during Hispanic Heritage Week, his true background did not come to light until seventy-one years after he gave his life for his country. When interviewed for a Telemundo documentary film that appeared in 1993, *Héroes Hispanos,* Rubén Barkley Hernández stated that his great uncle had kept his heritage a secret because "in those days Hispanics and Blacks were not regarded as intelligent enough for combat" and "he saw fit to keep his heritage hidden and to use the name Barkley to advance—to prove himself as a soldier." In his letters home to his mother, he asks his mother "not to mention the fact that he was Hispanic and not to use the name Cantú. And so for all practical purposes, he was just David Barkley" (*Héroes Hispanos*).

As an example of how anti-Mexican beliefs were in the air before Webb wrote his history and even with the threat of a true common enemy, an American soldier who was able to "pass" because of his appearance and name felt it necessary to deny his identity and experience. Today, politicians in their ignorance draw attention to the absence of Mexican American contributions in labor and in the defense of this country. Cited later in *Hispanic Magazine* for the absurdity of his comments, Patrick Buchanan made the following statement to the *Washington Times:* "Hispanics were never enslaved in America for three hundred years. Nor were they victims of one hundred years of racial discrimination. There were few Hispanics even in the United States forty years ago. How then can the Feds justify favoring sons of Hispanics over sons of White Americans who fought in World War II or Vietnam?" (Buchanan: 10).

Reference to the contributions Mexican Americans have made to the nation's defense remain very scattered, but there was "a Senator from New Mexico who published in the Congressional Record an honor roll of New Mexican Hispanics killed in France during World War I" (U.S. Dept. of Defense: 25–26). But the state of Texas had no such senator. It is in the *corrido,* as Américo Paredes has argued, that events affecting the Mexican American community have most often been recorded, especially in the absence of any external documentation that records their struggles. The impact of the 1918 draft, when Texas Mexicans were called upon to serve in France, is depicted in the *corrido "El registro de 1918"* [The Draft or Registration of 1918]:

Registro de 1918	[Registration of 1918
Les cayeron sus tarjetas	The cards arrived
al domicilio a cada uno	at home for each one
ser verificó el registro	verifying the registration
del veintiuno al treinta y uno.	those twenty-one to thirty-one.
Adiós Laredo lucido	Goodbye Laredo, highlighted
con sus torres y campanas,	by your towers and bells
pero nunca olvidaremos	but we shall never forget

a tus lindas mexicanas.	your beautiful Mexican women.
Ya nos llevan a pelear	They are taking us to fight
a unas tierras muy lejanas	to some distant land
y nos llevan a pelear	and taking us to fight
con las tropas alemanas.	the German troops.
Ya nos llevan a pelear	They are taking us to fight
a distintas direcciones	in various directions
y nos llevan a pelear	and taking us to fight
con diferentes naciones.	with different nations.]
(U.S. Dept. of Defense: n.p.,	
illustration)	

The return home by one of World War I's Mexican American soldiers in Beatriz de la Garza's story also parallels the events that occurred three decades later in Texas when the body of a World War II soldier, Felix Longoria, was returned to his hometown of Three Rivers. Regardless of his having given his life in the service of his country, he was received by his hometown as nothing more than a poor Mexican when "the funeral home owner initially refused the Longoria family's request to use its chapel saying white residents would oppose it" (Rhonda Smith: G8). In 1948 Dr. Hector P. García, founder of the American GI Forum, brought attention to the disregard for the corpses of Mexican American servicemen returning from war and to the discrimination the survivors faced at home, when he drew national attention to the fact that Longoria had been denied a funeral in his hometown. One of his letters of protest calling for action on the part of the community read and was posted as follows (Héctor P. García 1992):

GRAN JUNTA DE PROTESTA
AHORA EN LA NOCHE EN LA ESCUELA LAMAR
Ubicada en calles 19 y Morris a las ocho de la noche habra una
Gran Junta Protesta debido a que se le han negado los servicios de una
casa Funeraria en Three Rivers, Texas, a los Restos de un Soldado,
llamado Felix Longoria de Three Rivers, Texas.
EL AMERICAN GI Forum
de CORPUS CHRISTI
Requiere su presencia para que venga a oir los datos acerca de esta
CRUEL HUMILLACION a uno de nuestras HEROES Soldado de
esta última gran GUERRA. Todos los VETERANOS y sus familias
y público en general deben asistir sin FALTA o sin EXCUSAS.
Cuando una casa Funeraria se Niega a Honrar a los RESTOS de

un Ciudadano Americano solamente porque es de mejicano
entonces es TIEMPO que no unicamente el America GI Forum
sino todo el pueblo se levante a protestar esta injusticia.
Se la Ruega Respetuosamente a las MADRES de Soldados
Muertos en la GUERRA se sirvan ASISTIR.
Hoy esta Noche, Martes 11 de Enero de 1949
Estará presente la Sra. Beatriz Longoria Viuda
del Valiente Soldado Felix Longoria.

[LARGE PROTEST MEETING
TONIGHT AT LAMAR SCHOOL
Located on 19th and Morris streets. At 8:00 p.m. there will be a
large protest meeting due to the denial of funeral services for the
remains of Felix Longoria by a funeral home in Three Rivers, Texas.
The American GI Forum
of Corpus Christi
Requires your attendance to hear the facts pertaining to this cruel
humiliation of one of our hero soldiers in this last war. All veterans,
their families, and the general public should attend without fail or
excuses. When a funeral home refuses to honor the remains of an
American citizen, solely because he is of Mexican origin, then it is
time for not only the American GI Forum, but the entire community,
to rise in protest of this injustice. We respectfully beg the attendance
of the mothers of fallen soldiers in the War, this evening, Tuesday, the
eleventh of January of 1949. Mrs. Beatriz Longoria, widow of the
brave soldier, Felix Longoria, will be in attendance.
American GI Forum
Dr. Hector P. Garcia, Pres.]
(my translation)

Eventually, after media attention and with the help of then U.S. Senator
Lyndon B. Johnson, Longoria was buried in Arlington National Cemetery.
Through the close-up view that the fictional portrayal "The Candy Vendor's
Boy" provides for us, the narrative also reinscribes a lost history into the
minds of the readers, who might not otherwise have been drawn to see the
contradictory experience of sacrifice for one's country coupled with the discrimination and denigration that disappointed so many returning minority
servicemen. Their plight has generally gone undocumented in history as
framed by the rhetoric of dominance.

"THE KID FROM THE ALAMO"

Though "The Kid from the Alamo" brings us closer to our own times, it also returns us to the all too familiar scene of a famous battle of an older war. This story is particularly relevant in our own times; it is a telling portrayal of the pressures felt by a new generation of children and young adults to accommodate and assimilate to an American educational system that refuses to validate their own culture. It is also a particularly relevant story with which to end this analysis, for it puts in perspective some of the themes of the works examined here in relation to the lasting effects of an educational system which still teaches the Battle of the Alamo as the great historical event of the nineteenth century. This story, however, is told from the perspective of the narrator, Ruben Morales. Upon his return to South Texas thirty years after the event he recalls, he recognizes Osvaldo Esparza, a friend from out of his childhood. The encounter takes him back to events surrounding his sixth-grade teacher's assignment of a class project for in-depth reports on the Battle of the Alamo hero of the students' choice. He recognizes the proprietor of the business as the *pachuco* of his sixth-grade class who rebelled imaginatively by asserting that in his assignment he would report on his own ancestor, Gregorio Esparza, who, he claimed, died at the Alamo alongside the better-known heroes. Class questions come to bear here, as the narrator remembers how the *pachuco* was shunned by conservative, upwardly mobile, even middle-class Hispanics, who see him as a deviant from mainstream American values.

> This was 1958 or 1959 and the heyday of *pachucos* was already over.
> Some people said that *pachucos* went back to the early forties and
> remembered the Zoot Suit Riots in California which had happened
> at that time. They had been strongest in the barrios in California
> and in the larger cities of the Southwest, like Albuquerque and San
> Antonio. Also, it was funny, but *pachucos* had been mostly Mexican-
> American and not Mexican-Mexican. Anyway, *pachucos* were when
> I was a kid what the hippies were later: something that your parents
> hoped you would not grow up to be. (De la Garza 1994: 203)

In the story, Osvaldo's attempt to reinscribe a Texas Mexican hero into Texas history is indicative of a public education curriculum that excludes Hispanics or depicts them in disparaging ways. This exclusion, coupled with an acute awareness of the "material conditions of their existence" in the absence of any historical context that could demonstrate how things got to be as they are, still has the effect of driving a large portion of young Hispanics to less fruitful endeavors than completing high school:

> Texas history was something that I wasn't particularly interested in. A few things about it struck me as odd, though. I remember that the textbook started at first with a few pages on the Indians, then there was a little about the Spanish explorers and how they called the place "Tejas," after an Indian tribe, and that the word meant "friends." Then there was another bit about the missionaries and the missions they built, several of which were just a ways up the road from us. Then it jumped to the arrival of the Anglos.
>
> That is what struck me as odd. I mean, all you had to do was look around, and you would see that there were a lot of us, Mexicans, in Texas. So where did we come from? We came in at the Alamo, where we killed Davy Crockett, and at San Jacinto, where we were whipped by Sam Houston. That was it. Santa Anna and the wicked Mexicans were taken care of in a couple of chapters, and then we went on to the Civil War and a lot of boring governors after that. And not another Spanish name was mentioned again. (210)

With this description and the example from the story of history taught as hero worship replete with omissions, stereotypes, and distortions, De la Garza points to the alienating effects this kind of "official history" continues to have on present-day Hispanics.

The effect of the dominant culture's view of history makes itself known through the resistance and accommodation and retrieved memory of the author's character/narrator, who on his return home recognizes the boyhood friend whose courage he once admired. In the story, the teacher's assignment of a report on one of the Battle of the Alamo "heroes" has various results. The class becomes divided with conflict, with Mexicans on one side and Anglos on the other, as if they were reliving the Battle of the Alamo. One child, Lupita, stays home, claiming a stomach ache, because she cannot face the confrontation for which the teacher's assignment has set the stage: "Here I stopped being furious, and the image of Lupita, staying home from school and confounding the doctors with her stomach aches, came to mind. I would stay home too. I would not go to that school where all they did was put us down" (215).

Generational differences and values also come to light in the midst of this struggle over history as Ruben Morales's father becomes furious over his son's deliberate absence from school, for he had "worked to make sure all his kids got an education in the face of all Gringos who didn't want Mexican kids in school" (216). His father's view is pragmatic rather than ideological; his struggles had been defined by traditional values and older struggles over property, by the effort to leave something to his children after his death and to lead a life with at least some dignity, even if he got no respect from the Anglos. His advice to his son is that he not let himself get distracted from real, present-day issues. He must never let his guard down, and he must focus on his education and thus his own potential for prosperity:

> He did not care about the Alamo and other ancient history. What did it matter who was or was not at the Alamo over a hundred years ago? What mattered was who had the jobs at Fort Sam Houston in San Antonio today. Did they hire Mexicans there? Not very many. What was important was, did you have property, did you have a good job? Where other Mexicans had been pushed out and run off, he had bought land, like his father before him, and worked it from sun up to sun down and improved it, so that even the Gringos respected him—well, maybe not respected him, they didn't respect Mexicans at all—but they gave him his due and didn't try to push him around. He had learned to take care of himself. (217)

As a former Carrancista in the Mexican Revolution, Morales belongs to a certain generation, to "the kind of people who believed you had to leave something to your children" (206). His struggles echo the very same struggles and values depicted in various ways by other writers in this study: Lupita, who never returns to school, is victimized like Chonita in Paredes's "The Hammon and the Beans"; Morales, with his fierce independence, is like the new leader in Jovita González's *Dew on the Thorn* and Feliciano in Américo Paredes's *George Washington Gómez*. On the other hand, as a grown man, Osvaldo Esparza appears to have gone through the same process of accommodation as George W. Gómez. The *pachuco* at first looks like Guálinto Gómez fighting battles over the history of the Alamo in school. As a businessman, Oswald Esparza caters and tries to fit in with his Anglo clientele. He does not care to reminisce with Ruben. His memories of his once claimed relative appear to have completely faded, much to the narrator's disappointment: "I wanted to stick out my hand and call him *Vato* and start talking in Spanish, throwing in a few *pachuco* words that I had learned from him, but he was standing behind the counter with the look of 'What else can I do for you, and will that be all?'" (201). When he asks Osvaldo if Gregorio Esparza was really his ancestor, he replies, "'Who? . . . Never heard of him . . . I made him up,' he said" (220).

Despite his initial disappointment at meeting Osvaldo, Ruben, upon reflecting, eventually comes to understand his father's meaning: "As I got out to open the gate to the ranch, I was wondering where Osvaldo had heard of Gregorio Esparza. He was not in the history books that we had read. Even Miss Gibbs didn't know of him. Then it struck me that Valdo had already been to the Alamo before us. I could not help laughing and shaking my head at the thought. Rufus and his road repairs. Osvaldo and his famous ancestor. My father would have been pleased" (220).

Osvaldo had learned to outsmart the system at an early age by claiming an important ancestor with his own last name, in order to make a point in the face of bigotry. For his own success and at the cost of the repression of his identity and memory, he again maneuvers as best he can. He has a business of his own; running for reelection to political office, Ruben's brother, Rufus, had suddenly gotten busy fixing roads, and that is what would have counted for Ruben's father. Who got the jobs and who owns the property? He realizes in the end that a lot of progress had been made: "It struck me all of a sudden that we had come a long way. Not just Rufus, but all of us, since the days when the Plantation Café in Poggendorf had had a sign that said, 'We Do Not Serve Mexicans'" (219).

Despite progress defined in this sense, the author is also careful to point to an unhappy legacy left by an educational system that refuses to change in its most fundamental teachings. Refocusing our attention on the children like Lupita who get turned away, the author reveals that she was in fact the reason why Osvaldo had taken his unique approach to the Battle of the Alamo. In the only comment to Ruben in which he does "re-member," Lupita, we learn, is the very cause of his resistance:

I stopped, and before I could ask him why [he made it up], he added, "I got tired of that kid that was always crying, that girl who said the Anglo girl was picking on her. Lupita. What happened to her? Did she stay in school?"

I could not remember what had happened to Lupita. All I remembered was that I did not remember her after the sixth grade. "No," I answered him. "I don't think that she stayed in school."

"That's too bad." He went back to the table with the truck driver and his passenger, and I left. (220)

Under a democratic system of government, Mexican American students must have access to schooling, for access must be guaranteed if a false representation of a democratic system is to be upheld. But as future disciplined workers forming part of the labor force, with little of the kind of independence that owning a business or property can give one, they must not only possess skills but also the proper attitudes toward their future (subordinate) work in the labor force. The danger for schoolchildren in places like the South Texas town in this story, when they are made to believe that it is they who have failed, not the system that was so "available," is that they turn away from institutionalized learning altogether. The absence of themselves in the history they are taught, as well as in the literature and in the illustrations in their books, indicates early on to these children that they need not try too hard to belong, because they are already scripted out.

The obvious absence of the Mexican American in the "history" of this state within the educational experience is still very much the subject of discussions concerning today's curriculum in the schools, as Oralia Garza de Cortes points out:

> In an era in which the school dropout rate among Hispanics is already alarmingly high and increasing, we must pay heed to Walter Dean Myers's thoughtful essay "The Reluctant Reader" if we wish to empower children with a sense of positive self-identity and self-esteem about who they are. Through reading the literature that reflects their own cultural experiences, through learning of their history, and through seeing themselves in the literature for children then perhaps minority youngsters too can begin to see a future for themselves in a society that everyday continues to demand more intellectual output than they are currently prepared for. (cited in Garza de Cortez 1992: 123)

Students, unlike Lupita, feel compelled to either pretend to believe the lies and "go along to get along" or to negate who they are, as we have seen with Guálinto's experience in *George Washington Gómez*. But perhaps the best way to show how fiction recovers history or criticizes it is to look to autobiographical accounts of the effects of this type of distortion. José María Salazar, Jr., describes the South Texas educational system in our own day:

The honors system at San Benito [neighboring city to Harlingen] was instrumental to my assimilation. I simply never interacted with the *pachucos* because I was told I was so much better than them. I wasn't even considered a Mexicano. I was an honors student and that meant that I was segregated from other Chicanos. I was encouraged to do well so that I could continue to qualify to be in these privileged classes. What I never noticed was that virtually all of the Anglo students (only 5% of the student body) were in these classes. It all worked very well. After four years of segregated classes with primarily white people, you *felt* superior. We were socialized to think we had a right to be honored because we had been permitted to be in these classes. The fact that it was the domain of the *gringos,* taught us to associate success with whiteness. We were encouraged to be as much like them as we could. It meant nothing that 98% of the Valley population was Chicano/Mexicano because they weren't represented in the media. They were nothing; they didn't count. But I was close to being something because I now *acted* just like them. (8–9)

Worse than the self-hate brought about by this type of internal segregation is the placing of many students at terrible odds with an institution that holds the keys to their success and potential intellectual contributions to a society that more than ever needs their full participation.

o o o

With a close-up view, Beatriz de la Garza offers through "fiction" a reinscribing of a lost history in the minds of the readers who might not otherwise be drawn to view history as a contradictory experience of struggle against dominance and contribution to a just society. De la Garza's manner of recording the history of her people's complex struggles does not yield to the flattened concepts of the rhetoric of dominance. Her life and her writings distinctly articulate the struggles that come from the crossing of geographic as well as social-class and gender-constructed lines, in search of a sense of belonging in a place. Expressing the fluidity of her own cultural borders, her intelligence captures a whole realm of historical experience, individual and social, which was marginalized or denied by the school of historiography exemplified in the writings of Walter Prescott Webb.

The plight of those who for the most part have remained without a voice in U.S. literature cries out for the social and historical relevance provided by these stories. The stories of Beatriz de la Garza help fill a long-standing hiatus in evaluation of an educational process by which, even in the face of continuing obstacles and obstinate refusals, minoritized sectors in a mixed society might be acknowledged in all their independent reality. Even if fusion might not be desirable, reciprocal antagonism of the kind that De la Garza attends to, by portrayal and innuendo, not by propaganda, can only shrink into what needs to be actualized: the human potential for inspired consciousness that has sometimes induced cultural integration—and flowering—in recorded history.

EPILOGUE

En un barrio pobre llamado La Mina
Allá en Laredo, Tejas
Don Luís nació un día . . .
Se crió con nopales, frijoles, tortillas
con tacos y liebres, con huevos y migas . . .
Señalaba trabajos por todito Tejas
y por mal sueldo se fue a otros estados
con todo sufria, cubrió tantas millas,
que en un surco largo pasaron los años
Cuando ya sus hijos todos se casaron
Don Luís ya cansado volvió para Tejas
Encontró lo mismo que un día había dejado
pa' los campesinos, la misma pobreza . . .

—"Don Luís el Tejano," contemporary *corrido*/waltz
by Juan Barco, recorded by The Latin Breed[1]

 Patricia Limerick at the end of her chapter "Racialism on the Run" is looking for a center in the absence of the coherence once available when the principal concern of the Western historian was merely "the advance of white male pioneers across the continent" (291). In searching for some clue to the center that would lend coherence to the larger story she tries to offer, "whether in Indian removal or Mormon migration," she points to the fact that "[e]ach group may well have had its own, self-defined story, but in the 'contest for property and profit,' those stories met" (292). The center may be derived from the larger story that emerges from the coming together of these individual cultural group narrative histories. A larger story of diversity, power, and privilege that contains many multifaceted conflicts and struggles that are more telling of the complexities of our nation's history would come in sharp contrast to any one history forced into a prefabricated story of advance, of progress based on an ethic of imperialism. The stories of a *gente decente* and my story emerge out of the authors' strong identification with the recurring themes of struggle and migration in search for a better life—a life with dignity as reflected in the song excerpted above and in the stories that Limerick examines.

The small South Texas town of Pharr, where I grew up during the 1960s, was predominantly a Mexican town ruled by an Anglo oligarchy. In 1960, the death of my oldest sister, then only nine, made it necessary that my family return from Chicago to this Rio Grande Valley border town, where my mother, maternal grandmother, and great-grandparents all lived. Before leaving the South Side of inner-city Chicago, one of my aunts had said to my father, "En el Valle la gente todavía se muere de hambre" [In the Valley, people still die of hunger]. We did not die of hunger, but I gradually became aware of the way Chicanos were taught to view themselves and how they were treated in society and particularly within the public school system—a segregated system reflecting the social, political, and economic conditions of the Mexican American people as a whole. This experience and what I am about to relate has great bearing on the project I have tried to carry out in this book as well as on the career paths I have chosen. For me it becomes an essential story that explains a driving force and commitment to education that I could not escape even if I desired to do so.

Attendance in the first grade of a Chicago Catholic school where I was one of only two "white" students in my class gave me the basis by which to make important comparisons in those early years. Life as a South Side Chicago factory worker's child, living in a predominantly black neighborhood, with Catholic German, Irish, Polish, and Italian Americans as immediate neighbors and friends, contrasted sharply with this new experience on the South Texas Border. Most of my mother's siblings had moved to Chicago during the 1950s seeking better employment opportunities than those that had been available in the Valley in their youth when they had migrated seasonally north to do farmwork. Most of them, after twenty to thirty years of primarily factory work, eventually began moving back to the Valley during the 1980s and were able to buy property. In Chicago during the 1950s, we thought the reason my family was allowed to move into the large house in which we lived in our Chicago neighborhood was that my father had convinced the landlord that he could fix anything that was in disrepair; but, as we later found out, it was really because the landlord was afraid he would have to rent it to African Americans. He would rather have it empty. Apparently in that particular neighborhood, our Latino identity helped us to enjoy some of the privileges that came with whiteness.

On the other hand, in the Valley of the 1960s we came closer to living the experience of the Chicago African Americans. It did not matter that we were the majority. Choices for employment for my father were varied but of the same kind. Most of the women in the neighborhood who worked outside the home worked in the *bodegas,* the packing sheds, and the men did manual labor. Cattle trucks would go down our streets in the early morning hours picking up men and women of all ages, from great-grandfathers to children—all went to work in the local fields. Some men were fortunate enough to be *troqueros* hauling produce and other products in and out of the Valley, but most were wage laborers on the farms in and around the small and clustered surrounding towns. Our particular neighborhood was mostly made up of migrant farmworkers. Just as my maternal grandmother and her ten children had done for many years, these families boarded up their frame houses every year around early April and were not to be seen again by those of us who stayed behind until around November of the same year.

In order to avoid this "option," my father, the son of a cattle rancher/farmer just on the other side of the Rio Grande in the city of Reynosa Tamaulipas, had migrated north seeking industrial work. Before that, in 1953, he had brought his young family to Corpus Christi, where my grandfather (according to family history) had once owned land. Given his experience and training with PEMEX (Petroleros Mexicanos) and despite his family's opposition, my father sought work as an offshore oil driller, a job that was paying five dollars an hour at the time. He was quickly informed that *those* jobs were not for Mexicans, but they could use him to paint the sides of the ships as did other Mexican laborers. My parents were nearly destitute soon after. In Port Lavaca, where I was born, my father was digging ditches for the Brown & Root Company, and we were living in a labor camp. Again, seeking a better life, we went north to Chicago where we were to spend the next six years under somewhat improved circumstances. Upon our return to the Valley, my father took a job as a gasoline station attendant, while my mother sewed for the neighborhood, raised chickens, sold eggs, and occasionally worked at the *Casa de Matas* (nursery for plants). Meanwhile, my siblings and I became students in the Mexican schools of the Pharr—San Juan—Alamo Independent School District.

Recent revisionist historical accounts of Mexicano life in South Texas during the early part of the century have mapped what I had the opportunity to witness and live for myself in this small town. In Jovita González's reflections on the Río Grande Valley of the late 1920s and 30s, we obtain a clear view of the wage earner's circumstances and how that related to his children's experience in schools: "The friendly feeling which had slowly developed between the old American and Mexican families had been replaced by a feeling of hate, distrust and jealousy on the part of the Mexicans" (as cited in Montejano: 114–115). The "Mexican schools" were attended by the Mexicanos from the barrio, while the "grammar schools" served the Anglo school children and the few more affluent Mexicanos:

> Segregated schools were a straightforward reflection of the racial divisions of the farm towns. In the Lower Valley, the towns of Edinburg, Harlingen, and San Benito segregated their Mexican school children through the fourth and fifth grades. And along the dense string of newcomer towns of Highway 83—the "longest mile" of McAllen, Mercedes, Mission, Pharr–San Juan, and Weslaco—Mexican school segregation was an unbroken policy. On the Gulf Coast plains, Raymondville, Kingsville, Robstown, Kenedy, and Taft were among the new towns where segregation was practiced. And in the Winter Garden area, Mexicans were segregated through the fifth grade in Crystal City, Carrizo Spings, Palm, Valley Wells, Asherton, and Frio Town. There was no need for segregation beyond the fifth or sixth grade, as many school authorities and growers noted, because Mexicans rarely "get that far." Once sufficient numbers began passing the sixth grade in the late 1920's, the segregated system was expanded and Mexican junior and senior high schools began to appear. (Montejano: 168–169)

This in large part was still true of the Valley as I came to know it in the early 1960s. The Mexican and grammar school system, as it had been set up for the elementary schools since the 1920s, remained in place up until the late 1960s, despite the 1954 desegregation law. As children we were not conscious of this overtly "separate but unequal" system, but by the time all the students were joined together in the sixth grade, the ethnic disparity in the basic skills and background, especially in the social sciences, math, and science, made us inferior even in our own eyes. Certainly, we did not see this situation as a deliberate program or policy of domination, or as a way of ensuring the continued presence of the Mexicano primarily as a labor force. Instead, we marveled at how much the Anglo children "knew" compared with us, without questioning the system we were trained to accept, and we felt fortunate just to be receiving an education, for most of our parents had not. We were thus taught by our parents to have a reverence for our schools and our teachers, even when they were brutal to us for the great offense of speaking Spanish, or when they shamed us for following and believing in our traditions and eating our foods. This moment of integration was significant and necessary, for the school district could no longer afford to keep us apart and because originally the school system had not expected many Mexicanos to make it that far.

Integration had its most significant impact on the minds of the South Texas Mexicano children. We learned to view ourselves as inferior because of the Anglo advantages. They not only knew more and possessed advanced skills, but they also had obvious material advantages. There were constant references to the "barrio *americano,*" the "American" neighborhood, or the *americanos,* as if we were not Americans as well. Their brick houses looked nothing like our small frame homes, many of which were boarded up, with *escusados* (outhouses) lining the alleys. The type of history taught in these schools where the struggles of our people were either absent or distorted, coupled with our material conditions, made us believe less and less in ourselves as valuable people. I believe it was at this moment that large groups of Mexicano children, thrust for the first time against their Anglo counterparts, became convinced of the "rightness" of their social and economic status in the community—of their "proper" place.

At the same time that this was our experience as citizens on this side of the border, close proximity to Mexico generated a sort of social as well as linguistic heteroglossia. The Mexicano experience there is imbued with a sense of historic identity that never quite fits the schemes proposed and imposed by texts read in the schools. Many families gained what I can best call an "oppositional" sense of our history. We had close family ties with relatives across the river. In my case, one half of the family, my father's relatives, resided mostly in the town of Reynosa. In fact, my father's ancestors, the Garza-Zamoras, had been among the original founders of that city. My paternal grandmother's father had been a captain under Venustiano Carranza during the 1910 Revolution; later he had ridden up and down the river on horseback looking for contraband, such as coffee. At the turn of the century, the recently widowed mother of my paternal grandfather had moved her seven children from the Camargo–Rio Grande city area and bought a ranch outside Reynosa where her brother-in-law's ranch had been established generations earlier along the old *Carretera* Monterrey. With her death, my grandfather, the eldest son, took on the responsibility of raising his younger siblings, and later in life he with his younger brother became the owner of the dairy in town. While the Partido Revolucionario Independiente (PRI) was gradually taking a totalitarian grip on Mexico, there was much discontent among the very people who had once been ardent revolutionaries. These included my paternal grandmother's *Carrancista* father and his son-in-law, my grandfather. The former could do little more than publicly criticize the local administrators, a privilege he could get away with in his advanced years and as a respected member of the community. My grandfather, on the other hand, rode horseback during the early part of the 1940s, gathering all the *rancheros* living on the outskirts of the city and encouraging them to come into the city to show their support for the Partido Acción Nacional (PAN). Together, the rancheros he gathered rode into the middle of Reynosa showing their support for candidate General Juan Almazán against the PRI candidate, General Manuel Avila Camacho, who was running for *Presidente de la República*. This he did at the request of his first cousin, General Tiburcio Garza-Zamora, who supported change in the national and local government.

Frequent visits to Mexico while I was growing up showed me some of the complexities of our culture; later I saw in these the ideological diversity which was based on a class system. My paternal grandmother's family, for instance, were all of the merchant class. They owned restaurants, theaters, curio shops, and liquor stores in town; but my grandfather's family were all rancheros. Though my grandfather and a friend of his were the only men to own a car in Reynosa for some time, in general they were unlike the city people. Though they had money as well as property, they did not go in for showing off material wealth. Other than the abundance displayed at family gatherings on the ranch on the occasion of a wedding or baptism, where animals were slaughtered for the feast and musicians were hired for the dance, their lives were simple, for the most part consisting primarily of putting in a hard day's work. On the other hand, the city people were more openly conscious regarding their material wealth. They were more dramatic and flamboyant, at times even *presumidos,* or pretentious, at social events held at exclusive *casinos,* or private clubs. Even within this fraction of the family, their various forms of speech, their nationalistic attitudes as Mexicanos, as well as their view of us, the *pochos* in the family, collided against the mixed South Texas languages on the "other" side, where various levels of Spanish and English came together and were combined. This could only contradict or at least throw in doubt the flattened versions of our identity that formal education sought to impose on us. How could it all be so simple, so stereotyped through literature, history, and the media when our immediate experience was so complex and multileveled? The question could not then be answered by us, given the forces of our immediate, daily environment. The question of relations between two border cultures was too complex for most of us. We were well schooled under a system set up to make good citizens of us all and thus to dominate our culture through "education." Yet *preparación* was always of the utmost importance, for my mother struggled as did other parents to continue her education at the night classes offered at our neighborhood schools. And we had some excellent teachers, both Anglo and Mexican American, who despite the system did their best for us and did in fact make a difference. To add to the heteroglossia of our borderlands existence, many of us were heavily schooled in Catholicism. The religious instruction we received was for the most part influenced by the Irish priests and nuns, many of whom were recently arrived from Dublin. They formed a meaningful part of our *preparación.*

The issue of "progress" comes powerfully to bear on this experience and on our "imagined relationship to the world around us." While relatives on the other side of the border had their traditions and history, we had "progress," and the opportunity to succeed. Despite the conflicting images of ourselves, many of us growing up in this era also experienced a time of great transition which gave us our particular view of reality. Many parents were able to work themselves out of their poverty. My father benefited from a major oil company that moved into the Valley and promoted him to an administrative position over many stations throughout South Texas and Corpus Christi. In turn, he saw this as an opportunity to employ other Mexicanos and help others of his community who were trying to build their own businesses. My mother, in the meantime, spent ten years of her youth working long hard hours in a garment factory that also established itself in a neighboring Valley town. A very intelligent and beautiful woman, my mother in one form or another always persisted in her determination to continue her education despite her large family and multiple responsibilities. I credit her for my not having ever limited my expectations and goals in life, and both my parents for providing the sound example of disciplined hard work, goal setting, and aspirations for a better life.

Some parents eventually began to acquire property, perhaps some of the same land lost generations earlier. They did this either by forming cooperatives or through individual investment costing many years of hard work and sacrifice. Many of us who grew up in the migrant neighborhoods and attended segregated schools finished school despite discouragement by counselors and the general school environment. With the help of college loans, grants, or scholarships that became available during the later 1960s and '70s, we were able to acquire college educations and become professionals and public officials.

With the Chicano Movement initiated in San Antonio in 1967 and politically significant events in our immediate vicinity, such as the farmworkers' strikes in 1966 and subsequent school walkouts, power began to shift hands—though sometimes that too was also an illusion, for some of the old structures survived with a new face. But overall more choices did become available to the Valley Mexicanos. Many Anglos who didn't like the changes and were not bound by property holdings such as small farms or by some merchant endeavor began to leave our town or move into the still Anglo-dominated towns such as McAllen or Harlingen, while there were others who were at ease with transitions. Witnessing this growing empowerment with a community base made some of us true believers in the American Dream. All we had to do was work hard, as our parents had.

Given the drastic improvement we had experienced in our own lives, and even in the face of the Vietnam era, when a disproportionate number of our Valley Mexicanos were being called up to serve in the armed forces, the large majority of us were conservative Democrats and very patriotic Americans. We believed in the system that we saw: it allowed for change and we were more than willing to fight for that. In general, because of what we perceived as progress, it was a time of great optimism in the Valley, even with the Vietnam War claiming so many of the lives of the sons of our old neighborhoods. What was not immediately apparent to a lot of us was that we were but a few out of that generation who managed to squeeze through a window of opportunity before the Nixon and Reagan eras closed off what had finally become available to us during the Johnson years. Left behind were those who could not or did not want to move out of the old neighborhoods. Many continued to live as their parents had. Maybe their houses were slightly improved; maybe their children now finished school or even went on to college; but the general poverty remained—a permanent underclass once again became painfully evident. Even with our generation who did "succeed," it would be interesting to trace how many of us were able to actually sustain our progress. How many of us were able to pay for our own children's college education—and how many were loaded down with student loan debts or, worse still, not even able to benefit from legally imposed affirmative action, which of late has also come under attack?

In terms of our relationship to "America," it becomes clear that we drew strength from feelings that we at least to some degree had participated in a larger story of a progress. I suppose we believed that somewhere hidden in that positivist image of history replete with its hero-type "winning of the West" images that looked nothing like us, were our story and our values. The same narrative strategy often used in the construction of false histories in a myth-making process still shapes the way we compulsively act with regard to one another and makes significant comment on our "characteristic attitudes toward ourselves, our culture, and our racial subgroupings, and our land" (Slotkin: 17–18).

As we have seen, Walter Prescott Webb, as self-proclaimed frontiersman, becomes an actor in the very history he writes: he channeled and perpetuated the mainstream of contempt toward the Plains Indian and the Texas Mexican. Webb offers us a close-up view not so much of a very specific history but of a myth-making process that has repeatedly taken place when justification for past acts of aggression as well as cultural cohesion was necessary for a national identity. Slotkin notes the importance of the storyteller's role in uniting a fragmented people against some kind of constructed villain and the repetitive nature of these narratives when he demonstrates the important role that the earlier Daniel Boone narratives (which appeared in 1784) played in uniting colonial society: "This figure caught and held national attention for half a century, despite varying sectional evaluations of the moral and social character of the frontier hero" (23). He also notes how the success of this kind of narrative is dependent upon "the extent that its assumptions about life, America, Indian, God, and the wilderness coincided with those of its particular audience" (23). In the Valley that I grew up in, John F. Kennedy, Robert Kennedy, Dr. Martin Luther King, Jr., and Lyndon B. Johnson were our national heroes; our local heroes were our parents, our teachers, and the community leaders who strove to bring about equity and social justice for our times.

On the other hand, just as Webb's story provided a Western pioneer mythology for the new frontiersman, a similar "unifying" narrative which reappears, on demand, to promote the image or "feeling" of a cohesive, unified culture is necessary for any community. Our common enemy was the racist who tried to either exploit or humiliate the Mexican. Our heroes, as were Webb's, were the hard workers who managed to succeed with dignity despite great odds. Left out of this story of progress are the overwhelming obstacles that have nothing to do with the harsh environment, as is the story of the non-survivors.

Reaction to a 1991 National Museum of American Art exhibit at the Smithsonian dramatizes how this positivist image of history persists to this day and is still upheld as a paradigm of American values. The authors of the catalog "redress what they see as an inaccurate, flag-waving version of the West that smoothes over the many ways in which powerful special-interest groups, backed with considerable money, wrested control of the land not only from Indians but also from homesteaders, who are normally considered to have triumphed" (Lubin). Elizabeth Broun, Director of the NMAA, is critical of these paintings. She views them as an example of how art, servicing a particular ideology, has reinforced specific notions about our country's past: "The idea of progress implies some ultimate goal or at least occasional plateaus from which to gaze back with satisfaction over the path just traveled" (Brown: viii). She also notes how Frederick Jackson Turner's 1893 thesis that "the filling of the continent from ocean to ocean had called forth aspects of character that were now to be writ large as national identity" was "based on his interpretation of the 1890 census, which did more than declare the continent fully settled. It documented what many had suspected, that the stock of Anglo-Saxon 'founders' was being rapidly diluted through immigration" (viii). Because of the fear of the diluting effect of immigration on the national identity, art of this nature was called for at a particular time in history and had the power in effect not only to reinforce notions of the past but also to rewrite historical events as they were already written or being written into dominative versions of American history.

The reaction to the exhibit itself provides interesting testimony to how Turner-like concepts of western expansionism are still upheld and defended. In a *San Antonio Express News* article entitled "Cultures Clash at the Smithsonian" (June 9, 1991), Craig Donegan reports that former Librarian of Congress Daniel Boorstin and Senator Ted Stevens (R-Alaska) are "sputtering mad" because they take issue not with the paintings on exhibition, but with the "words that so-called revisionist historians have supplied to explain, or interpret, the pictures." According to Donegan, "Right wingers got mad because they saw the exhibit as besmirching the good name of American mission, progress and Manifest Destiny."

Donegan dismisses the efforts on both sides either to reinterpret history or to defend long-standing conceptual images by crediting the present-day American public with the ability to automatically discredit images that have been given a prominent position in American culture. He denies the power that a media in the service of this "American mission" has exercised since the days of Remington to perpetuate the "mythic fabrication glorifying the West through the work of various artists, filmmakers, politicians, and land promoters" (Lubin). For him, however consciously or unconsciously these images were meant to make their influence felt on the minds of the American public, they have failed to do so. Donegan states with regard to the exhibit:

> Moreover, it is beating a dead horse because few fools alive today— besides Stevens—are still wedded to westward-ho myths such as that in the *Ballad of Davy Crockett.*
>
> Even as kids we knew that Davy Crockett was born on a table top in Joe's cafe, the dirtiest place in the USA, drank a bottle of beer when he was only 9, grew up to look just like Frankenstein.
>
> Thus we deconstruct the man that wore—and the West that was—the coonskin cap, the cavalry charge and the cowboy hat.

Donegan's view is diametrically opposed to Broun's, for she assigns to language and especially art the power to revise "history"—by recording events as they supposedly occurred. She sees the need to produce these images glorifying the West as a reaction to the immigration of various peoples into the United States, which called for a more fixed definition of American culture:

> [Turner's] announcement that free land in the West was fully claimed, decades before anyone had anticipated, came just at the moment that the country was discovered to be filling with a polyglot population demanding accommodation. The need to define a unique American spirit—preferably one that validated the established order—took on a new urgency.
>
> American artists responded by revising history through art, presenting in their work a privileged role for a largely eastern elite. Ignoring the much earlier Hispanic settlements and the long record of Indian tribal life, they wrote a "creation myth" for America that focused on the primacy of colonial English settlers in the New World. (Broun: viii)

With regard to the power of language in shaping this American concept of the West and thus an American cultural identity, Broun also notes that in the innumerable treatises on declining Anglo-Saxon influence (as with the labeling device), key words were given new meanings: "'original Americans' and 'native Americans' refer to early English colonists, as if both Indians and Hispanics could be erased from the American past through the manipulation of language" (ix).

The historians who made heroes of themselves by doing a romantic spicing up in their own scholarly work at the service of a particular ideology are resurrected and honored for all to remember their great contributions to knowledge. This became evident with the recent erection of a statue honoring "Texas literary greats" J. Frank Dobie, Roy Bedichek, and Walter Prescott Webb in Zilker Park in Austin, Texas, where mostly Mexican American children play (see Morris: F1). The purpose of erecting this statue, which cost approximately $240,000, was to restore the "memory of these three great men [which is] beginning to fade. Statues help create memory for a community," said Larry Wright, author and one of the fund-raisers.

With a growing circulation and mainstreaming of literary and historical works by authors who write outside the "ideological American consensus" of what constitutes life and struggle in the United States, there will come about a gradual awareness that not only contradicts the progress mythology of our history but succeeds in adding fresh dimensions to what we define as constituting the "real" or the "natural." If scholarship can clarify past complexities that have been overshadowed, if it can restore to the light stories as well as documents which have been either suppressed or neglected, then histories such as Walter Prescott Webb's will eventually begin to appear more like fictions, as outmoded examples of the rhetoric of dominance, slanted for the particular purposes of the past. On the other hand, the recovering of literary works which anticipated the present movement in Chicano/a letters such as those of González, Mena, Guerra, Paredes, Viramontes, and de la Garza provides, at a particular moment in history, a more telling historical truth. By responding to dominative histories and questioning them, these literary "fictions," as well as contemporary ones, could make the reappearance of any rhetoric of dominance more immediately discernible in the domains of popular culture and of scholarly research. While there is much work to be done in recovering the work of precursors such as these, the works of contemporary Chicano/a writers who today continue to struggle against Webb's influence must continue to be the subject of more critical studies. This book, I hope, has made a contribution in that direction.

Appendix A
SHANNON'S APPRAISAL

The question of the extent to and method in which a historian links causal units in the formation of his narration and the story he chooses to tell was taken up in 1939 when the Committee on Appraisal of the Social Science Research Council chose Webb's *The Great Plains* for its series of critiques. According to Arthur M. Schlesinger, who wrote the foreword to the publication of "The Appraisal," Webb's comments, and the proceedings that followed (see Shannon), the purpose of the series of critiques was to "focus the attention of scholars more sharply on the underlying principles of social science and to assist in developing criteria of judgment and standards of performance that would help students to identify good work as well as to produce it" (vii).

On September 9, 1939, five members of the committee met with Professors Walter Prescott Webb and Fred A. Shannon and nine specialists in history and other social sciences to discuss Shannon's appraisal and to hear Webb's rejoinder. Shannon offers his "Appraisal" based on the following criteria: "What are the major theses of the author? How well does he substantiate them? Has the evidence on all sides of the question been given due consideration? Is any particular hypothesis a new one or merely an old one in a new dress? If it is well established by the author, what is its importance?" (5).

Shannon dispels Webb's "magic line" theory and shows how the Great Plains fails to be defined in any way that proves the great generalization that Webb makes about the *"singularly unique* type of life on the Plains [which] necessitated the evoking of a new philosophy of historical research, which the author calls *patterns of truth.*" Shannon goes on to state that Webb's "patterns of truth" idea sounds "like the older dictum: 'First decide what you want to prove, and then hunt up and assemble facts to support your conclusions'" (my emphasis; 8–9). Repeatedly, Shannon, though admittedly not a specialist on the Southwest, points to faults in Webb's thesis and to his persistent failure to consult sources available to him at the time of his research, those Webb ignores because they do not support his thesis of uniqueness on the Plains that called for exceptional measures of adaptability on the part of the settlers.

Shannon brings attention to Webb's exaggeration and time and time again offers specific examples of exceptions to Webb's assertions of uniqueness, thus putting to the test the integrity of Webb's entire work. Through Shannon's criticism Webb begins to look more like an exaggerator and teller of tall tales about the enduring Plains settlers than a historian. Webb appears to be trying desperately to force all of the Great Plains on to the Texan model with which he is more familiar. Using quotes from Webb, Shannon's appraisal states:

> "West of the great river [Mississippi], the surface is plane, comparatively speaking, to the foothills of the Rocky Mountains . . . " (page 4). This is an example selected from many loose generalizations. The fact is that much of the area mentioned is rough or rolling. . . . The author says (page 179) that events in Texas ". . . illustrate more forcibly some of the problems of the Plains than do those of the Northern section." He should know more about the area north of Texas. Let a resident of the border of the northern Plains check his impressions with those of the dweller on the edge of the Texan Plains. The former, after years of rather detailed familiarity with the whole of the United States west of the ninety-eighth meridian, agrees that some parts of the Texas Plains are pretty bad, but he insists that the Plains as a whole cannot be generalized on the Texan model. In other words, the Great Plains, regardless of the ubiquity of the cattle industry, are far from being the cultural or even the geographic unity pictured by Webb. (15)

Other examples of Webb's exaggeration include the stress he puts on the lack of water and nonnavigability of Great Plains rivers and of course the fierceness of the Indians. All of this, according to Shannon, "results from a confusion of thought" on Webb's part. "It was the mountains which provided the first great obstacle; the bleached bones of travelers were found mainly in the inter mountain deserts rather than on the Great Plains" (Shannon 18). Shannon cites *The Expeditions of Zebulon Montgomery Pike* for an account of just how hard a trip across the Great Plains was for this traveler during the years 1805–1807:

> Let Pike speak in place of Webb. His hardest marching was in the Flint Hills, before he reached the Plains, and there he says, he "passed very ruff [rough] flint hills. My feet blistered and very sore . . ." Did he suffer from lack of water on the Plains? About the worst he could say was that on September 18, when leaving one water camp near Salina, it was actually six hours before another river was reached. Less than half a day without water is no hardship. On November 9, he noted that he found *springs and hills* in the present Kearny County, Kansas. He had found but slight trouble with Webb's fierce horseman Indians. (27)

According to Shannon, there was no one "cultural unit" either among the Native Americans or among the pioneers as Webb claims. Citing many instances of similar migrations throughout the world, Shannon dispels the assertion upon which Webb's thesis hinges, that "there had been no other phenomenon like this in American history, and it is doubtful if world history offers a parallel case" (Shannon: 45):

The long hesitation of the Anglo-American before they occupied the Plains is discussed with more poetic license than judicial restraint. The reader is asked to stand on the ninety-eighth meridian where it crosses the thirty-first parallel (the only place where the line divides forests from treeless plains) and join the author in looking northward. He should watch ". . . a nation of people coming slowly but persistently through the forests . . ." (page 140), pursuing the same tasks and living the same lives that had engrossed their ancestors in exactly the same way on all the previous frontiers. This nation of people ultimately reaches the ninety-eighth meridian (or roughly thereabout) and bursts forth from the forest upon a desert-like country where there are ". . . no forests . . . , few springs and running streams. Before them is a wide land infested by a fierce breed of Indians, mounted, ferocious, unconquerable, terrible in their mercilessness" (page 141).

The reader, however, recalls that prairies had been encountered in Ohio, Indiana, Illinois, Missouri, Iowa, and eastern Kansas and Nebraska from one to two generations before the High Plains were reached and that most of the fundamental problems of prairie farming had slowly but certainly been solved. But the author says,

> As we gaze northward we see on the right side [of the meridian] the forested and well-watered country and on the left side the arid, treeless plain (page 140).
>
> This statement needs no comment—it condemns itself. The unconquerable Indians will have to await another section of this analysis for their ultimate conquest. (34)

Shannon goes on to quote more of Webb's creation of a unified "onward marching nation" on page 297:

> As one looks along this line [ninety-eighth meridian] he may see in his imagination some millions of people working their way out of the forests where fences could be made, and into the Plains where they could not be made.
>
> Here, the millions actually enter the Plains, apparently for farming purposes. The census figures show that in 1870, when there was no barbed wire, there were 293,024 persons over ten years of age. . . . In 1880, the figure was 718,242, and in 1890 it was 1,110,393. . . . Nearly all this population in 1870, and the bulk of it in the next two decades, must have been east of the ninety-eighth meridian in Texas, Oklahoma, Kansas, Nebraska, and the Dakotas. Another large number was in the mines of New Mexico, Colorado, Wyoming, and Montana, as well as South Dakota and the coal mines on the eastern fringe. . . . One could well venture to guess (and label it as such) that no "millions of people" ever did move out onto High Plains farms and ranches. Biological processes add to population there as effectively as elsewhere. (Shannon: 34–35)

The proceedings prove to be a fascinating story of academic relations in and of themselves. Whether this battle is framed as a North vs. South or a midwestern elitist's highly empiricist scholarship against a more rugged, romantic, and more artfully presented narrative history, Webb hardly had to speak for himself; his defenders viciously attacked Shannon for his assertions demanding that he provide them with the accurate information. Shannon, as if his own scholarship had been the focus of the meeting, repeatedly comes to the defense of his critique, and then apparently tires from the committee members' badgering and far cruder remarks made to him that were later deleted from the transcript:

> I heard somebody say something once about the tradition of gentility that has grown up in the historical profession. It has become common to take a thing with which you disagree and treat it somewhat tenderly, to give credit for a "serious effort." At this meeting today, we have had a good deal of that tradition of gentility: praising plausible generalizations and pooh-poohing the factual accuracy upon which sound generalizations must be built. I claim that generalizations can be established if you collect enough data of the proper kind and analyze them sufficiently; that only by this means can epochal contributions to historical science and significant new interpretations be made. . . . We should first collect our data, test their validity, dispose of all contradictory material properly, and then make our generalizations. Such work may not be so brilliant, it may not attract so many readers, but it will be sound. (Proceedings: 187)

Almost half a century later, Peter Novick viewed what went on during the proceedings in this way:

> Shannon was a hyperempiricist, deeply skeptical of claims for the heuristic value of frames of reference not arrived at inductively. He produced a lengthy recital of errors and alleged errors, which was so devastating that Webb, in a state of shock, decided not to accept it as an appraisal. . . . "I did not undertake to conform to professional standards", Webb wrote Schlesinger, "but to make a new synthesis that would give a better understanding to western life. . . . It happens that I like the book and my opinion of it is in no way dependent on the opinion of others. . . . It is its own defense, its sole defense. I shall never question it by defending it." Webb reluctantly agreed to attend the conference, but said that he would not foolishly charge the matadors, but rather, like Ferdinand, would "sit on his tail and sniff the fragrant flowers."
>
> In the circumstances the conference was something of a shambles. Shannon's 109-page critique did not lend itself to discussion—though the deliberations were enlivened by splenetic outbursts by Webb's defenders which were later deleted from the transcript. (201)

One can only speculate as to the reasons for the fervor with which Webb's defenders attacked Shannon, from the concern for "gentlemanly reviewing" Novick cites (202) to perhaps the Good Ol' Boy network it could be attributed to. Webb's thesis was defended because it was a more comprehensive version of the Turner thesis (172), because it lent validity to Max Weber's thesis on "the material conditions of existence" in his *Calvinism and Capitalism* (201), and because "the people who live in the area . . . generally regard Mr. Webb's book as the best one available that gives a general picture of the area and its significant characteristics" (199). The whole of Shannon's criticism was reduced to nothing more than the question of generalities versus specifics or, as noted elsewhere in the proceedings, "insight versus proof" (142). Webb, in the end, is credited with the gift of insight while Shannon's criticism is reduced to nit-picking:

> Mr. Hicks: I don't see that any good purpose is served by making issues out of minor points, even minor errors in the book. . . . Mr. Webb probably has missed some facts and slurred over others, but at least he has tried to portray a large picture on a sizable canvas. Sometimes he may give us only half a tree, or a suggestion of a tree, but we still get his general idea about the woods.
>
> While I think all historians value precision in detail, we also realize it is almost impossible to write a book of this size and not make errors. We also realize that one of the untruest pictures of a book that you can possibly make is to enumerate and emphasize all the petty blunders of an author. Mr. Webb may have made too many of them, but his general picture is pretty valid. (192)

Webb's motives for having painted the picture he did are never questioned, nor are his credentials as a historian. Read Bain in his "Commentary on the History Conference," which concludes the Social Science Research Council's publication of the critique, rejoinder, and proceedings, is hard pressed to discredit Shannon, and yet he cannot bring himself to discount Webb:

> There was a division of opinion as to whether Webb had established his thesis, and even those who held that he had done so in a general way, were of the opinion that further research would modify it in many details. . . . Mr. Shannon said every member of the Conference seemed to have read a different *Great Plains* and that the Conference had restated Webb's thesis. To the extent that this is true, it would seem to be a serious criticism of the work. Mr. Webb concurred in some of the criticisms, such as the loose use of the term Great Plains, and some overstatements, but he stuck to his essential thesis with reference to the role of the horse, windmill, revolver, and barbed wire in making the Plains habitable to white men and that there had been institutional adaptations in the Plains area with respect to the use of land, water, and tim-

ber which were singularly different from those prevalent in the Eastern humid woodland area. (232)

Bain gives little more credit to Shannon for what had amounted to his bold challenge to the motives behind the writing of such a history than to say that in the future historians must watch their language and facts:

> One of the most valuable results of Mr. Shannon's *Critique* is his constant reminder that one cannot be too careful in his use of language, or in the interpretation of records. At the behest of the Appraisal Committee he was frankly looking for all the weaknesses of the book. This is altogether fitting and proper. The most searching criticism that is possible should be brought against every thesis and every scholarly work. Some criticism was levied against Shannon for "picayunish attention to minutiae." No "fact" that is open to reasonable doubt can legitimately be regarded as "picayunish." Facts are important. So is careful and judicious statement. (233)

Bain, after citing that Shannon "could find in *The Great Plains* no recommendations for social action except by implication" and that Webb's work also by implication may have "no practical value," concludes by quoting Flexner's statement that "the most useful knowledge may be that which at the moment appears to be most useless" (237). How "useful" Webb's work became is evident by the impact and influence his work had, despite the errors admitted to but never corrected.

By his own admission many years after these proceedings were long forgotten and with his history now thoroughly sanctioned and "institutionalized," Webb spoke of his lack of preparation or even credentials to call himself a historian. The overall impression one gets after reading his texts and several of the speeches and commentary he made throughout his career is that to a certain extent Webb is swept away by a current he perhaps never had expected to help create. At his inaugural address as president of the American Historical Association, "History As High Adventure," delivered in New York in 1958, he states:

> My presence here is one of the most improbable accidents in the history of the profession . . . my field of study has been the plebeian field of Western America. All my degrees are from a state university [The University of Texas at Austin], the one in which I teach. I have never taught anywhere else except temporarily. I am one of the few persons who did not have to leave home to get a job. I am an example of institutional inbreeding which frightens all universities save the two that practice it most, Harvard and Oxford. . . .
>
> Actually I have never been ambitious in the profession as witnessed by the fact that I have a poor record of attendance at the national meetings, have served on no committees, written few book reviews, and have never submitted an article to either of the national journals, although a former

presidential address was published. This indifference illustrates two points: first, that I never expected national recognition; second, that I have followed my own interests, acquiring in the process severe penalties and occasional reward. (1969: 5–6)

Webb's mystification of the West comes from the inspiration regulated by a vision of what were, for him, pioneering times. This vision was nourished by certain beliefs that were rooted in eighteenth-century ideas about *organic* development. History as a progressive organic growth was also the great theme of German historians in the nineteenth century: historians who vindicated imperialist expansionism. This version of history had specific technical features, and Webb, by his own account, learned those from Lindley M. Keasbey, who had taught a course in institutional history at the University of Texas at Austin before he was eventually fired: "This technique consisted of taking an environment, in this case the Great Plains, as a unit, and superimposing layer after layer of its components with geology as the foundation and the latest human culture, literature, as the most final product, the flower growing out of the compost of human effort and physical forces" (Webb 1969: 13–14).

Webb himself questioned openly how it came about that with so little preparation and only a superficial knowledge of the various fields from which he drew his synthesis, he "knew beforehand [what] was there":

There was a compelling logic in this plan for him who would follow it, but to plough through such unknown fields as geology, climatology, botany, anthropology to arrive finally at the sixteenth century—when men began to make a record of their puny efforts, many failures and few successes—in order to write the heroic and tragic history of the American West, was no small task. But it was high adventure. I have never worked so hard or with such exaltation as in those days when I carved out of the books piece after piece of folklore or science or history and found that they all fit together to form a harmonious pattern which I knew beforehand was there.

Yes, this was the easy field. No matter how hard I worked, I was still a western historian. No one understood the trouble or the fun I was having in relating the many fields to my topic. In commenting one day to a colleague in a more scholarly division of history, I said: "Never have I felt so keenly the need of an education. The fact that I didn't get one is most unfortunate!"

"Yes," he said, "but think how lucky you were in getting into a field where you don't need it!" (1969: 13–14)

Appendix B
BIOGRAPHICAL OUTLINE OF
JOVITA GONZÁLEZ'S LIFE

1899   Born in Roma, Texas (according to Texas Folklore Society records);
1904 according to Benson Collection archives.

1905*   Attends for one year a one-teacher school in English taught by Miss
Elida García at the San Román Ranch. A few years later, her father,
Jacobo González, moves family to San Antonio so that his children can
be educated in English.

1909*   At age ten, enters the fourth grade.

1917*   By attending summer school, she finishes the equivalent of the high
school course when she is eighteen.

1918   Enrolls in Summer Normal School.

1920   Acquires a teaching certificate in two years.

1920   With the help of her uncle, Encarnación Salinas, county and district
clerk, and Mr. Sam P. Vale, county superintendent of schools, González
acquires a position in the Rio Grande City Schools. She lives with her
uncle and aunt in Rio Grande City and saves for her college fund.

1921   The following fall, González enrolls at the University of Texas at
Austin and completes her freshman year.

1922–24   Returns to San Antonio, out of money; teaches at Encinal for next two
years as head teacher of a two-teacher school.

1924   Enters Our Lady of the Lake College in San Antonio, where the dean
of the college, Mother Angelique, offers her a scholarship for the following year that includes a private room, board, and tuition. González
worries about continuing the courses in Spanish she had started at UT
Austin with Miss Lilia Casis. She tutors at Our Lady of the Lake in
order to continue studies at UT, as she cannot "consider anyone else."

1925   Meets J. Frank Dobie. "Heretofore the legend and stories of the border
were interesting, so I thought, just to me. However, he made me see
their importance and encouraged me to write them. Which I did, publishing some in the Folk-lore Publications and *Southwest Review*."

1927   The *Times-Picayune* review (Sunday, October 16, 1927) gives first and
special mention to her work "Folklore of the Texas Mexican Vaquero,"

*These dates are only my calculations, for González rarely gives exact dates in her
memoirs.

published as part of *Texas and Southwestern Folklore,* edited by J. Frank Dobie.

1927   Nov. 13 review in *New York Book Review* of Dobie's *Texas and Southwestern Folklore* credits González's "Folk-Lore of the Texas Mexican Vaquero," as "perhaps the best piece in the collection."

At the end of her sophomore year, González is offered a position teaching Spanish, half a day, at Saint Mary's Hall, an Episcopal school for girls. She continues her summer studying at UT, enjoying her friendship with the Dobies, Miss Casis, and Dr. and Mrs. Carlos E. Castañeda; the last were old family friends.

1927   Receives B.A. degree from Our Lady of the Lake and becomes full-time teacher at Saint Mary's Hall in San Antonio.

1927   April 22–23   Thirteenth annual meeting of the Texas Folk-Lore Society. González presents her "Folk-Lore of the Texas-Mexican Vaquero" on Saturday evening with ballads sung to accompaniment of guitars by native Mexican cowboys. Reelected secretary, J. Frank Dobie praises her work as "unusually well done." This selection was also included in *Texas Southwestern Lore,* Publications of the Texas Folklore Society 6. Also that year, she speaks on the "Social Conditions in Southern Texas" five or six generations ago at the Texas Historical and Landmark Association meeting held at the St. Anthony Hotel in Houston. The other featured speaker is Miss Evelyn Sterling, who speaks on John Austin.

1928   Completes a B.A., Our Lady of the Lake College.

1928   Gives a reading to the Fourteenth Annual Meeting of the Texas Folklore Society entitled "The Woman Who Lost Her Soul," April 27, held in the YMCA Auditorium, across from The University of Texas campus.

1929   April 20   Fifteenth meeting of the Texas Folklore society at Texas Christian University. Vice-President Jovita González presents "Legend and Song of the Texas-Mexican Folk" accompanied by Miss Argentina Blanca of San Antonio. Professor Newton Gaines of Texas Christian University praises González as one of the folklore society "stars."

Through the recommendations of Miss Ruth Coit, Headmistress of Saint Mary's, and J. Frank Dobie, González is awarded the Lapham Scholarship at the University of Texas to study and collect folklore on the border and to advance her studies toward her M.A. Spends summer traveling in Webb, Zapata, and Starr Counties. Letters of introduction from Catholic Archbishop Droessarts and Episcopal Bishop Capers, Episcopal bishops of San Antonio to the clergy of border counties, facilitate her research along with the fact that "She is maestro Jacobo's daughter, or she is Don Francisco Guerra's granddaughter from Las Viboras Ranch." Begins teaching and takes charge of the Spanish Department in St. Mary's Hall.

1930   Completes master's degree, University of Texas. Dr. Eugene C.
        Barker directs her master's thesis, "Social Life in Webb, Starr and
        Zapata Counties," but is somewhat hesitant at first to approve the thesis
        due to insufficient historical references. Barker signs after Carlos E.
        Castañeda comments, "This thesis will be used in years to come as
        source material." Dr. Barker's comment to her is, "an interesting but
        somewhat odd piece of work."

1930   Sixteenth annual TFS meeting elects González president at a meeting
        held at Garrison Hall, University of Texas Campus, Austin. John K.
        Strecker of Baylor University is the retiring president. González pre-
        sents "The Devil on the Border," later published in "Tales and Songs
        of the Texas-Mexicans," *Man, Bird and Beast,* Publications of the Texas
        Folklore Society 8.

1931   Seventeenth annual meeting of the Texas Folklore Society reelects
        Jovita González as president. The meeting is held at the Menger Hotel
        in San Antonio.

1932   González gives the President's Address, "Among My People" to the
        Texas Folklore Society's Eighteenth Annual Meeting, held in the
        Austin YMCA Auditorium. "Among My People" is later published
        in *Tone the Bell Easy,* Publication of the Texas Folklore Society 10.

1934   Through recommendation of J. Frank Dobie, González is awarded a
        Rockefeller grant.

1935   Bishop Mariano Garriga marries González and Edmundo E. Mireles
        at the Mission of La Purisima Concepción in San Antonio. Dr. and
        Mrs. Carlos E. Castañeda are *padrinos,* (godparents). "The Bullet Swal-
        lower" is published in *Puro Mexicano,* Publications of the Texas Folk-
        lore Society 8.

1935–36 The front page of the January 1935 issue (vol. 18, no. 1) of Mary *Im-
        maculate,* a publication of the Missionary Oblates of Mary Immaculate
        in San Antonio, announces the forthcoming appearance of "a series of
        articles on the folklore of the Border country by the well known author,
        Jovita González." "Among My People" appears as promised in various
        installments in the February, March, April, May, June, July, Septem-
        ber, October, and December issues of that same year. The second half
        of the December 1935 folktale "The Woman Who Lost Her Soul"
        appears in the January 1936 issue.

1936   "Stories of My People" published in *Mexican Tales,* Publications of the
        Texas Folklore Society 26.

1935–39 Upon the recommendation of Carlos Castañeda to Alonso S. Perales,
        founder of LULAC, and Santos Garza, president of the San Felipe
        School Board, Mireles and González are recruited to the San Felipe
        School District. Mireles becomes principal of San Felipe High School
        and González an English teacher.

1939   The couple moves to Corpus Christi. Edmundo organizes the Spanish

Program in the elementary grades from third to sixth grades. They both confront "a period when the walls of racial prejudice [were] still hard to be torn down." She begins teaching in the Corpus Christi High School until W. B. Ray High School opens. During 1936, '37, and '39, she teaches a course on "Methods of Teaching Spanish to Anglo American Children" in the Summer School of Our Lady of the Lake College.

1941   The Spanish-language teaching movement spreads through Texas and the Spanish Southwest. With Eleanor Roosevelt as a chief force and influence, the U.S. Congress revokes the 1917 law barring the teaching of all foreign languages in the state's public elementary schools.

1947   Presents "Nana Chita's Symptoms" at the Thirty-first annual meeting of the Texas Folklore Society in Corpus Christi, April 18 and 19.

1948   Presents a paper, "The Marquis de Aguoyo's Ghost," at the Thirty-second annual meeting of the Texas Folklore Society held at the University of Texas at Austin on April 16 and 17. Neither the 1947 or '48 papers were published.

1949   W. S. Benson & Co. in Austin publishes *Mi libro español,* an eight-volume textbook series to teach Spanish to elementary students. It is the result of Edmundo and Jovita's collaborative effort with Roy B. Fisher and is based on courses Edmundo introduced in the Corpus Christi Independent School District classrooms in 1940. The series incorporates Mexican American historical figures and the contributions of the Spanish-speaking population to the United States; it contains illustrations and songs with music. Adopted by the State of Texas. *El español elemental* was also published and used in Texas and the Spanish Southwest.

1967   After two decades of teaching Spanish and Texas History at Miller and W. B. Ray High Schools, González de Mireles retires from teaching.

1969   February 15, Mrs. Jovita Mireles is honored by the Spring Conference of the Texas Foreign Language Association, at Stephen F. Austin State College in Nacogdoches, Texas. Dr. D. Lincoln Canfield of the University of Rochester speaks on "Culture and Communication."

1983   Suffering from diabetes, Jovita González de Mireles dies after having collapsed on her kitchen floor.

1987   After years of depression and failing health following his wife's death, Edmundo E. Mireles dies. He leaves their house and all its belongings to Isabel Cruz, longtime companion, housekeeper, and caregiver for the Mireleses.

1992   CCSU receives the Mireles Collection from Isabel Cruz. She was encouraged to donate the papers by Ray J. García, lay historian, and Thomas Kreneck, whose relationship with this community member facilitates the donation.

1996   *Caballero,* edited by José E. Limón and María Cotera with a foreword by Thomas Kreneck, is published by Texas A&M University press.

NOTES

1. Herbert J. Muller traces the origins of the idea of progress in history from ancient civilizations to eighteenth-century Europe and to the positivist nature of Western history in his *The Uses of the Past: Profiles of Former Societies:* "In short, our feeling about time—however vague or unconscious—ultimately involves a philosophy of history. It leads to a momentous question. Given all the drama of human history, what is the plot, the grand design, the final meaning of the whole show? Positivists will tell us that this is a meaningless question. Manifestly we cannot give it a precise, positive answer: we cannot state it in terms that permit either empirical verification or rigorous logical analysis. But neither can we escape it. . . . Thus Westerners have declared that history is a progress, and in this faith have made extraordinary history" (74).

Muller goes on to explain that "the faith in progress . . . is the most original contribution of the eighteenth century," and that if "philosophers overlooked possibilities of evil, they recognized real possibilities of betterment" (303). He adds that these philosophers of the eighteenth century considered "progress the natural tendency, at least from their time on; and their too easy assumption of its naturalness was a threat to actual progress. They could not foresee the perils of freedom, the new possibilities of tension and dissension that it would inevitably create. They slighted even the immediate perils. Believing that the tyranny of priests and kings was the only real barrier to the natural unity of mankind, they overlooked the increasing sharpness of racial, national, and class differences. Lacking sympathy for the tragic ardors of the past, they tended not only to a rhetorical enthusiasm for the future but a limited sympathy for the present, especially for the common people who had to bear the brunt of history" (299).

2. See José E. Limón (1981) for a discussion of how the term "Chicano" has been and remains controversial in the "Mexicano" community. I mainly use "Mexicano/a" to refer to people with a strong identity rooted in their Mexican traditions and values because to this day many Southwest and Texas Mexicans are more likely to call themselves "Mexicanos" than Mexicans or Chicanos. In the field of letters, however, it is more likely that we would refer to "Chicano Studies" because of the strong nationalism and notions of Aztlán depicted by the writers of the initial "Quinto Sol" phase of literary production and beyond.

3. María Cristina Mena and later Beatriz de la Garza are not U.S. born, although de la Garza became a naturalized citizen. Chicano literature has at times been defined strictly as the literary production of those permanent residents and U.S. citizens of Mexican descent, but as Charles Tatum points out in his *Chicano Literature* when discussing the literature of the Southwest before 1848 by Spanish-

born soldiers and members of expeditions, John Smith, William Bradford, and Nathaniel Ward, well-known forerunners of "American" literature, were all English born (13).

4. When my fifteen-year-old son was eleven, he came home with a Texas history textbook that stated that when Stephen F. Austin came to what was then *Tejas* accompanied by Anglo settlers, the Mexicans living there "went back to Mexico." Later, when discussing the Texas Rangers in his class, my son questioned their hero status: "Didn't they kill many Native Americans and Mexicans?" His Mexican American teacher (who at the age of fifty could testify to the most blatant forms of exclusion and racism in the school system just twenty to thirty years ago) responded, "Yes that's true, but on the test, let's answer according to what the textbook says."

CHAPTER ONE

1. See Saldívar (1990b: 19), who calls this process "the ideological rewriting of [the Mexican American's] banished history."

2. My use of the word "function" has to do with Vladimir Propp's use of the word in his *Morphology of the Folktale* (1958), where "function" is applied to each isolated action, when each action is seen for its usefulness to the story. The "story" here would be the construction of the "winning of the West" as part of the larger construction of the American Dream.

3. Henry Nash Smith offers Turner's metaphor of the West as a "safety valve for social danger" in an America where "No grave social problem could exist while the wilderness at the edge of civilizations opened wide its portals to all who were oppressed, to all who with strong arms and stout heart desired to hew out a home and a career for themselves" (254). Richard Slotkin, who is indebted to Smith's work (first published in 1950 by the president and fellows of Harvard College), explains how myth comes into play in such a thesis as Webb's, which in many ways responds to Turner's: "The ultimate, archetypal questions of human existence are spoken to by the myth; but the success of the myth in answering these questions for a people depends upon the creation of a distinct cultural tradition in the selection and use of metaphor. It is in their development of traditional metaphors (and the narratives that express them) that the mythologies of particular cultures move from archetypal paradigms to the creation of acculturated, even idiosyncratic myth-metaphors" (14–15).

4. Herbert J. Muller in *The Uses of the Past* (1952) traces the origins of the idea of progress in history from ancient civilizations to eighteenth-century Europe, and to the positivist version of Western history. Regarding a divine purpose in history, Muller explains how only through struggle was the reward of success and the redemption of the people to be achieved: "The prophets had evolved a more rational, responsible theory of history than any other people had yet conceived. Instead of foisting history on Fate, they explained it by human character and con-

duct. Even in their utopian visions of the Messiah and the restoration of Israel they retained their moral realism. The idea of progress implicit in these visions was no automatic progress; man would first have to learn, through suffering, to be righteous and just. Meanwhile the prophets saw history as tragedy, and they did not soften it by easy promises of heaven for their followers or hell for their enemies" (Muller: 104–105).

Chapter Two

1. Bain's summation of Webb's thesis appears in the context of comments made at a history conference held by the Social Science Research Council in 1940. The conference focused on a critique of *The Great Plains* by Fred A. Shannon, commissioned in 1939 by the Committee on Appraisal of the Social Science Research Council to do a "thoroughgoing critique" of the text. Shannon's critique cited numerous errors both in Webb's generalizations and in the "factual" evidence with which he supports his thesis. Some of these errors will be discussed later in this chapter, but because the critique and reaction to the critique that took place during the proceedings prove to be a fascinating story and history of academic relationships in and of themselves, some of Shannon's comments and those of the committee members are included in Appendix A.

2. In his "Comments on Shannon's Critique" Webb's basis for the accusation that "[Shannon] doesn't seem to think very well of Texas or of Texans" (120) comes from an error Webb found in "Mr. Shannon's estimable work on the Union Army stating that Robert E. Lee deserted the United States Army." After quoting from Shannon's work and pointing out that Robert E. Lee had resigned his commission, Webb states: "I would not tarnish the name of Robert E. Lee by debating before any group the treason of Robert E. Lee, who, if a deserter, was also a traitor. I would not prostitute *The Great Plains* by accepting the Shannon manuscript as an appraisal. I propose to show that its acceptance would be an absurdity" (120).

Webb never shows any such thing; his colleagues and defenders speak for him and on behalf of his work throughout the proceedings. Shannon states that he regrets the error, has "always had a great admiration for Texans," and admits to his "careless use of terms." He insists that "a careful reading of the book will show that I then had a great deal of sympathy for the South and certainly no animosity toward it" (Shannon 141).

3. From a more personal perspective, E. C. Barksdale, in his "An Explanation," a preface to Webb's *History as High Adventure*, credits Webb's writing with poetic qualities: "Webb was proud of being a historian. To him the profession should not be that of an academician, the fabled egghead. He introduced with pride the phrase, 'As a Professional Historian I . . .' He stated that his only technical writing ability lay in the field of exposition, that he was not a novelist or a poet, though he had tried his hand at poetasting once when as a very young man he thought he

was in love. Webb did not think of himself as possessed of the lyric gift, yet some of his passages sang: 'And there it is, clothed in magic, a vision of truth never perceived so clearly by any other man'" (xii).

4. "Literary felicity" and "soft luminosity" may be elements Fielding had identified as rendering literary "histories" more inviting to the reader than the official histories written with "little charm, and few vivid figures of speech" (Braudy: 94). Fielding had certainly questioned what in the narrative/novelistic mode captivated the reader and had the power to convince as regards the historical evidence. He considered this aspect of literary presentation, which renders history more compelling of a "reader's assent," to be nothing more than a narrative that employs the same literary devices as those available to the imaginative writer. As he points out, narrative comprises a variety of imaginative patterns, evaluative epithets, and suggestive language, yet his observations also concern an aspect of control that would regulate both the overscreening of life and the overromanticizing of it. "All of Fielding's novels [as Braudy sees them] are basically exercises in the reinvigoration of perceptions that have been dulled by the overheated fantasies of the romance writers and 'romancing historians'"(94–95). Strangely enough, what Webb criticizes in the novels discussed in his chapter "The Literature of the Great Plains and about the Great Plains" are the very features his own "history" manifests. He attacks in literary art the narrative style he himself employs when writing, not novels as Fielding had done, but a very specific history.

5. I am indebted to Rolena Adorno's *Guaman Poma: Writing and Resistance in Colonial Peru* (1988) for its analysis of a parallel Hispanic literary tradition in historiography, particularly that of conquest. In her chapter "Searching for a Heroic Conception," she demonstrates "the homogeneity of the tradition of 'Moralistic, biographical exempla' where the moral lesson to be learned from these histories is emphasized. This feature in historical writing drew the portrait first and outlined the lesson afterward, . . . ordered discourse according to moral topics and gave anecdotes about historical figures to illustrate the principle, and . . . combine intimate and mundane details" (43).

6. It would be the subject of another study to investigate to what extent Webb's influence and such images still remain in contemporary, state-adopted textbooks which enshrine his assumptions and generalizations. The fact that misinformation about settlement history was still being passed on to children as late as 1977, thus perpetuating the myth, is noted in *Stereotypes, Distortions and Omissions in U.S. History Textbooks:* "The presence of at least 75,000 Mexicans when the U.S. conquered those lands [the Southwest] in the 1846–1848 war is rarely recognized [in most textbooks]. They were not the 'Spaniards' that some textbooks mention as living in the area. The vast majority were mestizos—the mixture of peoples called Raza—the original Chicanos.

"The Chicano also has a second set of roots, dating from more recent migrations of Mexicans to the U.S., especially—but not only—since the early 1900's. Those arrivals supplemented the existing population. By ignoring the first set of roots and mentioning only the latter, textbooks inaccurately portray Chicanos as 'foreign immigrants,' facing the same problems faced by all previous 'immigrants' and starting to 'climb the ladder of opportunity.' Thus, not only is the origin and much of the history of a whole people truncated, but the racist and colonialist nature of their oppression is ignored" ("Chicanos": 56).

That the general concept of erasure and exclusion has held up was proved for me seven years ago, during the 1990 Census. The U.S. Bureau of the Census (which according to the three-fifths rule did not count Native Americans as full persons until 1930) was still conducting training sessions for temporary employees which included government-produced films in which the Mexican history in the Southwest was completely ignored except for the depiction of Mexicans as poor immigrants in search of economic opportunity in the land of plenty. Nothing is said in these films of the U.S. War with Mexico, of conquest or displacement, of the contribution that Mexican cheap labor has made to the building of the American Southwest, or of the service of Mexican Americans for the defense of this nation.

7. See Gordon W. Allport's *The Nature of Prejudice,* especially chap. 11, "Linguistic Factors," for a comprehensive discussion of this linguistic device.

8. Although Webb presents the history of the Native Americans and the Spaniards on the Plains as two separate stories, Ramón A. Gutiérrez documents how, by the eighteenth century, the history of these two peoples had become integrated, though the people themselves continued to label themselves as different for sociopolitical and economic reasons. The "middle" group, as he indicates on pages 148–149, is the most populous and is "mestizo" or of mixed Native American and Spanish blood. Thus the two stories in many ways are inseparable and actually constitute the history of the Mexicano of the Plains, the *Mexicano* in whose veins, to varying degrees, both bloods flowed.

9. In *No Separate Refuge* Sarah Deutsch acknowledges the failure of historians to depict the world of village women (42). Recent historians and literary critics have also done much to unearth less widely known roles of Hispanic women on the frontier during and after colonization: "Although the exploration and colonization of the northern frontier has been attributed to military men and priests, shortly after the first explorations the areas were settled by colonists: families that included a goodly number of women. Indeed, in early expeditions to New Mexico, which was the first area beyond what we now know as Mexico to be colonized, there was at least one woman who accompanied the soldiers. In the Espejo expedition of 1582, Casilda de Anaya and her three sons accompanied her husband Miguel Sánchez Valenciano. We know she became pregnant on the journey . . . In the Juan de Oñate expedition of 1598, forty-seven wives accompanied the soldiers" (Rebolledo and Rivero: 2).

Antonia Castañeda has done the most significant work on the Hispanic woman of the frontier; see the bibliography for three of her relevant works. Also see Mario T. García, "The Chicana in American History."

10. See Gerard Jones, *Honey I'm Home!*.

11. In an interview (March 4, 1995), Américo Paredes remarked, "[Folklorist] Mody Boatright once corrected me when I referred to Webb as 'Doctor' Webb, telling me Webb was not a Ph.D."

CHAPTER THREE

1. At the keynote dinner of this conference, González and Américo Paredes were paired up when both were honored by the conference for their contributions to the preservation of the folklore, history, and literature of the Mexican people of Texas. But in fact, as a woman struggling at a time before Paredes had broken new ground, González contended with forces few Chicanas or Chicanos today could even imagine. While Professor Ricardo Romo stated in his address that "Don Américo's work has many historical dimensions and an understanding of Tejano history and culture begins with his published material," Acosta questioned whether this understanding began with Paredes. Adding a distinctly female dimension, Jovita González was resurrected and honored as a "México Tejana" folklorist, historian, writer, and educator who preceded Paredes. She was honored as a Chicana who distinguished herself as a pioneer in collecting the folklore of Texas Mexicans in the Río Grande Valley in the late 1920s and '30s. Her research, "her promotion of the teaching of Spanish in the public schools, and her stance claiming a México Tejano heritage" was said by Acosta "to have stood in sharp contrast to most Anglo-produced studies of the time, which viewed Mexicans as a social problem."

Though the conference directly challenged the way in which the history of Texas had been told and taught for the past 157 years, Acosta's comments revealed another ignored struggle, a struggle specific to women, one that no Chicano historians (and much less historians such as Webb) had ever remotely approached. The psychology of a "decent" woman, a decent Mexican woman with a mind urging her to go out and take on the traditionally male work of the folklorist and historian, is a complex one. I will explore some aspects of this complexity in this chapter.

González's work had been acknowledged previously by its inclusion in one of the first anthologies of Mexican American literature, *Mexican American Authors,* compiled and edited by Américo Paredes and Raymund Paredes (1972). Because of this very important anthology, González first came to my attention when I was teaching for the Bilingual Program at Berkeley High School in 1976. At this time, for teachers attempting to infuse multiculturalism into the public school curriculum, an anthology such as this was rare. Chicano publishing houses such as Quinto Sol, also in Berkeley, had been just recently established, and eventually they made the writings of Chicanos more accessible. The trend after 1972, after Américo and Raymund Paredes's initial efforts to include women writers, tended more toward an exclusion of Chicana writers until the early 1980s.

2. In an eighteen-page autobiography written in her own hand, González does not mention her birthdate. The Texas Folklore Society publications list her as having been born in 1899, though some later publications list her birthdate as 1904. From that autobiography and various articles collected in her scrapbook (from the "Mireles Papers," interviews, articles, notes, reviews, Texas Folklore Society records, and other bibliographical sources), I have composed a likely sequence of her life's most important events. See Appendix B for those dates and events.

3. J. Frank Dobie was a contemporary and ardent ally of Webb. Dobie's explanation during the Prohibition years of the etymology of the word "wetback" is similar to the astounding logic Webb applied to the "short-legged" Comanches' success with the horse (see Chapter 2). It is an explanation Américo Paredes has often recalled, when Dobie came to speak at either his high school or the junior college graduation in Brownsville, Texas, but it also speaks of how the stage was set during a particular course of events in U.S. history for "scholars" to come on the scene to legitimize and perpetuate a set of beliefs already in the air: "Wetbacks could not be called 'Wets' because those were the days of prohibition when you had the Wets and the Drys. So Dobie offered this explanation. He said that when a Mexican crossed the river his clothes would get wet, given that he hadn't sense enough to take off his clothes and place them above his head at the end of a stick to keep them dry. Upon getting to the other side, being a Mexican, the first thing he did was take a *siesta*. Because he lay in the sun and on his back, when he awoke, all his clothes were dry except the back portion of his shirt. Thus we have the word 'wetback'" (My recollection of Paredes's retellings of Dobie's explanation during his various talks between 1988 and 1993 to my students of Chicano/a literature in the English Department of UT Austin).

The problem of encoded authority—artfully presented—is thus a persistent one. A prominent figure in the inscription of dominative views of Texas Mexicans, Dobie would come to influence some Tejana writers like González and Fermina Guerra, whose work I examine in the following chapter.

4. *Caballero* literally means horseman, but in the historic, cultural sense, the way the term is used in the novel, it connotes a gentleman, one who, through his comportment, exemplifies and defends the old ways and traditions.

5. A series of articles on "the folklore of the Border country" appeared in the *Mary Immaculate* magazine, all under the general title "Among My People." An advertisement for this series appears below a picture of Jovita González on the first page of volume 18, no. 1, in the January 1935 issue. As promised, "Among My People" appeared in various self-contained installments in the February, March, April, May, June, July, September, October, and December issues of 1935 and in the January issue of 1936. This book was already in proof stage when a special compilation of these articles came to my knowledge; therefore, my comparisons to these publications are not extensive.

6. It is in great part due to this relationship between a member of an institution of higher education and a community member, Ray J. García, that these papers were saved from near destruction (see Eleanor Mortensen, "CCSU Preserving Papers of Teaching Pioneers," and Thomas Kreneck, "Credit Is Due"). As a result, we now know much more of González's attempts at a literary career. It is from her papers in this collection that I take a great deal of the information for this chapter. Too often the transfer of knowledge is thought to go in only one direction, and not enough credit is given to the knowledge we gain from the communities surrounding our institutions of "higher" learning.

7. The manuscript I read and examined had no title page, nor does this title have anything to do with the novel, but when the U.S. Hispanic Literary Heritage Recovery Project announced the appearance of a second novel-length manuscript, this is the title it was given (see "Coming Soon: *Dew on the Thorn*"). Probably it is Professor Limón's belief that this is the novel to which González makes some reference in a letter she wrote to J. Frank Dobie in 1935. In this letter the author refers to her having sent him "her own book-length manuscript, a novel then called *Dew on the Thorn* with which she expresses dissatisfaction, though she promises to continue working on it so that 'when it is properly done, it will be something that will make you proud that you were my padrino'" (Limón 1994: 60–61). It is unlikely, however, that this is the novel to which the author referred in her letter to Dobie, because by 1935 she had already had many of her stories derived from this "novel" published by the Folklore Society, beginning with "Folk-Lore of the Texas-Mexican Vaquero" in 1927 and soon following with "Tales and Songs of the Texas-Mexicans."

Other possibilities exist, however: She may have sent Dobie what would have amounted to a novella with all the folklore digressions from the main plot line already deleted, or Dobie could have suggested the excerpts in the first place. More than likely, what González referred to in her letter to Dobie was her much more sophisticated second novel, *Caballero,* written at least a decade later, of which the carbon copy version was typed on the backs of late 1930s and 1940s correspondence and fliers. In any case, for lack of a better title and because this manuscript for all intents and purposes has already been misnamed, I will also refer to this novel as *Dew on the Thorn.*

It is also important to note that José Limón's edited version of this novel may eventually be published with the chapters in a different order and with some of the material described below deleted. All description and criticism that follows here is based on the logic and evidence Thomas Kreneck so generously made available to me, which indicates that the chapters and pages would originally have been ordered before the excerpting of the folklore stories took place. As far as editing, I make only minor corrections in the spelling of this manuscript, and I usually insert the handwritten notes that appear in the author's own hand and delete the crossed-through words and phrases. I will not refer to page numbers but only to the chapters from which excerpted material is drawn. Those chapter numbers are not as clearly discernible in *Dew on the Thorn* as they are in the *Caballero* manuscript, which was prepared for publication. I will note chapter numbers when I can discern them.

8. According to José Limón, "to a considerable degree" González's narrative style is due to Dobie's influence, though he also discovers in it a "double-consciousness": "for within the body of her work—the work of an often disorganized intellectual won over to the side of domination, perhaps won over from the very beginning—we nonetheless find some key instances of a counter-competing vision on questions of race, class and gender domination, a bedeviled consciousness that ultimately finds the devil for its best articulation" (1994: 61).

9. Ironically, Lydia Mendoza (b. 1916) is today well known throughout Mexicano and Anglo communities alike as one of the pioneers of Texas Mexican music and a great contributor to its development. Yet relatively few know of González's existence even within her own Corpus Christi community, where she later spent most of her postretirement years in relative obscurity, or even within the academy, into which González had tried so hard to fit. In light of González's concern for not being identified with "las otras," it is also ironic that her "presence" at the "Mexican Americans in Texas History" conference was in fact shared with such politically active, working-class women as Doña Manuela Solís de Sager, who was among the elders also recognized and honored. Doña Manuela helped organize the Mexican Workers Union during the 1920s and '30s and became involved in the Pecan Shellers' Strike of 1938. Labeled as a Communist, Sager did crucial work in the organization of the United Canning and Agricultural Packing Workers Association. Yet she, too, appears not to have been "proper" enough to claim González's attention.

10. The March 1935 issue of *Mary Immaculate* magazine notes: "He furnished their living quarters, and besides the payment of a small sum of money, six *reales* a day, provided them with some articles of food. The salary, '*cuatro reales y la comida o seis reales y comen de ellos,*' four bits and meals or six *reales* and furnish your own, was in effect until the first decade of the twentieth century" (González 1935–36: 76).

11. A version of this story appeared in the September 1935 issue of *Mary Immaculate,* combined with a more condensed version of the story of the cattle thieves that follows (González 1935–36: 230).

12. Based on Thomas Kreneck's examination of some correspondence between Jovita González and E. E. Mireles, where González indicates that she is again reading *Gone With the Wind,* Kreneck believes the author may have been trying to give *Caballero* a literary appeal to that market. Given the romanticizing and exaggerated descriptions of the antebellum-style aristocracy of South Texas in the novel, I believe Kreneck's assessment to be sound.

13. The page numbers in the following citations match the carbon copy manu-

script I first viewed from the Mireles-González papers in 1993, and not the 1996 Texas A&M University Press publication of the novel, *Caballero: An Historical Novel.*

14. The carbon copy shows "the land whence they came" crossed out and replaced with "their own country."

15. Though I spell the names here with the accent mark and with a *"tilde"* over the "ñ," in the manuscript none of the Spanish names are spelled in this way. Spanish words, such as "Americanos," are sometimes underlined, but for the most part they are included in the text as if they were in English. In the published novel, the editors, Limón and Cotera, add an accent mark to the name "Soria," resulting in an additional syllable because it breaks up the "ia" diphthong, but in fact the name is pronounced with the stress over the first syllable, making the orthographic mark unnecessary.

16. As in *Dew on the Thorn,* throughout the novel, "Indians" are consistently referred to stereotypically, as thieves and people to be feared, who threaten "civilization" and must be gotten rid of.

17. Don Santiago's refusal to compromise with the changing times and conditions and his clinging to the old ways and customs—for him the only permissible form of life—contrast with another story of a landowning patriarch on the other side of the Southwest. María Amparo Ruiz de Burton's 1885 novel, *The Squatter and the Don* (published in 1992 by Arte Público), depicts Don Mariano Alamar's attempts at compromise and litigation. In the end, they are both tragic figures as they lose everything that was precious to them and in so doing represent the plight of all Mexicanos as they have come to be treated by the United States and in American history.

18. The phrase "the brew salted with greed" is crossed out in the carbon copy manuscript.

19. See Ramón Saldívar's extensive reference to ongoing research being done by Clara Lomas and others to "modify the traditional misperception that Chicanas did not produce significant literatures until the postmovement era" (1990b: 171). In addition, the case of María Amparo Ruiz de Burton's two recently recovered novels gives us an example. In *The Squatter and the Don,* we see the author's attempt to mask her strong criticism of the Mexican experience of what is defined as American "democracy" with the genre of the nineteenth-century romance novel. Her compassionate patriarch tries to accommodate but loses everything, including his life. It is no wonder that her work, despite her initial success at publication, had been lost until very recently. Both Ruiz de Burton and Jovita González contend with land loss, class, and gender issues, in both their lives and in their literary expressions; but despite Gonzalez's aspirations to educate her people, and her marriage, she did not publish, while Ruiz de Burton's writing was the very expression of her efforts to survive and make a living for herself and her children. Without her husband's death she may never have tried to publish her novel or felt angry enough to express her loss.

Chapter Four

1. See Crane's letter to Samuel Loveman (1931), in Robinson, p. 68.

2. Velásquez-Treviño attributes the use of the name Próspero to "the noble and intelligent hero from the Shakespearean drama, *The Tempest,* [which] illustrates Popo's comical image" (52). Ironically, in this narration Próspero appears foolish to the reader. The nickname 'Popo' further enhances the comical image of this character who is supposed to represent Mexican bourgeois values. I am more inclined to think that the name 'Próspero' refers not to the noble qualities of this character, but to his 'prosperidad' or economic wealth.

3. On this description, Velásquez-Treviño comments that it is through "Popo's relationship to Miss Cherry, who functions as the stereotype of the *'gringa'* or American woman, that the narrator reveals a negative attitude about the role of women in American society" and "the myth that other countries have created about the superior status of the United States" (53).

4. Eduardo Galeano criticizes the effect of mass media on Latin American populations of a later time than Mena's, when mass media has had a more profound effect than any writer of her time could have anticipated. He speaks about a people "whose identity has been destroyed by successive conquering cultures, and whose ruthless exploitation is part of the machinery of world capitalism, the system [that] creates a 'mass culture'" (190). He sees "culture for the masses" as a "degraded art with a massive circulation, which manipulates consciousness, masks reality and tramples on the creative imagination." But he also speaks to literature's capacity to directly oppose or expose the process of creating a "mass culture" and how the latter is exchanged for a more authentic reality: "Useless for revealing identity, it is a way to wipe it out and deform it, to impose ways of life and patterns of consumption which receive massive diffusion through the media. What is called 'National culture', is the culture of the ruling class, which lives an imported life and limits itself to copying, abortively and in bad taste, so-called 'world culture', or what that is understood to be by those who confuse it with the culture of the dominant countries. . . . The centres of power export to us not just machines and patents but also ideology" (172–179, 190–191).

5. I am indebted to Margo Gutiérrez, librarian and head of the Mexican American Library Project of the Latin American Collection of the Benson Library of the University of Texas at Austin, for her research into the author's background. All efforts failed to unearth further biographical information such as her birthdate and her whereabouts if she still lives.

Chapter Five

1. At the keynote dinner of the "Mexican Americans in Texas History" conference held May 2–4 at the University of Texas Institute of Texan Cultures at San Antonio in 1990, Ramón Saldívar read a message Paredes sent. In it he gave this account of how the *viejos* inspired his work.

2. Webb argued that "history was a branch of literature and should therefore

be written with imagination and feeling. He deplored the way most historians wrote, attributing much of the problem to their early training in graduate school. In 1955 Webb was asked by the editor of *American Heritage* to do an essay on how historians write. The essay was not published because Webb's views were considered much too strong on the subject, and he was unwilling to tone them down" (Wolfskill: 7).

3. Even at the height of Chicano nationalism, during the Chicano Movement, Paredes had not hesitated to speak to this different kind of power. At the Thompson Conference Center of the University of Texas at Austin in November 1970, he dared to suggest that what was of primary importance was to create a literary climate out of which a "tradition" of Mexican American literature could be created: "to get some really good [Chicano/a] writers we must have a lot of mediocre ones. And to have many mediocre writers we must begin with many bad works, works groping toward a goal yet to be reached" (Paredes 1983: 131). According to his own account, Paredes was not prepared for the "verbal thunder and lightning" that descended upon him from the young writers who felt that "all" Chicano literature had to be "an expression of the Chicano soul, of Aztlán itself" (1983: 131). At the risk of alienating himself from his own people, Paredes said lucidly and honestly what few had the courage to say and effectually launched the whole trajectory of Chicano history gainsaying the rhetoric of dominance (Garza-Falcón 1991).

4. In Mexico a form of this type of execution of prisoners was known as *la ley fuga;* a prisoner would be given the opportunity to try to escape. Usually released in an open plain, with little to hide behind, the prisoner would hardly have a chance of outrunning a bullet despite the head start he would be given (conversation with Roberto Garza Maciel, my father, September 16, 1994). Whether one form of this practice evolved out of the other or whether the Texas prisoners thought they were being given an opportunity to escape due to the custom, is an intriguing question this study can unfortunately not engage; however, we know that the *rurales* of Mexican President Porfirio Díaz's time were modeled after the Texas Rangers (A. Paredes, personal interview, March 4, 1995).

5. The notion of "place" of course requires definition. For the purposes of this analysis, "Place" refers to an area either fixed in space or present in moments actually lived, symbolically or in spirit, where resistance to the colonization of the mind or to hegemony is at least possible, regardless of whether that resistance manifests itself in open aggression. Focusing on what forces in the novel serve to eradicate the existence or at least obstruct the reclaiming of this place makes its absence more noticeable. The *tierra* is *desaparecida.* Successful obstruction to securing that place brings the systematic and fully conscious securing of the ruling class ideology.

6. Having struggled to get "The Hammon and the Beans" into print, something he finally accomplished in *The Texas Observer,* April 18, 1963, Paredes knew

publishing houses would spurn *George Washington Gómez.* This novel makes a statement for his people that would later be made in a different way with the publication of what grew out of his dissertation on the *corrido,* the Texas Mexican border ballad. The story of Gregorio Cortez would emerge as the well-known *With His Pistol in His Hand* (1958). With its publication, Paredes formally and publicly challenged Webbian notions of the Texas Mexican in his analysis of the *corrido* or the Texas Mexican ballad of resistance. Even *With His Pistol in His Hand* would sit on bookstore shelves collecting dust until a decade later, when the Chicano movement took notice of Paredes's scholarly defense of his people, or a decade after that, when it would be interpreted as "The Ballad of Gregorio Cortez," a PBS film.

George Washington Gómez, in its published form, was not completely finished, though what we have is by no means a rough draft (see Rolando Hinojosa's introduction to the novel). Paredes had every intention of revising Part 5 to bring his character back to South Texas as a lawyer who would establish a law practice.

7. The child is named George Washington because the family wants him to have the name of an important man in U.S. history, what they hope the child will also become. But because the old grandmother cannot pronounce George Washington, his name soon is adapted into Guálinto, which stays with him for most of the novel. When Feliciano enrolls his nephew in school, he is asked if it is an Indian name, and Feliciano assents to the supposition. The choice of name and its association with Mexican American patriotism and this population's identification with revolutionary, colonial America can perhaps be explained by the cover of the 1952 issue of *Revista Latino-Americana: Revista Mensual de Cultura Popular,* 5, no. 3 (Sept. 1952). The caption under a picture of George Washington reads, "Uno de los hombres más insignes de los últimos tiempos. Fundador de los Estados Unidos de América" [one of the most renowned men of recent times, founder of the United States of America]. This publication as a reflection of South Texas cultural and literary production also reflects the need that Mexican Americans have felt to show their patriotism to the United States. Other expressions of this are the week-long celebrations that take place to this day in Laredo, Texas, commemorating George Washington's birthday, as well as the impressive history of voluntary enlistment and heroism of Mexican Americans in the U.S. military since World War I (see Chapter 6).

8. The distribution of Mexican illiteracy, to which I referred earlier in this chapter, shows that in "Anglo counties," that is, those counties where the Anglos, particularly one Anglo family, were the *caudillos,* or bosses, and where *Mexicanos* had no political presence, Mexican illiteracy rates were high. Where only their presence as workers existed, the average illiteracy rate was 38.5 percent as compared with the Mexican counties, where the average was 23.5 percent (Montejano: 249). Today, propositions such as California's 187 reveal how attempts to create a permanent underclass of laborers during times of economic change repeat them-

selves. Without access to education and health care, to what can recent immigrants aspire for their children's future other than their perpetual service in the low-paying, primarily unskilled labor force?

9. More specific dynamics and local controlling factors contributed to the forming of this system. As Montejano notes in his chapter "The Web of Labor Controls," the lifestyle of the Mexican and his low wages discouraged "the settlement of Anglos [in South Texas] who did not have capital or some skill or profession to offer" (199). At the same time, other controls were exerted over the existing and emerging labor force, such as restricting the Mexican's mobility by discouraging road building and ownership of cars, or by guarding the existing labor force against agents for other farmers who might pay higher wages.

10. Aguirre went on to complete her undergraduate degree in 1942 from Southwest Texas State Teachers College in San Marcos and spent thirty-seven years teaching in Edgewood and Harlandale Independent School Districts. The San Marcos Independent School District would not have such aggressive reformers as Aguirre on its teaching faculty; however, she succeeded in paving the way for more accommodating, and less "radical" Chicana/o public school teachers (Davila 1995).

11. See Richard Johnson, "What is Cultural Studies Anyway?" on subjective forms by which we live.

12. Gramsci's analysis and criticism of the educational system, undergoing the "reform" the Mussolini government had enacted in 1923, has a bearing on the issues here. His critique of these "rhetorical" schools in the service of a corrupt political order can be applied to U.S. public school systems as described in the novel and, to a certain extent, even as we see them today. Along with his hope for the emergence of intellectuals from the working class, he can see how "the pupil's destiny and future activity are determined in advance [when the] . . . imparting of a general, humanistic, formative culture" is absent from the schooling those destined for productive work (i.e., labor) receive in the vocational schools to which working-class children are generally sent (Gramsci, "On Education": 27). Though his ideas on education as well as on organic leadership (found in "On Intellectuals") are culture specific, they are no less relevant when children are identified as early as kindergarten as the gifted and talented and are later groomed for honors programs, while "others" get left behind.

13. Anthropologist John U. Ogbu, of the University of California at Berkeley, points to the present-day consistent failure of involuntary minorities to score well on IQ tests. His article, "Human Intelligence Testing: A Cultural-Ecological Perspective," questions the very validity of those testing instruments and thus the standards by which they are designed. Involuntary minorities develop "an oppositional cultural frame of reference . . . [causing] minorities to perceive learning certain things or acting in certain ways as problematic. They associate certain skills and behaviors with their 'oppressors,' their 'enemies,' i.e., White Americans. The mastery of these skills by the White community has made it difficult and/or

painful for minorities" (28). Often such arguments overlook what Paredes's narrative describes, namely the actual state structuring and unconstitutional funding of even today's school systems that discriminate against involuntary minorities. This structuring often forms the "oppositional frame of reference" which was well established and sanctioned by the state prior to the development of any "oppositional identity" as Ogbu describes it. Unfortunately, arguments such as these usually focus on what problems minorities present to educational institutions, rather than on how institutions can change so that they cease to cause those problems.

14. This episode probably refers to the train derailment that occurred at the Tandy Station, eight miles north of Brownsville, Texas, on October 18, 1915. The seditionist Luís De la Rosa was supposedly responsible (Sandos: 101).

15. Emma Tenayuca was a leader and activist during the struggles of the Pecan Shellers' Strike in the San Antonio area during the 1930s. In a conversation with the author (November 1992), Paredes remarked that this is what he would have had Chonita grow up to be had she lived and that his inspiration for the creation of this character was Tenayuca, a woman he greatly admires.

CHAPTER SIX

1. In the Introduction to the collection of short stories from which this story is taken, *The Moths and Other Stories,* Yvonne Yarbro-Bejarano indicates that the "crazy" woman in the story is from El Salvador, but the reference in the story to the "Contras" would indicate that the woman is actually from Nicaragua. In the story, when the woman goes looking for her "disappeared" son, Geraldo, and asks some official about him, he says, "'Anyone who so willfully supports the contras in any form must be arrested and punished without delay.' . . . 'Contras are tricksters. They exploit the ignorance of people like you' . . . He throws the stub [of his cigarette] on the floor, crushes it under his boot. 'This,' he says, screwing his boot into the ground, 'is what the contras do to people like you'" (69).

We know that the Contras were the remaining members of Somoza's National Guard after the Sandinista Revolution and that they set themselves up for the most part in Honduras from where they could enter Nicaragua. They, in essence, are counterrevolutionaries whom President Reagan called "freedom fighters" while calling the campesinos struggling for agrarian reform "communists," another example of "labeling" as I shall develop the concept in this chapter. It remains doubtful that the woman is indeed from El Salvador, though there are strong indications in the story that this is inner-city Los Angeles, to which many Salvadoran political and economic refugees have immigrated.

2. The first trial of the L.A. police officers accused of the beating of Rodney King provided an example of how reality was redefined for the jury. They were convinced through words and prescribed notions, despite a video to the contrary, that a man lying on the ground while being beaten could somehow be "in control of the situation." Oddly enough, the events depicted in "The Cariboo Cafe" pre-

sumably also occur in Los Angeles, with the Los Angeles police taking the final decisive action. Since I first wrote this chapter, other similar events of unchecked police brutality have come to the fore with similar outcomes: the shooting of Tyron Lewis, a St. Petersburg, Florida, eighteen-year-old, on October 24, 1996, in which the white policeman, James Knight, was not indicted; the suffocation of thirty-one-year-old Jonny Gammage by several policemen in Pittsburgh on October 12, 1995; and the videotaped beating in 1996 of Mexican immigrants in Riverside County, California.

3. Michael Riffaterre makes the case that "truth in fiction is not based on an actual experience of factuality, nor does the interpretation or esthetic evaluation of fictional narrative require that it be verified against reality. Rather, truth in fiction rests on verisimilitude, a system of representations that seems to reflect a reality external to the text but only because it conforms to a grammar" (1990: xiii–xiv). Later Riffaterre elaborates on this idea of a "grammar" when he refers to "a consensus about reality already encoded in language" (xiv). We already believe a "truth" to be certain, regardless of verisimilitude, because we are swayed by the words used to describe events, words that already carry with them an encoded reality. In "The Cariboo Cafe" words such as *illegal alien, kidnapper, police, owner, rescue,* and *resisting arrest* become labels carrying ideological meaning which in and of themselves define reality for us, a reality completely devoid of the consciousness we can enter through narrative imagination.

4. Jean Franco has stated in her essay "Killing Priests, Nuns, Women, Children": "In common with Mediterranean countries, public space in Latin America was strictly separated from the private space of the house (brother), home and convent, that is spaces which were clearly marked as 'feminine.' These spaces gave women a certain territorial but restricted power base and at the same time offered the 'felicitous' spaces for the repose of the warrior" (1985: 417).

5. In her introduction to the collection of Viramontes's short stories, *The Moths and Other Stories* (18).

6. This information is from a talk given by Esperanza de Cabrera and women like herself who were instrumental in the formation of this organization when they were hosted by the University Catholic Center in Austin, Texas, on March 24, 1992.

7. The phrase "where the toilet was one's own" (Viramontes: 61) could also be read as a criticism of Anglo American feminism, with its echoing of Virginia Woolf's "A Room of One's Own."

Chapter Seven

1. De la Garza's grandfather wrote a short history of the city called *La Antigua Revilla en la leyenda de los tiempos.* According to the author, "This is what Guerrero Viejo, or la Antigua Revilla, has become"—"a legend, a myth of survival and endurance" (De la Garza 1995b: p. 14).

2. Recently, historians have also done much to unearth less widely known roles

of Hispanic women. George J. Sánchez, upon whom Deutsch relies heavily, has done much work on the Mexican immigrant woman's resistance to Americanization in his "Go After the Women: Americanization and the Mexican Immigrant Woman, 1915–1929." Vickie Ruiz, in her "A Promise Fulfilled: Mexican Cannery Workers in Southern California," has recorded the struggles and organization of Mexican women as well as the contribution of their work to a growing U.S. economy when that contribution was most badly needed. Additionally, the anthropologist Patricia Zavella has done work on female workers and food processing workers.

EPILOGUE

1. *[One day in a poor neighborhood named La Mina*
    over there in Laredo, Texas
    Don Luís was born . . .
    He was raised on prickly pear, beans and tortillas
    on tacos, jackrabbits, eggs and on migas. . . .
    Throughout all of Texas, he would find jobs,
    but because of poor pay, he left for other states.
    With all that he suffered, he covered so many miles
    that within the large furrow he followed, the years did pass.
    Once all his children were married,
    Don Luís, now tired, returned to Texas.
    He found the same thing he had once left—
    for the farmworkers, the same poverty remained.]
    (my translation)

BIBLIOGRAPHY

ABERNETHY, FRANCIS EDWARD. 1992. *The Texas Folklore Society, 1909–1943, Volume I.* Publication of the Texas Folklore Society 51. Denton: University of North Texas Press.

———. 1994. *The Texas Folklore Society, 1944–1971, Volume II.* Publication of the Texas Folklore Society 52. Denton: University of North Texas Press.

ACOSTA, TERESA PALOMO. 1990. Address given at the Keynote Dinner of the "Mexican Americans in Texas History" Conference held at the University of Texas Institute of Texan Cultures, San Antonio, May 2–4.

ACUÑA, RODOLFO. 1988. *Occupied America: History of Chicanos.* Third Edition. New York: Harper and Row. (First edition published 1972.)

ADORNO, ROLENA. 1988. *Guaman Poma: Writing and Resistance in Colonial Peru.* Austin: University of Texas Press.

ALLPORT, GORDON. 1958. *The Nature of Prejudice.* New York: Doubleday.

ALTHUSSER, LOUIS. 1964/1971. "Freud and Lacan." In *Lenin and Philosophy and Other Essays by Louis Althusser.* New York: Monthly Review Press.

———. 1969/1971. "Ideology and Ideological State Apparatuses." In *Lenin and Philosophy and Other Essays by Louis Althusser.* New York: Monthly Review Press.

ANZALDÚA, GLORIA. 1987. *Borderlands/La Frontera: The New Mestiza.* San Francisco: Spinsters/Aunt Lute.

Association of American Colleges and Universities. 1995, January. "American Pluralism, American Commitments and the College Curriculum: A Draft Report from the American Commitments National Panel," Washington, D.C.: author.

AYALA, RAMÓN. 1990. "Un puño de tierra." In *El disco de oro, Ramón Ayala y Los Bravos del Norte.* Corpus Christi, Tex.: Freddie Records.

BAIN, READ. 1979. "Commentary on the Conference." In *Critiques of Research in the Social Sciences III: An Appraisal of Walter Prescott Webb's The Great Plains: A Study in Institutions and Environment,* by Fred A. Shannon. Westport, Conn.: Greenwood Press. (Reprint of the 1940 edition published by the Social Science Research Council, New York.)

BAKHTIN, MIKHAIL MIKHAILOVICH. 1981. "Discourse in the Novel." In *The Dialogic Imagination: Four Essays by M. M. Bakhtin,* edited by Michael Holquist, trans. Caryl Emerson and Michael Holquist. Austin: University of Texas Press.

BARCO, JUAN. 1991. "Don Luís el Tejano," recorded by Latin Breed. In *Texas Triangle: Ram Herrera, Latin Breed, Xelencia.* Hollywood: Capital Records.

BARKSDALE, E. C. 1969. "An Explanation." In *History As High Adventure,* by Walter Prescott Webb, edited by E. C. Barksdale. Austin: Pemberton Press.

BARRERA, AIDA. 1990. Audiotaped interview of Jovita González and Américo Paredes for a radio series entitled *Sabor del pueblo,* as heard at "Mexican Americans in Texas History" Conference held at the Texas Institute of Texan Cultures, San Antonio, May 2–4. In author's possession.

BARZUN, JACQUES. 1985. "Walter Prescott Webb and the Fate of History." In *Essays on Walter Prescott Webb and the Teaching of History,* edited by Dennis Reinhartz and Stephen E. Maizlish. College Station: Texas A&M University Press.

BERGHOFF, ED, and LARRY BASTIAN. 1988. "Cowboy Bill." In *Garth Brooks* (Debut Album), by Garth Brooks. Major Bob Music Co./Ed's up Music.

BONILLA, RUBÉN. 1996, August 6. Personal interview. Corpus Christi, Tex.

BOOTH, WAYNE C. 1983. *The Rhetoric of Fiction.* Second Edition. Chicago: University of Chicago Press.

BRAUDY, LEO. 1970. *Narrative Form in History and Fiction.* Princeton, N.J.: Princeton University Press.

BROOKS, A. PHILLIPS. 1996, October 2. "New Curriculum Strays from Traditional." *Austin American-Statesman* p. A1.

BROOKS, A. PHILLIPS, and JEFF SOUTH. 1995, April 9. "School-Choice Plans Worry Resegregation Critics." *Austin American-Statesman,* p. A1.

BROOKS, GARTH, and CYNTHIA LIMBAUGH. 1988. "In Lonesome Dove." In *Roping the Wind.* Major Bob Music Co. (CD Produced by Allen Reynolds, Jack's Tracks Recording Studio, Nashville, Tenn., by Mark Miller.)

BROUN, ELIZABETH. 1991. Foreword to *The West As America: Reinterpreting Images of the Frontier: 1820–1920.* Washington, D.C.: National Museum of American Art, Smithsonian Institute.

BUCHANAN, PATRICK. 1996, April. Remarks quoted from the *Washington Times* (Jan. 23, 1995) in *Hispanic Magazine,* p. 10.

CÁRDENAS, BLANDINA. 1995, March 13. Personal interview. Southwest Texas State University, San Marcos.

———. 1995, April 13. Personal interview. Southwest Texas State University, San Marcos.

———. 1996, May 5. Personal interview. San Antonio.

CARR, HELEN. 1996. *Jean Rhys.* Plymouth, England: Northcote House Publishers.

CASTAÑEDA, ANTONIA. 1990. "The Political Economy of Nineteenth Century Stereotypes of Californianas." In *Between Borders: Essays on Mexicana/Chicana History,* edited by Adelaida R. Del Castillo. Los Angeles: Floricanto Press.

———. 1992, November. "Women of Color and the Rewriting of Western History: The Discourse, Politics, and De Colonization of History," *Pacific Historical Review* 61: 501–533.

———. 1993. "Presidarias y Pobladoras: The Journey North and Life in Frontier California." In *Chicana Critical Issues: Mujeres activas en letras y cambio social.* Berkeley, Calif.: Third Woman Press.

CERVÁNTEZ, YRENIA. 1996. "Black Legs." In *Chicana Creativity & Criticism: New Frontiers in American Literature,* edited by Maria Herrera-Sobek and Helena Viramontes. Albuquerque: University of New Mexico Press.

CHAPLIN, J. P. 1985. *The Dictionary of Psychology.* New York: Del Publishing.

"Chicanos." 1978. In *Stereotypes, Distortions and Omissions in U.S. History Textbooks.* New York: Racism and Sexism Resource Center for Educators, A Division of the Council on Interracial Books for Children.

"Coming Soon: *Dew on the Thorn:* A Novella of Folklore and History in the South Texas-Mexican Border Country, by Jovita González, Edited and With an Introduction by José E. Limón . . . ," 1996. *Recovering the U.S. Hispanic Literary Heritage* 5, no. 1 (Spring).

CORTÁZAR, JULIO. 1984. "Something More Than Words." In *They Shoot Writers, Don't They?,* edited by George Theiner. London: Faber and Faber.

COTERA, MARTA. 1993, March 8. Personal interview. Austin, Tex.

CRUZ, ISABEL. 1996, August 2. Personal interview. Corpus Christi, Tex.

———. 1996, August 6. Personal interview. Corpus Christi, Tex.

DAVILA, MIKE. 1995, February. Personal interview. San Antonio.

DE LA GARZA, BEATRIZ. 1994. *The Candy Vendor's Boy and Other Stories.* Houston: Arte Público.

———. 1995a. "The Border, from a Human Perspective." *Laredos: A Journal of the Borderlands* 1, no. 2 (February): 6.

———. 1995b. "Guerrero Viejo: A Myth of Survival and Endurance." *Laredos: A Journal of the Borderlands* 1, no. 3 (March): 14.

Democratic Party 1996 Platform, as adopted by the Democratic National Convention on August 27, 1996. www.demoparty.com.

DEUTSCH, SARAH. 1987. *No Separate Reality: Culture, Class, and Gender on an Anglo-Hispanic Frontier in the American Southwest, 1880–1940.* New York: Oxford University Press.

DONEGAN, CRAIG. 1991, June 9. "Cultures Clash at the Smithsonian." *San Antonio Express News.*

DUGGER, RONNIE. 1967. *"The Great Plains."* In *Three Men in Texas, Bedichek, Webb, and Dobie: Essays by Their Friends in the Texas Observer,* edited by Dugger. Austin: University of Texas Press.

EVANS, EVERETT. 1993, January 5. "Reclaiming Hispanic History: Project to Preserve 300 Years of Literature." *Houston Chronicle,* pp. 1D, 6D.

FEAGIN, JOE R., and CLAIRECE BOOHER FEAGIN. 1996. *Racial and Ethnic Relations,* 5th ed. Upper Saddle River, N.J.: Prentice Hall.

FRANCO, JEAN. 1985. "Killing Priests, Nuns, Women, Children." In *On Signs,* edited by Marshall Blonsky. Baltimore: The Johns Hopkins University Press.

Furman, Necah Stewart. 1976. *Walter Prescott Webb, His Life and Impact.* Albuquerque: University of New Mexico Press.

Galán, Héctor (producer/director). 1991. *"Los mineros,"* for *The American Experience,* a production of the Public Broadcasting System. Austin: Galán Productions.

Galeano, Eduardo. 1984. "In Defense of the Word." In *They Shoot Writers, Don't They?,* edited by George Theiner. London: Faber and Faber.

García, Héctor P. 1992. Remarks from the Dr. Héctor P. García Papers on a poster printed for the occasion of their formal dedication, Texas A&M University Library Archives, Corpus Christi, Tex., April 3.

García, Mario T. 1980, May. "The Chicana in American History: The Mexican Women of El Paso, 1880–1920—A Case Study." *Pacific Historical Review* 49: 315–337.

Garza de Cortes, Oralia. 1992. "United States: Hispanic Americans." Chapter 3 in *Our Family, Our Friends, Our World: An Annotated Guide to Significant Multicultural Books for Children and Teenagers,* edited by Lyn Miller-Lachmann. New Providence, N.J.: R. R. Bowker (a division of Reed Publishing).

Garza-Falcón, Leticia. 1991, March 22. "Setting Texas Straight." *The Texas Observer,* pp. 22–23. (Expanded version: "Américo Paredes: A True Texas Hero," *Arriba* [1 May, 1991], pp. 6, 16, 18.)

Garza-Falcón-Sánchez, Leticia. 1993. "The Chicano/a Response to the Rhetoric of Dominance." Dissertation, University of Texas at Austin.

Gay, Peter. 1974. *Style in History.* New York: McGraw Hill.

Gómez, Rogelio. 1990, September 16. "Rules of the Game." *The Texas Observer.*

González, Jovita. 1927. "Folklore of the Texas Mexican Vaquero." In *Texas and Southwestern Folklore,* edited by J. Frank Dobie. Publication of the Texas Folklore Society 6. Austin: University of Texas Press.

———. 1930a. "America Invades the Border Towns." *Southwest Review* 15, no. 4 (Summer): 467–477. (Cited in Montejano 1987: 115.)

———. 1930b. "Tales and Songs of the Texas-Mexicans." In *Man, Bird and Beast,* edited by J. Frank Dobie. Publication of the Texas Folklore Society 7. Austin: University of Texas Press.

———. 1935. "The Bullet Swallower." In *Puro Mexicano,* edited by J. Frank Dobie. Publication of the Texas Folklore Society 8. Austin: University of Texas Press.

———. 1935–1936. Compilation, special bound edition of series of articles under the general title of "Among My People" in the magazine *Mary Immaculate* published by the Missionary Oblates of Mary Immaculate of San Antonio. Mireles Papers. Special Collections & Archives, Corpus Christi Bell Library, Texas A&M University, Corpus Christi.

———. 1972. "Among My People." In *Mexican-American Authors,* edited by Américo Paredes and Raymund Paredes. Dallas: Houghton Mifflin.

(Reprinted from *Tone the Bell Easy,* edited by J. Frank Dobie. Austin: Texas Folklore Society, 1932.)

————. 1990. "Mexican Americans in Texas History" (recorded interview played at keynote dinner). Conference held at the University of Texas Institute of Texan Cultures, San Antonio, May 2–4.

————. Undated. *Dew on the Thorn.* Unpublished manuscript. Mireles Papers. Special Collections & Archives, Bell Library, Texas A&M University, Corpus Christi.

————. Undated. Memoirs. Mireles Papers. Special Collections & Archives, Bell Library, Texas A&M University, Corpus Christi.

GONZÁLEZ, JOVITA, and EVE RALEIGH. *Caballero.* Unpublished manuscript. Corpus Christi, Tex.: Corpus Christi State University Library.

GRAMSCI, ANTONIO. 1989a. "The Intellectuals." In *Selections from the Prison Notebooks of Antonio Gramsci,* edited and translated by Quintin Hoare and Geoffrey Nowell Smith. New York: International Publishers.

————. 1989b. "On Education." In *Selections from the Prison Notebooks of Antonio Gramsci,* edited and translated by Quintin Hoare and Geoffrey Nowell Smith. New York: International Publishers.

GUERRA, ANDREA. 1990, October. "At the TEA, It's Called the Great Texas History Purge." In *Tejas* (University of Texas Student Publication) 2: 14–15.

GUERRA, FERMINA. 1972. "Rancho Buena Vista, Its Ways of Life and Traditions." In *Mexican-American Authors,* edited by Américo Paredes and Raymund Paredes. Dallas: Houghton Mifflin. (Reprinted from *Texian Stomping Ground,* by J. Frank Dobie. Austin: Texas Folklore Society, 1931.)

GUTIÉRREZ, RAMÓN A. 1991. *When Jesus Came, the Corn Mothers Went Away: Marriage, Sexuality, and Power in New Mexico, 1500–1846.* Stanford, Calif.: Stanford University Press.

HALL, STUART. 1980. *Culture, Media, Language: Working Papers in Cultural Studies, 1972–79.* London: Hutchinson.

————. 1986. "The Problem of Ideology—Marxism without Guarantees." *Journal of Communication Inquiry* 10: 28–44.

HALL, STUART, et al. 1978. "The Social Production of News." In *Policing the Crisis: Mugging, the State, and Law and Order.* New York: Holmes and Meier.

HAY, DOUGLAS. 1975. "Property, Authority and the Criminal Law." In *Albion's Fatal Tree: Crime and Society in Eighteenth-Century England,* by Hay, Peter Linebaugh, John G. Rule, E. P. Thompson, and Cal Winslow. New York: Pantheon.

HAZELTON, JARED E. 1996. "Socioeconomic Trends in Texas and Their Implications for Higher Education." Paper presented to the Higher Education Symposium, the Hispanic Association of Colleges and Universities, Austin, September 23–24.

Héroes Hispanos: Two Centuries of Valor in American History. 1993. A Telemundo Production.

HILLS, PATRICIA. 1991. "Picturing Progress in the Era of Westward Expansion." In *The West as America: Reinterpreting Images of the Frontier.* Washington, D.C.: Smithsonian Institution Press.

JOHNSON, RICHARD. 1986, Winter. "What Is Cultural Studies Anyway?" *Social Text* 16: 38–80.

JONES, GERARD. 1992. *Honey I'm Home! Sitcoms: Selling the American Dream.* New York: Grove Weidenfeld, a division of Grove Press.

KINGSTON, MIKE. 1985. *Walter Prescott Webb in Stephens County.* Austin: Eakin Press.

KRENECK, THOMAS. 1992, July 30. "Credit Is Due." *Corpus Christi Caller Times,* p. A10.

———. 1996, August 2. Personal interview. Corpus Christi, Tex.

LAMAR, HOWARD R. 1992. "Regionalism and the Broad Methodological Problem." In *Regional Studies: The Interplay of Land and People,* edited by Glen E. Lich. College Station: Texas A&M University Press.

LIMERICK, PATRICIA. 1987. *Legacy of Conquest: The Unbroken Past of the American West.* New York: W. W. Norton.

LIMÓN, JOSÉ E. 1981. "The Folk Performance of *Chicano* and the Cultural Limits of Political Ideology." In *And Other Neighborly Names: Social Process and Cultural Image in Texas Folklore,* edited by Richard Bauman and Roger Abrahams. Austin: University of Texas Press.

———. 1987, April 15. Address presented for the "Inaugural Américo Paredes Distinguished Lecture Series" at the University of Texas at Austin.

———. 1992. *Mexican Ballads, Chicano Poems: History and Influence in Mexican-American Social Poetry.* Berkeley: University of California Press.

———. 1994. *Dancing with the Devil: Society and Cultural Poetics in Mexican American South Texas.* Madison: University of Wisconsin Press.

———. 1996. Introduction to *Caballero: A Historical Novel,* by Jovita González and Eve Raleigh, edited by Limón and María Cotera. College Station: Texas A&M University Press.

LOTTINVILLE, SAVOIE. 1976, 1990. *The Rhetoric of History.* Norman: University of Oklahoma Press.

LUBIN, DAVID. 1991, April 30. "Art and the Real Old West." *Washington Post,* p. A23.

MARTIN, WALLACE. 1986. *Recent Theories of Narrative.* Ithaca, N.Y.: Cornell University Press.

MEGILL, ALLAN. 1989, June. "Recounting the Past: Description, Explanation, and Narrative in Historiography." *American History Review* 94, no. 3: 627–653.

MENA, MARÍA CRISTINA. 1992. "The Education of Popo." In *North of the Río Grande: The Mexican-American Experience in Short Fiction,* edited by Edward Simmen. New York: Mentor.

Mireles, E. E., Roy B. Fisher, and Jovita González de Mireles. 1941. *Mi libro español.* Austin: W. S. Benson & Co.

Montejano, David. 1987. *Anglos and Mexicans in the Making of Texas, 1836–1986.* Austin: University of Texas Press.

Moquin, Wayne, with Charles Van Doren, eds. 1971. "Mexican Americans: Native and Alien, 1911–39." In *A Documentary History of the Mexican Americans,* edited by Moquin with Charles Van Doren. New York: Bantam.

Morris, Anne. 1993, February 21. "Literary Events to Benefit Statue Fund." *Austin American Statesman,* p. F1.

Mortensen, Eleanor. 1992, July 20. "CCSU Preserving Papers of Teaching Pioneers." *Corpus Christi Caller Times.*

Muller, Herbert J. 1952. *The Uses of the Past: Profiles of Former Societies: A Bold Analysis of the Meaning of History.* Oxford: Oxford University Press.

Novick, Peter. 1988. *That Noble Dream: The "Objectivity Question" and the American Historical Profession.* Cambridge, England: Cambridge University Press.

Ogbu, John U. 1988. "Human Intelligence Testing: A Cultural-Ecological Perspective." *National Forum: Phi Kappa Journal* (Spring): 23–29.

Padilla, Genero. 1993. *My History, Not Yours: The Formation of Mexican American Autobiography.* Madison, Wisc.: University of Wisconsin Press.

Paredes, Américo. 1958. *With His Pistol in His Hand.* Austin: University of Texas Press.

———. 1971. "The Hammon and the Beans." In *The Chicano: From Caricature to Self-portrait,* edited by Edward Simmen. New York: New American Library. (Reprinted from *Texas Observer,* April 18, 1963.)

———. 1976. *A Texas-Mexican Cancionero: Folksongs of the Lower Border.* Urbana: University of Illinois Press.

———. 1983. "Nearby Places and Strange-Sounding Names." In *The Texas Literary Tradition,* edited by Don Graham, James W. Lee, and William T. Pilkington. Austin: College of Liberal Arts and the Texas State Historical Association at the University of Texas at Austin.

———. 1990a. *George Washington Gómez: A Mexicotexan Novel.* Houston: Arte Público Press.

———. 1990b. "Mexican Americans in Texas History" (recorded message played at keynote dinner). Conference held at the University of Texas Institute of Texan Cultures, San Antonio, May 2–4.

———. 1991. *Between Two Worlds.* Houston: Arte Público Press.

———. 1992, August 17. Personal interview. Austin.

———. 1995, March 4. Personal interview. Austin.

Paredes, Américo, and Raymund Paredes, eds. 1972. *Mexican-American Authors.* Boston: Houghton Mifflin.

Paredes, Raymund A. 1982. "The Evolution of Chicano Literature." In *Three*

American Literatures: Essays in Chicano, Native American, and Asian-American Literature for Teachers of American Literature, edited by Houston A. Baker. New York: Modern Language Association of America.

POCOCK, J. G. A. 1985. *Virtue, Commerce and History.* Cambridge, England: Cambridge University Press.

PROPP, VLADIMIR. 1958. *Morphology of the Folktale.* Edited by Svatava Pirkova-Jakobson, translated by Laurence Scott. Bloomington: Indiana University Research Center.

Publishers Clearing House Advertisement for *The Burning Hills* and *Radigan,* by Louis L'Amour. 1993.

REBOLLEDO, TEY DIANA. 1995. *Women Singing in the Snow: A Cultural Analysis of Chicana Literature.* Tucson: University of Arizona Press.

REBOLLEDO, TEY DIANA, and ELIANA S. RIVERO. 1993. Introduction to *Infinite Divisions: An Anthology of Chicana Literature,* edited by Rebolledo and Rivero. Tucson: University of Arizona Press.

RIFFATERRE, MICHAEL. 1990. *Fictional Truth.* Baltimore: The Johns Hopkins University Press.

RIMMON-KENAN, SHLOMITH. 1983. *Narrative Fiction: Contemporary Poetics.* New York: Methuen.

ROBINSON, CECIL. 1963. *With the Ears of Strangers: The Mexican in American Literature.* Tucson: University of Arizona Press.

RODRÍGUEZ, ROBERTO. 1993, October 15. "Abuse in the Barrio, Still." *Texas Observer,* pp. 12–13.

ROMO, RICARDO. 1990. Address presented at the keynote dinner of the "Mexican Americans in Texas History" Conference held at the University of Texas Institute of Texan Cultures, San Antonio, May 2–4.

RUIZ, VICKI. 1990. "A Promise Fulfilled: Mexican Cannery Workers in Southern California." In *Unequal Sisters: A Multicultural Reader in U.S. Women's History,* edited by Ellen Carol DuBois and Vicki L. Ruiz. New York: Routledge.

RUIZ DE BURTON, MARÍA AMPARO. 1992. *The Squatter and the Don,* edited by Rosaura Sánchez and Beatrice Pita. Houston: Arte Público Press.

RUNDELL, WALTER, JR. 1963a. "A Dedication to the Memory of Walter Prescott Webb, 1888–1963." *Arizona and the West* 5, no. 1 (Spring): 1–3.

———. 1963b. "Walter Prescott Webb: Product of Environment." *Arizona and the West* 5, no. 1 (Spring): 4–28.

SALAZAR, JOSÉ MARÍA, JR. 1990. "Dilemma of a Gay Chicano: Parallels between Cultural and Sexual Identities." *Tejas* (University of Texas Student Publication) 2 (October): 8–9.

SALDÍVAR, RAMÓN. 1990a. Address presented at keynote dinner of the "Mexican Americans in Texas History" Conference held at the University of Texas Institute of Texan Cultures, San Antonio, May 2–4.

————. 1990b. *Chicano Narrative: The Dialectics of Difference.* University of Wisconsin Press.

————. 1991. "Narrative, Ideology, and the Reconstruction of American Literary History." In *Criticism in the Borderlands: Studies in Chicano Literature, Culture, and Ideology,* edited by Héctor Calderón and José David Saldívar. Durham, N.C.: Duke University Press.

SÁNCHEZ, GEORGE J. 1990. "Go After the Women: Americanization and the Mexican Immigrant Woman, 1915–1929." In *Unequal Sisters: A Multicultural Reader in U. S. Women's History,* edited by Ellen Carol DuBois and Vicki L. Ruiz. New York: Routledge.

SÁNCHEZ, ROSAURA. 1989. "Ethnicity, Ideology and Academia." *Americas Review* 15: 80–88.

————. 1995. *Telling Identities: The California "Testimonios."* Minneapolis: University of Minnesota Press.

SÁNCHEZ, ROSAURA, and BEATRICE PITA. 1992. Introduction to *The Squatter and the Don,* by María Amparo Ruiz de Burton. Houston: Arte Público Press.

SANDOS, JAMES. 1992. *Rebellion in the Borderlands: Anarchism and the Plan of San Diego: 1904–1923.* Norman: University of Oklahoma Press.

SANTOYO, JULIO-CÉSAR. Undated. "Spanish Loan-Words in American English: A Testimony against Some Historical Prejudices." In *The Origins and Originality of American Culture.* Budapest: Publishing House of the Hungarian Academy of Sciences.

SCHLESINGER, ARTHUR M. 1979. Foreword to *Critiques of Research in the Social Sciences III: An Appraisal of Walter Prescott Webb's* The Great Plains: *A Study in Institutions and Environment,* by Fred A. Shannon. Westport, Conn.: Greenwood Press. (Reprint of the 1940 edition published by the Social Science Research Council, New York.)

SHAFER, ROBERT JONES, ed. 1974. *A Guide to Historical Method.* Homewood, Ill.: Dorsey Press.

SHANNON, FRED A. 1979. *Critiques of Research in the Social Sciences III: An Appraisal of Walter Prescott Webb's* The Great Plains: *A Study in Institutions and Environment.* Westport, Conn.: Greenwood Press. (Reprint of the 1940 edition published by the Social Science Research Council, New York.)

SIMMEN, EDWARD. 1992. Introduction to *North of the Río Grande: The Mexican-American Experience in Short Fiction,* ed. Simmen. New York: Mentor.

SLOTKIN, RICHARD. 1973. *Regeneration Through Violence: The Mythology of the American Frontier, 1600–1860.* Middletown Conn.: Wesleyan University Press.

SMITH, HENRY NASH. 1978. *Virgin Land: The American West As Symbol and Myth.* Cambridge, Mass.: Harvard University Press.

SMITH, RHONDA. 1994, May 22. "Héctor P. García: A Legacy Overlooked: G.I. Forum's Founder Lost in History." *Austin American Statesman,* pp. G1 & G8.

HERRERA-SOBEK, MARIA, and HELENA VIRAMONTES, eds. 1996. *Chicana Creativity & Criticism: New Frontiers in American Literature.* Albuquerque: University of New Mexico Press.

TATUM, CHARLES. 1982. *Chicano Literature.* Boston: Twayne.

THOMPSON, E. P. 1996. *The Making of the English Working Class.* New York: Vintage, 1966.

TODOROV, TZVETAN. 1990. *Genres in Discourse.* Translated by Catherine Porter. Cambridge, England: Cambridge University Press.

U.S. Department of Defense, Office of the Deputy Assistant Secretary of Defense for Military Manpower and Personnel Policy. 1988. *Hispanics in America's Defense.* Washington, D.C.: GPO 0–253–424, vol. 3.

VARGAS LLOSA, MARIO. 1984. "The Writer in Latin America." In *They Shoot Writers, Don't They?,* edited by George Theiner. London: Faber and Faber.

VELÁSQUEZ-TREVIÑO, GLORIA LOUISE. 1985. "Cultural Ambivalence in Early Chicana Prose Fiction." Dissertation, Stanford University.

VILLANUEVA, TINO. 1994. "History Class." In *Crónica de mis años peores.* La Jolla, Calif.: Lalo Press.

VIRAMONTES, H. M. 1985. *The Moths and Other Stories.* Houston: Arte Público Press.

VOLOSINOV, V. N. 1973. *Marxism and the Philosophy of Language.* Cambridge, Mass.: Harvard University Press.

VON REZZORI, GREGOR. 1989. *The Snows of Yesteryear.* Translated by H. F. Broch de Rothermann. New York: Knopf.

WALKER, STANLEY. 1927, Nov. 13. "Some Frontier Ballads That Are Fit to Print." *New York Book Review.*

WATT, IAN. 1957. *The Rise of the Novel: Studies in Defoe, Richardson and Fielding.* Berkeley: University of California Press.

WEBB, WALTER PRESCOTT. 1931. *The Great Plains.* New York: Ginn and Company.

———. 1935. *The Texas Rangers.* Cambridge, Mass.: Houghton Mifflin.

———. 1969a. "History As High Adventure." In *History As High Adventure,* edited by E. C. Barksdale. Austin: Pemberton Press.

———. 1969b. "The Story of Some Prairie Inventions." In *History As High Adventure,* edited by E. C. Barksdale. Austin: Pemberton Press.

———. 1979. "Comments on Shannon's Critique." In *Critiques of Research in the Social Sciences III: An Appraisal of Walter Prescott Webb's* The Great Plains: A Study in Institutions and Environment, by Fred A. Shannon. Westport, Conn.: Greenwood Press. (Reprint of the 1940 edition published by the Social Science Research Council, New York.)

WEBER, DAVID J. 1987. "American Westward Expansion and the Breakdown of Relations between Pobladores and 'Indios Bárbaros' on Mexico's Far Northern Frontier, 1821–1846" in *Myth and the History of the Hispanic Southwest: Essays by David J. Weber.* Albuquerque: University of New Mexico Press.

WHITE, HAYDEN. 1978. *Tropics of Discourse: Essays in Cultural Criticism.* Baltimore: The Johns Hopkins University Press.

———. 1987. *The Content of the Form: Narrative Discourse and Historical Representation.* Baltimore: The Johns Hopkins University Press.

WILLIAMS, RAYMOND. 1976. *Keywords: A Vocabulary of Culture and Society.* New York: Oxford University Press.

———. 1977. *Marxism and Literature.* Oxford, England: Oxford University Press.

WINKLER, KAREN J. 1990, September 26. "Scholars Say Issues of Diversity Have Revolutionized Field of Chicano Studies." *Chronicle of Higher Education* 37, no. 4: A6–10.

WOLFSKILL, GEORGE. 1985. Introduction to *Essays on Walter Prescott Webb and the Teaching of History,* edited by Dennis Reinhartz and Stephen E. Maizlish. College Station: Texas A&M University Press.

YARBRO-BEJARANO, Y. 1985. Introduction to *The Moths and Other Stories,* by Helena María Viramontes. Houston: Arte Público Press.

ZAVELLA, PATRICIA. 1985. "'Abnormal Intimacy': The Varying Work Networks of Chicana Cannery Workers." *Feminist Studies* 11, no. 3 (Fall): 541–57.

INDEX